THE THANKSGIVING COOKBOOK

The
THANKSGIVING
COOKBOOK

❧

HOLLY GARRISON

Macmillan Publishing Company   *New York*
Maxwell Macmillan Canada   *Toronto*
Maxwell Macmillan International
New York   Oxford   Singapore   Sydney

To Gerry, for whom I give thanks every day.
And in memory of Didi.

Macmillan Publishing Company
866 Third Avenue, New York, NY 10022

Maxwell Macmillan Canada, Inc.
1200 Eglinton Avenue East, Suite 200
Don Mills, Ontario M3C 3N1

Library of Congress Cataloging-in-Publication Data

Garrison, Holly.
    The Thanksgiving cookbook / Holly Garrison.
        p.   cm.
    Includes index.
    ISBN 0-02-542750-4
    1. Thanksgiving cookery.   I. Title.
TX739.2.T45G37   1991   91-27408   CIP
641.5'68—dc20

Macmillan books are available at special discounts for bulk purchases
for sales promotions, premiums, fund-raising, or educational use. For
details, contact:

Special Sales Director
Macmillan Publishing Company
866 Third Avenue
New York, NY 10022

10 9 8 7 6 5 4 3 2 1

Printed in the United States of America

Acknowledgments

✿

My own list of things to be thankful for this year begins with those wonderful people who have been so helpful in seeing this cookbook through to its completion, at last, just three weeks after Thanksgiving of 1990.

Thank you:

Marisa Smith, of Smith and Kraus, for putting all my disconnected thoughts about how "somebody ought to write a Thanksgiving cookbook" into action by calling one morning and suggesting that I do it, and for all your good ideas, and for being so supportive of my work.

Pam Hoenig, for your patience and for being every writer's dream of what a good editor should be, always expecting the best from me and, hopefully, getting it.

Stephanie Curtis, for always being there when I've needed you, and for your willingness to leave Paris, not once, but twice, to come and help me. I hope you know how much I appreciate all that you did: food shopping, testing and retesting recipes in a sweltering kitchen, and then staying up late at night to get those recipes into the computer because you knew I needed to work on it during the day.

Anne Bailey, for coming to work for me in the first place and making every workday a happy one, for the recipes you developed for this book, and the other recipes that you so efficiently tested.

Carol Gelles and Christine Smith-Koury, for picking up your telephones at least a thousand times during the past year, and never being too busy to share your enviable knowledge of food and cooking techniques, and checking things out so I wouldn't have to take the time.

Doug Flynn and Al Bolton, for all the good cooking we've enjoyed in your company, and for letting me use so many of your recipes, and for being such good neighbors, friends, and "uncles."

James Baker, Director of Museum Operations at Plimouth Plantation, Massachusetts, for making sure our historical information was accurate.

Virginia Prescott, for proving once again that mothers can be best friends, too, by washing the food processor and mixer—how many times? But, mostly, for instilling in me the appreciation for good food.

My husband, Gerry Repp, for never expecting me to cook when I have deadlines, and for your enthusiasm and help in everything I do.

My children, Kimberly Roberts and Timothy Garrison, for having always been such good eaters and believing that I'm the world's greatest cook, and for being such good kids, too.

Didi, Ginger, and Taco, for being my most enthusiastic little tasters, and who think everything I drop on the kitchen floor is just great!

I would also like to express my appreciation to the following food companies and trade associations for supplying me with up-to-date information and, in many cases, for sending their products for recipe testing: Almond Board of California; American Spice Trade Association; Argo/Kingsford's Corn Starch/CPC International, Inc.; Borden, Inc.; Bridgeford Foods Corporation; Butterball Turkey Talk-Line, sponsored by Swift-Eckrich, Inc., makers of Butterball Turkeys; California Iceberg Lettuce Commission; California Olive Industry; California Pistachio Commission; California Prune Board; California Raisin Advisory Board; California Tree Fruit Agreement; California Turkey Industry Board; Delmarva Poultry Industry, Inc.; Food and Wines From France, Inc.; Lea & Perrins; Libby's, a division of the Carnation Company; Louis Rich Company; Molasses Information Network; Mushroom Council; National Broiler Council; National Goose Council; National Turkey Federation; Norbest Turkey Growers Association; Ocean Spray Cranberries, Inc.; Pacific Coast Canned Pear Service, Inc.; Pam Cooking Spray; Perdue Farms, Inc.; Potato Board; Rice Council; State of Maryland, Office of Seafood Marketing; The Pillsbury Company; Timber Crest Farms; Vanilla Information Bureau; Walnut Marketing Board; and Wisconsin Milk Marketing Board.

Contents

❦

CONTENTS
❦

Foreword

❦

Thanksgiving may very well be the sentimental favorite of all the American holidays, yet somehow it manages to remain unsullied by unrealistic expectations and unbridled commercialism.

More people go home for Thanksgiving than for any other holiday, most of them looking forward to nothing more than a good meal and the companionship of immediate and extended family and friends.

Aside from a seemingly unlimited supply of food, we all have things to be thankful for, starting with the Pilgrims, of course, and later *Godey's Lady's Book*, where the relentless campaign for a national day of thanks went on until Abraham Lincoln finally gave in and made it official. In a country where plenty of everything has always been taken for granted, it probably does us all good to stop once a year and reflect upon our personal, and collective, good fortune.

Thanksgiving customs haven't changed a whole lot over the years. Considering the many culinary revolutions during the last hundred or so years, cookbooks from the late nineteenth century offer menus and recipes that are remarkably like the ones we serve today. We may give a nod here and there to modern-day conveniences, and even convenience foods, but I'm certain that if my great-great-grandmother could join us for Thanksgiving this year she'd feel quite at home. She might even enjoy experimenting with my microwave oven, which, like most others across the land, will have been blessedly silent all day.

During the years I was the food editor at *Parents Magazine*, our department got more mail and phone calls in November concerning Thanksgiving than for the rest of the year combined. Questions ranged from when to start thawing the turkey to instructions for preparing a dish vaguely remembered from childhood. The degree of these readers' cooking skills varied, but they had one thing in common: They wanted to re-create at least some of the foods that were served (or they wish had been served) when they were growing up, and they were adamant about maintaining cherished traditions. They wanted to cook a dinner that they could be proud of, that everyone would enjoy and remember, and, for a generation that almost always considers faster better, with surprisingly little regard for time—or money.

Why, I wondered year after year, hadn't someone written a definitive Thanksgiving cookbook, with no trendy recipes or real or implied put-downs of those old-time foods we all love so much? We sometimes forget that nowadays families are often continents and sometimes oceans apart, and usually there's no reassuring mom or auntie around the corner to answer questions and instill in young cooks the confidence they need to plan for and cook a dinner of such proportions. Consider, too, that many would-be Thanksgiving cooks were raised in households where learning kitchen skills was low on the list of child-rearing priorities.

Researching and writing this cookbook has been a happy experience for me, although I admit I may have been less than joyful on a few brutal summer days when there were turkeys to be roasted and stuffings to be baked.

In these troubled times, when a threatening and often violent world has made a return to more secure lifestyles and old values an appealing option for more and more American families, it seemed to me that a book devoted to all the familiar and comforting foods of Thanksgiving would be a timely addition to even the most complete cookbook library.

A FEW NOTES ABOUT USING THIS BOOK
☙

Knowing that many of the cooks who might use this book would be less than expert, I've tried to be as explicit as possible and, at least for the most part, I've not called for any outlandish food or equipment. If you cook from this book I will only ask you to take the time to read through a recipe completely—not just the ingredients—before going to the store and getting out the spoons and bowls. Many a good dish has been ruined because the cook didn't take the extra couple of minutes to do this. I know. I've done it myself. It would also be a good idea if before you start baking or roasting, you make sure your oven is properly calibrated.

The only thing about which I've been less than definite is whether the butter that's called for in so many of the recipes is salted or unsalted. Professional cooks always test recipes with unsalted butter. I don't, because experience has told me that in most cases Americans use salted butter, no matter what the recipe says, and so adjustments have been made to allow for this. Obviously, if you use unsalted butter, you may have to add a little salt. And although I've not given it as an alternative, margarine can always be substituted for butter.

Unfortunately, because the preponderance of traditional Thanksgiving recipes were developed years before we all became so health aware and food smart, many are more than a little indulgent in butter, cream, sugar, and other things that we now eat in limited amounts. In those recipes where I considered the use of these things to be overkill, I went ahead and reduced them as much as possible without losing the characteristic flavor or texture of the dish. Of course, its always possible to make any recipe more Spartan, and you can do so, if you like, but for Thanksgiving I believe it may be better to simply recognize these foods as the special-occasion, once-in-a-while treats that they are.

ONE

Special Ingredients

❦

Although most of the ingredients called for in this book are quite common and familiar, a few may require some further explanation and directions for preparation.

CHESTNUTS

❦

At one time chestnut trees flourished in the United States until a blight in the early twentieth century eventually killed them right down to the last one. Lately, attempts to reestablish them here have been more or less successful, but the great majority of fresh chestnuts you find in the market come from France, Italy, and Japan.

Fresh chestnuts come into the market in the fall. They are at peak supply in October and November, but may be gone soon after, so if you have any idea of using chestnuts for the December holidays, buy nice ones when you see them, since whole nuts can be frozen, then thawed and cooked when you're ready for them.

For all their rich, sweet flavor, chestnuts are actually low in calories and fat, about 95 calories per ¼ cup, with less than a gram of fat. There are about 36 large chestnuts in a pound, which will yield about 2½ cups of peeled nuts.

Buying, Storage, and Preparation

Look for large glossy specimens that feel heavy for their size. Check that the shell adheres closely to the nut meat. An air pocket indicates that the nut meat has started to dry and shrivel. Buy just a few more nuts than you actually need, since a chestnut can look perfect on the outside but still be spoiled on the inside. They keep well for a week or so in a cool environment, and refrigerated for about two weeks.

Chestnuts must be peeled before they are used, and in order to do that they have to be precooked by either boiling or roasting.

To boil. Cut an X with the tip of a knife on the flat underside. Place the nuts in a large saucepan and cover with cold water. Bring to a boil over high heat. Lower the heat slightly and boil slowly for 15 minutes. Drain the nuts, and the moment they are cool enough to handle, peel off the shell and also the dark skin that covers the nut, which is rather bitter. As the nuts cool down they will become harder to peel. In that case, reheat them in boiling water.

To roast. Cut an X with the tip of a knife on the flat underside. Preheat the oven to 425°F. Spread the nuts in a shallow pan and roast for 20 minutes. Follow the preceding instructions for peeling.

Substituting Preserved Chestnuts

When fresh chestnuts are not available, it's also possible to buy them cooked, peeled, and packed in a small amount of water in a 16-ounce can or jar. These almost always come from France and are marked *marrons entiers*. They have a flavor and texture that is very similar to fresh. (These should not be confused with *marrons glacés*, which are chestnuts packed in sugar syrup.) When used in a recipe, canned chestnuts should be treated like peeled fresh nuts, including further cooking if the recipe calls for it.

CHICKEN AND BEEF BROTH

Many of the recipes in this book call for chicken broth and, less frequently, beef broth. It's easy enough to open a can or dissolve a bouillon cube, of course, but nothing beats having your own stash of homemade broth. Making broth from scratch is easy, it has an incomparable flavor, and certainly it's cheaper.

4 pounds chicken necks, backs, or wings
  or
4 pounds beef bones with just a little of
  the meat left on them
2 large onions, coarsely chopped (2 cups)
2 or 3 celery ribs, coarsely chopped (1 cup)
1 or 2 carrots, coarsely chopped (1 cup)

1 large onion, unpeeled and cut into large
  pieces (the onion skin will add some
  color to the broth)
2 whole cloves
1 bay leaf
4 or 5 fresh parsley sprigs
½ teaspoon dried thyme leaves, crumbled
8 peppercorns

Combine all of the ingredients in a large pot and cover with 4 quarts of cold water. Bring to a boil over high heat, skimming off the foam and scum with a large spoon as it rises to the surface. Lower the heat to medium-low and simmer gently, partially covered, for about 3 hours. Strain the broth into a large bowl through a colander that has been lined with a double thickness of damp cheesecloth. Discard the solids and set the broth aside to cool. When it has cooled, cover and refrigerate for several hours. As the broth chills, the fat will rise to the surface and solidify. Remove the congealed fat and discard it. Pour the broth into 1- to 4-cup containers with tight-fitting lids. The broth can be refrigerated for several days. Freeze for longer storage, up to six months. If freezing, allow about ½ inch of headspace for expansion in each container.

YIELD: ABOUT 12 CUPS

Note: For a dark, rich-looking broth, the chicken or beef can be browned before making the broth. Preheat the oven to 450°F. Spread the chicken or beef in a shallow roasting pan that has been lightly greased or coated with nonstick vegetable spray. Roast for 20 to 30 minutes, turning occasionally, until nicely browned.

A Better Canned Chicken or Beef Broth

The flavor of canned broth can be freshened and improved by simmering briefly with fresh vegetables and seasonings.

Four 13¾- or 14½-ounce cans clear
  chicken or beef broth
4 or 6 celery ribs, coarsely chopped
  (2 cups)
1 large onion, unpeeled and coarsely
  chopped (1 cup)

1 or 2 carrots, coarsely chopped (1 cup)
2 cups water
2 or 3 fresh parsley sprigs
1 bay leaf
½ teaspoon dried thyme leaves, crumbled
6 peppercorns

Combine all of the ingredients in a large pot and bring to a boil over high heat. Reduce the heat to medium-low and simmer, partially covered, for about 30 minutes. Strain the broth into a large bowl through a colander that has been lined with a double thickness of damp cheesecloth. Cool the broth and then pour it into 1- or 2-cup containers with tight-fitting lids. The broth can be refrigerated for several days. Freeze for longer storage, up to six months. If freezing, allow about ½ inch of headspace for expansion in each container.

YIELD: ABOUT 6 CUPS

CRÈME FRAÎCHE

This is what the French use in place of heavy or whipping cream. It is thicker than cream but less thick than sour cream, and is formed by the action of the culture, which thickens it and gives it a pleasantly sour, nutty flavor. Crème fraîche is widely available here, but if you can't find it, it's easy enough to make at home. However, you must use regular pasteurized heavy cream, not ultra-pasteurized cream, which does not have enough bacteria to curdle the cream properly.

To make it, add 1 tablespoon of buttermilk or plain yogurt to a half-pint container of heavy or whipping cream. Hold the top closed and shake well to mix. Allow the container to stand undisturbed at room temperature for 12 to 24 hours, at which point it will have thickened and turned slightly sour. Refrigerate and use within a week.

Another method is to whisk together equal parts of heavy or whipping cream and sour cream until slightly thickened. Refrigerate and use within a week.

DRIED CHERRIES

Several years ago I tasted my first dehydrated sour cherry at a fancy foods show, and right away I figured this product would be a winner. It took awhile, but now dried cherries (as well as dried blueberries and dried cranberries) are available in specialty food stores, loose or packaged, and I can't say enough wonderful things about them. I use dried cherries for both cooking and for snacking, although at their current price they aren't likely to become daily lunch-box fillers very soon.

Dried cherries should be handled about the same as other dried fruits. If purchased loose, transfer them to a zip-top plastic bag or a container with a tight-fitting lid (they need not be refrigerated if used within a week). If storage is to be longer, freeze in a zip-top plastic bag. Most recipes for dried cherries call for them to be plumped in some liquid before they are used.

If you have trouble finding dried cherries, you can order them from American Spoon Foods, P.O. Box 566, Petoskey, Michigan 49770.

(SUN-) DRIED TOMATOES
❦

Who knows for how many centuries Italian housewives were sun-drying their home-grown tomatoes for a rainy day before the idea caught on here. Dried Roma or plum tomatoes are available almost everywhere these days, and are sold both loose and packed in olive oil. They are so immensely popular that it's also possible to buy them chopped and packed in olive oil, or simply chopped into bits, all ready to sprinkle on salads.

The vast majority of so-called sun-dried tomatoes are actually dried by means of mechanical dehydration. And although this method lacks the charming image of to-matoes drying in the sun on a screen, it does guarantee an evenness and quality of the product, to say nothing of cleanliness and price.

I generally buy dried tomatoes loose (they're cheaper that way) and marinate some of them in a jar filled with olive oil to which I've added some slivered garlic and a few dried rosemary leaves. As long as the oil stays fresh, tomatoes that are completely covered with oil can be stored at room temperature. Refrigerate for long-term storage, but bring to room temperature for an hour or so before serving, as the olive oil will solidify when it is chilled. Since I use the tomatoes and the oil, I keep adding more of each for a while before starting a fresh batch. Any extra tomato-flavored oil can be used for cooking and in dressings. It never goes to waste.

Loose dried tomatoes should be stored in a zip-top plastic bag or a container with a tight-fitting lid (they don't need to be refrigerated). They can be rehydrated quickly in a little boiling water.

MUSHROOMS
❦

Until a few years ago, of all the many edible mushroom species on earth, only the regular white (or tan) button mushrooms, sold loose or in plastic-covered containers, were readily available unless, of course, you were an expert and could go foraging in the forest, or could afford to buy dry mushrooms imported from Europe.

Wild mushrooms defy cultivation, but lately mushroom producers in the United

States have discovered whatever the secrets are for growing a few of the more exotic varieties, and are marketing them at an affordable price range. The produce market where I shop usually has five or six exotic mushrooms to choose from all the time. The ones I reach for most often are the shiitake and crimini varieties.

Shiitake mushrooms. Also known as black forest and golden oak mushrooms, these are my favorite. They have broad, fleshy caps and skinny, woody stems, which are usually discarded or thrown into the stock pot. Shiitakes have a rich, almost smokey taste that withstands other strong flavors, and a meaty consistency that is also a little bit chewy.

When selecting shiitake mushrooms, look for caps that are dry and springy. The edges may be a bit ragged, and the color can range from pale brown to almost black. The cap size can range from an inch or so to several inches in diameter. Most recipes call for the caps to be sliced into strips, after they have been briefly rinsed and patted dry on paper towels.

Crimini mushrooms. When freshly picked, these look very much like ordinary button mushrooms, to which they are closely related, but that's where the resemblance ends. Within a few days the crimini cap naturally turns from light to deep brown and develops a deep, rich flavor. Handle these mushrooms and their stems just like the button mushrooms, slicing the caps or using them whole.

Other varieties that you are likely to come upon and may like to try are Chinese cloud ears, enoki, oyster, chanterelles, porcini (cèpes), and morels.

NUTS, TOASTED

Nuts take on greater flavor depth when toasted, and although a bit of a nuisance, the results are well worth the small effort.

Nuts can be toasted chopped (slivered or sliced) or whole, on the stove top or in the oven, usually depending on the amount being toasted. For much more than a cup, you may want to use the oven method.

Although it takes a few minutes for the nuts to start toasting, once they do it's only a matter of seconds until they burn, so watch carefully or, I should say, smell carefully, since it's actually the aroma that tells you when the nuts are perfectly toasted.

To pan toast. Place the whole or chopped nuts in a dry skillet that is large enough to hold them in a single layer. Cook over medium heat, stirring and tossing them constantly, just until the nuts begin to smell toasty. Immediately remove from the heat and continue stirring for a minute or two, since the heat retained by the skillet can cause the nuts to burn.

To toast in a conventional oven. Spread the whole or chopped nuts in a single layer in a shallow pan and place in a cold oven. Set the oven temperature to 350°F. Toast whole nuts for 12 to 15 minutes, and chopped nuts for 9 to 11 minutes, stirring occasionally, or until the nuts smell toasty. Remove from the oven and continue to stir for a minute or two.

To toast in a microwave oven. Spread the whole or chopped nuts on a microwave-safe plate or tray. Microwave on high power for 4 or 5 minutes for whole nuts and 3 minutes for chopped nuts, stirring halfway through toasting time. Cool on the counter.

NUTS, BLANCHED
❦

Blanched almonds are called for frequently in this book. It's possible to blanch your own natural almonds (those still in their brown skins) if you want to, although I can't imagine going to the bother, since almonds that are already blanched are readily available, whole, slivered, and chopped.

   To blanch whole almonds, cover them with boiling water and let stand for 3 minutes, then test to see if the skins slip off easily. Remove the almonds from the water, one by one, and slip off the skins by squeezing the almond between two fingers. Let dry on paper towels for several hours. Store in a tightly covered container.

NUT OILS
❦

These delicate oils are derived from nuts. Since heat destroys their flavor, nut oils are used only as a flavoring ingredient, and a rather expensive one at that. But since they are almost always called for in small amounts, the cost per serving is minimal after the initial cash outlay. Walnut, hazelnut, and almond oils are the main nut oils. They are very fragile and turn rancid quickly, but will keep in the refrigerator for six months to a year.

PEPPERS (ROASTED)

If you've never tasted a roasted pepper, you have no idea what a difference it can make. Roasting gives bell peppers (and other members of the pepper family as well) a mellowness and depth of flavor that will surprise you.

Roasting peppers is no big deal. There are two ways to do it—in the oven under the broiler, or on the stove top using a direct flame. The stove-top method is handy for roasting a single pepper.

To oven roast, place the peppers on the rack in a broiling pan. Roast about 4 inches from the source of the heat until the skins are charred and blistered, turning frequently to roast evenly, which will take 10 to 15 minutes. The peppers should be almost black, but don't overdo it so much that they actually cook and start to collapse. Remove the peppers from the oven and immediately place them in a paper bag, twisting the top closed. Set aside until the peppers have cooled enough to handle them. Remove the peppers from the bag and, using your fingers and a paring knife, strip off the skins.

To roast on the stove top, place the pepper directly on the grate over a medium flame, turning often until the skin is evenly charred and blistered. Place the pepper in a paper bag and proceed as instructed.

PUMPKIN

Those giant-size pumpkins for sale along the side of the road are great for carving into jack-o'-lanterns but not for dessert. The United Fresh Fruit and Vegetable Association recommends a 3- to 5-pound sugar pumpkin for eating. Look for these in stores specializing in fancy produce, and then select one that has a hard rind, is free of bruises, and is heavy for its size.

VINEGARS

Along with ever-increasing numbers of vegetable and nut oils is an expanding selection of flavored vinegars to go with them.

Before the days of *nouvelle cuisine*, besides cider and white vinegar, the most exciting distillations on the shelf were strong-flavored red and white wine vinegars. The wine vinegars are still there, of course, but now they have been greatly refined and have been joined by a whole array of fresh-tasting companions, including champagne and sherry vinegar, and slightly sweet rice vinegar, as well as those that are herb- and fruit-flavored, and the famous aged Italian balsamic vinegar. In fact, some vinegars have such exquisite, delicate flavors that they can be used as flavorings in drinks—vinegar spritzers, so to speak.

Good vinegar is worth spending the extra money that it's likely to cost. Vinegar has a lot in common with wine, which is the way many vinegars begin life, and like wine you may have to taste quite a few before you find a brand to settle on. And they won't last forever, either, so store fine vinegars in a cool, dry place where they will keep for about six months.

WILD RICE
❦

Wild rice is not rice at all but rather the seed of an aquatic grass native to the Great Lakes region. For centuries it was harvested from canoes by Native Americans using centuries-old techniques, hence the high price it has always commanded. For years wild rice resisted all attempts at cultivation, but it is now being successfully grown and mechanically harvested in California. Still it is a difficult and temperamental crop, so the price has not dropped significantly.

Wild rice has an unusual texture that ranges from slightly crisp to chewy, and a glorious flavor that is often described as "woodsy" or "earthy."

There are three grades of wild rice: select, extra-fancy, and giant (the giant grade having the longest grains with little or no breakage), which are priced accordingly. The flavor and color of different brands can vary quite a lot, but the giant grade will always look the best.

There are 5 to 6 ounces of wild rice per cup. One cup of raw wild rice will yield about 4 cups of cooked rice.

TWO

Making Things Look Pretty

❦

DECORATING THE FOOD
AND SETTING THE TABLE

Hand a food editor a food photograph and chances are she'll be able to tell you almost exactly when the picture was taken just by looking at the way the food is garnished, styled, and arranged on the plate.

From the time the ancient Greeks and Romans turned the simple act of serving food into flamboyant fantasies, food styles and decorations have reflected, and continue to reflect, the era and lifestyles of the times in which they were created, often very precisely, subtly changing from year to year.

Right now we're in what I'd call a minimalist period, when one look at the food photos in magazines can say more than a thousand words about our busy lives and growing appreciation of natural things, as well as which foods we choose to eat. Fancy, fussy food styles and ditsy decorations are out, left behind in a time when the home cook had all day, almost any day, to spend in the kitchen.

This isn't to say that food shouldn't be presented attractively and appetizingly, even for so-called family meals, but I would encourage the cook to direct his or her energy into making the food itself look appealing and keep decorations and plate garnishes to a minimum.

The art of decorating and garnishing food can be an involved subject, and one that has been explored in depth in lavishly illustrated books on the subject. I can only hope to hit some of the high points and try to give you a few hints that have worked well for me.

I'll start by suggesting that you clip pages from magazines that show interesting food treatments and file them in different categories. It's amazing how inspirational these can be when you're stuck for ideas.

Special Touches for Thanksgiving

When a lot of time and money are spent on one meal, it's only natural to want to make the food look special, even spectacular, and in so doing, make those who have come to dine feel just as special.

Where does the cook begin to make food look more beautiful than it is already? First of all, food *is* beautiful, so begin with the food itself. Buy the best you can afford and treat it with the respect it deserves even before the cooking begins, by caring for it and storing it properly. All the garnishes in the world won't help a salad if the greens are wilted.

Overcooking is probably the greatest potential disaster when it comes to nice-looking food. Even Julia Child might have a hard time making a roast turkey look good if the legs are falling off.

Food as Art

Think of the food you are about to serve as a still life, the plate being the canvas and the food on it the picture that is being painted. Sometimes just the arrangement of the food on the plate, with nothing else, looks great. Other times a little bit of something is needed—a dab of color, an interesting shape—on or near the food to create an eye-appealing, edible picture.

A garnish should have some connection with the food it decorates. One of my favorite spur-of-the-moment garnishes was a few raspberries scattered over a platter of sauced chicken. The connection was the raspberry vinegar I'd used to deglaze the cooking pan. The raspberries tasted good with the chicken, and besides being colorful, they added important elements of surprise and whimsy.

A Palette of Ingredients

Parsley. As innocuous as it seems, curly or flatleaf parsley can still be the perfect garnish, but its presence should appear deliberate and not as if it were plopped on the plate as an afterthought. For example, strip away most of the leaves on the sprig to accentuate the long stem, laying down two or three as if they were long-stemmed flowers. Or a strategically placed sprig, barely the size of a ladybug, may be exactly what's needed.

Fresh herbs. You wouldn't know it to look at dried herbs, but fresh herbs have marvelous colors and shapes, from wispy dill to long, frosty-looking leaves of sage, as well as dark, shiny bay leaves and graceful chives. And, of course, there is mint, which needn't *always* be relegated to desserts.

Although pricey, little bunches of fresh herbs are regularly starting to appear in the produce sections of ordinary supermarkets. Specialty food stores usually carry a grander array. In the winter I keep two or three pots of the hardier varieties to winter over on my windowsill, so that I always have a little something on hand for cooking and garnishes.

Use fresh herbs sparingly or lavishly: A lacy dill sprig or a branch of rosemary on the side of a first-course plate or bunches of sage surrounding the turkey are both striking in different ways.

Salad greens. We're not talking big branches and stalks here. Look for more unusual and diminutive varieties with interesting colors, textures, and shapes. Spriggy watercress, spidery Italian endive, bright maroon radicchio, angular red oakleaf lettuce, and tiny spinach leaves are all good candidates, even celery leaves.

Sprouts. They're all tasty, but wee green radish sprouts, especially, and alfalfa sprouts are the ones I use most often for decoration.

Miniature vegetables. If you're fortunate enough to be able to find them, miniature carrots, squash, eggplant, radishes, zucchini, tiny Brussels sprouts, and pearl onions are especially eye-catching when arranged here and there on large platters, particularly with poultry and roasts.

Fruits and nuts. Small fruits and berries can add color and brightness when tucked into green garnishes. Some of my autumn favorites are kumquats, grapes, cranberries, and pomegranate seeds. In-shell nuts are extremely attractive, almonds and walnuts being two of the showiest.

Simple Cutting and Slicing Techniques

Not long ago I had dinner at a Chinese restaurant where the Peking duck was served on a platter that included a hollowed-out turnip with an intricately carved top, lit from the inside by a tiny battery-powered bulb. I'm not talking turnip lights for the turkey, but a few simple cuts and slices can add attractive dimensions to fruits and vegetables.

Citrus twists. Cut a lemon, lime, or orange into transparently thin slices. With the tip of a knife, make one cut from the center of the slice through to the edge. Pick up the slice and twist it into a simple spiral.

Channels. With the tip of a paring knife, cut narrow channels lengthwise in a lemon, lime, or orange. The channels will appear as decorative edges when the fruit is sliced.

Citrus spirals. Use a sharp knife or a vegetable parer to cut the rind from a lemon, lime, or orange into one continuous spiral, the narrower the better. Wind the spiral around the handle of a wooden spoon, taping the ends so it won't come loose, and set aside for an hour or so until it "sets." Slip the curl from the handle. Loose curls look wonderful around the edge of a platter.

Cutouts. Strip or peel the rind from lemons, limes, oranges, or grapefruit, keeping the pieces as large as possible. Scrape away the white pith. Cut the pieces of rind into small shapes, such as diamonds, teardrops, or stars.

Whole-vegetable spirals. Any long, straight fruit is suitable for this technique, such as cucumbers, zucchini, or fat carrots. Cut off the ends, then insert a wooden kebob stick straight through the center of the vegetable. With a paring knife, cut slices around and around the vegetable, going through only as far as the stick. Very carefully pull out the stick, being careful not to tear the slices apart. Gently arrange into a semicircular spiral.

Fancy slices. Cut cucumbers, zucchini, or carrots into ¼-inch slices. Use a slightly smaller cookie cutter to cut out the centers of the slices. Use either the cutouts or the rim that's left for decoration. These vegetables can also be channeled using the method described for citrus fruit, or with the tines of a fork, before slicing.

Fans. Suitable for pickles, small carrots, and oval radishes. Lay the vegetable on its side and make very thin cuts, starting just below the root end down to the tip. Gently press the fan open.

Radish flowers. There are many ways to make radish flowers. This is one of the easiest and prettiest: Trim the root tip and, with the stem end down, make as many parallel cuts as possible through the radish down to within ⅛ inch of the stem. Turn the radish and make parallel cuts in the opposite direction. Place the radish in ice water until it opens, about one hour.

Green onion (scallion) brushes. There are two ways to make brushes. For a double brush, cut off most of the green leaves, leaving an overall piece about 3 inches long. With a sharp knife, cut slashes in one or both ends, turning the onion to make as many cuts as possible and leaving about ½ inch uncut at one end, or in the center if slashing both ends. Place the brushes in ice water until the slashes curl, about one hour.

Green onion frills. Trim the onion, leaving the green leaves. With a sharp knife, starting just above the white portion, make as many cuts as possible in the leaves. Place in a bowl of ice water until the leaves curl, about one hour.

Onion chrysanthemums. Peel a red onion, the size depending on the size flower you need. With the stem end down, cut the onion into quarters down to about ¼ inch above the root. Cut each quarter in half and in half again in the same manner, until there are sixteen divisions. Place the onion in ice water until it opens, about one hour.

Citrus rind and tomato roses. Trim off the rind of a lemon or orange with a sharp paring knife or a vegetable parer, going around and around in one continuous spiral, leaving behind as much of the white pith as possible. Roll the spiral into a rose, tightly at the center and becoming looser toward the edge. Secure with a toothpick. Use the same method for a tomato rose.

Julienne. Almost all vegetables and some fruits can be cut into julienne, which is best described as matchsticklike pieces, or finer. The julienne can be sprinkled anyplace a touch of color is needed.

Flowers and Plant Leaves

Any number of plants and flowers make lovely food decorations and plate garnishes. The only precautionary measure you must take before using them on food is to make sure that they have not been treated with toxic chemicals. Other than that, simply rinse the leaves in cold water and dry them on a rack. I have an old grapefruit tree that's hardly a beauty, but I keep it around for the express purpose of using its glossy, green leaves both as a garnish and for making chocolate leaves (see page 16). Although more typical of Christmas, holly leaves are also pretty, but remember that the berries are poisonous.

In the autumn the flower selection is rather sparse, so I usually opt for small yellow and dark red chrysanthemums, which I frequently use to garnish the turkey platter, tucked in among lots of glossy green leaves.

Sugar-Frosted Fruit

To give small fruits and berries a more festive appearance, they can be frosted with sugar. This looks especially nice when used on grapes, cranberries, and raspberries. Unfortunately, since raw egg white is used, these fruits should not be eaten.

Beat an egg white in a small bowl until well combined. With an artist's brush, paint the beaten white onto dry fruit, then sprinkle lavishly with granulated sugar. Set the sugared fruit on a rack to dry in a cool place for an hour or so. The same technique can be used for flowers (see page 16).

Dessert Decorations

Desserts are probably the biggest challenge for the cook who enjoys food decoration. The skills needed to artfully decorate cakes and other sweets don't develop overnight. Professional food stylists and talented home cooks have usually invested many hours, icing bag in hand, practicing a dizzying number of roses, swags, leaves, shells, zigzags, and stars, and other decorating techniques.

Fortunately, any number of simple tricks can add a lot of dazzle to desserts, even if you've decided you're all thumbs. Here are a few:

Nuts. Chopped, sliced, slivered, or whole, even a sprinkling of nuts can be most effective. Pressed onto the side or top of a cake, nuts are also elegant and easy cake decorations. If the cake is not iced, you can make the nuts stick by first giving the cake a jelly glaze.

The best way to chop nuts that will be used for decoration is the old-fashioned way: with a chef's knife. After chopping, shake the nuts through a fine- or medium-mesh sieve to eliminate any pieces that have been chopped too fine; rechop those that are too large. The chopped nuts should be more or less uniform in size. Toasting pale-colored nuts (see pages 6–7) is a good idea since it not only brings out their best flavor, but gives them a rich color.

Dusting and stenciling. Nearly everyone knows the old trick of sifting confectioners' sugar through a doily placed on top of a cake, but cocoa or even ground spices can be used, too. Take the stenciling one step further by using cardboard or plastic stencils (available where crafts and quilting supplies are sold) to make other kinds of fancy decorations and borders, even numbers and initials. You can even use two or three stencils and contrasting colors. Shake the coatings through a fine-mesh sieve, and always practice first on a piece of waxed paper.

Sometimes all that's needed is a light dusting of cocoa powder or confectioners' sugar. Other little touches can be added, such as mint leaves, raspberries, strawberries, or sugar-frosted fruit (see page 14).

Chocolate. Curls, swirls and grated chocolate give cakes and desserts that luscious look we all love. To make curls, pull a vegetable parer along a piece of semisweet chocolate that has been warmed to room temperature. Then, as professional food stylists do, arrange the curls with a toothpick so they don't melt from the heat of your fingers or fall apart.

Grate chocolate cold and, if possible, directly onto whatever is to be decorated. It's almost impossible to handle grated chocolate.

To make melted-chocolate swirls and other designs, place melted chocolate (milk chocolate, semisweet, or white) in a small zipper-top plastic bag. Cut a tiny piece off one lower corner and use like a decorating bag to make swirls and scrolls, or to write messages on cakes, cookies, and other desserts. Practice first on waxed paper.

Chocolate leaves. Melt semisweet, white, or milk chocolate pieces in the top of a double boiler over barely simmering water, stirring until smooth. With a small artist's brush, paint the warm, melted chocolate over the veined *underside* of a clean, dry, nontoxic leaf. Coat the leaf from the stem to the edges. Place the coated leaves, chocolate side up, on a plate or in a shallow bowl. To ensure that all the leaves aren't flat, lay some of them in the curve of the bowl so that the leaf will be slightly rounded. Refrigerate the leaves until hardened, at least one hour. Remove the leaves from the refrigerator and, working quickly, peel the leaf away from the chocolate. Chill the leaves until ready to use.

Chocolate dipping. Use the same method for melting the chocolate as for chocolate leaves. Place the dipped piece on waxed paper to dry. Nearly any clean, dry fruit can be coated with chocolate to use for decorating or eating, or both.

Supermarket supplies. Maybe the easiest decorations of all start at the supermarket. Cookies and candies can be used whole, crushed, or chopped. Also have a look at the various decorating supplies. Tubes of decorating icings and gels are very handy for the occasional decorator. It's also a good idea to have colored sugars, sprinkles, and dragées (those little silver balls that look like shotgun pellets) in the cupboard, since they keep practically forever.

Sugar-frosted flowers. Tiny roses, rosebuds, and freesia are all good candidates for this luxurious treatment. The only thing you will have to ascertain is that the flowers have not been treated with toxic chemicals or are inherently toxic. I have a florist who stocks flowers that are meant to be used with food. If I weren't sure, I'd probably put the sugared floral arrangement on a piece of cut-to-size plastic wrap to keep the food and flowers separate. The method for sugar-frosting flowers is exactly the same as sugar-frosted fruit on page 14.

Whipped cream. Dollops of whipped cream always look luscious, but for a more glamorous effect, remember that whipped cream can be piped just like icing. All you need is a big pastry bag fitted with a large decorating tip. When holding the bag, be gentle so that the cream is deflated as little as possible.

The recipes that follow are some of my favorite garnish recipes that have been mentioned elsewhere in this book.

PUFF PASTRY CUTOUTS

I use these tiny cutouts to float on top of cream soups and sometimes to decorate salads.

One sheet frozen puff pastry from a 17¼-
ounce box, thawed according to package
directions

Preheat the oven to 475°F. Roll out the pastry on a baking sheet that has been lightly greased or coated with nonstick vegetable spray. With tiny cookie cutters, cut out small rounds, squares, or other simple shapes. Remove the excess pastry from the baking sheet, lifting and cutting it away with the tip of a knife. Bake for about 5 minutes, or until the cutouts are puffed and golden. Cool on the baking sheet, then remove and store in a dry place until ready to serve.

YIELD: 48 TO 60 CUTOUTS

CANDIED ORANGE OR CITRUS RIND

A garnish that doubles as a confection. The strips can be dipped in chocolate, too.

4 large navel oranges   *Sugar for coating*
1½ cups sugar

Remove the rind from each orange in four large sections. With a spoon, scrape all of the bitter white pith from each piece of the rind and discard. Cut the rinds lengthwise into strips ¼ to ½ inch wide. (The strips can be cut into even finer slivers after they are cooked and before they are coated with sugar.) Place the strips in a large saucepan and add water to cover by about 2 inches. Bring to a boil over high heat. Reduce the heat to medium-low and simmer, uncovered, for 30 minutes. Drain the rind, add water to cover as before, bring to a boil, and simmer for another 30 minutes. *Do not drain.* Stir in the sugar and an additional ¾ cup water. Bring to a quick simmer over medium heat, stirring occasionally. Simmer for 25 minutes, then drain *very thoroughly.* When the peel is just cool enough to handle, roll in sugar that has been sprinkled on a piece of waxed paper. Spread out on another piece of waxed paper for about an hour to dry. Store in a tightly covered container until needed. The sugared rind will stay soft for a couple of weeks.

YIELD: ABOUT 3 CUPS

MUSHROOM-STUFFED MUSHROOMS

A luxurious garnish for elegant poultry and meat—for instance, squab and roast beef. The stuffing is actually a *duxelles*, which is a mixture of chopped mushrooms, vegetables, and seasonings. A *duxelles* is a very handy recipe to know since you can use it to stuff and fill many things (omelets, for instance), or stir it into gravy or sauce. You can also add it to a light white sauce to make cream of mushroom soup. The *duxelles* can be made ahead. Tightly covered, it keeps well for a few days in the refrigerator, and for months in the freezer.

12 large regular white mushrooms with
  caps about 2 inches in diameter (about
  ½ pound)
2 tablespoons butter
1 medium-size onion, finely chopped
  (½ cup)

1 small carrot, scraped and finely chopped
  (⅓ cup)
½ teaspoon soy sauce
¼ teaspoon salt
¼ teaspoon sugar
1 tablespoon finely chopped fresh parsley

Gently twist the mushroom stems to remove them and set aside. Reserve eight of the caps (without rinsing) in the refrigerator until you're ready to stuff them (if it will be awhile before you stuff them, place them in a brown paper bag). Rinse and trim the reserved stems and the four remaining mushroom caps. Pat dry on paper towels. Place the stems and caps on a cutting surface and chop into very small pieces with a long, sharp knife. You should have about 2 cups. Melt the butter in a large skillet over medium heat. When it is hot, add the onion and carrot and cook, stirring, until the onion is transparent. Add the chopped mushrooms, soy sauce, salt, and sugar. Continue to cook, stirring occasionally. As the mushrooms begin to cook and give up their liquid, the mixture will become very soupy, but as the liquid evaporates the mixture will cook down and become very pasty. The whole cooking procedure should take no more than 15 minutes. Remove the pan from the heat and set aside to cool. If not using immediately, cover tightly and refrigerate.

When ready to stuff, preheat the oven to 400°F. (This may be done right after the poultry or meat is removed from the oven.) Rinse the eight reserved caps and pat dry on paper towels. Place in a lightly buttered baking dish that is just large enough to hold them comfortably, cavity side down. Bake for 5 minutes. Remove from the oven and set aside to cool slightly. Mix the parsley with the mushroom mixture. Stuff the caps, mounding each one slightly. Return the filled caps to the baking dish, filled side up. Bake for about 10 minutes, or until heated through. Garnish the meat platter with the stuffed mushrooms.

YIELD: 8 STUFFED MUSHROOMS

CANDIED CRANBERRIES
❦

I won't lie to you. These take some time to make, although they're not difficult. I like to have them on hand to use as a garnish for Thanksgiving and Christmas meals. The trouble is, they also make a nice little snack, so you'll be lucky to have any around when you need them.

1¾ cups sugar　　　　　　　　　*One 12-ounce bag fresh cranberries, rinsed*
¾ cup water　　　　　　　　　　　　*and picked over (3 cups)*

　　Combine the sugar and water in a medium-size saucepan. Bring to a boil and stir constantly until the sugar dissolves. Place the cranberries in a small bowl and pour the boiling syrup over them. Place the bowl on a rack set in the bottom of a 6-quart saucepan. Pour enough water into the pan to come up to the bottom of the bowl. Cover the pan tightly, first with aluminum foil and then with the lid. Reduce the heat to medium and steam the berries for 45 minutes. Remove the pan from the heat. When the bowl is cool enough to handle, remove it from the pan and let the bowl of berries stand, uncovered, for two days. Remove the cranberries from the bowl with a slotted spoon to a rack set over a piece of waxed paper to catch the drips. Set the rack in a cool, dry place for about three days, turning the berries now and then. Pack the cranberries in a container with a tight-fitting lid. The berries will keep well at room temperature for several weeks.

YIELD: ABOUT 2 CUPS

Setting the Table

The Thanksgiving dinner table is the setting, or stage, for all of your production work in the kitchen. Just as a painting deserves a flattering frame, a painstakingly prepared meal deserves a worthy setting to show it off to its most appetizing advantage.

　　If you're fortunate enough to have inherited any of Grandma's silver or china, this is the time to enjoy it. However, elegant doesn't have to mean elaborate or expensive.

　　First, take an inventory of what's on hand. You'll probably be surprised. With menu in hand, go over everything, making sure there are plates and bowls and serving utensils for all the things you plan to serve. Remember that everything doesn't have to match. In fact, I think a table is much more interesting if everything is not precisely alike right down to the last salt spoon. Mixing different colors and patterns can be very effective as long as the overall look is harmonious and pleasing.

　　Through the years I've collected a lot of tableware just because I liked it. I started married life with a plain, white china pattern with a gold rim, but since then I've added many things in different and often much more elaborate patterns—for instance, several different sets of dessert and salad plates, a dozen or two cups and saucers, soup bowls, and a whole collection of demitasse, no two of which are alike and which I frequently use all together. The same is true of my flatware. Although the knives, dinner and salad forks, and most of the spoons are all one pattern, nothing else is. The soup spoons, bread-and-butter knives, and coffee spoons, for example, are all different, things I've picked up now and then, usually in antique shops and at flea markets, but they all look nice together.

Place mats and napkins are other things I buy when I see them at a good price. Usually I never get less than eight of anything because that's the number that most often sits down at my table on special occasions. Hidden away in a drawer is a damask tablecloth and umpteen linen napkins for more elaborate affairs.

A dining table is almost certain to mirror the taste and lifestyle, and very often the personal flair, of the person who sets it. The only hard-and-fast rule for setting a table "properly" is that it be attractive and welcoming.

What Goes Where

If you want to set a traditional table, these are the most common arrangements, one more formal than the other.

1. napkin
2. service plate
3. water goblet
4. red wine glass
5. white wine glass
6. salad fork
7. dinner fork
8. dessert fork
9. dinner knife
10. coffee spoon
11. soup spoon

PLACE SETTING FOR A FORMAL DINNER

These days few people have all of the china, flatware, and glassware necessary to set a table like this one, which can actually be even *more* elaborate, and can include salad knives, fish forks and fish knives, and individual salt and pepper servers, among several other possibilities. This is more or less the basic setting from which all place settings, even the most casual ones, are based. It's easy to know what goes where if you just remember the general rule of placing everything in the order in which it will be used, from the outside in, and from top to bottom. Bread-and-butter plates and knives are often not included in a formal place setting, but they are almost always needed at Thanksgiving and are placed as shown in the less formal diagram. The salad is served as a separate course, and the dessert spoon and/or fork is laid out when dessert is served.

PLACE SETTING FOR A LESS FORMAL DINNER

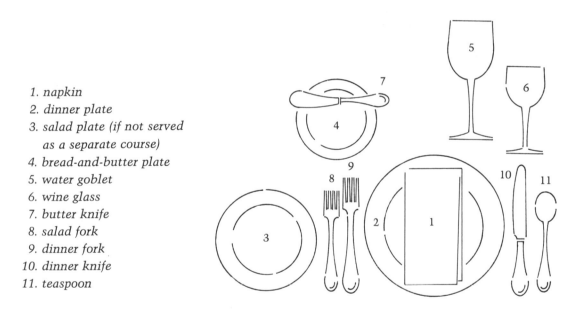

1. napkin
2. dinner plate
3. salad plate (if not served
   as a separate course)
4. bread-and-butter plate
5. water goblet
6. wine glass
7. butter knife
8. salad fork
9. dinner fork
10. dinner knife
11. teaspoon

This is simply a scaled-down version of the formal place setting, which can be scaled down even more, if necessary.

The Centerpiece

In the middle of everything else that's on the table, you'll probably want to leave room for a centerpiece, and my major advice about this would be to keep it small.

A centerpiece needn't be limited to flowers. In keeping with the spirit of Thanksgiving, anything that suggests a bountiful harvest would be appropriate and undoubtedly colorful, and usually less expensive and more durable than a floral arrangement. If you want to use or include flowers, consider a small flowering plant, usually chrysanthemums at this time of year.

Some of the things from which to choose include tiny pumpkins and other squash or gourds, miniature ears of dried corn, real autumn leaves (collected earlier in the season), bittersweet, and dried sheaves of grain. Ivy vines from your garden or other green leaves can also be added to soften the arrangement and tie things together.

If the table will be very crowded, you might want to have an arrangement that can be moved after the first course is served, and then put back on the table for dessert. And remember to keep the centerpiece low so that those facing each other across the table don't have to crane their necks or peek around it.

If the dinner is served in the evening, candles can also be set on the table as part of the centerpiece. Light them before the guests sit down to dinner, and extinguish them after everyone has left the table. Tall, tapered candles are always beautiful and come in an array of colors. There are also short, fat candles that can be set into the centerpiece. Remember that Thanksgiving dinner usually goes on and on, so make sure the candles are big enough to burn for several hours.

THREE

Beverages and Wine

❦

Accounts of the 1621 harvest festival at Plymouth contain few references to any beverages that may have been served with the meal. However, records do show that Indian chief Massasoit broke into a sweat when served "aqua vitae," a ginlike, distilled spirit that the Pilgrims brought with them from England. But reserves of this "strong water," used mainly for medicinal purposes and sometimes for special occasions, must have been severely depleted nearly a year after the *Mayflower*'s arrival. Any other liquid provisions, notably ale, the Coca-Cola of seventeenth-century England, would undoubtedly have been long gone.

"Contrary to one popular myth," says James Baker, Director of Museum Operations at Plimouth Plantation, "the Pilgrims are not likely to have pressed and brewed wine from local grape crops." It would simply not have been English to do so, even though wine was not unknown in England at the time. In fact, the *Mayflower* had regularly carried wines from France's Bordeaux area to England before taking on her historic human cargo. The lack of orchards during the first years of the colony would also have ruled out cider or other fruit juices as options for the Pilgrims' table.

The odds are good, according to Baker, that the Pilgrims washed down their bird with beer or, more accurately, a type of low-alcohol ale brewed from the first scanty barley crop. It was what they were used to drinking at home, contrary to another popular myth that the Pilgrims were rigid ascetics who equated alcohol with sin. The modern Thanksgiving indulger will be happy to learn from scholars like Baker that the Pilgrims were hearty eaters who loved a good feast accompanied by a frothy ale or a splash of aqua vitae. The fundamentalist asceticism that gives Pilgrims their prim and proper reputation didn't show up until the early nineteenth century.

Aside from ale, and maybe a little goat whey, the most revolutionary beverage set out on the Pilgrims' table may have been New England's sparkling clean water, something to be particularly thankful for in contrast to the contaminated water in England.

Wine: Getting to Know the Varietals

Up until the middle of this century, milk for children and water for adults remained the traditional beverage accompaniments through scores of all-American Thanksgiving dinners. But during the last decade or two, prodigious culinary experimentation has altered the patriotic feast in some ways, above all, perhaps, in the choice of accompanying beverages. As a result, wine has increasingly found its way to the Thanksgiving table. Today's thriving American wine industry has raised our wine consciousness like nothing else. The range of domestic and imported wines, along with increasing sophistication about matching wines with foods, regardless of their respective colors, could make the task of selecting the right bottle, or bottles, for this special dinner mind boggling. Nevertheless, the choice need not be intimidating.

Several key factors come into play when choosing a wine. For the devoted connoisseur, settling on the wine may be the first step in planning the Thanksgiving feast, but for most families the bird is the centerpiece of the celebration and the wine is a secondary consideration.

The primary rule to remember when choosing a wine to accompany any menu is that there are no ironclad rules. The old axiom of "white wine with fowl and fish, and red wine with red meat" is a generality based on sound logic, but is by no means intractable. For instance, the white wine you might choose to serve with roast turkey stuffed with herbed winter vegetables would certainly be too light a partner for a goose with a kumquat and corn bread stuffing. The latter would call for a more assertive wine, either a very rich, slightly sweet white or a hearty, full-bodied red to balance the intense flavors of the goose and its stuffing.

Remember, too, that wine choices are a matter of personal taste and style. Open four different wines selected to complement the roast turkey and its trimmings, and you'll probably find as many different opinions about which one makes the best match.

Since Thanksgiving is a uniquely American feast, this is a particularly appropriate occasion to experiment with American wines. And since most American wines take their names from the varietals from which they are made, it helps the novice wine buyer to know the characteristics of these main grape varietals.

THE WHITES

Chardonnay. This noble varietal, grown widely in California, produces particularly rich and complex wines. Although styles vary, the prevailing characteristics are low to moderate acidity, and medium to full body, with nuances of apricot and spiced green apple. Often oak aged, this wine has a distinctive style that allows it to stand up well to a menu with a full range of flavors. Chardonnay is the grape used in France's luscious white burgundies, and is one of the grapes in champagne.

Chenin blanc. This produces lively, light-bodied whites that can be dry, slightly sweet, or very sweet. Acidity is often high, and its very subtle flavors include melon and peach. This is the predominant white grape of France's legendary Loire Valley.

Sauvignon blanc. Fuller-bodied than chenin blanc, but lighter than chardonnay, this herby varietal results in dry, crisp whites that are often very aromatic, occasionally smokey, and are frequently lightly aged in oak. Wines made from this grape are also often labeled fumé blanc. This is the grape used in the wines of France's upper Loire Valley, as well as in the white wines of the Bordeaux region.

Gewürztraminer, or traminer. The German *Gewürz* translates as "spicy" or "seasoned" and aptly describes this particularly pungent grape. It produces very rich wines that can be vinified from dry to sweet. Despite their pronounced character, these moderately acidic wines can be quite soft, manifesting hints of lychee and other tropical fruits, as well as allspice. In addition to American versions, there are, of course, excellent gewürztraminers from the Alsace region of France, and Germany where they originated.

Riesling. Germany's noblest grape variety, riesling, has adapted well to American soil. Riesling is vinified from dry to sweet, but is frequently thought of as a sweet wine. Some of the best rieslings, often labeled Johannisberg riesling in the United States, achieve a pleasant balance between moderate acidity and relatively low sweetness. Late-harvest versions are full-bodied and sweet. German and French (from Alsace) versions are generally labeled just riesling. Flavor nuances include green apple, honeysuckle, and acacia.

THE REDS

Cabernet sauvignon. The primary grape of the Médoc and France's prestigious bordeaux wines, cabernet also produces some of the best of the California reds. It is available in a variety of styles at a wide range of prices. It has a marked herbaceous character, laced with touches of red fruit and spice. Traditional versions are highly tannic and require aging, although many California cabernets are now being vinified for early maturity. American cabernets are generally full-bodied and quite rich, just the right accompaniment for a magnificent holiday beef roast.

Pinot noir. The pride of Burgundy's regal reds, pinot noir at its best produces satin-smooth, moderately acidic and medium- to full-bodied wine, with hints of cherry and other red fruits, cinnamon, smoke, and violets. California versions vary greatly in quality, for this temperamental grape needs ideal conditions to flourish. Look for pinot noir from Sonoma, Monterey, Russian River Valley, and the Lost Carneros district. This wine is a good match with game.

Merlot. This mellow grape, used as the softening element in France's red bordeaux wines, has been widely planted and experimented with in California. The result is a diversity of aromatic, smooth wines with hints of black currants, cherries, and herbs.

Gamay. The grape used in France's famous beaujolais. It produces light, fragrant, fruity wines to be drunk fresh and young. In California, it is known as Napa gamay and shouldn't be confused with gamay beaujolais, a California variety of pinot noir.

Zinfandel. A fruity varietal of European origin that has dropped deep roots in California soil. Extremely versatile, this grape of low to moderate acidity, with hints of berries, spice, and flowers, runs the gamut from light- to full-bodied, from hearty and deeply colored and often zesty reds to delicate blush and lightly spiced whites.

SELECTING AND SERVING A DINNER WINE

With the main characteristics of these varietals in mind, the job of choosing a wine suited to your Thanksgiving menu becomes a little less intimidating. According to David Rosengarten, co-author of *Red Wine with Fish* (Simon & Schuster, New York, 1989), one of the most practical primers on the art of matching wine with food, the mating game can be approached in one of two ways: Decide to choose a wine that is strikingly similar to the elements of your menu, or aim for contrast by choosing a wine markedly different in some way from the menu's main flavor elements.

Remember to consider all the parts of the menu, not just the bird and its stuffing, but side dishes, too. The more diverse the flavor elements in the menu, the more universal the wine should be. (Bear in mind that serious wine drinkers may serve a different wine with every course.) Rich California chardonnays are good bets to match with a roast bird and the complex flavors that surround it. Fruity reds, including some pinot noirs, are also safe candidates. Another possibility for those who don't mind introducing a foreign element into this American celebration is a French Beaujolais. The *nouveau* versions of this light, fruity wine come onto the market in mid-November, and the hoopla that surrounds their appearance grows annually and makes them a very timely and festive choice for Thanksgiving.

And, of course, there are the sparkling wines, notably the American versions of champagnes, which are extremely versatile and certainly a celebratory choice. Sparkling and still hard ciders, with a low-alcohol content (around 6 percent) are yet another option, as well as apple wine.

California and New York are the largest and best known of the wine-producing states, but wine is vinified almost everywhere, and one can hardly drive ten miles on a back road without seeing a sign for a local winery. Most of these places eagerly invite passersby in for a taste, so why not? You might discover something eminently "quaffable," as the wine people say.

As always, when in doubt consult an expert, who may very well be a local wine merchant, and who will undoubtedly be happy to assist in the selections based on your Thanksgiving menu.

Some of the traditional stands on the proper way to serve wine are open to debate, mainly the question of how long in advance to open a red wine. The old dictum that tannic red wines should be opened several hours in advance to allow them time to aerate is not strictly adhered to by all. Many modern experts maintain that most wines do not need such long breathing periods. An hour or so should be more than enough time.

One rule that does hold is that wines, both red and white, suffer from temperature extremes, especially temperature fluctuations, and should not be subjected to rapid changes. Store wine bottles on their sides, with the tops tilted slightly downward so that the corks stay moist. Few homes today have a wine cellar, but a small one, not intended for long-term storage, can be created with a rack or two set away from light and heat, and where the temperature, if not perfect (50° to 57°F is ideal), is fairly stable.

White wines are generally served chilled and most red wines perform best at a little under room temperature. Opinions vary on ideal serving temperatures. Generally, dry whites and sparkling whites, including champagne and other sparkling wines, should be served at between 42° and 50°F, and full-bodied reds are best between 60° and 65°F, or what was once considered to be room temperature before the days of overheated houses.

To appreciate all of the aspects of wine—the look, aroma, and flavor—it should be served in a clear, stemmed wineglass, filled to just a third of its capacity.

Other Beverage Options

Although it was hardly a deliberate selection, the Pilgrims' choice of ale was an excellent one to accompany the conglomeration of meat and fowl and other foods that may have appeared on the first Thanksgiving table. Ale, and beer, too, are still good choices for the Thanksgiving meal, although British-style ale, heavy, with a good smack of hops, may take a bit of getting used to by Americans who are accustomed to the lighter domestic brews.

Nowadays many people have decided to eschew alcohol-containing beverages, and happily for them, the selection of nonalcoholic alternatives couldn't be better. It wasn't always that way. Specialty food stores are the first place to look for both imported and domestic nonalcoholic beers, sparkling or still wines, grape juices, and cider. Some of the sparkling drinks are even sealed with a cork so that they produce the festive "pop" when they are opened.

Fresh-pressed, unfiltered apple cider is another option. But don't confuse apple cider with the clear apple juices that are marketed mainly for children. Some fruit juices, especially cider, which are sweet and heavy, can be lightened by the addition of sparkling water or club soda.

Taking a lead from the Pilgrims, water, as mundane as it seems, can be quite a refreshing and welcome drink, and is currently enjoying a surge of popularity as the newest status drink, served with or without ice and maybe a slice of lime or lemon. The vast array of sparkling and still mineral waters, imported and domestic, flavored and non, that are now on the market offer possibilities that would have floored Pilgrim menu planners.

Before- and After-Dinner Drinks

What is served to drink before dinner is usually a matter of family and social custom. The only words of advice on the subject that I might offer to the inexperienced host is to remember that while a small amount of alcohol can stimulate the appetite, much more than that can dull it very effectively. Be sure to offer some light alcoholic beverages, as well as hard-liquor cocktails and drinks. Dry sherry, wine, of course, and some of the aperitifs, such as Campari, Dubonnet, Cinzano Bianco and Rosso, and Lillet, are a pleasant segue into a substantial meal. And spritzers or fizzes, in which sparkling water is poured over fruit juice or wine, are most refreshing. It's also up to the host to keep the cocktail hour from going on too long, usually by simply serving dinner on time.

With few exceptions, most hot and cold punches are not suitable pre-dinner beverages since most are much too heavy and sweet. Better to serve these at a holiday open house or cocktail party later on.

After dessert is the time to bring out the fancy cordials, brandy, Madeira, sweet sherry, and port. The cordials may be served as is in tiny glasses, or over crushed ice or ice cubes. The others are generally taken at room temperature in a glass large enough to allow the drinker to be able to savor the aroma as well as the flavor. One after-dinner drink is usually enough for most people.

When serving alcoholic after-dinner drinks, be mindful and considerate of those who have to drive home. And never, in a desire to be an expansive host, insist that anyone have a drink who seems the least bit recalcitrant about accepting it.

FOUR

Appetizers and Hors d'Oeuvres
❦

I have ambivalent feelings about serving appetizers on Thanksgiving. Too often I've watched a beautifully executed and delicious Thanksgiving dinner go half eaten and seemingly unappreciated because famished diners mindlessly filled up on tempting appetizers and hors d'oeuvres, which were, of course, intended to whet the appetite, not kill it. What a pity, and what a waste of time and money, to say nothing of the precious food for which we're supposed to be giving thanks.

On the other hand, the Thanksgiving celebration begins in many homes hours before dinner, so it seems only reasonable and gracious to offer some light sustenance to keep everybody from fainting while the tantalizing aromas of turkey and pumpkin pie drift through the house.

Other things to be taken into consideration when deciding whether or not to serve include such practical matters as how much time is available for preparation, the size of your kitchen and the amount of refrigerator space, whether or not a first course will be served, and even the amount of money you feel you want to spend on just one meal.

The answer, as in nearly all things, is moderation. It helps if everyone knows what time dinner will be served so they can pace themselves throughout the day. Be specific when the invitation is extended and then try to serve dinner promptly. No matter what, don't, in your great enthusiasm and eagerness to serve the most bountiful dinner the world has ever seen, set out trays and trays of agonizingly appetizing little snacks.

One or two appetizers, three at the most, are about the right amount to precede a big dinner. In making appetizer selections, try to achieve a balance between plain and fancy, rich and bland, crisp and soft. For instance, Walnut Duxelles and Saga Blue (see page 42), a big bowl of seasoned but not too heavily buttered popcorn, and a tray of seedless red and green grapes (even strawberries, if you dare) would seem to me to be a perfect sort of prelude to Thanksgiving dinner. When in doubt, remember that it is far better to err on the side of too few than too many.

Obviously, you should choose those things that need not be cooked or fussed with at the last minute. If time is more important than money, also have a look at what's available, both packaged and fresh, in specialty food stores and the gourmet departments in supermarkets. Supplementing a home-cooked Thanksgiving dinner with a couple of prepared items is not a sin and can free you to concentrate on the rest of the meal.

CHARLOTTE'S TOASTS

Charlotte Adams, friend and mentor, author of the original *Four Seasons Cookbook* (The Ridge Press, Inc., and Holt, Rinehart and Winston, New York, 1971) and so many others that I've lost count of them, gave this recipe to me many years ago and it is one of the handiest in my collection. I use the toasts in the bread basket with meals, for setting out with snacks, to eat plain or spread with something. Mostly I find myself eating them as a snack whenever they're on hand. I like the toasts plain, but I suppose there's no reason you couldn't season the butter with garlic, herbs, or Parmesan cheese, for instance, or sprinkle the toasts with chili powder or other seasoning powders while they're still warm from the oven.

8 slices firm, homemade-style bread,   *4 tablespoons (½ stick) butter, softened*
  crusts removed

Preheat the oven to 250°F. Spread one side of each slice of bread with butter. Cut the slices into four equal strips, quarters, or triangles and place them, buttered side up, on an ungreased baking sheet. Bake for about 45 minutes, without turning, or until golden, watching carefully toward the end of the baking time so they don't get too brown. When cool, store at room temperature in a tightly covered container for up to two weeks.

YIELD: 32 TOASTS

PLAIN COCKTAIL TOAST

If you take the time to make these, they'll save you a lot of money, for they are much less expensive than even the most mundane water crackers and, in my opinion, much better. Use either thinly sliced (about ¼-inch-thick) French or Italian bread, or plain, thin-sliced white bread, crusts removed and cut into quarters, strips, or triangles.

Preheat the oven to 250°F. Place the bread on an ungreased baking sheet and bake for about 30 minutes, turning occasionally, until crisp and golden. Store at room temperature in a tightly covered container.

TINY CHEESE BISCUITS

Each biscuit is just one spicy bite!

*5 ounces extra-sharp cheddar cheese (half
   of a 10-ounce package), cut into large
   pieces
¼ pound (1 stick) butter, softened
1 cup all-purpose flour*

*½ teaspoon salt
⅛ teaspoon paprika
½ teaspoon Worcestershire sauce
½ teaspoon liquid red pepper seasoning*

Place the cheese in a food processor or blender and process until finely chopped. In a medium-size bowl, thoroughly blend the cheese with the remaining ingredients. Gather the dough into a ball and cut it into quarters. Roll each quarter into a cylinder measuring about 10 inches in length. Wrap tightly in plastic wrap or aluminum foil and place in the refrigerator until well chilled. (The cylinders can also be frozen. In that case, thaw in the refrigerator for an hour or so before slicing.) When ready to bake, preheat the oven to 350°F. Unwrap the dough and cut the cold cylinders into ½-inch slices. Place the slices on a baking sheet that has been lightly greased or coated with nonstick vegetable spray. Bake for about 15 minutes, or until firm and golden. Cool on wire racks. Store at room temperature in a tightly covered container. They will keep for a couple of weeks, or can be frozen longer and thawed at room temperature.

YIELD: ABOUT 6 DOZEN

CORNMEAL CRISPS

These are very much like the expensive crackers that I occasionally resort to when I have none of these on hand. I almost always have a bag of crisps in the freezer and pull them out when needed. By the time the drinks are made, the crisps are just about at room temperature and ready to serve.

½ cup yellow cornmeal
1 cup all-purpose flour
1 teaspoon salt

5 tablespoons (½ stick plus 1 tablespoon)
 butter
½ cup shredded cheddar cheese
¼ cup milk

Preheat the oven to 350°F. Thoroughly mix the cornmeal, flour, and salt in a medium-size bowl. Cut in the butter with two knives or a pastry blender until the mixture resembles coarse crumbs. Stir in the cheese, then add the milk and stir only until the mixture is moist and holds together. Turn out onto a lightly floured surface and knead for just a few seconds. Cut the dough into quarters. Roll each quarter out to a ⅛-inch thickness on a lightly floured surface. Cut into 1½-inch rounds with a biscuit or cookie cutter, placing each one as it is cut on a baking sheet that has been lightly greased or coated with nonstick vegetable spray. Bake for 12 to 15 minutes, or until crisp and lightly browned. Cool on wire racks. Store at room temperature in a tightly covered container for up to two weeks.

YIELD: ABOUT 4 DOZEN

FRENCH TWISTS
❦

Purchased at a French bakery, these twists cost several dollars a pound. They are always very popular, so it pays, quite literally, to keep some in the freezer.

One sheet frozen puff pastry from a
 17¼-ounce package, thawed according
 to package directions

1 large egg, slightly beaten
⅓ cup grated Parmesan cheese
1½ teaspoons chili powder

Unfold the sheet of pastry onto a piece of waxed paper. Brush half of the beaten egg over its surface. Mix the cheese and chili powder in a small bowl, then sprinkle half of the mixture over the pastry, pressing it in lightly. Cover the pastry with another sheet of waxed paper and invert. Peel off waxed paper on top. Brush the other side of the pastry with the remaining egg, then sprinkle with the remaining cheese mixture and press in as before. Fold the dough in half lengthwise and cut into ⅜-inch strips with a sharp knife, making 20 strips. Unfold the pastry. Pick up each of the strips and twist it while holding both ends. Lay the twist on an ungreased baking sheet, pressing the ends onto the baking sheet to anchor. Place the baking sheet in the freezer for 10 minutes. Preheat the oven to 425°F. Bake the twists for 7 or 8 minutes, or until crisp and golden. Cool on a wire rack. Store at room temperature in a tightly covered container for up to a week. To serve the twists warm, reheat in a preheated 400°F oven for 5 minutes.

YIELD: 20 TWISTS

HARVEST CREAM PUFFS

It's impossible to eat just one of these, but that's okay. The puffs are so airy they're not likely to spoil appetites.

1 cup water
¼ pound (1 stick) butter
⅛ teaspoon freshly ground black pepper
1 cup all-purpose flour

4 large eggs
1¾ cups grated Asiago, Parmesan, or
    Romano cheese

Preheat the oven to 375°F. Combine the water, butter, and pepper in a 2- or 3-quart saucepan over high heat until the water boils and the butter is melted. Reduce the heat to low. Add the flour all at once and cook, stirring vigorously, until the mixture forms a ball and leaves the side of the pan. Remove from the heat. Beat in the eggs, one at a time. Continue to beat vigorously until the mixture is smooth and glossy. Stir in 1½ cups of the cheese until well blended. Drop by scant measuring tablespoonfuls, leaving about 2 inches between each mound, onto two baking sheets that have been lightly greased or coated with nonstick vegetable spray. (The puffs will nearly double in size when baked.) Lightly press a little of the remaining cheese onto the top of each mound. Bake for 25 to 30 minutes, or until evenly browned. Remove the puffs from the oven and lower the temperature to 300°F. Prick each puff a couple of times with a wooden toothpick to allow the steam to escape and dry out the insides. Return the puffs to the oven for 5 minutes. Cool completely on wire racks. Serve the puffs at room temperature, or rewarm and recrisp for 5 minutes in a preheated 350°F oven. Store for only a day or two in a tightly covered container at room temperature.

YIELD: ABOUT 3 DOZEN

Note: The cheese puffs can be securely wrapped and frozen for up to one month. Thaw in the refrigerator for several hours and refresh on a baking sheet in a preheated 350°F oven for 5 minutes.

BIG BOWLS OF POPCORN

As one of the oldest American foods, popcorn deserves a place of honor in the Thanksgiving celebration. The story goes that the Pilgrims were introduced to popcorn when Indian chief Massasoit's brother brought along a deerskin bag full of it to the first Thanksgiving feast.

A big bowl or two of popcorn is a very appealing appetizer that can have lots of flavor and few calories. In case you've forgotten, ½ cup popping corn makes 4 quarts (16 cups) popcorn. The corn can be popped a day in advance for each recipe, but season on the serving day.

Parmesan Pop. Melt 4 tablespoons (½ stick) butter and drizzle over 8 cups freshly popped, unseasoned popcorn. Immediately sprinkle with ½ cup grated Parmesan cheese and toss until well blended.

Lightly Herbed. Melt 4 tablespoons (½ stick) butter and combine in a small bowl with 1 teaspoon dried thyme leaves, crumbled, and ½ teaspoon each dried basil, oregano, and rosemary leaves, crumbled. Drizzle over 8 cups freshly popped, unseasoned popcorn and toss until well blended.

Curry Corn. Melt 4 tablespoons (½ stick) butter and combine in a small bowl with 1 teaspoon curry powder and ¼ teaspoon each ground cinnamon and ground ginger. Drizzle over 8 cups freshly popped, unseasoned popcorn and toss until well blended.

Border Corn. In a small bowl, mix 1 cup shredded Monterey Jack cheese with 2 teaspoons each chili powder, paprika, and ground cumin. Sprinkle over 8 cups freshly popped, unseasoned popcorn and toss until well blended.

Cajun Corn. Melt 4 tablespoons (½ stick) butter and combine in a small bowl with 1 teaspoon each paprika and lemon pepper and ½ teaspoon each onion powder, garlic powder, and ground cayenne (red) pepper. Drizzle over 8 cups freshly popped, unseasoned popcorn and toss until well blended.

Cock-Trail Mix. Melt 4 tablespoons (½ stick) butter and drizzle over 8 cups freshly popped white popcorn. Add 1½ cups dark raisins and toss until well blended.

Sonoma Pop. Drizzle ¼ cup extra virgin olive oil over 8 cups freshly popped popcorn. Sprinkle with ½ cup dried-tomato bits (half of a 3-ounce jar) and toss until well blended.

Note: For even fewer calories, coat popcorn with olive oil- or butter-flavored nonstick vegetable spray (instead of drizzling with butter) before seasoning. (Spray and toss at the same time.)

A PLATTER OF AMERICAN CHEESE

Because Thanksgiving is a celebration of American food, this is a good time to serve (and cook with) American cheese—or at least those varieties of cheese that are produced in the United States, which includes many of the major varieties in the world.

The number of "true" American cheeses is pitifully small. Apparently the cheese makers in this country directed most of their talent and energy into reproducing great European cheeses that would satisfy the tastes of our melting-pot population, rather than creating new ones that would be uniquely American. We have only to taste to know how well they succeeded.

Wisconsin, which has long been known as America's Dairyland, is probably the best known of the cheese-making states, and produces nearly half of the nation's supply. Other states contribute their fair share, but anywhere there are cows (or sheep or goats) there is cheese. This might be a good time to scout out small, local cheese makers and taste what they have to offer. You may discover something really special.

When laying out a cheese platter, try to include as many different textures and flavors as possible, with a representation from the three main types of cheese.

Soft-cheese varieties include Brie, Camembert, feta, mascarpone, Liederkranz, and all of the unripened goat cheeses, often referred to by their French name, *chèvre*. Supplement these with semisoft Port Salut, Muenster, brick, baby Swiss, jack, blue, Gouda, and Edam. Finish off the platter with pieces of firm cheddar (there are many American varieties of cheddar, including Colby, coon, pineapple, tillamook, and Vermont Sage), Swiss, or provolone. There are also pasteurized process cheeses to choose from, as well as cold pack cheeses, with or without added flavors, and the American versions of the herb- or pepper-flavored French triple-cream cheeses, of which Boursin is probably the most famous. The soft cheeses will require toast, crackers, or thinly sliced bread on which to spread them. Keep in mind that these are simply a vehicle to get the cheese to the mouth, and should have no particular flavor of their own to compete with or overshadow the cheese.

Embellish the cheese platter with fruit, if you like. Nearly any fruit that's ripe and pretty would be wonderful, with the possible exception of citrus fruits. The rule is delicate fruit with delicate cheese and more flavorful fruit with more flavorful cheese. Nuts and nut meats would also be an attractive addition to the platter.

HONEY-ROASTED ALMONDS

From the home economists at Blue Diamond, here is the recipe for their famous honey-roasted almonds. And very generous of them, too, considering how much money you'll save by making these nuts instead of buying them.

2 cups whole almonds	*2 tablespoons honey*
¼ cup sugar	*2 tablespoons water*
½ teaspoon salt	*2 teaspoons almond or vegetable oil*

Spread the almonds in a single layer in a shallow ungreased baking pan and place in a cold oven. Bake at 350°F, stirring occasionally, until the internal color of the nuts is tan to light brown, 12 to 15 minutes. (Keep in mind that the nuts will continue to roast a little more after they are removed from the oven.) Set the roasted almonds aside. Mix the sugar and salt on a piece of waxed paper and set aside. Stir together the honey, water, and oil in a medium-size saucepan and bring to a boil over medium heat. Stir in the roasted almonds and continue to cook and stir until all of the liquid has been absorbed by the nuts, about 5 minutes. Immediately transfer the almonds to a medium-size bowl. Sprinkle the sugar mixture over the almonds and toss until they are evenly coated. Spread the almonds out on waxed paper. When cool, store at room temperature in a tightly covered container or plastic bag for up to two weeks.

YIELD: 2 CUPS

BARBECUED WALNUTS

Everyone who tastes these (and the Honey-Roasted Almonds, preceding recipe) will want the recipe. Be prepared.

1 tablespoon butter	*2 or 3 drops liquid red pepper seasoning*
2 tablespoons Worcestershire sauce	*2 cups walnut halves*
2 teaspoons catsup	*Salt to taste*

Preheat the oven to 400°F. Melt the butter in a medium-size skillet over medium-high heat. When hot, stir in the Worcestershire, catsup, and red pepper seasoning and remove from the heat. Add the walnut halves and stir to coat them thoroughly. Spread the walnuts in a single layer in an ungreased shallow baking pan. Bake for 20 minutes, stirring frequently. Turn out onto paper towels and sprinkle with salt. When cool, store at room temperature in a tightly covered container or plastic bag for up to two weeks.

YIELD: 2 CUPS

TOASTED PUMPKIN SEEDS

Waste not, want not. Roasted pumpkin seeds are a wonderful snack. The amount of seeds depends on the size of the pumpkin, but count on about one cup from an average-size jack-o'-lantern.

Seeds from the Halloween pumpkin   *Salt to taste*

After the pumpkin has been hollowed out, separate the seeds from the fiber. Rinse the seeds with cool water and lay them out on newspaper to dry completely. Store the seeds at room temperature in a plastic bag or tightly covered container until ready to toast. Preheat the oven to 400°F. Spread the seeds in one layer on one or two baking sheets that have been lightly greased or coated with nonstick vegetable spray. Bake for about 15 minutes, or until lightly browned. Sprinkle with salt to taste. They can be stored covered at room temperature for at least a couple of weeks.

DONNA FERRARI'S LIGHT DIP FOR RAW VEGETABLES

Donna served this simple dip at a gathering of food editors several years ago. I'm not crazy about dips, in general, but I have served this one at least twenty times since then. That's how good it is. Plenty of garlic is what makes the dip outstanding. Don't be afraid to use plenty of it.

½ pint plain low-fat yogurt   *Mayonnaise to taste*
2 or 3 cloves garlic, put through a garlic
  press

In a small bowl, mix the yogurt with the garlic and just enough mayonnaise (a couple of teaspoons to start with) to give the yogurt a little body and richness. Serve with an assortment of colorful raw vegetables. My choices would be jicama or parsnip sticks, bell pepper strips (any color but green), snow peas, and short lengths of green onions (scallions).

YIELD: 1 CUP; 6 TO 8 SERVINGS

MEDITERRANEAN EGGPLANT SCOOP

A zesty blend of Mediterranean flavors that's so good it's hard to believe it's actually healthy.

¼ cup olive oil
1 large onion, finely chopped (1 cup)
1 large clove garlic, minced
1 small eggplant, finely chopped (about 4 cups)
1 medium-size red bell pepper, finely chopped (about ¾ cup)
1 medium-size zucchini, finely chopped (about 2 cups)

½ teaspoon salt
½ teaspoon dried basil leaves, crumbled
¼ teaspoon dried oregano leaves, crumbled
¼ cup water
One 14- to 16-ounce can whole plum tomatoes, drained and finely chopped
6 pita breads, split in half and the halves cut into quarters

Heat the oil in a large heavy saucepan or Dutch oven over medium-high heat. Add the onion and garlic and cook, stirring frequently, until softened. Stir in the eggplant and red pepper and cook for 5 minutes, stirring frequently. Reduce the heat to medium-low. Stir in the zucchini, salt, basil, oregano, and water. Cover and continue to cook, stirring occasionally, until the vegetables are tender but still fairly firm and hold their shape, about 10 minutes. Stir in the tomatoes and cook for 5 minutes longer. Remove from the heat and cool slightly. Turn into a serving bowl, cover, and chill until ready to serve. Serve at room temperature, accompanied by pita pieces for dipping.

YIELD: 4 CUPS; ABOUT 16 SERVINGS

GRAPES UNDER WRAPS

Everyone looks so surprised when they bite into these attractive cheese balls and find refreshing little grapes in the center.

One 8-ounce piece Jarlsberg cheese, cut into large pieces
One 8-ounce package cream cheese, softened
1 teaspoon grated onion

1 tablespoon Dijon mustard
½ teaspoon Worcestershire sauce
1½ to 2 cups very finely chopped pecans
Small seedless grapes (about 50)

Place the Jarlsberg in a food processor and process until very finely chopped. In a medium-size bowl, beat the cream cheese with the onion. Add the Jarlsberg, mustard, and Worcestershire and beat again until well blended. Spread the nuts out onto a sheet of waxed paper. With damp hands, press as little as possible of the cheese mixture (about 1 measuring teaspoonful) around each grape. Roll each cheese-covered grape in the nuts, setting on a baking sheet as it is finished. Cover and chill until serving time.

YIELD: 40 TO 50 GRAPES; ABOUT 18 SERVINGS

DRIED TOMATOES AND PARMESAN CHEESE

The uses I find for dried tomatoes are nearly endless. This spread was concocted in an emergency and immediately found its way into my permanent recipe file.

2 cups (34 to 36) dried tomatoes (see page 5)
1 cup olive oil
2 cloves garlic, cut into pieces
2 to 4 teaspoons grated Parmesan cheese

8 ounces plain unripened goat cheese or cream cheese
Plain Cocktail Toast (see pages 30–31) or plain crackers

Soak the tomatoes in the oil for several hours or overnight at room temperature, turning them occasionally, to soften. Drain the tomatoes, reserving the oil. Place the tomatoes in a food processor or blender and process until as finely chopped as possible. (Because of their texture it's not likely that the tomatoes will ever turn into a puree, so don't worry about that.) Add 2 tablespoons of the reserved oil and the garlic and process again. Add the Parmesan cheese to taste and enough of the remaining oil to give the mixture a good spreading consistency (it should not be too moist) and process again, just to blend. I usually pack the tomato mixture into a 1-cup dry measure and turn it out onto a serving plate in a neat little mound. Serve with goat cheese or cream cheese. Spread the cheese on toast or crackers and top with the spread.

YIELD: 1 CUP; ABOUT 8 SERVINGS

CALIFORNIA TAPENADE

If the tapenade will be stored for more than a day or two, cover it with a very thin layer of olive oil and it will keep in the refrigerator for several months.

½ pound Greek Kalamata or French
   Niçoise olives, pitted
2 teaspoons anchovy paste (optional)
1 large clove garlic, minced
2 tablespoons drained capers
2 tablespoons olive oil

¼ teaspoon freshly ground black pepper
8 ounces plain unripened goat cheese or
   cream cheese
Plain Cocktail Toast (see pages 30–31) or
   plain crackers

Place the olives, anchovy paste, garlic, capers, olive oil, and pepper in a food processor or blender and process briefly until the mixture is blended but still coarse in texture. Spoon into a container with a tight-fitting lid, cover tightly, and store in the refrigerator. Serve with goat cheese or cream cheese. Spread the cheese on toast or crackers and top with the spread.

YIELD: 1 CUP; ABOUT 8 SERVINGS

AL BOLTON'S CHEDDAR-AND-PIMIENTO SPREAD

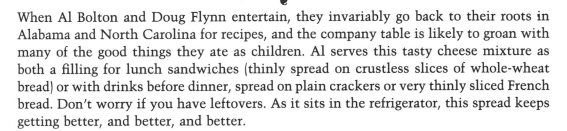

When Al Bolton and Doug Flynn entertain, they invariably go back to their roots in Alabama and North Carolina for recipes, and the company table is likely to groan with many of the good things they ate as children. Al serves this tasty cheese mixture as both a filling for lunch sandwiches (thinly spread on crustless slices of whole-wheat bread) or with drinks before dinner, spread on plain crackers or very thinly sliced French bread. Don't worry if you have leftovers. As it sits in the refrigerator, this spread keeps getting better, and better, and better.

One 10-ounce package extra-sharp
   cheddar cheese
One 4-ounce jar chopped pimiento,
   drained (reserve the liquid) and finely
   chopped

¼ cup mayonnaise
⅛ teaspoon Maggi seasoning or soy sauce
Plain crackers or thinly sliced French
   bread

Grate the cheese using the fine-shredding disk of a food processor or a hand grater. (It's important that the shreds are not too big or too clumpy.) Place the grated cheese in a medium-size bowl with the pimiento and its reserved liquid. Mix until well blended. Stir in the mayonnaise and Maggi seasoning and mix again. Cover and refrigerate for at least 8 hours, or overnight, to allow the mixture to "ripen." Bring to room temperature before serving, beating in a little more mayonnaise, if necessary, to give the mixture a good spreading consistency.

YIELD: 1½ CUPS; 8 TO 12 SERVINGS

CREAM CHEESE, RAISINS, AND WALNUTS

Sometimes I plump the raisins beforehand for about an hour in just enough white wine to cover them. Drain the raisins before adding them to the spread. Make this a day or so in advance so that the flavors have a chance to mingle.

*One 8-ounce package cream cheese,
softened
½ cup golden raisins
½ cup toasted (see pages 6–7) coarsely
chopped walnuts*

*½ teaspoon finely chopped crystallized
ginger
Plain crackers*

In a small bowl, mix the cream cheese, raisins, walnuts, and ginger. Cover and chill until near serving time. Serve at room temperature with plain crackers.

YIELD: 1¼ CUPS; 8 TO 10 SERVINGS

SMOKED SALMON MOUSSE

Every time I serve this I live in hope that there will be just a little left over for me to snack on the next day. There never is.

*6 ounces Nova Scotia, Scottish, or Norwe-
gian smoked salmon, cut into pieces
¼ pound (1 stick) butter, softened
¼ cup light cream or half-and-half
1 tablespoon snipped fresh dill*

*1 tablespoon minced fresh chives
1 tablespoon fresh lemon juice
3 or 4 turns of a pepper mill
Fresh dill sprigs for garnish
Pumpernickel cocktail bread*

Process the salmon in a food processor or blender until it is coarsely chopped. Slowly add the butter and cream, continuing to process until the mixture is very smooth. Add the dill, chives, lemon juice, and pepper and process again until well blended. Scrape the mixture into a serving bowl, swirling it into an attractive mound. Cover and refrigerate until shortly before serving. Bring to room temperature to soften slightly and garnish with a few sprigs of dill. Serve with pumpernickel cocktail bread.

YIELD: 1½ CUPS; ABOUT 8 SERVINGS

WALNUT DUXELLES AND SAGA BLUE

A *duxelles* is a mixture of chopped mushrooms and other ingredients that is cooked down to a nearly dry consistency with an intense flavor. It is usually used as a stuffing, or as the basis for a sauce or soup, and sometimes just by itself, as it is here, to enhance the flavor of a wedge of creamy Saga blue cheese. The only small drawback to a *duxelles* is that it is not very colorful. Sprinkling it with chopped greens of some sort is almost mandatory.

2 tablespoons butter
2 tablespoons finely chopped onion
1 clove garlic, minced
1 pound regular white mushrooms, finely
   chopped
¾ cup toasted (see pages 6–7) finely
   chopped walnuts

One 12-ounce wedge Saga blue cheese
Chopped chives or green onion (scallion)
   tops for garnish
Thinly sliced French bread or plain
   crackers

Melt the butter in a large skillet over medium-high heat. When hot, add the onion and garlic and cook, stirring frequently, until the onion is golden. Add the mushrooms and continue to cook, stirring frequently, until most of the moisture from the mushrooms has evaporated and the mixture has cooked down considerably and is almost pasty, about 10 minutes. Remove from the heat and stir in the walnuts. Cool to room temperature, then cover and chill until near serving time. To serve, place the cheese on a large plate and surround it with the *duxelles*. Lavishly sprinkle the *duxelles* with chives. Serve at room temperature with thinly sliced French bread or plain crackers.

YIELD: ABOUT 2 CUPS *DUXELLES*; ABOUT 12 SERVINGS

BEGGAR'S PURSES

The traditional filling for these purses is sour cream and caviar, but you can fill them with anything you like. A *duxelles* (see the preceding recipe) could be substituted for the caviar, or a blend of equal amounts of cream cheese and either blue cheese or finely chopped chutney, for instance, would make excellent fillings.

CREPES (SEE NOTE BELOW)
1½ cups all-purpose flour
½ teaspoon salt
4 large eggs
2 cups milk
6 tablespoons (¾ stick) butter, melted

FILLING
¾ cup sour cream
One 4-ounce jar golden or black whitefish
  caviar or red lumpfish caviar
24 chives or thin strips of green onion
  (scallion) tops, plus a few extra to re-
  place those that may break as they
  are tied

Sift the flour and salt into a large bowl. Beat the eggs with the milk in a medium-size bowl. Beat the egg mixture into the flour mixture until smooth. Stir 2 tablespoons of the melted butter into the batter. The crepes may be made immediately, or the batter may be covered and refrigerated for up to two days. In that case, beat the batter to reblend it before using.

Set a 6-inch (measured across the bottom) *nonstick* skillet over medium heat. (The skillet is ready when a few drops of water bounce around when sprinkled in the bottom.) Brush the skillet lightly with some of the remaining melted butter. Measure 3 tablespoons (about three quarters of a ¼-cup dry measure) of the batter into the skillet. Immediately tilt the skillet until the batter covers the bottom. Cook for about 1 minute, or until the top looks nearly dry and the edge of the crepe is starting to brown. Turn the crepe (I use a long icing spatula to do this) and cook on the other side for about 30 seconds. Slide the crepe out of the pan onto a plate. Repeat with the remaining batter, lightly buttering the skillet between making each crepe. (Remove the pan from the heat after each crepe is made to keep it from overheating.) Give the batter a stir from time to time to keep it well mixed. As the crepes are made, stack them on top of one another. You should have about 24 crepes. Cover the crepes with plastic wrap or aluminum foil and refrigerate until ready to make the purses.

Place each crepe on a flat surface with the most attractive side down. Spoon 1 generous measuring teaspoonful of the sour cream in the center of each crepe. Top with ½ teaspoon of the caviar. Pull up the edge of the crepe around the filling to resemble a purse and tie with a chive. Refrigerate until ready to serve. Set the purses on a platter and serve at room temperature garnished with green leaves (see page 14) and fresh cranberries.

YIELD: 24 PURSES

Note: If there's no time to make the crepes from scratch, you can buy them ready-made in packages of 24 in the produce department of many supermarkets.

MARINATED GOAT CHEESE

The longer it marinates the more flavorful the cheese becomes. This eye-catching appetizer is simple, yet elegant, and keeps well for at least ten days, so don't hesitate to make it ahead.

About 12 ounces plain unripened goat
  cheese
½ teaspoon dried rosemary leaves
½ teaspoon dried thyme leaves
4 or 5 turns of a pepper mill
4 cloves garlic, peeled and lightly mashed
1 bay leaf
1 large red bell pepper, roasted (see page
  8) and cut into slivers

2 cups small black olives, such as Greek
  Kalamata or French Niçoise, pitted and
  coarsely chopped
1½ to 2 cups extra virgin olive oil
Fresh rosemary sprigs for garnish
Plain Cocktail Toast (see pages 30–31) or
  plain crackers

Shape the cheese into several small disks and place them in the bottom of a wide bowl. Sprinkle with the rosemary, thyme, and pepper. Add the garlic, bay leaf, pepper slivers, and olives. Pour enough olive oil into the bowl to cover the cheese completely. Cover tightly and chill for at least a day (or up to several days) to allow the flavors to develop. (The olive oil may thicken and become cloudy when it is chilled for any length of time, but will clear again when it comes back to room temperature.) To serve, place the cheese disks in a shallow serving dish. Remove the garlic and bay leaf, then spoon the roasted peppers and olives over and around the cheese. Pour some or all of the olive oil over the cheese. Garnish with a sprig or two of fresh rosemary. Spread the toast with the cheese and a little of the flavored oil and top with olives and peppers.

YIELD: ABOUT 8 SERVINGS

CALIFORNIA-STYLE BRIE

This is a lovely way to serve one of the world's most prized cheeses, and because it's Thanksgiving, perhaps you'd like to try an American Brie. A nice way to present this is to set the Brie on a large round platter and surround it with tiny bunches of green and red seedless grapes and very thinly sliced French bread or plain crackers. The whole thing can be transformed into a dessert cheese by accompanying it with cordial glasses of the same black raspberry liqueur. (There are probably other black raspberry liqueurs, but the one with which I'm most familiar is Chambord.)

One 3-ounce package cream cheese,
 softened
3 tablespoons black raspberry liqueur

½ cup toasted (see pages 6–7) finely
 chopped almonds
One 4-inch wheel Brie, refrigerator cold
Plain crackers

Mix the cream cheese, liqueur, and almonds in a small bowl. Cut the wheel of Brie in half horizontally with a long sharp knife. Spread the cream cheese mixture on top of each cut half. Re-form the Brie and wrap it tightly in plastic wrap or aluminum foil. Refrigerate for 24 hours before serving. To serve, unwrap the cheese and bring it to room temperature. Serve with plain crackers.

YIELD: 8 TO 12 SERVINGS

A MOLD OF CREAM CHEESE WITH CHIVES AND CAVIAR

A very impressive appetizer, and one that will cinch your reputation as a cook. By the way, instead of one large mold, the cream cheese mixture may be molded in little custard cups (about ½ cup for each serving) and served as a first course.

2 envelopes unflavored gelatin
½ cup cold milk
1½ cups milk, heated to boiling
Two 3-ounce packages cream cheese,
 softened

¼ cup snipped chives or minced green
 onion (scallion) tops
One 4-ounce jar golden whitefish caviar
Fresh dill or parsley sprigs for garnish
Plain Cocktail Toast (see pages 30–31) or
 plain rounds of melba toast

Sprinkle the gelatin over the cold milk in a blender. Let stand for about 5 minutes to soften. Add the hot milk and blend at low speed until the gelatin is completely dissolved, 3 or 4 minutes. Add the cream cheese and blend at high speed until thoroughly mixed. Pour into a medium-size bowl and refrigerate until very thick but not set, 25 to 30 minutes. Fold in the chives until well distributed. Pour the mixture into a well-oiled 3-cup mold and chill until firm. To unmold, run a small sharp knife around the edge. Position a cutting board (or something similar) over the molded gelatin. (The cutting board will serve only as a work surface.) Firmly grasp both the mold and the cutting board and invert the two. Remove the mold from the gelatin mixture. (This unmolds rather easily, so it will probably not need the warm water dip required for most molds.) Using an icing spatula or a spreader, spread and press the caviar onto the top and sides of the mold. With a pancake turner, carefully transfer the mold to a serving platter. Garnish with dill sprigs. Serve with cocktail toast or plain melba rounds.

YIELD: 3 CUPS; ABOUT 12 SERVINGS

MACADAMIA-CHEESE BALL

Nearly everyone enjoys luxurious macadamia nuts, so this disappears quickly. If you like, you can freeze one of the balls (and the nuts to coat it with, separately) for another occasion.

Two 8-ounce packages cream cheese,
　softened
¼ pound (1 stick) butter, softened
2 tablespoons minced green onions
　(scallions)

One 7-ounce jar macadamia nuts, very
　finely chopped
2 teaspoons grated orange rind

In a medium-size bowl, beat the cream cheese and butter with an electric mixer until smooth. Stir in the onion, 1 cup of the nuts, and the orange rind until well blended. Divide the mixture in half and spoon each half onto the center of a square of plastic wrap. Pull the wrap up around each half of the cheese mixture and form into balls. Refrigerate the cheese balls until firm. Shortly before serving, unwrap and press the remaining nuts onto the balls. Soften slightly before serving with crackers or thinly sliced French bread.

YIELD: TWO 3-INCH BALLS; 16 TO 24 SERVINGS

Variation: This mixture also makes a wonderful celery stuffing, which can be served as an appetizer or on the relish tray along with dinner.

ANNIE'S VELVETY CHICKEN PÂTÉ

Traditional liver pâtés are often too liver-y for some tastes. This one is just right, with a texture so smooth that to call it velvety is not an exaggeration.

*5 tablespoons (½ stick plus 1 tablespoon)
    butter*
*2 boneless, skinless chicken-breast halves
    (about 4 ounces each), cut into pieces*
*¼ pound chicken livers, rinsed and cut
    in half*
1 medium-size onion, chopped (½ cup)
*1 medium-size apple, peeled, cored, and
    chopped (½ cup)*
1 tablespoon all-purpose flour

1 hard-cooked egg, quartered
½ teaspoon salt
¼ teaspoon freshly ground black pepper
¼ teaspoon ground allspice
¼ teaspoon ground nutmeg
2 tablespoons brandy
1 red apple
Fresh lemon juice
Plain Cocktail Toasts (see page 30–31)

Melt 2 tablespoons of the butter in a large nonstick skillet over medium-low heat. When hot, add the chicken pieces and livers and cook, stirring frequently, until the chicken is cooked through and the livers are firm but still pink in the center, about 10 minutes. Remove with a slotted spoon to a food processor. Melt the remaining 3 tablespoons of butter in the same skillet over medium heat. When hot, add the onion and chopped apple and cook, stirring frequently, until the onion is translucent. Sprinkle with the flour and continue to cook, stirring, for 1 minute. Scrape this mixture into the food processor. Add the egg, salt, pepper, allspice, nutmeg, and brandy and process until very smooth. Turn the pâté into a 2-cup crock or serving bowl. Press a piece of plastic wrap directly onto the surface. Refrigerate until close to serving time. Shortly before serving, core the apple and cut it in half. Cut each half into about 8 thin slices. Brush the slices with lemon juice to prevent darkening. Serve the pâté with the toast and apple slices.

YIELD: ABOUT 2 CUPS; ABOUT 16 SERVINGS

VERY GOOD TUNA PÂTÉ

I know, I know. This reads like a very ho-hum recipe, but I think you'll change your mind after you taste it. I like to serve this with small squares of thinly sliced black bread and skinny little green onions (scallions), but it is also very good spread on the stem ends of endive spears.

Two 6½-ounce cans white tuna packed in
   oil or water, drained
4 or 5 green onions (scallions), trimmed
   and cut into pieces, including some of
   the green tops
½ cup heavy or whipping cream
½ cup mayonnaise

3 tablespoons fresh lemon juice
¾ cup pitted ripe olives, finely chopped
1 envelope unflavored gelatin
½ teaspoon salt
½ cup water
Little green onions for garnish
Thin black bread, cut into small squares

Combine the tuna, green onions, cream, and mayonnaise in a food processor or blender. (If using a blender, the mixture will probably have to be processed in two batches.) Process until smooth. Turn the mixture into a medium-size bowl and stir in the lemon juice and olives until well blended. Sprinkle the gelatin and salt over the water in a small saucepan and set aside until softened, about 5 minutes. Set the pan over low heat and cook, stirring, until the gelatin is dissolved, 3 or 4 minutes. Stir into the tuna mixture. Spoon into a 4-cup mold that has been lightly greased or coated with nonstick vegetable spray. Cover and refrigerate for several hours, or overnight, until firm. Run the tip of a sharp knife around the edge of the mold and turn it out onto a serving plate. Garnish with little green onions and serve with small squares of dark bread.

YIELD: 8 TO 12 SERVINGS

A LITTLE TURKEY PÂTÉ

This goes together so easily that I make it while I'm preparing the stuffing. I consider it a cook's reward, so my Thanksgiving guests rarely get a taste, except for those fortunate ones who wander into the kitchen at the right moment.

2 slices bacon
1 turkey liver (the size doesn't matter
   since they are all roughly the same), cut
   into large pieces
2 teaspoons all-purpose flour

1 tablespoon coarsely chopped shallot
   or the white part of a green onion
   (scallion)
2 or 3 turns of a pepper mill
3 to 4 tablespoons heavy or whipping
   cream

Preheat the oven to 325°F. Grease a 1- or 1½-cup baking dish or mold, or coat it with nonstick vegetable spray. Drop the bacon slices into a small pan of boiling water for about 10 seconds and then remove them. Cut the slices into pieces. Place the liver and bacon in a blender or mini food processor and process until well blended. Add the flour, shallot, pepper, and 2 tablespoons of the cream and process until smooth, adding as much more of the cream as needed to give the mixture the consistency of a thick cream soup. Pour into the prepared baking dish. Set the baking dish in a larger pan and add enough hot water to come halfway up the side of the baking dish. Bake, uncovered, for 40 to 50 minutes, or until a knife inserted in the center comes out nearly clean. Cool slightly and eat while still warm, or cover and chill.

YIELD: ABOUT 1 CUP

LIGHTLY PICKLED SHRIMP

Serve with wooden toothpicks—and lots of napkins. A neater way is to provide small plates and forks next to the bowl of shrimp. (I always use my grandmother's cut-glass bowl for the shrimp and it looks very festive.)

1½ cups vegetable oil
¾ cup white wine vinegar
4 bay leaves
1 large clove garlic, quartered
2 tablespoons drained capers
1 tablespoon sugar
½ teaspoon salt

¼ teaspoon black peppercorns
¼ teaspoon liquid red pepper seasoning
2 pounds (40 to 50) medium-size shrimp,
* peeled and deveined*
1 cup small fresh parsley sprigs for garnish
Light-rye cocktail bread rounds

Combine the oil, vinegar, bay leaves, garlic, capers, sugar, salt, peppercorns, and red pepper seasoning in a medium-size bowl, stirring until the sugar dissolves. In a large saucepan, cook the shrimp in lightly salted, simmering water to cover until the shrimp are pink and firm, about 5 minutes. Drain the shrimp and immediately add them to the oil mixture, stirring the shrimp to coat them completely with the marinade. Cover and refrigerate for at least 8 hours or overnight. When ready to serve, drain off some of the marinade and spoon the shrimp mixture into a serving bowl. Tuck parsley sprigs here and there into the shrimp mixture and serve chilled with cocktail bread.

YIELD: 8 TO 12 SERVINGS

TRICOLORED ALMOND TORTE

A very pretty appetizer, and much less complicated than it looks.

Four 8-ounce packages (2 pounds) cream
cheese
1 large clove garlic, put through a
garlic press
1 tablespoon finely chopped fresh basil or
1 teaspoon dried basil leaves, crumbled
1 teaspoon fresh lemon juice
Few drops liquid red pepper seasoning

1 cup toasted (see pages 6–7) finely
chopped almonds
2 tablespoons prepared pesto sauce (available in small jars in the produce or refrigerated section of the supermarket)
1 tablespoon tomato paste
Fresh basil leaves for garnish
Thinly sliced Italian bread

Line a deep, 4-cup fluted mold or mixing bowl with cheesecloth, or coat generously with nonstick cooking spray. In a large bowl, beat the cream cheese with the garlic, basil, lemon juice, and red pepper seasoning until well blended. Stir in ¾ cup of the almonds. Remove ½ cup of the cheese mixture to a small bowl and beat the pesto sauce into it. Remove another ½ cup of the cheese mixture to another small bowl and beat the tomato paste into it. Press 1 cup of the plain cheese mixture into the bottom of the prepared mold. Press the pesto-cheese mixture in an even layer on top of the plain cheese layer. Press the tomato-cheese mixture in an even layer on top of the pesto-cheese layer. Pat the remaining plain cheese mixture in an even layer on top of the tomato-cheese layer. Cover the mold tightly and refrigerate overnight, or for at least 8 hours. Unmold the torte onto a serving plate. Lightly press the remaining chopped almonds onto the top of the torte and garnish with basil leaves. Serve with thinly sliced Italian bread.

YIELD: 24 TO 32 SERVINGS

COFFEE TABLE RACLETTE

La raclette is a traditional Swiss country dish, for which the cut side of a wheel of cheese is gradually melted by an open fire and scraped off onto a hot plate. (You may remember from your childhood reading that Heidi's grandfather made *raclette*, and I thought it sounded great even then.) Anyway, *raclette* caught on in the United States a few years ago, and with typical Yankee ingenuity, at least one small-appliance manufacturer produced a little cheese-heating device to circumvent the open fire. But even this isn't necessary. A one-burner, electric hot plate and a small nonstick (*very* important) skillet produce quite an acceptable *raclette*.

Serving a *raclette* for an appetizer is fun to do and a little out of the ordinary, although probably not a great idea if there are going to be more than a few gathered before dinner. In any event it's probably a good idea to enlist the services of a family member or a good friend (or one of those people who's always asking to help) to take charge of the cheese melting and serving.

Always included in a *raclette* are little boiled potatoes, tiny sour pickles (cornichons), and usually sour cocktail onions, although I often substitute green onion (scallion) brushes (see page 13) for the cocktail onions.

Several hours ahead, precook small, unpeeled red potatoes, one for each serving. Turn the drained potatoes into a microwave-safe bowl with a tight-fitting lid. Just before serving, reheat the potatoes in the microwave oven. (If you don't own a microwave oven, reheat the potatoes in the top of a double boiler over simmering water for about 20 minutes, or until heated through.) Set up the burner and skillet, along with the hot potatoes, pickles, and onions, on a table wherever the dinner guests are assembled. Lay a single layer of very thinly sliced (⅛- to ¼-inch-thick) cheese in the skillet. Set the skillet on the hot burner. When the cheese is melted and bubbling, spoon a small amount onto each plate, adding a potato, a pickle or two, and a few sour onions or a green onion brush. Serve and eat immediately (not waiting for everyone to be served), before the cheese has a chance to harden or become gummy. It helps some if the plates are not ice cold.

A specialty food store with a good selection of cheese is the best place to buy cheese for the *raclette*. Nowadays, special cheeses are imported just for this purpose and are referred to as *raclette* cheese or sometimes just *raclette*. In a pinch, another firm cheese with good melting properties (Muenster, Tilsiter, or Jarlsberg, for example) will work reasonably well.

FIVE

Soups, Salads, and Other First Courses

❦

I'd happily trade all of the appetizers and most of the desserts at Thanksgiving for One Very Special first course, for it is this small offering that can set the stage engagingly for what is to come. It can also give the cook a little extra time in the kitchen while the plates are being cleared away and loaded into the dishwasher, hopefully by a member of the family or a helpful friend.

The first course can range from soup, to salad, to seafood, and beyond, but whatever it is, let it express a certain thoughtfulness and how much the cook cares. Dinner plates may look positively scrumptious, piled high with turkey, stuffing, gravy, and six other things, but rarely are they picture pretty. On the other hand, since most first-course plates are prepared in the kitchen, a little time can be taken with the arranging and garnishing of the food so that the presentation is worthy of comment.

Visually appealing food begins with the plate on which it's served, so keep tableware in mind when planning this course. A multi-ingredient salad on a heavily decorated plate may look too busy to be taken seriously, and a brown pâté on a plain plate could induce yawns all around.

Ideally, nothing served in the first course should be repeated in the dinner course, so plan the rest of the menu first. The first course should be in balance with other parts of the menu, too. If rich side dishes and desserts will follow, as they usually do at Thanksgiving, the first course should be purposely lean.

For obvious reasons, keep servings conservative. A salad should be sparse, pâtés and other loaves very thinly sliced, and soups should barely cover the bottom of the bowl, no more than about ¾ cup per serving, especially if it is rich and creamy.

First courses needn't be served at the dinner table, either. If it works better for you, serve this course wherever the guests are assembled, whenever it's convenient. Serving the first course early might even eliminate the need for appetizers, or if the appetizers will be substantial, a first course might not be necessary at all.

RAW OYSTERS, ON AND OFF THE HALF SHELL

Elegant oysters have been enjoyed by sophisticated civilizations for centuries. The Chinese were probably the first to appreciate their briny, subtle flavor, closely followed by the Greeks and the Romans. The Native Americans ate their share, as did the early settlers. Oysters may not have been eaten at the first Thanksgiving dinner, but it probably wasn't too many years later when they became a traditional part of the feast. Food historians tell tales of monster oysters, measuring a foot or more, but the oyster's general size has been diminishing in direct proportion to its popularity.

In the United States, we're probably blessed with more varieties of oysters than any other country in the world. All oyster lovers have at least one favorite variety that they swear is better than all the rest. (This preference often has everything to do with where you were when you swallowed your first oyster—whole. Chewing comes later.) I feel that way about Chincoteague oysters from the Chesapeake Bay, and I make a great effort to serve them on Thanksgiving and Christmas, even though it's not always easy, living in the land of Long Island bluepoints, as I do.

If there will be just a few for dinner, I buy oysters in the shell and my husband, Gerry, good-naturedly opens them a few minutes before we eat, and I serve them on the half shell. Otherwise I buy them shucked by the pint or half-pint and serve an oyster cocktail, which is about six oysters per serving nestled on a bed of shredded lettuce.

The purists take their oysters neat, with just a squirt of fresh lemon juice and, perhaps, a little freshly ground black pepper. Others prefer a few drops of balsamic or other wine vinegar. And there are those who refuse to eat them any way other than slathered with red cocktail sauce.

Barbara Kafka, a noted New York food authority, recently wrote that all she asks of her oysters these days is that they come from clean waters. Amen. These days we are all wary about eating almost anything raw. However, I am assured by authorities on the subject that raw oysters, both in and out of the shell, are perfectly safe to eat as long as they are purchased from a reliable seafood merchant whose supply undoubtedly comes from a certified source. This means that the boxes of oysters he buys are tagged with the date and location of the harvest, which is kept on file in the unlikely event that any health problems should arise. Individual containers of shucked oysters will be marked with a freshness date, as well as a certification number of the rigidly inspected and monitored plant in which they were packed.

Buy oysters, in or out of the shell, as close to the time you plan to serve them as possible. Keep them icy cold, discarding any with gaping shells that do not close immediately when the oyster is given a light tap.

Here are two popular sauces for raw oysters.

MIGNONETTE SAUCE

¼ cup finely chopped shallots or the white
    part of green onions (scallions)
1 cup balsamic or tarragon vinegar

2 tablespoons minced fresh chives or
    green onion tops (optional)
1 teaspoon ground white pepper

Mix all of the ingredients together in a small bowl, cover, and chill. It will keep for a day or two in the refrigerator.

YIELD: 1¼ CUPS; 4 TO 6 SERVINGS

Variation: Substitute 2 tablespoons shredded fresh horseradish or ginger for the shallots.

CLASSIC AMERICAN RED COCKTAIL SAUCE

1 cup chili sauce or catsup
Prepared horseradish, well drained, to
    taste (about ¼ cup)
2 tablespoons fresh lemon juice

1 teaspoon Worcestershire sauce
2 drops liquid red pepper seasoning
Salt and freshly ground black pepper to
    taste

Combine all of the ingredients together in a small bowl, cover, and chill. It will keep for a day or two in the refrigerator.

YIELD: 1¼ CUPS; 4 TO 6 SERVINGS

VICHYSSOISE

This is the French soup that was created in America in 1910 by chef Louis Diat of the Ritz-Carlton Hotel in New York City. In making the famous cold soup, Diat drew from an old recipe for French leek and potato soup that was served hot, with butter and milk added at the last moment.

3 tablespoons butter
1 small onion, chopped (¼ cup)
1 pound all-purpose or Russet (Idaho) potatoes, peeled and cut into small pieces (2 cups)

3 or 4 leeks, trimmed, rinsed to remove any sand, and sliced, including some of the green tops (1½ cups)
4 cups chicken broth (see pages 2–4)
¼ to ½ cup heavy or whipping cream
Salt and ground white pepper to taste
Snipped fresh chives for garnish

Heat the butter in a Dutch oven or other large heavy saucepan. Add the onion and cook over medium-high heat, stirring frequently, until softened. Add the potatoes, leeks, and chicken broth and bring to a boil over high heat. Reduce the heat to medium-low and simmer, uncovered, for 30 minutes. Remove from the heat and cool slightly. Pour into a food processor or blender (if using a blender, this will have to be done in two batches) and process until very smooth. Add ¼ cup of the cream and process again. Pour into a bowl and add the salt and pepper. (Remember that anything served cold requires extra seasoning since chilling dulls flavors.) Cover and refrigerate. When ready to serve, add more cream (or milk) if the soup seems too thick. Taste and add more salt and pepper, if necessary. Ladle the cold soup into shallow bowls and garnish each serving with a sprinkling of chives.

YIELD: 7 CUPS; 8 SERVINGS

Sweet Potato Vichyssoise: Substitute sweet potatoes for the white potatoes.

OYSTER SOUP

The only thing that makes this soup significantly different from oyster stew is that it has fewer oysters per serving, in deference to the amount of food that will follow it.

3 cups half-and-half
1 cup heavy or whipping cream
2 pints small shucked oysters, drained
  and the liquor reserved
2 teaspoons salt

½ teaspoon freshly ground black pepper
⅛ teaspoon ground cayenne (red) pepper
3 tablespoons butter
2 green onions (scallions), thinly sliced,
  including some of the green tops (¼ cup)

Combine the half-and-half, cream, reserved oyster liquor, salt, and peppers in a large heavy saucepan. Place the pan over medium-low heat and cook until the mixture simmers. Add the oysters and cook over low heat just until the edges of the oysters curl—do not allow the mixture to simmer after the oysters have been added. Remove from the heat and stir in the butter until it is melted. Ladle into shallow soup bowls and garnish with the green onion.

YIELD: ABOUT 8 CUPS; 8 TO 10 SERVINGS

FRESH PUMPKIN SOUP

I think the very first pumpkin soups must have been very much like this one, which is simply a winter squash and root vegetable soup. Stirring in cream for enrichment would have been a much later addition.

1 small pumpkin, weighing about
  4 pounds (see page 8)
6 tablespoons (¾ stick) butter
1 medium-size onion, finely chopped
  (½ cup)
½ pound turnips, peeled and coarsely
  chopped (1 cup)

1 large parsnip, scraped and cut into
  1½-inch pieces
6 cups chicken broth (see pages 2–4)
½ cup heavy or whipping cream
Salt and ground white pepper to taste
Unsweetened whipped cream for garnish

Cut the pumpkin in half, scoop out the fiber and seeds, and discard them. Cut the pumpkin into large pieces. Peel off the skin with a vegetable parer and trim away any remaining fiber so that what remains is solid flesh. Cut the flesh into 1-inch pieces. Heat the butter in a Dutch oven or other large heavy saucepan. Add the onion and cook over medium-high heat, stirring frequently, until softened. Stir in the pumpkin, turnips, parsnip, and chicken broth and bring to a boil. Cover and simmer over medium-low heat for 1 hour. Remove from the heat and set aside to cool slightly. Place the vegetables in a food processor, add a cup or two of the broth, and process until smooth. Add the remaining broth and process again. (Depending on the size of your food processor, this may have to be done in more than one batch.) Rinse the saucepan in which the vegetables were cooked and return the pureed soup to it. Stir in the cream and cook over medium heat, stirring frequently, until heated through. Season with the salt and pepper. Ladle into shallow soup bowls and garnish with a small spoonful of whipped cream.

YIELD: ABOUT 8 CUPS; 8 TO 12 SERVINGS

ROASTED VEGETABLE SOUP

A deep-flavored soup, and a very pretty one, too. Pebbly bits of vegetables give it a nice mouth feel. This is one of my favorite soups—I continue to serve it long after winter is gone.

1 pound carrots, cut into 1½-inch pieces
2 or 3 medium-size all-purpose potatoes
  (about ¾ pound), peeled and quartered
1 large onion, quartered
4 cloves garlic, unpeeled
½ teaspoon salt

¼ teaspoon freshly ground black pepper
1 tablespoon vegetable oil
2 cups chicken or beef broth (see
  pages 2–4)
½ teaspoon dried thyme leaves, crumbled
2 cups half-and-half or light cream
1 tablespoon chopped fresh parsley

Preheat the oven to 500°F. Place the carrots, potatoes, onion, and garlic in a medium-size roasting pan and sprinkle with the salt, pepper, and oil. Toss to lightly coat the vegetables with the oil. Place the pan in the oven and immediately lower the temperature to 350°F. Roast the vegetables, uncovered, for about 1 hour, stirring occasionally, until they are tender and lightly browned. Remove from the oven and cool slightly. Remove the skin from the garlic and discard it. Also discard any pieces of onion that may be more burned than brown. Place the vegetables in a food processor, add the broth and thyme, and process until the mixture looks pebbly. (May be made ahead up to this point and chilled until ready to proceed.) Transfer the pureed vegetables to a large saucepan, add the half-and-half, and cook over medium heat, stirring frequently, until heated through. Season to taste with additional salt and pepper, if necessary. Ladle into shallow soup bowls and sprinkle with the parsley.

YIELD: 6 CUPS; 8 SERVINGS

PUMPKIN AND TOMATO BISQUE

Serving canned tomatoes is a very American tradition. It wasn't too long ago that almost every family had rows and rows of quart jars filled with tomatoes that had been put up in the late summer; they then made an appearance in as many recipes as possible all winter.

2 tablespoons butter
⅓ cup finely chopped red bell pepper
2 or 3 green onions (scallions), finely
  chopped, including some of the green
  tops (⅓ cup)
1 tablespoon finely chopped fresh basil or
  1 teaspoon dried leaves, crumbled

One 15-ounce can whole plum tomatoes
One 16-ounce can solid-pack pumpkin
2 cups chicken broth (see pages 2–4)
1 cup plain low-fat yogurt or sour cream
2 tablespoons chopped fresh parsley

Heat the butter in a Dutch oven or other large heavy saucepan. Add the bell pepper, green onions, and basil and cook over medium-high heat, stirring frequently, until the vegetables are softened, about 5 minutes. Stir in the undrained tomatoes, breaking them up with the side of a spoon. Add the pumpkin and chicken broth, stirring until well mixed. Reduce the heat to medium-low, cover, and simmer for 30 minutes, stirring occasionally. (May be made ahead up to this point and reheated before proceeding.) Remove the pan from the heat and rapidly stir in the yogurt until well blended. Do not boil the soup after the yogurt is added or it will curdle. Ladle into shallow soup bowls and sprinkle with the parsley.

YIELD: ABOUT 7 CUPS; 6 TO 8 SERVINGS

PUMPKIN-PEACH SOUP

It sounds like a strange combination, but don't let that put you off, for this soup is quite memorable. I suggest that you make it a day or two ahead. Besides saving time on Thanksgiving day, the soup will benefit enormously from giving the flavors a chance to mingle and mellow.

Two 16-ounce cans cling peaches in juice,
  pureed with their juice
Two 16-ounce cans solid-pack pumpkin
4 cups chicken broth (see pages 2–4)
½ teaspoon grated lemon rind

¼ cup fresh lemon juice
1 teaspoon dried fines herbes (see note on
  page 59)
½ teaspoon ground white pepper

In a large saucepan, mix together all the ingredients. Cook over medium heat, stirring frequently, until heated through. Ladle into shallow soup bowls. It may be served hot or chilled.

YIELD: 9 CUPS; ABOUT 12 SERVINGS

Note: This blend of delicate herbs can be purchased in the spice section of many supermarkets or a specialty food store.

PLAIN OLD CREAMY PUMPKIN SOUP

🍃

This is the pumpkin soup that everyone has been serving since Libby's started packing pumpkin puree in a can and everybody rushed to buy it, thrilled that they no longer had to cook a pumpkin from scratch.

4 tablespoons (½ stick) butter
1 large onion, chopped (1 cup)
1 or 2 celery ribs, sliced (½ cup)
1 clove garlic, crushed
½ teaspoon salt
¼ teaspoon ground white pepper

3 cups chicken broth (see pages 2–4)
One 16-ounce can solid-pack pumpkin
1 cup half-and-half or light cream
Plain or cheese-flavored popcorn for
*   garnish*

Melt the butter in a large saucepan over medium-high heat. When hot, add the onion, celery, and garlic and cook, stirring frequently, until softened. Stir in the salt and pepper and cook for 1 minute more. Stir in the broth and continue to cook over medium-high heat, uncovered, for 15 minutes. Stir in the pumpkin and half-and-half. Pour into a food processor or blender and process until smooth. (If using a blender, the mixture will have to be blended in two or three batches.) Return the soup to the saucepan and cook over medium heat, stirring, until heated through. (May be made ahead up to this point and reheated.) Ladle into shallow soup bowls and garnish with the popcorn.

YIELD: 6 CUPS; 8 SERVINGS

EASY CORN SOUP

So many people have told me that corn soup is one of their Thanksgiving dinner must-haves that I had to include a recipe for it. The bacon is my idea, and probably not at all traditional, so leave it out if you want to, substituting three tablespoons of butter for the bacon fat, and garnishing the soup with chopped fresh parsley or just a sprinkling of paprika.

10 slices bacon, cut into ½-inch pieces
1 large onion, finely chopped (1 cup)
2 or 3 celery ribs, finely chopped (1 cup)
½ cup finely chopped red bell pepper
3 tablespoons all-purpose flour
3 cups milk

One 10-ounce package frozen cut corn,
*   thawed and drained, or one 12-ounce*
*   can whole-kernel corn, drained*
One 17-ounce can creamed corn
¼ teaspoon freshly ground black pepper
Salt to taste

Cook the bacon in a Dutch oven or other large heavy saucepan over medium heat, stirring frequently, until crisp. Remove the bacon with a slotted spoon and set aside in a small bowl. Remove all but 3 tablespoons of the bacon drippings from the pan and discard. Add the onion, celery, and bell pepper and cook over medium-high heat, stirring frequently, until the vegetables are softened, about 5 minutes. Stir in the flour, mixing until it is well blended with the vegetables. Gradually stir in the milk. Add both kinds of corn and cook over medium-high heat, stirring frequently, until the mixture comes to a boil. Stir in about three quarters of the reserved bacon. Reduce the heat to medium-low and simmer for 5 minutes. Stir in the pepper and salt. Ladle into shallow soup bowls and sprinkle each serving with some of the remaining bacon.

YIELD: ABOUT 6 CUPS; 8 SERVINGS

CURRIED BUTTERNUT BISQUE

Getting out-of-season food is usually not a problem for magazine test kitchens, where recipes are cooked at least six months ahead, since almost everything now has an opposite growing season somewhere in the world and is available for a price. The notable exception is fresh pumpkin, which, if you notice, is why a real pumpkin rarely appears in magazine food photos. If it does, you can be sure the photo was taken the year before. The point to all of this is that in test kitchens, butternut squash is always substituted for fresh pumpkin when pumpkin is out of season. Butternuts apparently have a longer cold-storage life than pumpkins, and are almost identical in cooking properties and flavor. And that, to make a long story longer, is how this recipe came into being, the April creation of Susan McQuillan, a very talented cook and food writer.

2 pounds butternut squash, peeled, seeded, and cut into pieces (about 5 cups)
4 tablespoons (½ stick) butter
1 medium-size onion, chopped (½ cup)
¼ cup all-purpose flour

1 tablespoon curry powder
2 cups chicken broth (see pages 2–4)
1 cup light cream or half-and-half
2 cups milk
16 fresh chive blades for garnish

Place the squash in a Dutch oven or other large heavy saucepan. Cover by about an inch with lightly salted water and bring to a boil over high heat. Reduce the heat to medium-low, cover, and simmer for about 30 minutes, or until the squash is very tender. Meanwhile, melt 1 tablespoon of the butter in a small skillet over medium-high heat. When hot, add the onion and cook, stirring frequently, until softened; set aside. Drain the squash and place in a food processor, along with the onion. Process until smooth. Melt the remaining butter in a large saucepan over medium heat. When hot, stir in the flour and curry powder to make a smooth paste. Cook, stirring, until the mixture is bubbly. Whisk in the chicken broth gradually and continue to cook and stir over medium heat until the sauce is thick and smooth. Stir in the cream and milk, reduce the heat to low, and cook, stirring frequently, until heated through. (May be made ahead up to this point and reheated.) Ladle into shallow soup bowls and float two chive blades, crisscrossed, on each serving.

YIELD: 8 CUPS; 8 TO 10 SERVINGS

LIGHTLY CREAMED SWEET POTATO SOUP

Even without the cream, this soup is very rich tasting. The sweet potatoes give it body, as well as a delicate flavor that most people like very much but usually don't recognize.

2 tablespoons butter
1 medium-size onion, coarsely chopped (½ cup)
1 or 2 celery ribs, coarsely chopped (½ cup)
2 tablespoons all-purpose flour
3 cups chicken broth (see pages 2–4)
3 cups beef broth (see pages 2–4)

1½ pounds sweet potatoes, peeled and sliced (4 cups)
1 cup light cream or half-and-half (optional)
Salt and freshly ground black pepper to taste
Chopped fresh chives or Puff Pastry Cutouts (see page 17)

Melt the butter in a Dutch oven or other large heavy saucepan over medium-high heat. When hot, add the onion and celery and cook, stirring frequently, until softened. Reduce the heat to medium and stir in the flour, mixing until it is well blended with the vegetables. Gradually stir in the chicken and beef broths. Add the sweet potatoes and bring to a boil. Reduce the heat to medium-low, cover, and simmer until the potatoes are very soft, about 20 minutes. Remove from the heat and cool slightly. Spoon just the vegetables into a food processor. Add about a cup of the broth and process until very smooth. Add the remaining broth and process until well blended. (This will probably have to be done in two batches.) Return the puree to the saucepan and stir in the cream. (May be made ahead up to this point.) Cook over medium heat, stirring frequently, until heated through. Season with the salt and pepper. Ladle into shallow soup bowls and garnish with chopped chives or puff pastry cutouts.

YIELD: 10 CUPS; 12 TO 14 SERVINGS

MUSHROOM CONSOMMÉ

Don't be tempted to substitute regular white mushrooms in this consommé. They simply haven't got enough flavor.

½ pound shiitake mushrooms, rinsed and
    patted dry
4 cups beef broth (see pages 2–4)
2 tablespoons finely chopped onion
2 tablespoons finely chopped carrot
2 fresh parsley sprigs
½ small bay leaf

2 tablespoons butter
1 small clove garlic, put through a
    garlic press
One half of a 10-ounce package frozen
    chopped spinach, partially thawed
4 green onions (scallions), thinly sliced,
    including some of the green tops (½ cup)

Twist off the mushroom stems and set the caps aside. Chop the stems coarsely. In a large saucepan, bring the broth, chopped mushroom stems, onion, carrot, parsley sprigs, and bay leaf to a boil. Reduce the heat to medium-low, cover tightly, and simmer for 15 minutes. Strain the broth through a fine-mesh sieve into a 4-cup measure, pressing the vegetables with the back of a spoon to extract all of the liquid. Add enough water to the broth to make 4 cups. Discard the vegetables and set the broth aside.

Cut the mushroom caps into ¼-inch strips. Melt the butter in the same saucepan used to simmer the broth over medium-high heat. When hot, add the mushroom strips and cook, stirring and tossing, until they are limp. Stir in the garlic, spinach, green onions, and reserved broth. Reduce the heat to medium-low, cover, and cook for 5 minutes. Ladle into shallow soup bowls and serve very hot.

YIELD: 7 CUPS; ABOUT 8 SERVINGS

ALISON ON DOMINICK STREET'S FRESH FRUIT SOUP

I failed in my attempt to re-create this very unusual soup after tasting it at Alison on Dominick Street, one of the best restaurants in New York, a city where it is never easy to be one of the best of anything. Rather than have me suffer, Thomas Valenti, the chef, was gracious enough to send the recipe to me to be included in this book. I thought it would be just right for Thanksgiving. The only small difference between this soup and the one Tom makes is that his version also calls for five ounces of chopped lemon grass, an ingredient that is not easy to come by in most places.

Finely grated rind of 2 large oranges (see note below)
Finely grated rind of 2 limes (see note below)
1½ quarts water
1¼ cups sugar
1 piece (about 1 inch) fresh ginger, peeled and finely chopped

½ cup fresh mint leaves
Pinch of salt
3 tablespoons fresh lemon juice
2 turns of a pepper mill
About 4 cups ¼-inch-diced mixed fruits (peeled oranges, halved seedless grapes, pears, apples, peeled kiwi fruit, etc.)

In a large saucepan, combine the grated rinds, water, sugar, ginger, mint, salt, lemon juice, and pepper. Bring to a boil, then reduce the heat to medium-low and simmer for 1 minute. Remove from the heat, cover, and cool to room temperature. Strain the broth through a cheesecloth- or paper towel–lined sieve into a medium-size bowl, discarding the residue in the sieve. Cover the broth and chill until ready to serve. To serve, divide the diced fruit among 8 soup cups. Pour the chilled ginger broth over the fruit, dividing evenly.

YIELD: 3½ CUPS BROTH; 8 SERVINGS

Note: Be careful not to include any of the bitter white pith just beneath the rind.

AVOCADO AND PEAR SALAD
WITH POPPY SEED DRESSING

The avocados must be ripe, but not overly so, for this salad to look its best. You'll know when they're just right if they give very slightly when lightly pressed between the palms of your hands. Place perfectly ripened avocados in the refrigerator for a day or so. If the avocados are not quite ripe, place them together in a paper bag, close the bag, and ripen at room temperature.

2 medium-size avocados, peeled, pit removed, and thinly sliced lengthwise	DRESSING
½ cup fresh lime or lemon juice	¾ cup almond or vegetable oil
Two 16-ounce cans pear halves in light syrup or juice, drained and thinly sliced lengthwise	⅓ cup tarragon-flavored white wine vinegar
	⅓ cup mild honey
Watercress sprigs for garnish	2 tablespoons Dijon mustard
	2 teaspoons poppy seeds

Gently turn the avocado slices in the lime juice in a large bowl to prevent darkening. Alternate the avocado and pear slices, dividing them evenly among 8 salad plates. Whisk together all the dressing ingredients in a medium-size bowl, then spoon over the slices, dividing evenly, about 3 tablespoons per serving. Garnish with watercress sprigs.

YIELD: ABOUT 1½ CUPS OF DRESSING; 8 SERVINGS

POMEGRANATE AND ENDIVE SALAD

When pomegranates are in season I serve this salad often. Besides being a bit offbeat, it is very beautiful. Everything can be done ahead except for slicing the endive, which turns a sort of pale brown-purple color if done too far in advance.

1 pomegranate (see note on page 65)	¼ cup plus 2 tablespoons vegetable oil
2 tablespoons raspberry vinegar (see pages 8–9)	Salt to taste
	Sugar (optional)
2 teaspoons minced shallot or the white part of a green onion (scallion)	4 medium-size Belgian endive
2 teaspoons Dijon mustard	1 bunch watercress, trimmed and rinsed

❦

Cut the pomegranate in half through the blossom. With the tip of a pointy spoon (a grapefruit spoon works best), dig out the juicy red seeds and place them in a small bowl, making sure to discard any bits of the bitter white pith. Pour any juice that remains in the fruit cavities over the seeds. Mix the vinegar, shallot, and mustard in a small bowl, then gradually whisk in the oil. Add the salt and, if the mixture seems exceptionally tart, a pinch of sugar. Stir the vinegar mixture into the seeds and set aside. (May be done ahead up to this point.) Trim off the endive roots. Cut each endive, crosswise, into thin slices. (You should have 4 to 5 cups.) Divide the endive equally among 8 salad plates. Divide the watercress leaves among the salads, placing them here and there between the endive rings. Stir the dressing to distribute the seeds evenly, and spoon about 1 measuring tablespoonful over each of the salads. Serve immediately.

YIELD: 8 SERVINGS

Note: Pomegranates are in plentiful supply in November. If you're not familiar with them, they are almost perfectly round, usually bright red, and have a leathery skin with a pretty, six-pointed blossom end. My kids used to call them "Christmas ball fruit." The juice stains, so be careful.

BEET AND TURNIP SALAD WITH MUSTARD DRESSING
❦

Root vegetables were the very backbone of the early settlers' menus, so I like to include them as much as possible at Thanksgiving. Although there's nothing old-time about this recipe, it shows just how nicely these vegetables can be integrated into today's way of eating.

1 pound medium-size beets, trimmed,
   peeled, and cut into matchstick pieces
   (2 cups)
1 tablespoon pickling spice
¾ teaspoon salt
½ pound medium-size white turnips,
   trimmed, peeled, and cut into matchstick pieces (1 cup)
3 tablespoons cider vinegar

1½ tablespoons prepared mustard
2 teaspoons chopped fresh dill or
   ½ teaspoon dried leaves, crumbled
Freshly ground black pepper to taste
½ cup vegetable oil
4 green onions (scallions), thinly sliced,
   including some of the green tops (½ cup)
8 Boston lettuce leaves, rinsed and dried

Cover the beets with water in a medium-size saucepan. Tie the pickling spice in a cheesecloth bag and add to the pan with ½ teaspoon of the salt. Bring to a boil over high heat. Reduce the heat to medium-low and simmer for about 5 minutes, or until the beets are tender-crisp. Remove from the heat and let the beets cool to room temperature in the cooking liquid. Drop the turnip pieces into a medium-size saucepan of lightly salted boiling water. Reduce the heat to medium-low and cook just until tender-crisp, about 2 minutes. Drain well and set aside to cool to room temperature.

In a small bowl, mix together the vinegar, mustard, dill, the remaining salt, and the pepper. Gradually whisk in the vegetable oil. Drain the cooled beets and toss them with half of the dressing in a medium-size bowl. In a small bowl, toss the drained turnips with the remaining dressing. Cover both bowls tightly and refrigerate overnight, or for up to two or three days. Just before serving, remove the beets and turnips from the refrigerator. In a medium-size bowl, toss them together with the green onions. Place a lettuce leaf on each of 8 salad plates. Spoon the salad onto the lettuce leaves and serve immediately.

YIELD: 8 SERVINGS

ORANGE AND RED ONION SALAD

It's always been a mystery to me why oranges and onions are such excellent companions, but who am I to question perfection? On a black plate, this simple salad looks terrific.

⅓ cup plus 1 tablespoon olive oil
1 cup chopped almonds
3 large navel oranges
½ teaspoon dried thyme leaves, crumbled
½ teaspoon salt

¼ teaspoon garlic powder
¼ teaspoon ground cumin
¼ teaspoon ground white pepper
2 small red onions, thinly sliced and
    separated into rings

Heat 1 tablespoon of the oil in a medium-size skillet over medium heat. Add the almonds and cook, stirring constantly, until they are crisp and lightly browned. Remove the skillet from the heat and set aside. With a small sharp knife or a vegetable parer, peel the oranges, making sure to cut away all of the bitter white pith just beneath the rind. Holding each orange over a large bowl, neatly cut between the segments, letting the segments and the juice fall into the bowl. Drain the segments, reserving 3 table-spoons of the juice, and set them aside. In a small bowl, mix the reserved juice, the thyme, salt, garlic powder, cumin, and pepper. Gradually whisk in the remaining ⅓ cup olive oil. (May be done ahead up to this point.) Arrange the orange segments on 8 salad plates, dividing them equally. Arrange the onion rings over the orange segments. Sprinkle the reserved almonds over the salads. Reblend the dressing and drizzle about 1 measuring tablespoonful over each of the salads. Serve immediately.

YIELD: ½ CUP OF DRESSING; 8 SERVINGS

WARM MUSHROOM SALAD

I prefer the plain, old, garden-variety mushrooms for this salad, but you can certainly substitute a more upscale variety, such as shiitake caps or crimini, if you like.

½ pound regular white mushrooms (about
   2 cups)
1 head red-tipped lettuce, rinsed, dried,
   and torn into pieces
1 cup extra virgin olive oil

¼ cup balsamic vinegar
1 teaspoon salt
¼ teaspoon freshly ground black pepper
3 or 4 celery ribs, diagonally sliced
   (1½ cups)

Rinse the mushrooms briefly and pat dry on paper towels. Trim the stem ends and thinly slice the mushrooms. (May be done several hours ahead, then covered and refrigerated.) Shortly before serving, arrange an equal amount of lettuce on each of 8 salad plates. Heat the oil, vinegar, salt, and pepper in a large nonreactive skillet over medium-high heat until the mixture is very warm. Add the mushrooms and celery and cook for a minute or so, stirring to coat the ingredients with the dressing, until the mixture is warmed through but not hot. Divide evenly among the prepared salad plates and serve immediately.

YIELD: 8 SERVINGS

OLD-FASHIONED FRUIT SALAD

Every time I eat this I'm whisked right back into my childhood (me and everyone else over the age of forty), when fruit salad was always the first course. The more elaborate the meal, the more ingredients that went into it.

2 large navel oranges
One 8¾-ounce can pineapple tidbits,
   drained
2 large red apples, cored and diced
   (about 2 cups)
2 large bananas, sliced (about 2 cups)
2 tablespoons fresh lemon juice

½ cup heavy or whipping cream
2 tablespoons confectioners' sugar
⅛ teaspoon ground cardamom or mace
½ cup toasted (see pages 6–7) slivered
   almonds
1 head iceberg lettuce, rinsed, drained,
   and cut into shreds

With a small sharp knife or a vegetable parer, peel the oranges, making sure to cut away all of the bitter white pith just beneath the rind. Holding each orange over a large bowl, neatly cut between the segments, letting the segments and the juice fall into the bowl. Drain off the juice. Add the pineapple, apples, bananas, and lemon juice to the oranges and stir to coat. (May be made a few hours ahead up to this point. Press a piece of plastic wrap directly onto the surface of the fruit to prevent discoloration.) Shortly before serving, whip the cream with the sugar and cardamom in a medium-size chilled bowl with chilled beaters until stiff peaks form when the beaters are lifted. Sprinkle the almonds over the fruits and immediately fold in the whipped cream. Divide the lettuce equally among 8 salad plates, then spoon the salad over the lettuce and serve immediately.

YIELD: 8 SERVINGS

THE RAYMONDS' SLUSHY FRUIT COCKTAIL

Anne Raymond Bailey says this fruit cocktail is as essential as turkey when her family gathers for Thanksgiving dinner. As a little girl it was her job to dish out the fruit cocktail, making sure that the cherries were evenly divided.

Two 16-ounce cans fruit cocktail in
   heavy syrup
One 6-ounce can frozen apple juice
   concentrate, slightly thawed
½ cup water

Four 3- or 4-inch cinnamon sticks, broken
   in half
6 whole cloves
8 maraschino cherries, quartered

Drain the syrup from the fruit cocktail into a medium-size saucepan. Set the drained fruit aside. Stir the concentrate, water, cinnamon sticks, and cloves into the syrup and bring to a boil over high heat. Reduce the heat to medium-low, cover, and simmer for 10 minutes, stirring occasionally. Remove from the heat and set aside, removing the cloves. Divide the drained fruit cocktail between two 8- or 9-inch square baking pans. Pour the syrup and cinnamon sticks over the fruit, dividing evenly. When the fruit is cool, cover the pans and place them in the freezer. To serve, let the frozen fruit cocktail stand at room temperature for 30 minutes, then break the slightly thawed mixture into chunks with the side of a spoon. Spoon the chunks and some of the slushy liquid into chilled bowls or compote glasses, evenly dividing the cherry pieces, and making sure that each serving has a cinnamon stick. Serve immediately.

YIELD: 6 TO 8 SERVINGS

MINTY MELON BALLS

If no children will be at the table, you might want to add a couple of tablespoons of light rum to this for added oomph, stirring it in at the same time the orange and lime juices are added to the mint mixture.

1 cup mild honey
⅔ cup water
½ teaspoon ground cardamom
2 tablespoons chopped fresh mint
⅔ cup fresh orange juice

½ cup fresh lime juice
1 teaspoon grated orange rind
2 cantaloupes
1 large honeydew melon
Fresh mint leaves for garnish

Combine the honey, water, and cardamom in a medium-size saucepan and bring to a boil. Reduce the heat to medium-low and simmer for 5 minutes. Pour over the mint in a medium-size bowl and set aside to cool. Stir the orange and lime juices and orange rind into the cooled mint mixture. Cut the melons in half and scrape out the seeds and fiber. With two or three sizes of melon-ball scoops, scoop out the melon flesh, placing the balls in another medium-size bowl. Strain the syrup over the fruit. Cover and refrigerate until serving time, stirring occasionally. Serve cold in sherbet glasses or small bowls, garnished with mint leaves.

YIELD: 8 SERVINGS

ANNIE'S SALMON AND CREAM CHEESE LOAF

In New York City, bagels, Nova Scotia smoked salmon, and a "shmear" (smear) of cream cheese are a popular combination, with chopped onion and capers sometimes added. Hence, Anne Bailey's inspiration for this molded loaf. Nova Scotia smoked salmon is not mandatory. Scottish or Norwegian smoked salmon, for example, can also be used, but I don't suggest the crumbly wood-smoked salmon that is so popular in the West and Northwest. Because it is quite rich, I wouldn't serve this as a first course if it will follow substantial appetizers. This loaf keeps well for up to a week.

Three 8-ounce packages cream cheese,
    softened
1 tablespoon fresh lemon juice
¼ cup drained capers, coarsely chopped
½ pound thinly sliced smoked salmon
8 green onions (scallions), thinly sliced,
    including both the white and green
    parts (1 cup)

2 or 3 large (4 to 5 inches in diameter)
    fresh bagels or frozen bagels, thawed (if
    the bagels are smaller, more may be
    needed)
Radish roses for garnish (see page 13)
Watercress sprigs for garnish

Line an 8½- × 4½- × 2½-inch loaf pan with aluminum foil, using one piece (cut to fit) in each direction. Fold any excess foil over the outside of the pan. In a large bowl, beat 2½ packages of the cream cheese with the lemon juice until fluffy. Stir in the capers until they are evenly distributed. Set the remaining plain cream cheese aside. Press one third (about 1 cup) of the caper and cream cheese mixture evenly in the bottom of the prepared pan. (This is easier to do if you wet your fingers so they don't stick to the cream cheese.) Lay half of the salmon slices on top of the cheese. Add another third of the caper and cream cheese mixture over the salmon, pressing it down evenly. Top with the sliced onions, spreading them evenly. Add the remaining third of the caper and cream cheese mixture, pressing it down evenly over the onions. Lay the remaining salmon over the cheese. Press the reserved plain cream cheese over the salmon. Cover the top of the loaf with a piece of plastic wrap, pressing down evenly on the wrap with the palm of your hand to make sure the layers are well compacted. Refrigerate the loaf overnight, or for at least 8 hours. To serve, remove the plastic wrap and, using the foil to assist, turn the loaf out upside down onto a cutting board. Carefully remove the foil. With a sharp knife, cut the loaf into 8 to 16 slices. Use a firm downward motion with the knife; don't saw or it may break apart. Shortly before serving, lay the bagels flat on a work surface. With a serrated knife, cut each bagel into ¼-inch perpendicular slices. (Do not allow the bagel slices to sit out for too long before serving, since they get hard very quickly.) To serve, arrange 1 or 2 slices of the loaf on each of 8 salad plates, then place 3 or 4 slices of bagel on each plate. Garnish with a radish or two and watercress sprigs. The loaf may be eaten with a fork, accompanied by the bagel slices, or it can be spread on the slices.

YIELD: 8 servings

Note: The loaf may be made ahead and frozen. In that case, wrap securely in aluminum foil after assembling. Thaw the loaf for several hours in the refrigerator. It does not have to be completely thawed before slicing.

CAROLE SAVILLE'S COUNTRY PÂTÉ

Carole says that one of the great joys of her life is her beautiful and aromatic herb garden that flourishes behind her Laurel Canyon home near Los Angeles. Carole is widely known as an authority on the subject of cultivating and using herbs, and one of the offshoots of her expertise has been a thriving little business of planning and managing "kitchen cutting gardens" for more than a few celebrity clients and stellar restaurants in the area. Carole is also unsurpassed at making glorious pâtés. At one time, when she lived in New Jersey, she supplied several New York restaurants with their *pâté du maison.* Carole suggests this pâté for Thanksgiving because it's easy to make and stays moist and fresh-tasting for two or three days before and after it's served.

1¼ pounds sliced bacon
1 pound ground veal
1 pound ground pork
½ cup Madeira or good brandy
2 large eggs
½ cup pistachio nuts (from uncolored
   shells), coarsely chopped
2 teaspoons salt
½ teaspoon dried thyme leaves, crumbled
¼ teaspoon ground allspice

¼ teaspoon freshly ground black pepper
2 tablespoons butter
½ pound chicken livers, rinsed and cut
   in half
2 or 3 bay leaves
Cornichons (tiny French sour pickles)
Thinly sliced toasted or untoasted French
   bread
Dijon mustard

Preheat the oven to 350°F. Chop ¼ pound of the bacon and set aside. Drop the remaining bacon slices into a large skillet of boiling water. Remove the slices almost immediately and pat them dry on paper towels. Line the bottom and sides of a 3-quart loaf pan or terrine with the blanched bacon, allowing the slices to hang over the sides. (Later the ends will be used to cover the pâté.) In a large bowl, combine the ground veal and pork, reserved chopped bacon, and Madeira. The best way to do this is with your hands. Add the eggs, pistachios, salt, thyme, allspice, and pepper. Mix again until thoroughly blended.

Melt the butter in a large skillet over medium-high heat. When hot, add the chicken livers and cook, stirring and tossing, until firm to the touch but still pink inside. Remove the skillet from the heat and set aside. Spoon half of the ground-meat mixture into the prepared loaf pan, patting it down evenly. Arrange the chicken livers evenly over the layer of ground meat. Spoon the remaining meat mixture into the pan, patting it down and smoothing the top with a spatula. Fold the overlapping pieces of bacon over the top of the pâté. Arrange the bay leaves on top. Cover the loaf pan tightly with aluminum foil. Place the loaf pan in a larger baking pan and set in the oven. Fill the larger pan with enough hot water to come about halfway up the side of the loaf pan. Bake for 1½ to 2 hours, or until an instant-reading thermometer inserted through the foil into the center of the pâté registers 170°F. Remove from the oven and set on a wire rack to cool.

Cut a piece of heavy cardboard to fit over the top of the pâté inside the pan and cover it with aluminum foil. Place the foil-covered cardboard on top of the cooled pâté and weigh it down with cans or other heavy objects. (I use a brick that fits neatly into my terrine.) Place the pâté in the refrigerator and chill overnight.

Remove the weights and cardboard, then run a knife around the edge of the pâté and invert the loaf pan onto a platter or cutting board. Remove the loaf pan and pat the pâté dry with paper towels. Turn right side up and, if not serving immediately, wrap securely in aluminum foil or plastic wrap and chill until ready to serve. You can remove the bacon strips, if you like, but I leave them on.

To serve, remove the bay leaves and cut the pâté into 16 thin slices, or however many are needed. For a first course, serve one slice of pâté per person. Just before serving, arrange a slice of the pâté on each salad plate and garnish with cornichons and thinly sliced toasted or untoasted French bread. Serve the mustard on the side in a small crock. Rewrap and refrigerate any remaining pâté.

YIELD: ABOUT 16 SLICES

SHRIMP MOUSSE WITH CHIVE MAYONNAISE

Seafood mousses were another preparation that gained popularity with the nouvelle cuisine. Because the recipe calls for egg whites, and because the servings are small, this mousse is not quite as sinful as most of them.

2¼ pounds raw shrimp, shelled, deveined, and cut in half (1½ pounds after shelling)
2 cold large egg whites
1½ cups cold heavy or whipping cream
1 teaspoon salt
½ teaspoon ground white pepper
A big pinch of ground nutmeg
One 10-ounce package frozen leaf spinach, thawed and squeezed dry

8 small cooked shrimp, peeled and deveined for garnish (optional)
Whole chives for garnish

CHIVE MAYONNAISE
1 cup mayonnaise
¼ cup minced fresh chives
½ cup sour cream
Heavy or whipping cream

Preheat the oven to 350°F. Butter a 9- × 5-inch, glass loaf pan. Pull off a piece of aluminum foil measuring about 16 inches. Cut the width of the foil so that it measures the same as the length of the loaf pan. Lay the foil crosswise inside and up the sides of the loaf pan, folding the excess foil over the outside of the pan.

Place the shrimp in a food processor and process with quick on/off pulses until coarsely chopped. Add the egg whites and process until smooth. Slowly add the cream, stopping once or twice to scrape down the side of the work bowl, processing only until the mixture is well blended. (If processed for too long, the cream will turn buttery.) Add the salt, pepper, and nutmeg and process quickly to blend. Spoon about half of the shrimp mixture into the prepared pan. Evenly spread the spinach over the shrimp mixture. Spoon the remaining shrimp mixture over the spinach.

Set the baking dish in a larger pan and place in the oven. Pour hot water into the larger pan until it comes about halfway up the side of the baking dish. Bake for 35 to 40 minutes, or until the mousse is firm to the touch and the sides are just barely beginning to pull away from the side of the pan. Remove from the oven and set the loaf pan on a wire rack to cool for about 20 minutes. Cover the pan tightly and refrigerate for at least 8 hours or overnight.

To prepare the Chive Mayonnaise, mix the mayonnaise, sour cream and chives in a small bowl until well blended. Stir in just enough of the cream so that the mixture is about the consistency of a thick cream soup. Cover and refrigerate until shortly before serving time.

Remove the mousse from the baking dish onto a cutting surface, using the excess foil to assist. Discard the foil and cut the mousse into ½- to ¾-inch slices. Beat the Chive Mayonnaise to reblend. Spoon 4 or 5 tablespoon-fuls of the mayonnaise onto each of 8 individual plates, spreading it into a large pool with the back of a spoon. Lay one slice of the mousse on each plate on top of the mayonnaise, which should surround the slice. Garnish each serving with one shrimp, then arrange two chive blades on top of each slice of mousse.

YIELD: 8 TO 12 SERVINGS; ABOUT 1¾ CUPS MAYONNAISE

HERRING AND APPLES

This was quite a daring first course back in the forties when my Grandmother Hanners frequently served it on important occasions, which probably included Thanksgiving, although I don't actually remember. At that time I doubt if herring came in handy little jars at the supermarket, so it's likely that she asked Grandfather to pick some up at a delicatessen in New York City, where he commuted to work every day. (I have to tell you that I hated this, almost as much as I hated jellied consomme, another one of her favorite first courses. Years later I learned to enjoy them both.)

2 large red apples, cored and thinly sliced
About ⅓ cup fresh or bottled lemon juice
1 or 2 Boston lettuce leaves, rinsed and
  dried, per serving

Two 8-ounce jars herring in sour cream
2 small red onions, cut into thin slices
  and the slices separated into rings
Coarsely ground black pepper

Dip the apple slices in lemon juice to prevent darkening. Place a lettuce leaf or two on each of 8 salad plates. Arrange equal numbers of apple slices on the lettuce leaves. Top with herring and then onion rings, dividing evenly. Sprinkle each serving with pepper.

YIELD: 8 SERVINGS

MUSSELS IN MUSTARD SAUCE

Now that clean, cultivated mussels are so readily available, I could not resist including one of my own favorite first courses. I first learned to love these at Georges Rey, an early New York French restaurant that is gone, but not forgotten. You don't have to use cultivated mussels, of course, but in that case look for small mussels, which are usually sweeter and more tender. Canned mussels, available at specialty food stores, may also be used, but they do lack the incomparable flavor of fresh mussels.

2 pounds (about 40) cultivated mussels
1 cup water
½ cup dry white wine or vermouth
1 small onion, minced (¼ cup)
1 cup mayonnaise
1 tablespoon Dijon mustard

1 tablespoon coarse-grain mustard
2 or 3 drops liquid red pepper seasoning
Four or five turns of a pepper mill
2 or 3 Boston lettuce leaves per serving
Chopped fresh parsley for garnish

Scrub the mussels under cold running water and scrape away any traces of the beard with a small paring knife. Place the mussels in a large kettle. Add the water and wine. Stir in the minced onion. Cover and bring to a boil. Cook over high heat, stirring the mussels that are on the bottom up to the top once or twice, until the shells open, 3 or 4 minutes. Remove from the heat and set aside until the mussels have cooled. In a small bowl, mix the mayonnaise, both kinds of mustard, red-pepper seasoning, and black pepper. Discard any mussels that have not opened. Remove the mussels from the shells, placing them in a large bowl as you do so. Gently stir the mayonnaise dressing into the mussels. Cover tightly and chill. When ready to serve, line 8 salad plates with two or three lettuce leaves. Stir the mussels and then divide them evenly among the prepared plates. Sprinkle with parsley.

YIELD: 8 SERVINGS

CROSTINI

Even though crostini seems more like a prelude to spaghetti than turkey, I can't imagine that you will receive any complaints if you serve this on Thanksgiving.

16 slices (½ inch thick) Italian bread
Two 15-ounce cans whole plum tomatoes
1 cup pitted ripe olives, finely chopped
¼ cup drained capers, coarsely chopped
2 large cloves garlic, put through a
  garlic press

2 teaspoons extra virgin olive oil
2 teaspoons red wine vinegar
Three or four turns of a pepper mill
2 bunches arugula leaves
Sprigs of flat-leaf parsley for garnish

Preheat the oven broiler. Spread the bread slices out on a baking sheet. Toast a few inches from the source of heat for a minute or two on each side, or until lightly browned. Remove from the oven and set aside. (This may be done a day or two in advance.) Drain the tomatoes and then turn them onto a work surface and scrape out as many seeds as possible. Chop the tomatoes rather fine and drain again. In a medium-size bowl, mix the chopped tomatoes with the olives, capers, and garlic. Stir in the oil, vinegar, and pepper. Spread the tomato mixture on the toast shortly before serving. Place three or four arugula leaves on each of 8 salad plates. Arrange two toasts per serving on the arugula leaves. Garnish the top of each toast with a parsley sprig.

YIELD: 8 SERVINGS

SIX

Relishes and Condiments

❦

"Oil, vinegar, sugar, and saltiness agree!"—Oliver Goldsmith

Sweet, savory, spicy, or tart, palate-pleasing relishes and condiments are the all-important flavor enhancers that have always played a major role on the Thanksgiving menu. Chow chow, chutney, pickled fruit rinds, brandied peaches, spiced crab apples, dilled and pickled vegetables, jams, jellies, tutti-frutti, salsas, and even the ubiquitous catsup: these, along with hundreds of other similar concoctions, emerged who-knows-when-or-where as just another way to preserve the goodness of a fleeting season.

Like so many things born of thrift and necessity, these tasty little side dishes have become an integral part of the way Americans dine. Although condiments are hardly unknown or unappreciated in other world cuisines, perhaps in no other food culture is quite so much importance attached to the pleasurable experience of blending piquant flavors with the rich offerings of the main course. In most regions of the country, but especially in those places where the Pennsylvania Dutch hold forth with their well-known sweets and sours, and throughout the South, where anything sweet is always appreciated, the more festive the meal, the more varieties are expected.

Before You Begin

Most relishes are easy to cook and don't take a whole lot of time. The only general warning I would give to the uninitiated is not to cook ingredients that are highly acidulated in aluminum or iron pans. Doing so causes a chemical reaction that, although not harmful, does brighten the inside of an aluminum pan considerably, and can give the food a decidedly metallic taste and sometimes an off color. Stainless steel, porcelain-lined, and other nonreactive pots and pans are best for cooking relishes and other things that contain high-acid ingredients.

Most relishes keep quite well as long as they are tightly covered and refrigerated. If you have leftovers, go ahead and continue to serve them after Thanksgiving has passed. You might be surprised at how much they can perk up a lazy appetite and more ordinary meals.

THE CRANBERRY SAUCES

This crimson sauce, made from that native American berry, in all its infinite forms, is perhaps the best known of all the relishes. The first cranberry sauce that was similar to what we serve today was probably made by crushing cranberries with sugar-maple sap.

Both cranberries and turkeys were around at the time of the first Thanksgiving feast, but the fact that the Pilgrims may have eaten neither has in no way diminished their place in history or our pleasure in eating them together.

PLAIN GOOD CRANBERRY SAUCE

A mildly spiced sauce that's hardly more trouble than opening a can, and keeps well for two or three weeks.

1 cup sugar
½ cup water
¼ cup white vinegar
6 or 7 whole cloves

One 2-inch cinnamon stick
2 cups fresh cranberries, rinsed and
   picked over

Bring the sugar, water, vinegar, cloves, and cinnamon to a boil in a 3-quart saucepan and continue to boil for 10 minutes. Leave in the cloves or remove them with a slotted spoon and discard. Add the cranberries and boil slowly for 5 minutes over medium heat, or just until the berries begin to pop. Remove from the heat and cool slightly. Turn into a bowl or container with a tight-fitting lid and refrigerate until serving time. Serve chilled or at room temperature.

YIELD: ABOUT 3 CUPS; 12 SERVINGS

SPICY CRANBERRY CONSERVE

My Grandmother Tilghman concocted this tasty turkey accompaniment many years ago. She peeled and cooked her own little onions, and you can do the same, if you like, but her handwritten recipe *does* call for canned pineapple. I serve this relish with fresh pork and ham, as well as turkey, and sometimes I double the recipe, since it keeps for at least a month in the refrigerator.

One 12-ounce jar orange marmalade
2 cups fresh cranberries, rinsed and
  picked over
½ teaspoon ground allspice
Big pinch of ground cloves
One 2- or 3-inch cinnamon stick

One 16-ounce can or jar small whole
  onions, drained
One 8-ounce can chunk pineapple,
  drained
1 cup toasted (see pages 6–7) coarsely
  chopped walnuts

Combine the marmalade, cranberries, allspice, cloves, and cinnamon in a medium-size nonreactive saucepan. Cook over medium-high heat, stirring frequently, until the cranberries begin to pop, about 5 to 10 minutes. Stir in the onions, pineapple, and walnuts and cook for 3 minutes longer, stirring constantly. Remove from the heat and let cool slightly. Turn into a bowl or container with a tight-fitting lid and refrigerate until serving time. Serve chilled, at room temperature, or slightly warm.

YIELD: ABOUT 4½ CUPS; ABOUT 12 SERVINGS

CRANBERRY-ORANGE RELISH

Of all the cranberry sauces I've cooked, tasted, and eaten over the years, this one remains my favorite. It's easy and has all the flavors and textures I like best in my cranberry sauce, and keeps well for about a month.

One 12-ounce bag fresh cranberries
  (3 cups), rinsed and picked over
¾ cup sugar
½ cup orange juice
⅓ cup orange liqueur
¼ teaspoon ground allspice

¼ teaspoon ground cloves
¼ teaspoon ground ginger
1 tablespoon shredded orange rind
½ cup toasted (see pages 6–7) coarsely
  chopped walnuts

Combine the cranberries, sugar, orange juice, orange liqueur, allspice, cloves, and ginger in a medium-size nonreactive saucepan and bring to a boil. Reduce the heat to medium-low and simmer, stirring frequently, until the cranberries begin to pop and the mixture has thickened slightly, about 10 minutes. Remove from the heat and let cool slightly. Stir in the orange rind and walnuts, then turn into a bowl or container with a tight-fitting lid. Cover and refrigerate until serving time, or up to several days. Serve chilled or at room temperature.

YIELD: 2¼ CUPS; ABOUT 8 SERVINGS

FRESH CRANBERRY RELISH

Long ago Native Americans crushed raw cranberries and mixed them with wild-animal fat to make a mixture they called pemmican. Whether or not this little mixture was served at the first Thanksgiving feast is unknown, but there is no doubt that it was the basis for the New World's first cranberry sauce. Whenever I make this, I find myself thinking of pemmican, probably because this cranberry relish isn't cooked either, although I'm sure it tastes better. In fact, it tastes *wonderful*—crunchy, tart, and refreshing—perfect with the fattier poultry, such as goose and duck.

One 12-ounce bag fresh cranberries
  (3 cups), rinsed and picked over
1 small navel orange, unpeeled and cut
  into small pieces (1 cup)

1½ cups sugar
1 teaspoon ground cinnamon
½ teaspoon ground cloves
Orange liqueur to taste (optional)

Place the cranberries and orange pieces in a food processor and chop into very fine pieces using a few on/off pulses, being careful not to puree the berries. Scrape the mixture into a medium-size bowl. Stir in the sugar, cinnamon, cloves, and the orange liqueur. Cover tightly and refrigerate for at least 24 hours before serving. If kept tightly covered and refrigerated, this relish keeps well for a week or two. Serve a little on the cold side.

YIELD: 4 CUPS; 12 TO 14 SERVINGS

CRANBERRY-APPLE BUTTER

My mother is so fond of this sauce that she doubles the recipe and packs it into small dishwasher-clean jars, which she stores in the back of the refrigerator. She likes to serve it with pork and ham, as well as turkey, and anyone who really enjoys the relish at her table usually gets a little jar of it—and the recipe—to take home.

*1½ pounds McIntosh or Granny Smith
  apples, peeled, cored, and coarsely
  chopped (4 cups)*
*2 cups fresh cranberries, rinsed and
  picked over*

1½ cups sugar
½ teaspoon ground cinnamon
¼ teaspoon ground cloves
¼ teaspoon ground nutmeg

Combine all of the ingredients in a heavy 4-quart nonreactive saucepan. Cook over medium heat, stirring constantly, until juices form and the mixture comes to a boil. Reduce the heat to medium-low and boil gently, stirring occasionally, until the mixture is thick and soft, about 20 minutes. Remove from the heat and let cool slightly. Turn into a bowl or container with a tight-fitting lid, cover, and refrigerate until serving time.

YIELD: 4 CUPS; 12 TO 14 SERVINGS

WEST INDIAN CRANBERRY RELISH

For maximum flavor, make this spicy sauce about a month before Thanksgiving so it has time to age.

1 tablespoon minced fresh ginger
*Two 3-inch cinnamon sticks, broken
  in half*
1 dried hot chile pepper
*1 vanilla bean, split and broken into
  pieces*
6 whole allspice
2 cups sugar

⅔ cup cold water
*1 large navel orange, unpeeled and finely
  chopped*
1 lime, unpeeled and finely chopped
½ cup golden raisins
½ cup dark raisins
*Four 12-ounce bags fresh cranberries
  (12 cups), rinsed and picked over*

Tie up the ginger, cinnamon sticks, chile pepper, vanilla bean, and allspice in a square of cheesecloth and set aside. Place the sugar and ⅓ cup of the water in a large heavy skillet or Dutch oven. Cook over medium heat, stirring, until the sugar has dissolved. Raise the heat to medium-high and boil slowly, without stirring, for 7 or 8 minutes, until the sugar mixture turns a pale amber color and smells like caramel. (Watch carefully so that it doesn't darken too much.) Add the chopped orange and lime (be careful—it will splatter) and the spice bag, and cook over high heat, stirring constantly, for 5 minutes. Stir in the raisins, cranberries, and the remaining water. Cook over medium heat, stirring constantly, until about half of the cranberries pop, about 10 minutes. Remove the skillet from the heat, then remove the spice bag and discard it. Spoon the relish into dishwasher-clean ½- or 1-pint jars. Cover tightly and refrigerate for about a month before using. This relish keeps quite well for about three months.

YIELD: 6 CUPS; SIX ½-PINT JARS

MOLDED CRANBERRY SAUCE

If you're going to make a plain cranberry sauce from scratch, you might as well go a step further and mold it. A molded sauce looks especially attractive when it's garnished with candied cranberries (see page 19) or sugared grapes (see page 14) and fresh mint leaves.

1 cup sugar	One 12-ounce bag fresh cranberries
1 cup water	(3 cups), rinsed and picked over
1 envelope unflavored gelatin	1 teaspoon grated lime rind

Combine the sugar and water in a medium-size nonreactive saucepan and stir until the sugar is dissolved. Sprinkle the gelatin over the sugar water and let stand for 5 minutes to soften the gelatin. Set the pan over low heat and stir until the gelatin is dissolved completely. Raise the heat to medium-high and bring to a boil. Stir in the cranberries and lime rind and return the mixture to the boil. Reduce the heat to medium-low and simmer, stirring occasionally, for 10 minutes. Remove from the heat. Puree half of the cranberry mixture in a food processor or blender, then stir back into the whole-berry mixture. Turn the berry mixture into a well-oiled 2-cup mold. Cool to room temperature, then cover and refrigerate until firm, at least 8 hours or overnight. To unmold, invert the mold onto a serving plate, then cover the mold with a warm, damp towel until the cranberry mold slides out easily. Garnish as suggested above. Cover and refrigerate leftovers.

YIELD: 2 CUPS; ABOUT 6 SERVINGS

THE REVEREND GEORGE MINNIX'S BAKED CRANBERRIES

George appreciates good cooking and he loves to travel. Between the two, he has been able to sample some of the finer food the world has to offer. But when it comes to Thanksgiving, George likes to stay home in Elkhart, Indiana, and cook homey Midwestern food, like this easy cranberry sauce.

1 pound fresh cranberries (4 cups), rinsed and picked over
⅔ cup sugar

One 8-ounce jar English orange marmalade
½ cup toasted (see pages 6–7) chopped walnuts

Preheat the oven to 350°F. Mix all of the ingredients in a large bowl. Turn into a 6-cup baking dish that has been lightly greased or coated with nonstick vegetable cooking spray. Bake for 30 to 35 minutes, or until hot and bubbly. Serve very warm, straight from the baking dish. Refrigerate leftovers and serve, reheated, within a week or so.

YIELD: 3 CUPS; 8 TO 10 SERVINGS

CRAN-RAISIN RELISH

This recipe, accompanied by a jar of the real thing, was given to me years ago by the California Raisin Advisory Board, and it has been one of my favorites ever since. There's something wonderful about raisins and cranberries together, probably the soft sweetness of the one against the crisp tartness of the other.

1½ cups sugar
¾ cup white vinegar
3 tablespoons frozen orange juice concentrate
1½ cups dark raisins
1½ cups golden raisins
1 medium-size and 1 small onion, finely chopped (¾ cup)

1 large clove garlic, put through a garlic press
1 pound fresh cranberries (4 cups), rinsed and picked over
1 teaspoon ground ginger
½ teaspoon salt
¼ teaspoon freshly ground black pepper
⅛ teaspoon ground cayenne (red) pepper

Combine the sugar, vinegar, and orange juice concentrate in a 3-quart nonreactive saucepan. Cook over medium heat, stirring, until the sugar is dissolved. Stir in the raisins, onions, and garlic and bring to a boil over medium-high heat. Reduce the heat to medium-low and simmer for 5 minutes, stirring almost constantly. Stir in the cranberries, ginger, salt, and both peppers. Raise the heat to high, bring to a boil, then return to medium-low and simmer, uncovered, for 10 minutes, stirring frequently. Remove from the heat and let cool slightly. Turn into a bowl or container with a tight-fitting lid, cover, and refrigerate until serving time. Serve chilled or at room temperature. This relish keeps well for at least a month.

YIELD: ABOUT 5 CUPS; 12 TO 16 SERVINGS

CRANBERRY CUTOUTS

For many of us, canned cranberry sauce—tart and sweet and firm-textured—is as indispensable at Thanksgiving dinner as the turkey. Sometimes the sauce is served spoon-cut into little pieces in a cut-glass or some other pretty serving dish. But all too often it goes straight from the can, ridges and all, onto an oblong relish dish, where it reminds us of a hundred Thanksgivings past and receives a yearly place of honor between the mashed potatoes and the gravy.

If plain, jellied cranberry sauce is one of your can't-do-withouts, you might like to serve these whimsical cutouts that often appeared on my grandmother's Thanksgiving table. Young diners find these particularly enchanting.

Two 16-ounce cans jellied cranberry sauce   *Fresh parsley sprigs for garnish*
Fancy cookie cutters, measuring no more
   than 2½ inches at the widest point

Open both ends of each can of the cranberry sauce and slide the sauce out onto a cutting board. With a long, sharp knife, cut the sauce into 8 round slices. Cut the slices into fancy shapes with the cookie cutters. Using a pancake turner, transfer the cutouts to a serving plate and chill until serving time. Tuck a few parsley sprigs between the cutouts for garnish. Scraps of the sauce may be stored in a tightly covered container and served with leftovers, or they may be coarsely chopped and served at dinner along with the cutouts.

YIELD: 16 SERVINGS

CANNED CRANBERRY SAUCE RELISH

Canned cranberry sauce can also be used as the foundation for slightly more elaborate sauces by adding fruits, nuts, and spices. Considering the small effort you'll expend making them, this and the following recipe are two of the best cranberry sauces you'll ever eat.

One 16-ounce can jellied or whole-berry
    cranberry sauce
16 pitted dates, cut into small pieces
½ cup golden raisins
½ cup toasted (see pages 6–7) chopped
    almonds
One 2- or 3-inch cinnamon stick, broken
    in half

4 or 5 whole cloves
Pinch of salt
Pinch of ground ginger
Pinch of ground allspice
⅔ cup cider vinegar
1 to 3 tablespoons sugar (optional)

Combine all of the ingredients except the sugar in a heavy, medium-size nonreactive saucepan. Bring to a boil, then cook over low heat, stirring frequently, for 15 minutes. If the mixture isn't sweet enough at this point, add the sugar to taste. Continue to cook for 10 to 15 minutes, or until very thick. Let cool slightly, then turn into a bowl or container with a tight-fitting lid. Cover and refrigerate until serving time.

YIELD: 2 CUPS; 6 TO 8 SERVINGS

THE QUICKEST CRANBERRY RELISH

Two 16-ounce cans whole-berry cranberry
    sauce
One 8-ounce can crushed pineapple,
    drained

½ cup toasted (see pages 6–7) coarsely
    chopped pecans

Combine all of the ingredients in a medium-size bowl. Cover tightly and chill until serving time.

YIELD: 4 CUPS; ABOUT 12 SERVINGS

PICKLES, CHUTNEY, AND OTHER POULTRY RELISHES

Besides the cranberry sauces, other condiments complement the main course and jog the palate. I usually serve two or three other little asides that, in addition to their piquant flavor, contribute unexpected color and texture to the Thanksgiving table and dinner plate.

PUMPKIN PICKLES

Most people have never cooked a pumpkin from scratch and are amazed to find out how easy it is. A pumpkin is, after all, nothing but a winter squash, and a tasty one at that. If you can carve a jack-o'-lantern, you can make these pickles. It's not likely that there will be leftovers, but if so, they'll keep for about a month.

*1 small pumpkin, weighing 3½ to 4
  pounds (see page 8)*
1⅔ cups sugar
¾ cup cider vinegar
1 cup water
*Two 3-inch cinnamon sticks, broken
  in half*

8 whole cloves
8 whole allspice
*Six 2-inch strips orange rind (make sure
  all of the white pith is scraped away)*

Cut the pumpkin in half and scoop out the fiber and seeds and discard. Cut the pumpkin into large pieces. Peel off the skin with a vegetable parer and trim away any remaining fiber so that what remains is solid flesh. Cut the pumpkin flesh into ½-inch cubes. Combine the sugar, vinegar, water, cinnamon, cloves, allspice, and orange rind in a 3-quart nonreactive saucepan or Dutch oven. Bring to a boil and cook over medium heat for 5 minutes. Add the pumpkin, reduce the heat to medium-low, and simmer, uncovered, for 10 to 15 minutes, stirring occasionally, until the pumpkin is just tender but not at all mushy. Remove the pumpkin from the syrup with a slotted spoon to a bowl or container with a tight-fitting lid. Continue to simmer the syrup until it is reduced to about 1 cup. Remove from the heat and cool to room temperature. Pour the syrup (it will be thick) over the pumpkin and stir to coat all of the pieces. Cover and refrigerate until ready to serve.

YIELD: ABOUT 3 CUPS; 8 TO 12 SERVINGS

SPICY APPLE BALLS

I couldn't resist including this old-fashioned relish. Kids love it. Most of the cooking liquid will be left over and I can never bear to throw it away, so sometimes I boil it down further to make a sauce for vanilla ice cream. Another time I poured seltzer water over the syrup, added ice cubes, and got a surprisingly good spritzer.

1 cup sugar
½ cup water
1 tablespoon white vinegar

¼ cup tiny hot cinnamon candies
4 large Golden Delicious or Rome Beauty
  apples (about 1¾ pounds)

Mix the sugar, water, vinegar, and candies in a medium-size saucepan. Bring to a boil and simmer over low heat for 5 or 6 minutes, stirring occasionally, until the candies have melted. Meanwhile, peel the apples and cut into balls (and half-balls) with a melon-ball cutter. Try to get as many balls as possible from each apple. Drop the balls into the syrup and boil slowly, stirring frequently, until tender, 6 or 7 minutes. Remove the apple balls with a slotted spoon to a bowl. Spoon 2 to 3 tablespoons of the cooking liquid over the balls, then cover tightly and chill until serving time. The balls will keep well for a week or two.

YIELD: ABOUT 2 CUPS; 6 SERVINGS

VERY SPICY PICKLED SECKEL PEARS

These firm little pears are frequently the first choice for cooking, although they are also good eaten out of hand, and their diminutive size makes them just right for tucking into a fruit bowl or garnishing a meat platter. For pickling, I search through the bin to find the very smallest pears.

2 cups sugar
1 cup cider vinegar
½ cup water
Two 3-inch cinnamon sticks

2 teaspoons whole cloves
2 teaspoons whole allspice
2 pounds (6 to 8) small Seckel pears

Combine the sugar, vinegar, water, cinnamon, cloves, and allspice in a large heavy saucepan or Dutch oven. Bring the mixture to a boil. Cover and boil slowly for 5 minutes. Meanwhile, peel the pears, cut them in half, and remove the core with a melon-ball cutter. Add the pears to the sugar mixture and continue to boil slowly, covered, for 10 to 15 minutes, or until just tender. Remove from the heat and let the pears stand, covered, for 8 hours or overnight in the syrup. Remove the pears to a bowl with a slotted spoon, reserving the syrup. Return the pan of syrup to the heat and boil over high heat, uncovered, for 5 minutes. Strain the syrup over the pears. Let cool slightly, then cover and refrigerate until serving time. You can store the leftover pears for a week or two in a covered bowl.

YIELD: 12 TO 16 PEAR HALVES

SAVORY CORN RELISH

Two 16-ounce cans whole-kernel corn, drained
1 small red onion, finely chopped (¼ cup)
¼ cup finely chopped fresh parsley
¼ cup red wine vinegar
2 tablespoons vegetable oil
Salt and freshly ground black pepper to taste

In a medium-size bowl, mix together the corn, onion, and parsley. Add the vinegar and oil and mix until well blended. Season with salt and pepper. Turn into a bowl or container with a tight-fitting lid, cover, and refrigerate until ready to serve.

YIELD: 2 CUPS; 8 SERVINGS

Variation: For a Southwestern flavor, substitute fresh cilantro for all or part of the parsley.

SWEET CORN RELISH

Two 12-ounce cans Mexican-style corn, drained
1 or 2 celery ribs, finely chopped (½ cup)
1 medium-size red onion, finely chopped (½ cup)
¼ cup white vinegar
¼ cup light corn syrup
½ teaspoon celery seed
¼ teaspoon dry mustard
¼ teaspoon salt
⅛ teaspoon freshly ground black pepper

In a medium-size bowl, mix together the corn, celery, and onion. Add the remaining ingredients and mix until well blended. Turn into a bowl or container with a tight-fitting lid, cover, and refrigerate until serving time.

YIELD: 2 CUPS; 8 SERVINGS

FRESH RED AND GREEN PEPPER RELISH

In some parts of Pennsylvania, pepper relish is as common on the table as salt and pepper. There are probably hundreds of variations of this popular relish, and this and the one that follows are typical. Most pepper-relish recipes call for only green peppers, but I like to use an equal number of red peppers, which are sweeter and less "peppery," and make the relish prettier. I usually chop the peppers by hand, but you can use a food processor if you're careful not to pulverize them. Both relishes keep well for about a week.

1 small red bell pepper, cored, seeded, and finely chopped (1 cup)

1 small green bell pepper, cored, seeded, and finely chopped (1 cup)

2 green onions (scallions), minced, including most of the green part

One 8-ounce can crushed pineapple, drained

2 tablespoons cider vinegar

1 to 2 tablespoons sugar

¼ teaspoon salt

⅛ teaspoon freshly ground black pepper

Combine the peppers, green onions, and pineapple in a medium-size bowl. Mix together the vinegar, sugar, salt, and pepper in a small bowl, then pour over the pepper mixture and stir until well blended. Turn into a bowl or container with a tight-fitting lid, cover, and refrigerate for several hours before serving.

YIELD: ABOUT 2¼ CUPS; ABOUT 6 SERVINGS

COOKED RED AND GREEN PEPPER RELISH

3 small green bell peppers, cored, seeded,
  and finely chopped (3 cups)
3 small red bell peppers, cored, seeded
  and finely chopped (3 cups)

1 large onion, finely chopped (1 cup)
1 cup white vinegar
¾ cup sugar
1½ teaspoons salt

Place the peppers and onion in a 3- or 4-quart nonreactive saucepan or Dutch oven. Pour enough boiling water over the vegetables to cover them and let stand for 5 minutes. Drain in a colander and return to the pan. Cover with boiling water again and let stand for 10 minutes before draining. Return the pepper mixture to the saucepan and stir in the vinegar, sugar, and salt. Bring the mixture to a boil, stirring constantly. Reduce the heat to medium-low and boil gently for 15 minutes. Remove from the heat and let cool. Turn into a bowl or container with a tight-fitting lid, cover, and refrigerate until serving time.

YIELD: ABOUT 4 CUPS; 8 SERVINGS

FRESH PEAR AND TOASTED WALNUT RELISH

Make this relish ahead of time, if it's more convenient, but don't add the pears until shortly before serving or they will turn dark and unappetizing looking.

⅓ cup firmly packed light brown sugar
⅓ cup fresh lemon juice
1 teaspoon mustard seeds
½ teaspoon curry powder
¼ teaspoon salt
¼ teaspoon crushed red pepper

⅓ cup finely chopped onion
⅓ cup finely chopped red bell pepper
½ cup toasted (see pages 6–7) chopped
  walnuts
3 ripe Bartlett pears, seeded and coarsely
  chopped (3 cups)

Combine the brown sugar, lemon juice, mustard seeds, curry powder, salt, and crushed red pepper in a medium-size saucepan. Bring to a boil over medium-high heat. Stir in the onion, bell pepper, and walnuts, then remove from the heat and let cool slightly. Stir in the pears shortly before serving.

YIELD: 3 CUPS; 8 TO 10 SERVINGS

GINGERY APPLE RELISH

I generally serve another big meal over Thanksgiving weekend that's designed to get rid of the bulk of the leftovers and the nice big pieces of meat off the turkey while they're still moist and tasty. I serve the turkey slices cold, and if there's not enough cranberry sauce left over I make this relish and serve it warm. The crystallized ginger and red pepper add a bit of heat to this relish, which, by the way, goes just as well with cold roast beef as cold turkey.

3 Golden Delicious apples, peeled, cored, and cut into small cubes (3 cups)
1 lemon, peeled, chopped, and seeded
One 2.7-ounce jar crystallized ginger, finely chopped
1 cup golden raisins

1 cup cider vinegar
1 cup firmly packed light brown sugar
½ teaspoon salt
Pinch of ground cayenne (red) pepper
One 4-ounce jar pimiento, drained and finely chopped

Combine the apples, lemon, ginger, raisins, vinegar, brown sugar, salt, and cayenne pepper in a large nonreactive saucepan. Cook over medium-high heat, stirring often, until the mixture comes to a boil. Reduce the heat to medium-low and simmer for 8 minutes, or until the apples are tender but still hold their shape. Stir in the pimientos. Remove from the heat and serve warm. If stored in a container with a tight-fitting lid, it will keep in the refrigerator for a week or two.

YIELD: 3½ CUPS; 8 TO 12 SERVINGS

CALIFORNIA RAISIN RELISH

A good accent for ham, duck, goose, or smoked poultry that is not being served with a sweet sauce or glaze. This is a very rich relish—a little goes a long way.

1¼ cups golden raisins
1 cup water
½ teaspoon whole allspice
½ teaspoon whole cloves

¾ cup sugar
⅓ cup cider vinegar
One 3-inch cinnamon stick, broken in half

Combine the raisins and water in a medium-size nonreactive saucepan and bring to a boil. Reduce the heat to medium-low, cover, and simmer for 5 minutes. Tie up the allspice and cloves in a square of cheesecloth. Add the spice bag, sugar, vinegar, and cinnamon stick to the raisins. Simmer, uncovered, for 20 minutes, or until the raisins are very tender and the mixture has thickened. Remove from the heat and let cool. Remove the spice bag and cinnamon stick and turn the relish into a bowl or container with a tight-fitting lid. Cover and refrigerate until serving time. This relish keeps well for several weeks.

YIELD: 1½ CUPS; 6 SERVINGS

CURRIED PEACHES

If you'd care to use them that way, this and the two relishes that follow also make eye-catching platter garnishes to encircle a duck or a ham, especially if the fruits are interspersed with shiny, dark green lemon leaves.

Two 16-ounce cans halved or sliced cling
  peaches (do not use freestone peaches)
  in heavy syrup
1 teaspoon grated lemon rind

1 teaspoon curry powder
2 tablespoons firmly packed light brown
  sugar
3 tablespoons white vinegar

Combine all of the ingredients in a medium-size nonreactive saucepan. Bring to a boil over medium-high heat. Remove from the heat and cool to room temperature. Turn into a bowl or container wtih a tight-fitting lid, cover, and chill until serving time. The peaches keep well for a couple of weeks.

YIELD: 6 TO 8 SERVINGS

Brandied Peaches: You can use this recipe to make a quick version of brandied peaches by omitting the curry powder and substituting ¼ to ½ cup brandy. Add the brandy before boiling if you want the alcohol to evaporate, or after the peaches have cooled if you don't.

SPICED APRICOTS

Two 15-ounce cans apricot halves in
  heavy syrup, drained and 1 cup of syrup
  reserved
⅓ cup firmly packed dark brown sugar
2 teaspoons pumpkin pie spice

2 tablespoons butter
2 tablespoons toasted (see pages 6–7)
  slivered almonds
½ teaspoon almond extract (optional)

Combine the drained apricots, reserved syrup, brown sugar, pumpkin pie spice, and butter in a medium-size saucepan. Bring to a slow boil over medium-high heat. Simmer over medium-low heat, uncovered, for about 10 minutes, or until the liquid is reduced by half. Remove from the heat and cool slightly. Stir in the almonds and almond extract and turn into a bowl. Cover and chill until ready to serve. Reheat and serve slightly warm.

YIELD: 6 TO 8 SERVINGS

KUMQUATS IN SYRUP

¾ cup water
¾ cup sugar

2 cups kumquats

Combine the water and sugar in a 2-quart nonreactive saucepan. Bring to a boil, stirring constantly, until the sugar has dissolved. Reduce the heat to medium-low and simmer for 5 minutes. Remove the pan from the heat and cool the syrup to room temperature. Rinse the kumquats, then cut a small X in the blossom end (as opposed to the stem end) of each one. Place the kumquats in the cooled syrup. Cover and bring to a boil over high heat. Reduce the heat to low and barely simmer, covered, for 15 minutes. Remove from the heat *(do not remove the cover at the end of the cooking time or the kumquats will shrink)* and cool to room temperature. Spoon the kumquats and syrup into a container with a tight-fitting lid, cover, and chill until serving time. The kumquats will keep well for a week or two.

YIELD: 2 CUPS; ABOUT 8 SERVINGS

PEACH-JAM CHUTNEY

The cook who's in a rush should consider this chutney. It's fast—15 minutes from start to finish—and it's good with just about anything, including curry.

1 cup peach jam
½ cup golden raisins
¼ cup toasted (see pages 6–7) coarsely
*   chopped pecans*

¼ cup cider vinegar
1 tablespoon chopped crystallized ginger
1 teaspoon minced onion
Pinch of salt

Combine all of the ingredients in a small, heavy nonreactive saucepan. Bring to a simmer over medium heat. Reduce the heat to low and cook, stirring frequently, for 5 minutes. Remove from the heat and let cool slightly. Turn into a bowl or container with a tight-fitting lid, cover, and refrigerate until serving time. Serve chilled, at room temperature, or slightly warm.

YIELD: 2 CUPS; 6 TO 8 SERVINGS

ALMOND AND APRICOT COMPOTE
❦

Other dried fruits, such as peaches or pears, can be substituted for the apricots in this recipe.

2 cups firmly packed dried apricots,
   quartered
4 cups apple cider
4 tablespoons (½ stick) butter, cut into
   small pieces

¼ cup sugar
½ cup toasted (see pages 6–7) slivered
   almonds

Combine the apricots and cider in a 4-quart nonreactive saucepan and let stand at room temperature for at least 8 hours or overnight to soften. Bring the mixture to a boil, then reduce the heat to medium-low and simmer for 10 minutes, or until the apricots are tender. Remove from the heat and add the butter and sugar, stirring until the butter has melted and the sugar has dissolved. Stir in the almonds. Let cool slightly and turn into a container with a tight-fitting lid. Cover and refrigerate until serving time. Serve at room temperature or slightly warm.

YIELD: ABOUT 4 CUPS; 6 TO 8 SERVINGS

GINGERED ONION CHUTNEY
❦

This is the condiment that I always serve with a standing rib roast. It reminds me of a chutney that I was once served at Simpson In The Strand—a grand old London restaurant—so you know it's got to be good.

3 large onions (about 1 pound), cut in half
   vertically and thinly sliced
2 lemons
⅓ cup dried currants

¾ cup sugar
½ cup white vinegar
2 tablespoons finely chopped fresh ginger
Pinch of ground nutmeg

Place the onions in a medium-size, heavy nonreactive saucepan. Cook over low heat, covered, until they are limp but not brown, stirring occasionally. While the onions are cooking, cut the lemons vertically into quarters. Cut each quarter into thin, vertical slices, removing the seeds with the tip of the knife. Stir the lemon slices, currants, sugar, vinegar, ginger, and nutmeg into the softened onions. Cook over low heat, uncovered, until the mixture thickens and has given up most of its liquid, stirring occasionally, and then more often as the mixture begins to thicken. Remove from the heat and let cool to room temperature. Scrape the cooled chutney into a bowl or container with a tight-fitting lid and refrigerate until shortly before serving time. Serve at room temperature or slightly warm. The chutney keeps well for two or three weeks.

YIELD: 2 CUPS; 6 SERVINGS

ENGLISH APPLE CHUTNEY

This is another relish that works well with beef or pork roasts, as well as turkey and other poultry. And if I happen to have some in the refrigerator, I serve it with curries.

1 pound Granny Smith or McIntosh
   apples, peeled, cored, and diced (about
   3 cups)
1 large onion, chopped (1 cup)
1¼ cups cider vinegar
1⅓ cups dark raisins

1 cup firmly packed dark brown sugar
1 tablespoon Worcestershire sauce
1 teaspoon grated lemon rind
3 teaspoons fresh lemon juice
½ teaspoon salt

Combine the apples, onion, and vinegar in a medium-size, heavy nonreactive saucepan. Bring to a boil, then reduce the heat to medium-low and simmer, uncovered, until the apples soften and cook down slightly, about 15 minutes. Stir in the remaining ingredients. Return to boiling, then reduce the heat to medium-low and simmer, uncovered, stirring frequently until the mixture has thickened, about 45 minutes. Cool slightly, then turn into a bowl or container with a tight-fitting lid. Cover and refrigerate until serving time. Before serving, bring to room temperature.

YIELD: ABOUT 2½ CUPS; 6 TO 8 SERVINGS

BAKED ONION FANS

When they're fanned out on a white platter, cut side up, onion fans resemble dark red chrysanthemums, so I often use them as an edible garnish, as well as a relish, with both poultry and meat.

6 medium-size red onions   *Freshly ground black pepper to taste*
1 cup balsamic vinegar

Preheat the oven to 350°F. Brush off any loose pieces of skin, but otherwise leave the onions unpeeled. Cut the onions in half from the root end through the stem. Place the halves, cut side down, in a glass baking dish just large enough to hold them comfortably. Pour the vinegar over the onions and cover the dish tightly with aluminum foil. Bake for 35 to 40 minutes, or until the onions are fork tender. When they are cool enough to handle, remove the skins but be sure to leave the roots intact. Cut each onion half in half again to make quarters. Place the onion quarters in a shallow dish, cover, and refrigerate until serving time. Before serving, fan the layers of each onion quarter slightly. Serve at room temperature or slightly warm, sprinkled with pepper.

YIELD: 24 PIECES; 6 TO 12 SERVINGS

FREEZER PICKLES

Call me picky, if you want to, but I've finally given up eating seedy, watery, wax-coated cucumbers. I much prefer the smaller Kirby cucumbers, which seem to be available most of the year. Kirby cucumbers have crisp flesh and, to me, taste most like cucumbers that have been freshly pulled from the vine. It's easy to recognize Kirby cucumbers because they look like big dill pickles, about four inches long with somewhat knobby, pale-to-dark-green skin. If Kirbys are absolutely not to be found, regular cucumbers can be substituted, but the wax will have to be scrubbed off the skins with a vegetable brush and very warm water. If you add mustard and celery seeds to this recipe, these will remind you of old-fashioned bread-and-butter pickles.

1 pound (4 or 5) Kirby cucumbers, rinsed   1 tablespoon uniodized *salt*
    and cut into ¼-inch slices (about   2½ cups sugar
    3½ cups)   1 cup cider vinegar
2 or 3 small onions, thinly sliced and   1 teaspoon mustard seed (optional)
    separated into rings (about 1 cup)   1 teaspoon celery seed (optional)

Place the cucumber and onion slices in a large bowl, sprinkle with the salt, and let stand for 2 hours, stirring occasionally. Turn into a colander and drain thoroughly. Return to the bowl. Mix the sugar and vinegar together in a small nonreactive saucepan and heat, stirring until the mixture simmers. Remove from the heat and cool slightly. Stir in the mustard and celery seeds and pour over the cucumber and onion slices. Pack into 1- or 2-cup containers with tight-fitting lids, leaving about ½ inch of headspace. Tightly cover the containers and freeze for up to six months. Once frozen, the pickles are ready to be thawed in the refrigerator and served. Thawed pickles may be stored in the refrigerator for a couple of weeks.

YIELD: 3½ CUPS; 8 TO 12 SERVINGS

CUCUMBERS IN CREAM

I suppose it's my Pennsylvania Dutch background, but I like the sugar added to this creamy cucumber mixture, particularly when it's served as a relish at Thanksgiving dinner. You may prefer to serve it without the sugar, especially if there are many other sweet offerings on the table. By the way, the cream dressing, made without the sugar, is also an excellent salad dressing for a tender-leaf green salad or, with the sugar mixed in, for shredded cabbage. See the preceding recipe for my feelings about Kirby cucumbers.

1 pound (4 or 5) Kirby cucumbers, rinsed
   and cut into ⅛-inch slices (about
   3½ cups)
1 teaspoon salt
½ cup heavy or whipping cream (not
   ultra-pasteurized)

2 tablespoons red wine vinegar
2 teaspoons sugar (optional)
¼ teaspoon freshly ground black pepper
3 or 4 green onions (scallions), thinly
   sliced, including some of the green tops

Place the cucumber slices in a colander and sprinkle with the salt. Set aside for 30 minutes to 1 hour, stirring occasionally. Mix the cream, vinegar, sugar, and pepper in a 1-cup measure. Turn the cucumber and onion slices into a medium-size bowl, add the cream dressing, and mix. Cover and refrigerate until serving time.

YIELD: 3½ CUPS; 6 TO 8 SERVINGS

Note: To reduce the fat, you can substitute light cream, half-and-half, or even milk for the cream, but the dressing will not thicken as much.

SPICED PRUNES

If you have a prejudice against serving prunes for dinner, then serve these for breakfast. But do serve them. They're wonderful.

3 orange-and-spice-flavored tea bags
3 cups boiling water
One 12-ounce box pitted prunes

One 3-inch cinnamon stick, broken
    in half
1 tablespoon sugar

Steep the tea bags in the boiling water, tightly covered, until cool. Remove the tea bags and discard. Combine the prunes and tea in a medium-size nonreactive saucepan, cover, and set aside for at least 8 hours or overnight. Add the cinnamon stick and bring the mixture to a boil. Reduce the heat to medium-low and simmer, uncovered, for 25 minutes, stirring occasionally. Stir in the sugar and continue to simmer for 5 minutes. Remove from the heat and cool. Turn into a bowl, cover tightly, and refrigerate for no more than a few days, until ready to serve, chilled or at room temperature.

YIELD: ABOUT 3 CUPS; ABOUT 8 SERVINGS

PICKLED MUSHROOMS

You might consider serving this as an appetizer with plain or toasted slices of French bread or as a salad in Bibb lettuce cups, as well as a dinner relish. One of the nicest things about this recipe is the way the sliced mushrooms look. However, the mushrooms tend to darken and shrink as the mixture ages, so don't make this more than a day before it is to be served.

1½ pounds medium-size regular white
    mushrooms
1 cup water
1 teaspoon salt
2 or 3 celery ribs, finely chopped (1 cup)
1 small red onion, chopped (¼ cup)
One 3-ounce can pitted black olives,
    drained and sliced

One 5-ounce jar pimiento-stuffed green
    olives, drained and sliced
1 tablespoon chopped fresh parsley
1 large clove garlic, put through a
    garlic press
¾ teaspoon freshly ground black pepper
¼ cup olive or vegetable oil
2 tablespoons white vinegar

Wipe the mushrooms with damp paper towels, or rinse them briefly in cool water and pat dry with paper towels. Trim the stems, then slice, from the rounded cap through the stem, into thick slices. You should have 7 or 8 cups. Bring the water with the salt to a boil in a large saucepan. Drop in the mushrooms. Reduce the heat to medium-low, cover, and simmer for 5 minutes. Drain, then pat the mushroom slices dry with paper towels. Combine the remaining ingredients in a large bowl and stir in the mushrooms. Cover and chill until serving time.

YIELD: 7 CUPS; 10 TO 12 SERVINGS

Note: If the mushrooms are not served soon after preparation, they will shrink considerably, reducing the yield to about 5 cups.

SWEET-AND-SOUR VEGETABLES

Other vegetables can be added or subtracted from this relish, as you choose. I steer away from green things, such as beans and broccoli, because they tend to lose their bright color rather quickly.

2 cups cauliflower flowerets, cut into
   small pieces
2 or 3 small red bell peppers, cored,
   seeded, and cut into strips
¼ pound yellow wax beans, trimmed and
   cut into 1-inch pieces
2 cups frozen small white onions, thawed

2 or 3 celery ribs, sliced (1 cup)
1 cup sugar
1 teaspoon salt
2 cups white vinegar
1 teaspoon celery seeds
1 teaspoon mustard seeds

Bring a large saucepan of lightly salted water to a boil. Add the flowerets, pepper strips, beans, onions, and celery. When the water returns to the boil, boil for about 4 minutes, or until the vegetables are tender-crisp. Drain the vegetables into a colander and rinse under cold running water. This stops the cooking and helps the vegetables retain their bright color. Drain well, then turn into a large bowl. Combine the remaining ingredients in a small nonreactive saucepan. Heat to boiling, stirring until the sugar has dissolved. Simmer for 15 minutes over low heat, or until the syrup is slightly thickened. Pour the syrup over the vegetables, cover, and refrigerate for at least 24 hours before serving.

YIELD: ABOUT 4½ CUPS; 8 TO 10 SERVINGS

MUSTARDY BEANS AND ONIONS

Some of the best food I've eaten in my life was served at Pine Tree Camp in the Pocono Mountains in Pennsylvania. This relish, or one very much like it, often accompanied dinner. No wonder we were all happy campers.

1 pound fresh wax beans or green beans,
or a 1-pound can, drained
1 cup sugar
½ cup cider vinegar
3 tablespoons prepared yellow mustard

¼ teaspoon salt
⅛ teaspoon freshly ground black pepper
1 jar (about 4 ounces) tiny cocktail
onions, drained

Cover the beans with lightly salted water in a medium-size saucepan, and bring to a boil over high heat. Then simmer over medium-low heat, covered, until tender-crisp, about 6 minutes. Drain the beans into a colander and set aside. In a medium-size saucepan, combine the sugar, vinegar, mustard, salt, and pepper and bring to a boil. Reduce the heat to medium-low and simmer, stirring, until the sugar dissolves. Add the beans and onions and simmer, uncovered, for 5 minutes. Remove from the heat and let cool. Turn into a bowl or container with a tight-fitting lid, cover tightly, and refrigerate until ready to serve, chilled or at room temperature.

YIELD: 2 TO 2½ CUPS; 6 SERVINGS

THE RELISH TRAY

At the very heart of Thanksgiving dinner is the relish tray, which has expanded over the years to become a relish *platter* for most families. On it you will generally find celery hearts, carrot sticks, fancy-cut radishes, green onions, and black and stuffed green olives. (Incidentally, giving the radishes and olives a light coating of oil will keep them bright and shiny for the duration of dinner.) And if you're lucky, you'll find stuffed celery.

The relish tray I've just described is straight out of the forties and fifties, and most people I know wouldn't have it any other way. However, if you're ready for a change, you might consider such up-to-date additions as sliced fennel bulbs, little yellow tomatoes, red and yellow pepper strips, jicama sticks, or any sort of offbeat raw vegetables that strike your fancy.

You might also want to expand the relish tray to include a separate plate of sliced fruits and melons, especially if there will not be many sweet condiments on the table.

STUFFED CELERY

Near and dear to most Thanksgiving celebrants is the presence of stuffed celery on the relish tray. Traditionally, most of these stuffings are of a pinkish hue and consist mainly of softened cream cheese mixed with one or two other ingredients. Other times the ribs are simply filled with the cheese spreads that come in little jars with flip-off lids, my own personal favorite, I confess, being olive-pimiento spread.

For old times' sake, I've included a few of the cream cheese–style stuffings, but I've also acknowledged our entrance into the nineties with a few updated stuffings.

If you're really determined to go to no end of trouble, some of these stuffings can be piped into pitted ripe or green olives, but you may need to thin them out a little with milk first.

The stuffings can also be used as appetizers, spread on crackers or toasted baguette slices. A tablespoon of the stuffing mixture will fill a 3- or 4-inch celery rib. The stuffing may be spooned into the ribs, or piped into them with a pastry tube fitted with a fancy tip.

3-ounce package cream cheese is ⅓ cup.

Pineapple-Horseradish. Mix one 3-ounce package softened cream cheese with ¼ cup drained, canned crushed pineapple and 1 teaspoon drained prepared horseradish. Makes about ⅔ cup

Ham-and-Cheese. Mix one 3-ounce package softened cream cheese with one 2¼-ounce can deviled ham, 2 tablespoons crumbled blue-vein cheese, and 1 tablespoon minced red bell pepper. Makes about ¾ cup.

Bombay. Mix one 3-ounce package softened cream cheese with ½ teaspoon curry powder and 3 tablespoons finely chopped chutney of your choice. Makes about ½ cup.

Cheddar-Olive. Mix 1 cup finely shredded cheddar cheese, ⅓ cup finely chopped ripe olives, ¼ cup thinly sliced green onions (scallions), 2 tablespoons mayonnaise, 1 tablespoon minced red bell pepper, and 1 teaspoon drained prepared horseradish. Makes about 1½ cups.

Pesto. Mix ¾ cup whole-milk or part-skim ricotta cheese with ½ cup prepared or homemade pesto sauce. Makes about 1¼ cups.

Tapenade. Puree ¾ cup pitted ripe olives, 2 teaspoons drained capers, ½ teaspoon an-chovy paste, and 1 teaspoon olive oil in a blender or food processor. Mix with ¼ pound softened fresh white goat cheese. Makes about ¾ cup.

Roquefort-and-Walnuts. Mix one 3-ounce package softened cream cheese with ⅓ cup crumbled Roquefort cheese and 2 tablespoons toasted (see pages 6–7) finely chopped walnuts. Makes about ⅔ cup.

Goat Cheese with Sun-Dried Tomatoes. Mix 6 ounces softened fresh goat cheese with 1 tablespoon finely chopped oil-packed dried tomatoes (see page 5), 1 teaspoon of the tomato oil, 1 medium-size clove garlic that has been put through a garlic press, ¼ teaspoon dried oregano, and ¼ teaspoon salt (the amount of salt will depend upon the saltiness of the goat cheese). Makes about ⅔ cup.

SEVEN

Vegetables and Side Dishes

❦

Thanksgiving dinner is not known for being a particularly well-balanced meal, at least not from a nutritional viewpoint. Bright, crisp-cooked vegetables, for example, are usually noticeable only by their absence, and salad greens, so highly regarded at other meals, are more often than not relegated to the gelatin-mold platter.

My research into Thanksgiving food confirms that whatever vegetables are served at this bountiful meal usually come to the table sauced, glazed, creamed, or otherwise adorned within an inch of their lives, and very often reflect a national fondness for sweet things. Surely the sales of brown sugar must skyrocket during the last two weeks in November.

In defense of our lopsided Thanksgiving menus, remember that this is a feast with roots deeply planted in tradition and repetition. Our forefathers established the basic menu that is more or less followed to this day, at a time when the only foods that were available were those that could be stored in a root cellar or dried. Later, canned produce and fruit came to the table, followed in more recent years by frozen food. Fresh vegetables and greens, at least in the less temperate parts of the United States, are virtual infants on the Thanksgiving food scene.

There's a lot to be considered when pulling together a meal of such proportions, especially for the cook with little or no experience in feeding a crowd. With so much going on in the kitchen during the last half hour before dinner, is it any wonder that recipes needing a lot of stove-top or other last-minute attention are put away for another day, at least if the cook is to arrive at the table in anything less than a state of near-collapse? Dishes that can be made ahead entirely and reheated, or need only minimal effort before they are served, are the ones most likely to be served.

Add to that the fact that most home kitchens have only one conventional oven, and guess what's in it. This means that if it's not small enough to fit in the oven with the turkey, then it must be baked or reheated during the short time the turkey is resting before it's carved.

Of course, those cooks who own a microwave oven, and are adept at using it, are not quite so constrained, since this miraculous appliance reheats almost anything, often right in the bowl or sauceboat in which it will be served. The microwave can even be used for cooking some recipes from scratch during the final countdown, as long as there's not too much covering, uncovering, turning, and stirring required.

In presenting the vegetable accompaniments for Thanksgiving dinner, I've kept all of these things in mind, for almost nothing annoys me more than contemplating a menu that would require two conventional ovens, an upright freezer, and possibly a kitchen assistant in order to get it to the table.

One last thought: Most of the recipes in this chapter will provide at least eight servings, but they are all easily divisible and multipliable, so that the quantities can easily be adjusted for the number of servings needed. Just remember that the number of servings means just that: the number of (reasonably generous) servings, not the number of people a recipe will serve. If there are big eaters at your table, that must be taken into consideration, although with so many offerings to choose from, things tend to go further at Thanksgiving dinner than they do at normal meals. The tendency is always to overcook, not undercook, so you can almost certainly count on having plenty of leftovers.

VEGETABLES, PLAIN AND SIMPLE

If you think you can handle it, you might want to consider at least one plain or lightly sauced fresh vegetable at your Thanksgiving table in deference to modern times. Besides adding a patch of unadorned texture and color among the browns, oranges, and often wishy-washy food colors of this feast, crisp-cooked vegetables are a welcome change of pace for the eye, the palate, and the teeth.

Cooking vegetables to the *al dente* (tender-crisp) stage is quick and easy, and at least to me, nothing looks prettier or more appetizing on the table than a bowl of plain vegetables with a big pat of butter melting on top.

If you want to go one or two steps further, you could also add a pinch of fresh herbs, a squirt or two of citrus juice, a few drops of flavored vinegar or oil, or even an understated sauce that enhances, not overwhelms.

In chapter 10, you will find additional suggestions for saucing vegetables, if you want to gild the lily a little more. These vegetables, abundant in November, are good candidates for the quick-cook treatment:

- *beets*
- *broccoli, green and purple*
- *Brussels sprouts*
- *carrots, sliced, or whole baby carrots*
- *cauliflower, white and purple*
- *celery, sliced*
- *fennel*
- *green or wax beans, whole or cut*
- *leeks, whole or cut*

- *mushrooms*
- *okra, whole or cut*
- *parsnips*
- *rutabagas*
- *snow peas*
- *turnips*
- *winter squash, peeled and cubed*
- *zucchini, sliced or cubed*

The herbs (fresh, if you can find them), juices, vinegars, and oils that I choose most often for seasoning plain vegetables are:

- *chervil*
- *chives*
- *cilantro*
- *dill*
- *marjoram*
- *fresh mint*
- *fresh parsley*
- *freshly ground black pepper*

- *thyme*
- *lemon, lime, and orange juices*
- *raspberry and other fruit vinegars (see pages 8–9)*
- *balsamic vinegar*
- *wine and liqueur*
- *nut oils (see page 7)*

To serve vegetables that still have some "tooth" left in them, cook whole or cut-up vegetables in lightly salted, briskly simmering water over medium heat just until they are tender-crisp. Drain in a colander, turn into a warm bowl, and serve promptly. If you plan to reheat the vegetables, briefly run cold water over them while they're still in the colander, which stops further cooking and helps retain their color. Microwave mavens will, of course, use their ovens, which turn out perfect, crisp-cooked vegetables every time. Frozen and even canned vegetables benefit enormously when prepared this way. Simple stir-frying is another technique that leaves vegetables with their integrity intact.

❦

STEAMED ASPARAGUS AND GREEN ONIONS

❦

Now that fresh asparagus is available year-round, it is often my "green vegetable" of choice at Thanksgiving, when it is always eagerly received, an unexpected little extravagance. Steamed green onions, tender and delicately flavored, are another surprise.

3 pounds slender asparagus spears
About 20 green onions (scallions)
Softened butter to taste

Freshly ground black pepper to taste
Fresh lemon juice (optional)

For a showy presentation, cut all the asparagus spears to the same length. With a vegetable parer, peel an inch or so at the bottom part of each spear. Also trim off all of the spines and rinse well. Trim the green onions and cut to the same length as the asparagus. With kitchen string, tie the asparagus at both ends into bundles of about 6 spears. Do the same with the green onions. Select a pan for cooking that is long enough to accommodate the asparagus and onions without bending them. Lay the asparagus in the bottom of the pan. Cover by about an inch with lightly salted water and bring to a boil. Lower the heat to medium-low, cover, and simmer for about 5 minutes. Lay the green onions on top of the asparagus. Continue to simmer, covered, for another 5 minutes, or until both vegetables are tender but still retain some of their bite. The exact cooking time will depend on the thickness of both the asparagus and the onions. Lift the bundles from the water, suspending them over the pan for a few seconds to allow the cooking water to drain and evaporate before arranging them on a serving platter. Cut away the string and spread with butter. Finish with a few turns of a pepper mill. A squirt or two of fresh lemon juice may also be added.

YIELD: 8 SERVINGS

GREEN BEANS WITH RASPBERRY VINEGAR

❦

Adding the vinegar sauce takes only a few moments and gives the beans a festive flavor without overwhelming them.

2 pounds green beans, trimmed and left
   whole
3 tablespoons butter

3 small onions, thinly sliced and sepa-
   rated into rings (about 1 cup)
¼ cup raspberry vinegar
Freshly ground black pepper to taste

Drop the beans into a large pan of lightly salted boiling water and simmer over medium-low heat for about 6 minutes, or until tender-crisp. Drain into a colander, then run cold water over the beans to stop further cooking and to help retain the color. Set the beans aside. Shortly before serving, melt the butter in the same saucepan in which the beans were cooked. Add the onion rings, cover tightly, and cook over very low heat for about 5 minutes, or until the rings are tender and transparent. Stir in the vinegar and a liberal amount of pepper. Add the green beans and cook over medium heat, stirring, until they are hot and well coated with the sauce.

YIELD: 8 SERVINGS

GREEN BEANS WITH MUSHROOMS

One of my most requested recipes. I prefer to use shiitake mushrooms, even if I have to occasionally resort to the dried ones.

2 pounds green beans, trimmed
½ pound shiitake or regular white
  mushrooms
4 tablespoons (½ stick) butter
¼ cup walnut or vegetable oil

½ teaspoon salt
Freshly ground black pepper to taste
½ cup toasted (see pages 6–7) chopped
  walnuts for garnish

Drop the beans into a large pan of lightly salted boiling water and simmer over medium-low heat for about 4 minutes, or until barely tender. Drain into a colander, then run cold water over the beans to stop the cooking and to help retain the color. Set aside. Remove the stems from the shiitake mushrooms and discard. (If using regular white mushrooms, trim the stems, but leave them attached to the caps.) Rinse the caps and pat dry on paper towels. Cut the caps (or the whole regular white mushrooms) into ¼-inch slices and set aside. (May be done ahead up to this point.) Combine the butter and oil in a large skillet or wok over medium-high heat. When it is hot, add the beans and mushrooms and cook, stirring and tossing, until the mushrooms are limp and the beans are hot and tender-crisp. Add the salt and a liberal amount of pepper. Turn into a warm serving bowl and sprinkle with the walnuts.

YIELD: 8 SERVINGS

JELLY BEANS

An old Southern favorite that takes just minutes to make. Once upon a time big lima beans were my most hated vegetable—until my mother cooked them this way.

Two 10-ounce packages frozen Fordhook
  lima beans
¼ pound (1 stick) butter

½ cup sugar
½ cup water

Cook the lima beans in a medium-size saucepan, according to package directions, but only until fork tender, 5 to 7 minutes, and drain well. While the beans are cooking, melt the butter in a medium-size saucepan. Stir in the sugar and water. Bring to a boil, lower the heat to medium-low, and simmer until the mixture is thick and creamy looking when removed from the heat, about 10 minutes. Add the beans to the syrup, coat them well, and cook over medium heat, stirring frequently, until most of the syrup has disappeared from the bottom of the pan and the limas are richly glazed, about 10 minutes. (May be made ahead and reheated.)

YIELD: 6 TO 8 SERVINGS

JACK PRESCOTT'S INDIAN SUCCOTASH

In the late summer, when fresh corn and limas were at their peak, my stepfather, Jack Prescott, could frequently be found in the kitchen making succotash according to an old New England recipe handed down by his Grandma Osgood. Although fresh corn and limas are long gone by November, succotash has always been a standard Thanksgiving side dish for many New Englanders. Before frozen food, dried corn, and limas were used when fresh were out of season.

Two 10-ounce packages frozen baby
  lima beans
Two 10-ounce packages frozen cut corn
4 tablespoons (½ stick) butter, softened

1 cup light cream or half-and-half
1 teaspoon salt
Freshly ground black pepper to taste

Cook the lima beans and corn separately as the packages direct and drain in a colander. In a large saucepan, combine them. (May be made ahead up to this point; reheat before proceeding.) Stir in the butter and cream and cook over medium-low heat, stirring frequently, until steaming. Season with the salt and plenty of pepper.

YIELD: 8 TO 10 SERVINGS

BEETS WITH LEMON SAUCE

Usually nothing surpasses fresh vegetables, but beets are one of the few that can be canned without much loss of the roots' integrity. You can use fresh beets, if you like, but in that case try to find very small ones, or cut larger ones into quarters. (If cooking fresh beets, do not peel the beets or cut off the stems until after they are cooked. Drain, then slip off the skins and cut off the stems when the beets are cool enough to handle.)

4 tablespoons (½ stick) butter
½ cup firmly packed light brown sugar
¼ cup fresh lemon juice
Three 16-ounce cans whole small beets,
* well drained*

⅛ teaspoon salt
Big pinch of freshly ground black pepper
½ teaspoon grated lemon rind

Heat the butter in a Dutch oven or other large heavy saucepan. Stir in the brown sugar and lemon juice and cook over medium heat, stirring frequently, until the sugar is dissolved. Stir in the beets until they are well coated. Cook over medium heat, stirring frequently, until the beets are glazed, about 20 minutes. Stir in the salt and pepper. (May be prepared ahead up to this point and reheated.) Sprinkle the beets with grated lemon rind and serve.

YIELD: 8 SERVINGS

BROCCOLI WITH WINE

A simple pan sauce that's good with other crisp vegetables, too, especially green beans.

2 large bunches broccoli or 3 smaller
* bunches*
4 tablespoons (½ stick) butter, melted

¼ cup dry white wine or dry vermouth
Freshly ground black pepper to taste

Rinse the broccoli and cut off the main stems. Break the bunches into even-size flowerets, leaving short stems. (May be done ahead up to this point, but keep the broccoli covered with cold water until ready to cook.) Cook the broccoli in a large saucepan of lightly salted, simmering water over medium-low heat until tender-crisp, about 5 minutes. Drain in a colander and rinse briefly in cool water to stop further cooking and help retain the color. Add the butter and wine to the pan in which the broccoli was cooked. Stir over medium heat until the butter is melted and about half of the wine has evaporated. Return the broccoli to the pan and stir gently over low heat until it is well coated and heated through. Turn into a warm serving bowl and finish with a few turns of a pepper mill.

YIELD: 8 SERVINGS

CAROL GELLES'S BROCCOLI WITH BACON AND CHESTNUTS

A good recipe from one of the best cooks I know. Carol says if you don't feel like fiddling with the chestnuts, big pecan pieces would be a good substitute.

8 slices bacon, cut into ½-inch pieces
2 tablespoons butter
2 large bunches broccoli or 3 smaller bunches

¼ pound chestnuts, roasted or steamed and peeled (see pages 6–7), and cut into small pieces
Freshly ground black pepper to taste

Cook the bacon in a medium-size skillet over medium-high heat until it is crisp. Remove the bacon and let drain on paper towels. Discard all but 2 tablespoons of the fat in the skillet. Add the butter to the skillet and set aside.

Rinse the broccoli and cut off the main stems. Break the bunches into even-size flowerets, leaving short stems. (May be done ahead up to this point, but keep the broccoli covered with cold water until ready to cook.) Cook the broccoli in a large saucepan of lightly salted, simmering water over medium-low heat until tender-crisp, about 5 minutes. While the broccoli is cooking, heat the butter and bacon fat in the skillet over medium-high heat. When it is hot, stir in the chestnuts and cook until heated through, about 2 or 3 minutes. Drain the broccoli and rinse it briefly in cool water to stop further cooking and help retain the color. Return the broccoli to the pan in which it was cooked. Add the hot chestnut mixture and the reserved bacon bits. Stir gently over low heat until well combined. Turn into a warm serving bowl and finish with a few turns of a pepper mill.

YIELD: 8 SERVINGS

BRUSSELS SPROUTS AND TANGERINES

Tangerines tone down the intense flavor of the sprouts, as well as make the finished dish look pretty.

2 pounds small Brussels sprouts
1 tablespoon sesame seeds
4 tablespoons (½ stick) butter

2 small tangerines, peeled, separated into
*   sections, and those cut into thirds*
½ teaspoon grated tangerine rind

Rinse and drain the Brussels sprouts. Trim the stems close to the base of the sprouts and remove any wilted leaves. Rinse in a colander and drain. Place the sprouts in a large saucepan and cover with 2 or 3 inches of lightly salted cold water. Bring to a boil, then reduce the heat to medium-low and simmer, uncovered, for about 10 minutes, or until just tender. Drain the sprouts in a colander and run under cold water to stop further cooking and help retain the color. Return the sprouts to the pan in which they were cooked and set aside. Heat the sesame seeds in a small skillet over medium heat, stirring frequently, until they are golden brown, about 5 or 6 minutes. (May be made ahead up to this point, but reheat the sesame seeds briefly before proceeding.) Stir the butter into the sesame seeds until melted. Pour the hot butter mixture over the Brussels sprouts and stir gently over low heat until the sprouts are well coated and heated through. Stir in the tangerine sections and sprinkle with the rind just before serving.

YIELD: 8 SERVINGS

ANNE BAILEY'S WILTED SPROUTS

Annie says that, as far as she's concerned, Brussels sprouts are nothing but little cabbages, and nothing goes better with cabbage than bacon—except maybe corned beef.

1½ pounds Brussels sprouts
6 slices bacon, cut into ½-inch pieces
1 large onion, finely chopped (1 cup)
3 tablespoons butter

1½ cups water
½ teaspoon salt
⅛ teaspoon freshly ground black pepper

Rinse and drain the Brussels sprouts. Trim the stems close to the base of the sprouts and remove any wilted leaves. Rinse in a colander and drain. Cut each sprout in half if it is small, and in quarters if it is larger. Place about half of the sprouts in a food processor and process with quick on/off pulses until they resemble homemade cole slaw. Transfer the processed sprouts to a large bowl. Repeat the process with the remaining sprouts. Cook the bacon in a Dutch oven or other large heavy saucepan over medium heat, stirring frequently, until crisp and lightly browned. Spoon all but a light coating of the fat from the pan. Stir the onion and 1 tablespoon of the butter into the bacon and drippings. Cook over medium heat, stirring almost constantly, until the onion is softened. Add the sprouts and stir to coat well. Stir in the water, cover, and cook over low heat for 5 minutes. Uncover and cook over medium heat, stirring frequently, until the sprouts are tender-crisp, adding a few drops of water to keep the mixture moist, if necessary. Stir in the remaining 2 tablespoons of butter, the salt, and pepper. (May be made ahead and reheated.)

YIELD: 8 SERVINGS

FANCY GLAZED CARROTS

Carrots, which can usually be counted on for leftovers, disappear quickly when they are prepared this way. If you can locate tiny baby carrots, they can be substituted for the sliced carrots. You'll need about twenty-four to thirty-two of them, cooked just until tender, about 15 minutes.

3 tablespoons butter
½ cup orange juice
⅓ cup honey
2 tablespoons orange liqueur (optional)
2 teaspoons grated orange rind

Pinch of ground nutmeg
10 to 12 medium-size carrots, cut into diagonal ½-inch slices (about 6 cups)
Chopped fresh parsley for garnish

Melt the butter in a large skillet over medium-high heat. When hot, stir in the orange juice, honey, orange liqueur, orange rind, and nutmeg. Add the carrot slices, stirring to coat well with the orange juice mixture. Reduce the heat to low, cover, and simmer for 10 minutes. Uncover and continue to cook over low heat, stirring occasionally, until the carrots are tender, about 10 minutes, and the cooking liquid has thickened into a glaze. (May be prepared ahead up to this point and gently reheated before serving.) Serve sprinkled with the parsley.

YIELD: 8 SERVINGS

CARROTS AND PARSNIPS À LA FLORENT
❦

Some of the recipes I enjoy the most are my interpretations of food I've eaten at restaurants. This one is named for the campy New York bistro where this—or something very much like it—was served one evening as the vegetable du jour. One forkful and, as far as I was concerned, they could have skipped whatever else I ordered. The only problem is that you really do need a food processor with a fine shredding disk to do the vegetable strands properly. You can use the large holes of a four-sided grater, but it's an arduous task.

1 pound carrots, trimmed and scraped
1 pound parsnips, trimmed and scraped
4 tablespoons (½ stick) butter

¼ cup water
½ teaspoon salt
About 5 turns of a pepper mill

Shred the carrots and parsnips with the 2 mm shredding blade of a food processor. (May be prepared ahead up to this point.) Melt the butter in a large skillet over medium heat. When hot, add the shredded vegetables, stirring and tossing until they are well coated. Stir in the water, cover tightly, and cook for about 5 minutes, or until tender-crisp. Stir in the salt and pepper and serve.

YIELD: 6 TO 8 SERVINGS

SKILLET CORN FRY
❦

Corn is one of the few vegetables that take well to freezing, and this easy dish is always popular at Thanksgiving. However, I urge you to try it with spanking fresh corn next summer.

4 tablespoons (½ stick) butter
Four 10-ounce packages frozen cut corn,
 thawed and drained
1 cup light cream or half-and-half
¼ cup minced fresh chives or green onion
 (scallion) tops

1 large clove garlic, put through a
 garlic press
1 teaspoon salt
Freshly ground black pepper to taste

Heat the butter in a Dutch oven or other large heavy saucepan. Stir in the corn, cream, chives, garlic, and salt. Cover and simmer for about 10 to 15 minutes over medium-low heat, stirring frequently, until the corn is tender. (May be made ahead up to this point and reheated.) Turn into a warm serving bowl and finish with a few turns of a pepper mill.

YIELD: 8 TO 12 SERVINGS

Skillet Hominy Fry: Substitute two 16-ounce cans yellow or white hominy, drained in a colander and rinsed, for the corn.

FRESH BUTTERED PUMPKIN

Most cooks are surprised to find that pumpkin is so simple to cook, but, after all, it's just another winter squash with a pleasant nutty flavor.

1 small pumpkin, weighing 3½ to 4 pounds
2 tablespoons butter

½ teaspoon dried thyme leaves, crumbled
½ teaspoon salt
¼ teaspoon freshly ground black pepper

Cut the pumpkin in half and scoop out the fiber and seeds and discard. Cut the pumpkin into large pieces. Peel off the skin with a vegetable parer and trim away any remaining fiber so that what remains is solid flesh. Cut the flesh into ½-inch cubes. Place the cubes in a large saucepan and cover with about an inch of cold water. Bring to a boil, reduce the heat to medium-low, and simmer, covered, just until tender, 10 to 12 minutes. Drain, leaving just a little bit of liquid in the pan to create a sauce. Add the remaining ingredients, stirring until the butter is melted and the pumpkin is coated. (May be made ahead up to this point; cover and reheat gently when ready to serve.)

YIELD: 8 SERVINGS

SECOND-HELPING TURNIPS

I wouldn't kid you. There will be no leftovers. This recipe is a longtime Thanksgiving favorite at the home of Mary T. Gordon, the sister of a dear, but now departed friend, Dianna Caulfield. The recipe was given to me several years ago by Dianna, who admitted that she didn't do much cooking herself, but obviously she knew a good recipe when she tasted it. Second-Helping Turnips have graced my Thanksgiving table ever since.

3 pounds turnips or rutabagas (see note on page 115)

½ pound bacon, cut into ½-inch pieces
¼ teaspoon freshly ground black pepper

Peel the turnips and cut them into even-size chunks. Cook in lightly salted boiling water over medium-high heat in a large saucepan until tender, 25 to 30 minutes. Meanwhile, fry the bacon in a Dutch oven or other large heavy saucepan over medium-high heat until crisp and brown. Remove the bacon to paper towels to drain. Pour off all but about 6 tablespoons of the fat from the pan. Drain the turnips and return the pan to low heat for a minute or so to remove all of the moisture. Mash the turnips with a potato masher or a large fork until they are fairly smooth but still have a few little lumps. (May be done ahead up to this point.) Heat the bacon drippings over medium heat, then add the mashed turnips, sprinkle with the pepper, and cook, stirring, until hot. Stir the bacon bits into the turnips, reserving a few pieces for garnish.

YIELD: 8 TO 12 SERVINGS

Note: Although they look quite different, turnips and rutabagas are very closely related, so one can be substituted for the other in every case. Rutabagas are larger than turnips and are pale yellow in color. Rutabagas also have a more intense flavor than turnips, which I actually prefer for this dish.

ED ROBERTS'S ZUCCHINI

Trust a vegetarian when it comes to making good meatless dishes. Take the time to hunt for small zucchini so that the slices will be small.

2 tablespoons butter
2 pounds small zucchini, rinsed, trimmed, and cut into ⅛-inch slices

½ teaspoon salt
2 tablespoons firmly packed light or dark brown sugar

Melt the butter in a large skillet or wok over medium-high heat. When it is bubbly, add the zucchini and salt and cook, stirring and tossing, until the slices are limp and tender, and a few may even be a bit brown around the edges, about 10 minutes. Sprinkle with the brown sugar. Continue to cook and stir briefly until the sugar is melted and the slices are glazed.

YIELD: 8 SERVINGS

CREAMED THINGS

Back in the old days, all mothers knew that any vegetable that was creamed was three times as likely to be eaten, so it's not surprising that virtually every person I've spoken to about favorite Thanksgiving food has mentioned at least one creamed vegetable.

Creaming cooked vegetables is quite simple. The creaming sauce is merely a medium-thick white sauce that the French call *béchamel,* and it can be made in a few minutes with butter, flour, and milk or cream. The sauce is stirred into the cooked, drained vegetable and there you have it: Creamed Anything. If you like, you can flavor the sauce with herbs, spices (nutmeg, mace, or curry, for instance), wine, cheese (Swiss, Gruyère, or Parmesan are good choices), mustard, and garlic, or minced onion or shallot can be wilted in the butter before the flour is added, but in that case a little extra butter may be needed.

Almost any vegetable, or combination of vegetables, can be creamed. Usually the vegetables are cut into pieces, but whole vegetables can be creamed, too.

Because béchamel is flavorful enough to stand on its own, it can be served alongside the vegetables at the table and spooned over them. Another way to use the cream sauce is to spoon it over cooked vegetables that have been arranged in a shallow baking dish. Sprinkle with grated cheese or buttered bread crumbs, if you like, and then run the baking dish under a preheated broiler until the sauce bubbles or the bread browns.

Creamed vegetables may also be made into a casserole and topped with cheese or buttered bread cubes or crumbs and baked in a 325° to 350°F oven until hot and bubbly.

BÉCHAMEL SAUCE

(A MEDIUM-THICK WHITE SAUCE)

2 tablespoons butter
2 tablespoons all-purpose flour
1 cup milk, half-and-half, or cream

Salt and ground white or black pepper to taste

Melt the butter in a medium-size saucepan over medium-low heat. When it is hot, add the flour and stir constantly until the mixture bubbles. Whisk in the milk slowly and continue to cook and stir until the sauce is thick and smooth. Stir in the salt and pepper. At this point any additional flavoring ingredients may be added. If cheese is added, stir until it is melted. Wine should be cooked long enough for the raw taste of the alcohol to evaporate, about 2 or 3 minutes.

Béchamel may be made ahead, but in that case press a piece of plastic wrap directly on the surface to keep a skin from forming. If the sauce is to be held for more than an hour or so, it should be refrigerated. Actually, I think it's easier just to cream the vegetables ahead of time. The sauce seems to hold them in a sort of state of suspension so that they reheat very nicely.

YIELD: 1 CUP; 1 CUP OF SAUCE WILL CREAM BETWEEN 2 AND 4 CUPS OF VEGETABLES, DEPENDING ON HOW CREAMY YOU WANT THEM

CREAMED AND GLAZED LEEKS
❦

Leeks have been called the poor man's asparagus, but not where I buy them. They are now as expensive as asparagus, sometimes more so, but worth every penny. If you don't want to cream the leeks, they are wonderful with just a little butter, or you can combine them with an oil and vinegar drooving and serve at room temperature

8 medium-size leeks
1 cup Béchamel (see recipe above)

2 tablespoons grated Gruyère, Parmesan,
or blue cheese

Leeks must be cleaned very well to remove the sandy soil that stubbornly lurks in them. Cut off the green tops to about 2 or 3 inches above the white part. Trim off the roots, but leave enough of the root end in place so that the leek will not fall apart. Lay each leek on its side and, starting just below the green portion, cut into quarters through the leaves. Hold the leek under cold running water, spreading the leaves slightly to flush away all the sand.

Lay the leeks in the bottom of a saucepan that is wide enough to hold them without bending. Cover with lightly salted water and bring to a boil. Reduce the heat to medium-low, cover, and simmer for 15 to 20 minutes, or until just tender. Drain the leeks thoroughly and arrange them in a shallow 1½- or 2-quart baking dish that has been lightly buttered or coated with nonstick vegetable spray. Pour the sauce over the leeks and sprinkle with the cheese. (May be made ahead up to this point.) Place the baking dish 4 to 6 inches beneath a preheated broiler. Broil until the cheese melts and the top looks slightly glazed, about 5 minutes.

YIELD: 8 SERVINGS

MUSHROOMS THERMIDOR

So named because it makes me think of Lobster Thermidor, a dish that some years ago used to appear regularly on *haute cuisine* restaurant menus, but is now very much out of fashion.

3 pounds small regular white mushrooms
  (see note below)
¼ cup vegetable oil
4 tablespoons (½ stick) butter
¼ cup all-purpose flour
2 cups half-and-half or light cream

⅓ cup dry sherry
¼ teaspoon paprika
1 teaspoon salt
¼ teaspoon ground white pepper
Chopped fresh chives or parsley for
  garnish

Trim the mushroom stems fairly close to the cap. Rinse the mushrooms briefly in cool water and pat dry on paper towels. Heat the oil in a large skillet over high heat. When it is very hot, add the mushrooms and cook, stirring and tossing, for about 5 minutes, or until they have shrunk down considerably and their liquid has been given off and evaporated. Remove from the heat and set aside. In a large saucepan, melt the butter over medium heat. When hot, add the flour and cook, stirring, until bubbly. Gradually stir in the half-and-half, sherry, paprika, salt, and pepper and continue to cook, stirring, until thick and smooth. Drain off any liquid that may have accumulated with the mushrooms and add the mushrooms to the sauce, stirring until heated through. (May be made ahead up to this point and reheated just before serving.) Turn into a warm serving bowl and garnish with the chives.

YIELD: 8 SERVINGS

Note: For this dish to look its best, the mushrooms should be quite small, no larger than small bite-size. Larger mushrooms can be substituted, but in that case cut them into quarters or halves.

Mushrooms and Peas Thermidor: When adding the mushrooms, also add a package of frozen tiny peas that have been cooked until barely tender and drained.

CREAMED ONION CASSEROLE
❦

Cooking little onions from scratch is largely a labor of love, since blanching and peeling them will take some time. If you like, you can substitute frozen onions, or even frozen creamed onions. Or to save time on Thanksgiving, put the casserole together the day before and refrigerate it. In that case, increase the baking time by about 10 minutes.

This method for creaming onions may be used with other vegetables as well. Cauliflower flowerets, and celery and carrot slices, for instance, all cream very nicely. It's also not necessary to make this into a casserole. If you want just plain creamed onions, simply heat the cooked onions (or any other vegetable that you like) in the cream sauce, omitting the bread cubes, and serve with a dusting of paprika.

3 pounds small white onions (the smallest
are called pearl onions)
¼ pound (1 stick) butter
⅓ cup all-purpose flour
1 teaspoon salt
¼ teaspoon ground white or freshly
ground black pepper

Pinch of ground nutmeg
3 cups milk
4 slices white bread, crusts removed and
cut into ½-inch cubes
Chopped fresh parsley for garnish

To loosen their skins, place the onions in a large saucepan and cover with boiling water for about 1 minute. Drain and cover with cold water. Slip off the onion skins and cut an X in the root ends. Place the onions in lightly salted boiling water in a large saucepan and cook for about 20 minutes over medium-high heat, or until barely tender. Drain well and turn into a 3-quart casserole that has been lightly buttered or coated with nonstick vegetable spray. Preheat the oven to 375°F. Melt 6 tablespoons (¾ stick) of the butter in a medium-size saucepan over medium heat. When hot, blend in the flour, salt, pepper, and nutmeg and cook, stirring constantly, until bubbly. Gradually stir in the milk. Continue to cook and stir until the sauce thickens and boils. Pour gently over the onions. Melt the remaining 2 tablespoons of butter in a large skillet. Toss the bread cubes in the melted butter to coat them on all sides, then scatter them over the onions. Bake for about 20 minutes, or until the mixture bubbles and the bread cubes are lightly browned. To serve, sprinkle with the chopped parsley.

YIELD: 8 SERVINGS

Variation: Sprinkle the casserole with shredded cheese instead of bread cubes. My choice would be about ½ cup shredded Gruyère.

CREAMED SPINACH

At one point in their lives, my kids wouldn't have considered sitting down to a celebratory meal, or almost any meal, for that matter, that didn't include creamed spinach. Their eating habits have changed over the years, but creamed spinach for Thanksgiving is still *de rigueur*. Although using fresh spinach would be an admirable endeavor on Thanksgiving, there's really not *that* much difference in the frozen spinach version, and it's certainly a lot less demanding.

2½ pounds fresh spinach or four 10-ounce packages frozen leaf spinach
6 tablespoons (¾ stick) butter (2 tablespoons of this are optional)
1 medium-size onion, minced (½ cup)

3 tablespoons all-purpose flour
1½ cups half-and-half or light cream
1 teaspoon salt
⅛ teaspoon ground white pepper
Big pinch of ground nutmeg

Rinse the fresh spinach in several changes of cold water. Cut out the tough stems with kitchen scissors. Place the spinach in a large pot with only the water that clings to the leaves and cook over medium-high heat just until the leaves have wilted and are cooked through. (If you're using frozen spinach, cook as the package directs, but only until the spinach is completely defrosted. Proceed as with fresh spinach.) Drain the spinach in a colander, pressing down on it with your hands to extract as much of the cooking liquid as possible. Place the spinach in a food processor or blender and process until finely chopped but not pureed. (This may have to be done in more than one batch.) Melt 4 tablespoons of the butter in a large saucepan over medium heat. When hot, add the onion and cook, stirring, until softened. Stir in the flour until bubbly. Gradually stir in the half-and-half until the mixture is thick and smooth. Stir in the salt, pepper, and nutmeg. Add the spinach and continue to cook, stirring, for 2 or 3 minutes, or until heated through. Remove from the heat and stir in the remaining 2 tablespoons of butter, if you wish. (The entire recipe may be made in advance and rewarmed over low heat, adding the optional extra butter after reheating.)

YIELD: 8 TO 10 SERVINGS

SPINACH IN CREAMY TOMATO SAUCE

This is not actually creamed in the true sense. Also, it has never struck me as a particularly Thanksgiving-y dish, and I was not going to include it, but I was outvoted by the spinach lovers who have eaten it.

Three 10-ounce bags fresh or three 10-
 ounce packages frozen chopped spinach
2 tablespoons heavy or whipping cream
 (optional)

1½ cups prepared tomato sauce
2 tablespoons butter

Rinse the fresh spinach in several changes of cold water. Cut out the tough stems with kitchen scissors. Place the spinach in a large pot with only the water that clings to the leaves and cook over medium-high heat until the spinach is wilted and well cooked down. Drain thoroughly. (If using frozen spinach, cook as the package directs, but only until the spinach is completely defrosted. Drain thoroughly and proceed as with fresh spinach.) Return the spinach to the pot in which it was cooked. Mix the cream with the tomato sauce and stir into the spinach with the butter. Cook over low heat, stirring, until heated through. (May be made ahead and reheated.)

YIELD: 6 TO 8 SERVINGS

ELEGANT PUREES

Pureed vegetables were once the darlings of *nouvelle cuisine*, the "new" French cooking that was so popular some years back. Like everyone else I finally got tired of eating so much baby food, but I still like vegetable purees, and they are especially handy when serving a big dinner because they reheat so well.

A puree is exactly what you think it is: a cooked vegetable that has been reduced to a pulp by means of an electric beater, a food mill, a blender, a food processor (except for potatoes because it destroys their texture), or just elbow grease and a potato masher. The puree is then thinned, usually with milk or broth, and suitably seasoned.

Mashed potatoes are a puree, and essentially the same methods apply when pureeing, or mashing, anything else.

Purees dry out a bit as they sit, some more than others, so when reheating, beat in some additional butter or liquid to return it to a creamy consistency.

CHESTNUT PUREE

If you've never eaten poultry, especially goose, accompanied by chestnut puree, you owe it to yourself to try it. Chestnuts have a delicate, incomparable flavor that is slightly sweet and so rich that servings should be small, barely more than a spoonful.

1 pound chestnuts, roasted or boiled and
shelled (see pages 1–2), or one 16-ounce
jar or can peeled chestnuts

3 cups chicken broth (see pages 2–4)
2 tablespoons butter
2 tablespoons heavy or whipping cream

Cook and peel the chestnuts. Place the peeled chestnuts in a medium-size saucepan with the chicken broth and enough water to cover by about an inch. Bring to a boil, then reduce the heat to medium-low so the mixture barely simmers. Cook, uncovered, for 40 to 45 minutes, or until the chestnuts are quite tender but not mushy. While the chestnuts are simmering, pick off any bits of skin that float to the surface with the tip of a spoon. Drain the chestnuts, *reserving the cooking liquid*. Place the chestnuts in a food processor. (If you don't own a food processor, the chestnuts can be passed through a food mill and the butter and cream can be beaten in by hand.) Process until smooth, scraping down the sides of the container a couple of times. The puree will be very thick and pasty. Add the butter and cream and process again. Add enough of the reserved cooking liquid to give the puree a spoonable consistency, keeping in mind that it will thicken somewhat as it cools. Ideally, chestnut puree should be served immediately. However, since this is asking a lot on Thanksgiving, the puree can be reheated satisfactorily in the top of a double boiler over simmering water, but you will have to add a little more of the cooking liquid to get it back to the proper consistency.

YIELD: ABOUT 2 CUPS; 8 TO 12 SERVINGS

A PUREE OF PEAS

Frozen peas are a pretty ordinary vegetable, but when transformed into a puree they suddenly become surprisingly special.

Three 10-ounce packages frozen peas
6 tablespoons (¾ stick) butter
3 teaspoons chopped fresh mint (optional)

½ teaspoon sugar or to taste
½ teaspoon salt
¼ teaspoon freshly ground black pepper

Cook the peas according to the package directions and drain thoroughly. Place the peas in a food processor and process until smooth. Return the pureed peas to the pan in which they were cooked. Add the remaining ingredients and beat by hand until well blended. (May be made ahead up to this point.) When ready to serve, cook over medium-low heat, stirring constantly, until hot, adding a little more butter, or milk, if the puree seems dry.

YIELD: 8 SERVINGS

THE ULTIMATE PUREE: MASHED POTATOES
❦

After the turkey and the gravy, mashed potatoes are probably the most important dish on the Thanksgiving table—and many other dinner tables throughout the year as well.

4 pounds all-purpose or Russet (Idaho) potatoes, peeled, rinsed, and cut into large even-size chunks
6 tablespoons (¾ stick) butter, softened

About 1¼ cups milk, warmed, if you like, although this isn't absolutely necessary
1 teaspoon salt or to taste
¼ teaspoon freshly ground black or white pepper or to taste

Place the potatoes in a large saucepan and cover them with about 2 inches of lightly salted cold water. (May be made ahead up to this point.) Bring to a boil, then reduce the heat to medium, cover, and boil slowly for about 20 minutes, or until the potatoes are very tender. Drain thoroughly. The potatoes may be mashed with a hand-held electric mixer or in the large bowl of a stand mixer, or even using a potato masher or a big spoon and old-fashioned elbow grease. (Please note that using a food processor will make the potatoes gummy and nearly inedible.) Add the butter to the hot potatoes, then mash or beat until no lumps remain. Gradually add the milk, beating until the potatoes are the consistency that you like, or at least the consistency that lends itself to making a big crater to hold gravy. Beat in the salt and pepper. Rewarm over low heat, beating constantly. If the potatoes are not to be served immediately, rewarm over very low heat, beating until hot and adding a little more milk if they seem dry. Do not cover the potatoes at any time after they are mashed or they will get mushy.

YIELD: 8 TO 12 SERVINGS

Extra Rich and Creamy Mashed Potatoes: Substitute half-and-half, light cream, sour cream, or evaporated (not condensed!) milk for all or part of the milk.
Mashed Potatoes with Onions: Cook about ½ cup thinly sliced green onions (scallions) in a tablespoon or so of butter, stirring, until tender. Stir into the potatoes after the salt and pepper have been added.

Note: Don't ever throw away leftover mashed potatoes, at least until you've made mashed potato pancakes. In fact, most people who have tried these like them so much that they deliberately mash more potatoes than they need. Refrigerate leftover mashed potatoes. When they are cold, shape them into 2- or 3-inch patties, about ½ inch thick. In a large skillet, fry the patties in a ¼-inch-deep mixture of butter and vegetable oil (or bacon fat, if you're not cholesterol or fat conscious) over medium-high heat until crisp-brown on both sides. If you like, you can add lightly browned chopped onion to the cold potato mixture before forming the patties.

MASHED POTATOES AND CARROTS

I served this for the first time last Thanksgiving and most of my guests preferred it over mashed potatoes. My daughter, Kimberly, the mashed-potato queen, now asks me to make this every time she visits.

3 pounds all-purpose or Russet (Idaho) potatoes, peeled, rinsed, and cut into large even-size chunks
1½ pounds carrots, trimmed, scraped, and cut into 2-inch lengths

3 tablespoons butter, softened
½ cup heavy or whipping cream
2 teaspoons salt
½ teaspoon freshly ground black pepper

Place the potatoes and carrots in a large saucepan and cover them with about 2 inches of lightly salted cold water. (May be made ahead up to this point.) Bring to a boil, then reduce the heat, cover, and boil slowly for about 20 minutes, or until both of the vegetables are very tender. Drain thoroughly, *reserving 1½ cups of the cooking liquid.* The potatoes and carrots may be mashed with a hand-held electric mixer or in the large bowl of a stand mixer, or even using a potato masher or big spoon and old-fashioned elbow grease. Add the butter and the reserved hot cooking liquid and beat until the mixture is fairly smooth. Beat in the cream, salt, and pepper until nearly smooth, although there will inevitably be small lumps of carrot throughout the mixture. Rewarm over low heat, beating constantly. If not to be served immediately, rewarm over very low heat, beating until hot and adding a little milk if the mixture seems dry. Do not cover the potatoes and carrots at any time after they are mashed or they will get mushy.

YIELD: 8 SERVINGS

POTATO AND TURNIP PUREE

Rather than adding any distinct flavor of their own, turnips seem only to intensify the flavor of the potatoes and add lightness and moisture to the texture of the finished dish. This is a nice substitute for plain mashed potatoes.

8 medium-size all-purpose potatoes (about 4 pounds), peeled, rinsed, and quartered
8 medium-size turnips (about 2 pounds), peeled and cut into eighths (they take longer to cook)
¼ pound (1 stick) butter, softened

¼ cup half-and-half, milk, or light cream
1 teaspoon salt
½ teaspoon ground white pepper
Chopped fresh parsley or paprika for garnish

Place the potatoes and turnips in a large saucepan and cover with about 2 inches of lightly salted cold water (May be made ahead up to this point.) Bring to a boil, then cover and boil slowly over medium-high heat for about 25 minutes, or until very tender when pierced with a fork. Drain well and mash with a potato masher or beat with an electric mixer. Beat in the butter, half-and-half, salt, and pepper. Set aside, uncovered, until close to serving time. Then rewarm over very low heat, beating constantly. Turn into a serving bowl and sprinkle lightly with chopped parsley or paprika.

YIELD: 12 SERVINGS

Note: To make 6 servings, this recipe may be halved. Cooking instructions remain the same.

SWEET POTATO PUREE WITH FRESH GINGER

When serving a puree, do as the chefs do and swirl an eye-catching pattern on top with the back of a spoon.

4 pounds sweet potatoes, peeled and cut
    into large even-size chunks
6 tablespoons (¾ stick) butter
2 teaspoons minced fresh ginger
6 tablespoons firmly packed light or dark
    brown sugar

¾ teaspoon salt
¼ teaspoon freshly ground black pepper
6 tablespoons milk or half-and-half
Finely chopped crystallized ginger for
    garnish

Drop the potatoes into a large saucepan of lightly salted boiling water. Cover and cook over medium heat until tender, about 20 minutes. Drain thoroughly. While the potatoes are cooking, melt the butter in a small saucepan over medium heat. When hot, add the ginger and cook, stirring, for 2 minutes. Stir in the brown sugar, salt, and pepper. Add the butter mixture to the hot drained potatoes and beat with an electric hand-held mixer until well blended. Add the milk and continue to beat until smooth. (May be made ahead up to this point.) When ready to serve, cook over medium-low heat, stirring constantly, until hot. To serve, sprinkle with crystallized ginger.

YIELD: 8 SERVINGS

QUICK BAKES

The day I got two ovens in my kitchen I thought I'd died and gone to heaven, even though one of the ovens isn't really full size. Even so, it's quite a luxury to be able to bake more than one thing at a time, especially on Thanksgiving when most cooks have to perform juggling tricks when there's anything besides the turkey that needs to be baked or reheated, and there's always *something* that needs to be baked or reheated.

The way around this is to combine precooked ingredients that only need to be reheated, or to bake ahead and reheat after the turkey is out of the oven and resting before it's carved.

By the way, most things don't need to be reheated at any precise oven temperature; 325°, 350°, or 375°F don't make that much difference, but you may have to adjust the times a little and watch carefully.

OLD-FASHIONED CORN PUDDING

Adding beaten egg whites to the batter produces a pudding that is lighter than most, but with all of the old-fashioned flavor that keeps us eating corn pudding generation after generation.

Two 16-ounce cans cream-style corn
4 tablespoons (½ stick) butter, melted
⅓ cup all-purpose flour
3 tablespoons sugar

1 teaspoon salt
⅛ teaspoon ground white pepper
3 large eggs, separated
1 cup milk

Preheat the oven to 350°F. In a large bowl, mix the corn and butter. Add the flour, sugar, salt, and pepper and mix until well blended. Lightly beat the egg yolks in a small bowl. Heat the milk over low heat in a small saucepan until it is steaming. Remove from the heat and rapidly stir in the yolks. Add to the corn mixture, mixing until well blended. In a medium-size bowl, beat the egg whites until stiff peaks form when the beaters are lifted. Stir about one quarter of the beaten whites into the corn mixture until well blended, then fold in the remaining whites. Pour into a deep 2-quart baking dish that has been lightly greased or coated with nonstick vegetable spray. Bake for about 1 hour, stirring the crust that forms on the top down into the pudding twice during baking, once after 20 minutes and again after 40 minutes. The pudding is done when it sets up on the spoon but is still slightly loose and creamy.

YIELD: 8 SERVINGS

ONION-RING GRATIN

In the spring, when Spanish onions are out of season, this gratin can be made with Vidalias, the sweetest onion of them all.

4 large Spanish onions (about 2 pounds),
   peeled and cut into ½-inch slices
Salt and freshly ground black pepper to
   taste

Ground mace to taste
1 cup shredded Jarlsberg cheese
1 cup light cream or half-and-half

Bring a large saucepan of lightly salted water to a boil. Drop in the onion slices and cook until tender, about 12 minutes. The slices will separate into rings as they cook. Drain the onion rings in a colander. Preheat the oven to 375°F. When the onion rings are cool enough to handle, arrange about half of them in a shallow 2-quart baking dish that has been lightly buttered. Sprinkle with the salt, pepper, mace, and half of the cheese. Arrange the remaining onion rings over the top. Again sprinkle with the salt, pepper, mace, and the remaining cheese. Drizzle the cream over the top. (May be made ahead up to this point.) Bake for 25 to 30 minutes, or until the cheese melts and the cream bubbles. Place under a hot broiler for a minute or two to lightly brown the top.

YIELD: 8 SERVINGS

STUFFED ACORN SQUASH I

Acorn squash don't really have to be filled with anything, but they make such nice little containers that it's hard to resist putting something in them. To serve plain, bake as directed in either of the following recipes, then turn right side up, put a lump of soft butter in each cavity, and sprinkle with brown sugar, if you like.

4 acorn squash, about 1 pound each
2 tablespoons grated orange rind
½ teaspoon ground nutmeg
½ teaspoon salt
2 cups golden raisins

1 cup half-and-half
½ cup orange juice
1 cup toasted (see pages 6–7) chopped
  walnuts
Ground nutmeg for dusting

Preheat the oven to 350°F. Cut the squash in half through the stems and scrape out the seeds and fiber and discard. Place the squash halves, cut side down, in one or two shallow baking dishes filled with ½ inch of water. Bake for about 30 minutes, or until the squash feel barely tender when pressed with protected fingers. (Be careful not to bake the squash too long, or they will collapse as they cool.) When the squash are cool enough to handle, scoop the flesh into a large bowl, leaving shells about ¼ inch thick. Reserve the shells. Add the orange rind, nutmeg, and salt to the squash in the bowl and mash coarsely with a fork. In a food processor or blender, combine 1 cup of the raisins, the half-and-half, and orange juice and process with quick on/off pulses just enough to finely chop the raisins. Stir the raisin mixture into the squash mixture. Add the walnuts and the remaining raisins, stirring to combine. Spoon the raisin mixture into the reserved squash shells and dust with additional ground nutmeg. (The squash may be prepared ahead up to this point, then covered and refrigerated.) Bake for about 15 minutes, or until heated through. Squash that has been refrigerated will need a little extra heating time.

YIELD: 8 SERVINGS

STUFFED ACORN SQUASH II
❧

Since I've found that most people who eat this seem to like the caramelized onions better than the squash, I sometimes serve just the onions and forget about the squash.

4 acorn squash, about 1 pound each
Two 16-ounce bags frozen whole onions
1 cup water
4 tablespoons (½ stick) butter

¼ cup sugar
½ teaspoon salt
Honey (optional)

Preheat the oven to 350°F. Cut the squash in half through the stems and scrape out the seeds and fiber and discard. Place the squash halves, cut side down, on one or two baking sheets that have been lightly greased or coated with nonstick vegetable spray. Bake for about 35 minutes, or until the squash feel tender when pressed with protected fingers. (Do not bake the squash too long, or they will collapse as they cool.) Remove from the oven, but leave the squash on the baking sheets.

Place the onions in a large skillet with the water. Stir in the butter, sugar, and salt. Bring to a boil, then reduce the heat to medium-low and simmer until the water evaporates and the onions are caramelized, stirring frequently toward the end so the onions brown evenly and don't stick. (This whole process will take about 20 minutes.) Set the onions aside. Turn the baked squash right side up. Brush the cavities and rims with honey, if you like. Fill each cavity with warm or room-temperature onions, dividing equally, about ⅓ cup each. (May be made ahead and reheated in a preheated 350°F oven for about 15 minutes.)

YIELD: 8 SERVINGS

Stuffed Squash III: If you prefer a savory onion stuffing, cook the onions in 1 cup beef broth instead of the water and omit the sugar, salt, and honey.
Stuffed Squash IV: Fill the squash with any buttered vegetable or combination of vegetables, such as peas and carrots, corn and baby lima beans, peas and pearl onions, baby carrots, corn and red peppers, or peas and mushrooms.

BAKED YELLOW SQUASH
❧

Rich and creamy, this is a nice change of pace when there will be a lot of sweet things on the table.

2 pounds yellow crookneck squash, rinsed
and cut into ¼-inch slices
7 tablespoons (1 tablespoon less than a
stick) butter
¼ teaspoon freshly ground black pepper
1¼ cups shredded cheddar cheese
1 cup sour cream

1 medium-size onion, finely chopped
(½ cup)
¼ cup dry white wine or dry vermouth
2 slices white bread, crusts removed and
whirled in a blender or food processor
to make soft bread crumbs (1 cup)

Place the squash in a large saucepan and barely cover with lightly salted water. Cover and bring to a boil. Reduce the heat to medium-low and simmer until tender, about 10 minutes. Drain off the cooking liquid and return the pan to low heat for a minute or so to remove all of the moisture. Add 4 tablespoons of the butter and the pepper and mash together until well blended but still a little lumpy. Stir in the cheese, sour cream, onion, and wine.

Preheat the oven to 350°F. Turn the mixture into an 11-inch (6-cup) gratin dish that has been lightly buttered or coated with nonstick vegetable spray. Sprinkle the bread crumbs evenly over the top. Melt the remaining butter and drizzle evenly over the bread crumbs. (May be made ahead up to this point.) Bake for 20 to 30 minutes, or until bubbly and golden.

YIELD: 8 SERVINGS

The Difference Between Sweet Potatoes and Yams

Right here might be a good place to try to end the confusion that has existed for centuries about sweet potatoes and yams. Although the two are both tubers, similar in taste and appearance, they come from completely different plants. Sweet potatoes are grown in the warmer climates of the United States and the Caribbean, whereas true yams originated in Africa. It is thought that the African slaves started calling the sweet potato a yam because it so closely resembles the African yam, both in appearance and cooking properties, and the name caught on, especially in the South. There are several different varieties of sweet potatoes, but what is marketed in the United States is almost always a variety of sweet potato, so it really doesn't make a whole lot of difference what they're called.

SWEET POTATO AND APPLE BAKE

This is a superb dish that is not too sweet. The brandy adds a wonderful flavor and aroma. A few golden raisins can also be sprinkled onto each layer and are a nice addition.

*2 pounds sweet potatoes, peeled and cut
into ¼-inch slices*
*2 pounds McIntosh or Golden Delicious
apples, peeled, cored, and cut into
¼-inch slices*

*6 tablespoons firmly packed light brown
sugar*
6 tablespoons (¾ stick) butter
*½ cup Calvados or other apple brandy,
or apple cider*

Drop the sweet potato slices into lightly salted boiling water and boil gently until fork-tender but not falling apart, about 5 minutes. Drain and set aside. Preheat the oven to 350°F. Butter an 8-cup soufflé dish or other deep baking dish. Arrange a layer of sliced apples over the bottom of the dish. Sprinkle with 1 tablespoon of the brown sugar and dot with 1 tablespoon of the butter that has been cut into small pieces. Cover the apple slices with a layer of sweet potato slices and sprinkle with another tablespoon of the sugar and dot with another tablespoon of the butter as before. Continue layering the apples, sweet potatoes, sugar, and butter in this manner until all of the ingredients are used, ending with a layer of apples. Drizzle the Calvados over the top. Cover tightly with aluminum foil and bake for about 1 hour and 20 minutes, or until the apples are very soft. (May be made ahead up to this point; leave covered at room temperature until ready to reheat.) Reheat in a 350°F oven, still covered with foil, for 25 to 30 minutes.

YIELD: 8 SERVINGS

TINY BAKED SWEETS

Tuck tiny little sweet potatoes here and there around and behind the turkey roasting pan to bake. Since they're so small they can also be used to garnish the turkey platter. If the potatoes cool during the carving, they can always be reheated briefly in the microwave.

*8 small sweet potatoes (the smallest you
can find)*

Solid white vegetable shortening

Preheat the oven to 325°F. Scrub the potatoes under running water and pat dry. Rub the skins with a light coating of shortening, then prick each potato once or twice with the tines of a fork to prevent them from exploding in the oven. Bake for 45 minutes to 1 hour, depending on the size of the potato. Test for doneness by squeezing gently with protected fingers; they will feel soft. To serve, cut the potatoes open and serve with a pat of butter in each.

YIELD: 8 SERVINGS

JUST FOR KIDS:
SWEET POTATO BALLS

Kids of all ages, of course. I am always amused by sophisticated diners who finally agree to have "just one" of these and then scrape the plate with their fork to get every last morsel.

2 pounds sweet potatoes, peeled and cut
    into large even-size chunks
4 tablespoons (½ stick) butter, softened
¾ cup firmly packed light or dark
    brown sugar

2 tablespoons milk or orange juice
½ teaspoon grated orange rind (optional)
¼ teaspoon salt
2 cups corn flakes
8 regular-size marshmallows

Place the potatoes in a medium-size saucepan and cover with water by about 1½ inches. Bring to a boil, then cover and boil slowly over medium-high heat until tender, about 20 minutes. Drain the potatoes thoroughly and mash until smooth with an electric mixer or by hand. (There should be 3 cups.) Beat in the butter, brown sugar, milk, orange rind, and salt. Sprinkle the corn flakes on a sheet of waxed paper and crumble them a little with your fingers. Scoop up about a heaping ⅓ cup of the sweet potato mixture and shape it around a marshmallow to make a 2- to 2½-inch ball. Gently roll the ball in the corn flakes and place it on a buttered baking sheet. (Rolling the balls in the corn flakes is much easier to do if you can enlist the aid of a helper, or you will have to rinse and dry your hands in between making each ball.) Repeat with the remaining sweet potatoes and marshmallows. Place the baking sheet in the freezer for two or three hours, or until the balls are frozen solid. (If frozen storage will be much longer than a few hours, cover the baking sheet with aluminum foil.) When ready to bake, preheat the oven to 350°F and bake the frozen potato balls for 20 minutes. Serve immediately.

YIELD: 8 BALLS

BAKED SWEET POTATOES AND MARSHMALLOWS

This is it. The recipe for sweet potatoes we all lived for as kids. Some of us still do.

*4 pounds sweet potatoes, peeled and cut
into large even-size chunks
4 tablespoons (½ stick) butter
½ cup pineapple or orange juice
½ cup half-and-half or milk*

*½ cup firmly packed light brown sugar
1 teaspoon salt
½ teaspoon ground cinnamon
Regular-size marshmallows*

Place the potatoes in a large saucepan and cover with cold water by about 1½ inches. Bring to a boil, then cover and boil slowly over medium-high heat until tender, about 20 minutes. Drain the potatoes thoroughly and mash until smooth. Add the butter and beat with a hand-held electric mixer (or in the large bowl of a stand mixer) until the butter is melted. Gradually beat in the juice, half-and-half, brown sugar, salt, and cinnamon.

Preheat the oven to 350°F. Turn the potato mixture into a shallow or deep 3-quart baking dish that has been lightly greased or coated with nonstick vegetable spray. Press as many marshmallows as you like into the top of the potatoes. (May be made ahead up to this point, covered, and refrigerated until ready to bake.) Bake for about 30 minutes, or until the marshmallows are oozing and golden brown.

YIELD: 12 SERVINGS

Note: To make 6 servings, this recipe may be halved and baked in a shallow or deep 1½-quart baking dish.

PAM PERCIVAL'S SWEET POTATO CASSEROLE

Pam swears that, in the South, this casserole is not a dessert but a side dish. You could fool me, and probably everybody else, too, if it were served after dinner with whipped cream.

2¼ pounds sweet potatoes, peeled and cut
  into large even-size chunks
¼ pound (1 stick) butter, softened
½ cup sugar
⅓ cup milk
2 large eggs, lightly beaten
1 teaspoon vanilla extract
⅛ teaspoon ground nutmeg

TOPPING
6 tablespoons (¾ stick) butter, melted
1 cup firmly packed light brown sugar
½ cup all-purpose flour
1 cup toasted (see pages 6–7) chopped
  pecans

Place the potatoes in a large saucepan and cover with cold water by about 1½ inches. Bring to a boil, then cover and boil slowly over medium-high heat until tender, about 20 minutes. Drain the potatoes thoroughly and mash until smooth with an electric mixer. (There should be 3 cups.) Beat in the butter, sugar, milk, eggs, vanilla, and nutmeg until well blended. Spoon the mixture into a shallow 3-quart baking dish that has been buttered or coated with nonstick vegetable spray. (May be made ahead up to this point.)

Preheat the oven to 350°F. To make the topping, mix the butter, brown sugar, and flour in a medium-size bowl. Stir in the nuts and sprinkle evenly over the top of the potato mixture. Bake for 35 to 40 minutes, or until the topping is lightly browned.

YIELD: 6 TO 8 SERVINGS

ELLEN MARTIN'S CANDIED YAMS

Ellen was my stepmother. She was raised in Birmingham, Alabama, and she was pretty, genteel, a talented dancer and choreographer, and a dedicated cook. Although she lived in the North for many years, Ellen never lost her Southern accent—or her love for Southern food. She also referred to sweet potatoes as yams.

4 pounds yams (sweet potatoes)
1½ cups firmly packed dark brown sugar
1½ cups granulated sugar
1 cup water
4 tablespoons (½ stick) butter
2 teaspoons grated orange rind

1 teaspoon grated lemon rind
½ teaspoon salt
½ teaspoon freshly grated or ground
  nutmeg
Two 3-inch cinnamon sticks, broken
  in half

Rinse the yams but do not peel them. Place the yams in a large saucepan and cover with water. Bring to a boil over high heat. Lower the heat slightly and boil for about 30 minutes, or until fork-tender.

Preheat the oven to 325°F. While the yams are boiling, make the syrup by combining the remaining ingredients in a heavy medium-size saucepan. Bring to a boil, stirring constantly. Lower the heat to medium-low and simmer for about 10 minutes, or until the sugars are dissolved and the mixture is clear. Drain the yams and, when they are cool enough to handle, slip off the skins. Cut the yams in half and arrange, cut side down, in a shallow 3-quart baking dish that has been lightly greased or coated with nonstick vegetable spray. Mash each yam half down slightly with the back of a fork. Remove the cinnamon and pour the warm syrup over the yams. Cover and refrigerate until ready to bake. Bake for about 30 minutes, occasionally spooning the syrup over the yams.

YIELD: 10 TO 12 SERVINGS

Note: To make 6 servings, this recipe may be halved and baked in a 1½-quart baking dish.

Variation: Add ½ cup golden or dark raisins or dried currants to the syrup after removing it from the heat.

AND A FEW OTHER GOOD SIDE DISHES

Some of these recipes just didn't seem to fit neatly into any of the foregoing categories. Others require long baking times and can't be baked ahead and reheated, thus necessitating two ovens. But many are old favorites and just too good to leave out.

BUTTERSCOTCH APPLE SAUCE

Brown sugar and butter are what give this dark apple sauce its rich, almost butterscotch flavor. The exact amount of sugar you add depends mostly upon the natural sweetness of the apples you use. This is an excellent accompaniment for poultry and ham, but it is superb with duck or goose. If time is scarce, you can take a shortcut and start with prepared apple sauce.

5 pounds apples (any variety you like), peeled, cored, quartered, and cut into ¼-inch slices

½ to ¾ cup firmly packed dark or light brown sugar
4 tablespoons (½ stick) butter
Pinch of ground nutmeg

Place the apple slices in a large saucepan, barely cover them with water, and bring to a boil. Reduce the heat to medium-low, cover, and simmer until the slices are very tender, about 15 minutes. Drain off and discard all but 2 or 3 tablespoons of the cooking water. Turn the apples and the remaining cooking water into a food processor and process until smooth. (The apples may be mashed by hand with a potato masher.) Scrape back into the saucepan and return the pan to medium heat. Stir in the brown sugar until melted. Continue to cook and stir until the apple sauce has reached a fairly thick consistency. Add the butter and stir until melted. Stir in the nutmeg. Serve slightly warm or at room temperature. (May be made ahead and reheated.)

YIELD: 8 SERVINGS

Shortcut Version: Heat three 16-ounce jars prepared apple sauce in a medium-size saucepan. Cook over medium-low heat, stirring often, until some of the liquid has cooked away and the sauce has thickened, 5 to 10 minutes. Stir in ¼ cup firmly packed brown sugar until melted. Add the butter and stir until melted. Stir in the nutmeg.

BRAISED ENDIVE AND PEARS

Endive, if you're not familiar with it, is the pretty, pale green to pale yellow, cigar-shaped vegetable that is usually wrapped in tissue paper. Even though it is commonly referred to as Belgian endive, much of what is available is actually grown in France, and it can be eaten either cooked or raw. The slight bitterness of endive, which is less intense when it is cooked, is very much an acquired taste, so this may not be everyone's dish. However, the combination of endive and pears is no less than heavenly. Unfortunately, this dish is better if it is not cooked ahead, but since it requires only a minimum of attention from the cook this is usually not a problem.

4 endive (about 1 pound), rinsed, trimmed, and cut in half lengthwise
4 small Bosc pears, ripe, but not too soft, peeled, quartered, and cored

½ cup chicken broth (see pages 2–4)
2 tablespoons butter
1 teaspoon sugar
Chopped fresh parsley for garnish

Arrange the endive, cut side down, in an 11- or 12-inch nonreactive skillet. Arrange the pear quarters among the endive, trying to keep the mixture as close to one layer as possible. Add the chicken broth and bring to a simmer over medium-high heat. Cover tightly and cook over very low heat for about 15 minutes, or until the endive and pears are tender. Remove to a serving platter, cover with aluminum foil, and set in a warm place. Add the butter and sugar to the skillet and simmer the pan juices over medium heat, stirring occasionally, until they become thick and syrupy, about 10 minutes. Pour over the endive and pears on the platter and sprinkle with the parsley.

YIELD: 8 SERVINGS

Variation: Medium-size fennel bulbs, trimmed and quartered, may be substituted for either the pears or the endive. However, if the fennel is replacing the pears, a little more chicken broth may be required and the fennel should be scraped before cooking because it is stringy.

ELLEN MARTIN'S GRITS SOUFFLÉ

Another one of my Southern stepmother's recipes, which she served frequently in place of potatoes or other starches with both poultry and red meat.

1 cup milk
1 cup water
½ cup uncooked regular hominy grits
2 tablespoons cold butter

3 large eggs, separated
1 teaspoon salt
Plain dried bread crumbs

Combine the milk and water in the top of a double boiler with a 6- or 7-cup capacity. Place the top of the double boiler over direct medium heat until the milk and water are just ready to simmer. Gradually stir in the grits and cook over medium heat, stirring, until the mixture boils and begins to thicken. Place the top of the double boiler over hot water and continue to cook for about 20 minutes, stirring occasionally, until thick and smooth. Remove from the heat and cool slightly. Gradually beat in the butter, egg yolks, and ¾ teaspoon of the salt. Set aside to cool to room temperature. Preheat the oven to 325°F. Butter an 8-cup soufflé dish and dust it with bread crumbs. In a medium-size bowl, beat the egg whites with the remaining ¼ teaspoon of salt until stiff peaks form when the beaters are lifted. Stir a big spoonful of the beaten whites into the grits mixture. Fold in the remaining whites and turn into the prepared soufflé dish. Bake for 45 minutes, or until the top is lightly browned.

YIELD: 6 SERVINGS

CREAMY OR BUTTERY HOMINY

Hominy is something like canned corn (it actually is corn) and should not be confused with hominy grits, which is dried, ground hominy.

*Two cans (about 16 ounces each) yellow
　or white hominy (although yellow will
　look better)*
2 tablespoons butter
¼ cup milk

½ teaspoon salt
¼ teaspoon ground white pepper
¾ cup sour cream
Chopped fresh parsley for garnish

　Drain the hominy in a colander. Rinse well with cold water and drain again. Melt the butter in a Dutch oven or other large heavy saucepan. Add the hominy, milk, salt, and pepper and cook over medium heat, stirring, until hot. Stir in the sour cream until well blended and hot, but do not allow the mixture to boil after adding the sour cream or it will curdle. Serve sprinkled with the parsley.

YIELD: 6 TO 8 SERVINGS

Buttered Hominy: Omit the sour cream.

AL BOLTON'S FRIED OKRA

It never occurred to me to include a recipe for fried okra in this book, and except for a happy happenstance, I may have forever been denied the pleasure of eating this simple, delectable dish. As it happened, I was speaking on the phone with Al about another recipe when he mentioned that he had found some nice little okras in the market that day and was just about to fry some for dinner. I'd heard of fried okra, of course, but I'd never eaten it, and, truthfully, I didn't think I'd like it. (You know all those notions we have about okra being slimy.) I should have known better because Al never cooks anything that I don't eat to the last bite. I followed his easy directions and now fried okra is one of our favorite vegetables. I may even serve it for Thanksgiving since I discovered that it doesn't have to be fried at the last minute. The only thing I would have to say against fried okra is that it is not a particularly pretty dish. But what it lacks in looks it makes up for in flavor. Al uses an equal mixture of flour and cornmeal to coat his okra. I like it better with just cornmeal. Either way, try it, if you haven't. You'll like it.

2 pounds firm, unblemished okra, preferably not much bigger than a man's
  thumb (3 or 4 inches), says Al
1 cup yellow cornmeal

½ teaspoon salt
¼ teaspoon freshly ground black pepper
1 cup olive oil

Rinse and drain the okra, then trim off the stem ends and cut each pod into two or three pieces. Mix the cornmeal, salt, and pepper together in a big bowl (or a paper bag) and toss the okra around in the mixture until it is well coated. Heat half of the olive oil in a large skillet over medium-high heat. When it is very hot, add half of the okra and cook, stirring and tossing, until it is well browned. Remove from the skillet and drain on paper towels. Rinse and wipe the skillet and repeat frying with the remaining oil and okra. Although fried okra is probably best served straight out of the skillet, it can be reheated in a 350°F oven for a few minutes.

YIELD: 6 TO 8 SERVINGS

Fried Zucchini: Cut the zucchini into ½-inch slices and prepare the same way as the okra.

HERB-ROASTED ONIONS

These are a snap to prepare and they do add a festive little touch to a holiday dinner. Since the onions can be baked in a very shallow roasting pan, it may be possible to fit them into the oven with the turkey. These are good with roast beef, too.

4 medium-size (8 to 10 ounces each)
  Spanish onions, peeled and cut in
  half lengthwise
3 tablespoons butter, softened
1 teaspoon fresh lemon juice

½ teaspoon dried thyme leaves, crumbled
½ teaspoon dried rosemary leaves,
  crumbled
½ teaspoon salt
Freshly ground black pepper to taste

Preheat the oven to 325°F. Arrange the onion halves cut-side up in a shallow greased baking pan that is just large enough to hold them comfortably. Combine the butter, lemon juice, thyme, rosemary, salt, and a liberal amount of pepper in a small bowl. Spread the mixture onto the onions. Bake for 1¼ to 1¾ hours, or until tender and appetizingly brown.

YIELD: 8 SERVINGS

SHALLOT CONFIT

The word *confit* usually means salted meat or poultry simmered in and preserved in its own fat, but the word has been bandied about and often refers to vegetables or fruits that have been cooked in fat and sugar until they are soft and glazed. Shallots, which are part of the onion family, grow in bulbs, like garlic, with a flavor more like an onion with just a hint of garlic. As well as a lovely side dish that complements most meat and poultry, glazed shallots can be used as a garnish. Servings should be small, about three or four shallots per person. Shallots can also be served as an appetizer spread on thin toast.

2 pounds small shallots (about 1 inch in diameter), peeled

6 tablespoons (¾ stick) butter, cut into pieces
⅓ cup sugar

Place the shallots in a Dutch oven or other large heavy saucepan. Add only enough water to cover about one third of the shallots. Stir in the butter and sugar and cook over medium heat until the water simmers. Reduce the heat to medium-low, or until the mixture barely simmers. Continue to cook, uncovered, stirring occasionally for about 45 minutes, more frequently toward the end, or until the water has evaporated and the shallots are soft, lightly browned, and shiny. Remove to a serving dish with a slotted spoon, leaving most of the glaze in the pan. Serve at room temperature or slightly warm.

YIELD: 8 servings

TOM GARRISON'S SAUERKRAUT

When I lived in Baltimore a number of years ago, my in-law family made it clear to me that, for them, Thanksgiving without sauerkraut was no Thanksgiving at all. This was something new for me, and it did taste good, all mushed up with the mashed potatoes and gravy. My father-in-law, Tom Garrison, was a great cook and he frequently made the sauerkraut. This is how he did it:

Depending on the number of people you will be serving, place one, two, or three 1-pound bags of sauerkraut in a deep baking dish. Chop the raw turkey neck into three or four pieces and bury it in the sauerkraut. Cover the baking dish tightly and put it in the oven with the turkey for three, four hours, or whatever. It's almost impossible to overcook sauerkraut as long as you keep it moist. After the turkey has been roasting for a while, spoon some of the drippings over the kraut. (The kraut can be made well ahead, and even refrigerated. Reheat, spooning some of the turkey drippings over the sauerkraut.)

YIELD: EACH 1-POUND BAG OF SAUERKRAUT WILL MAKE ABOUT 4 TO 6 SERVINGS

SAUERKRAUT SALAD
❦

This is one of those dishes that can't decide whether it's a relish or a side dish, but I think of it as a side dish, probably because everyone takes large helpings and seconds, too.

1½ cups sugar
¾ cup white wine vinegar
¼ cup vegetable oil
3 or 4 celery ribs, finely chopped (1½ cups)

2 small onions, thinly sliced and
  separated into rings
¼ cup finely chopped pimiento
2 teaspoons caraway or celery seeds
2 pounds sauerkraut, drained

Combine the sugar, vinegar, and oil in a medium-size nonreactive saucepan over medium heat, stirring until the sugar dissolves. Remove from the heat and set aside to cool. Stir in the celery, onions, pimiento, and caraway seeds. Place the sauerkraut in a large bowl. Pour the dressing over the sauerkraut and toss to coat thoroughly. Refrigerate for 24 hours and bring to room temperature to serve.

YIELD: 8 TO 12 SERVINGS

NEW ENGLAND–STYLE BUTTERNUT SQUASH
❦

Grains and root vegetables were an important part of the American settlers' diet, and so it's nice to give them a nod at Thanksgiving by serving this dish, which will remind you of the more familiar candied sweet potatoes.

2 cups cooked pearl barley (about ⅔ cup
  raw barley)
2 cups ½-inch-diced butternut squash
  (about ¾ pound)
1 cup chopped walnuts

1 cup apple cider
½ cup fresh cranberries
¼ cup honey
¼ cup firmly packed dark brown sugar
2 teaspoons ground cinnamon

Combine all of the ingredients in a heavy 3-quart Dutch oven. Cook over medium-low heat, stirring gently every now and then, until the mixture begins to bubble. Cover tightly and cook over low heat, stirring occasionally, until the squash is tender, 25 to 35 minutes. (May be made ahead and rewarmed by stirring gently over medium-low heat.)

YIELD: 8 TO 10 SERVINGS

VIRGINIA PRESCOTT'S WARM WILD RICE WITH FRUIT

This is my mother's recipe, which you will serve many times throughout the year, since it is as good at a picnic as it is for Thanksgiving.

1 cup uncooked wild rice (see page 9)	*2 tablespoons butter*
4 cups chicken broth (see pages 2–4)	*1 large onion, finely chopped (1 cup)*
12 dried apricots	*2 large red apples*
1 cup golden raisins	*Salt to taste*
½ cup dried currants	

Preheat the oven to 350°F. Place the rice in a fine strainer and rinse under cool running water. Drain thoroughly. Combine the drained rice and 3 cups of the chicken broth in a 3-quart casserole with a tight-fitting lid. Cover and bake for 1½ hours, checking the cooking liquid after 1 hour. If more is needed, add a little water or broth and fluff with a fork. At the end of the baking time, the rice should be moist, not dry. Set the covered baked rice aside.

At least 45 minutes before serving, combine the apricots, raisins, and currants in a medium-size bowl. Bring the remaining cup of broth to a boil and pour over the fruit. Let the fruit stand until softened, about 30 minutes.

Melt the butter in a medium-size skillet over medium heat, then add the onion and cook, stirring frequently, until softened. Core the apples and cut them into ¼-inch cubes. Uncover the baked rice and add the onion, apple, and fruits with the soaking liquid. Mix gently until well blended. Taste and add salt, if needed. Turn the dressing into a serving dish. Serve lukewarm or at room temperature.

YIELD: ABOUT 12 SERVINGS, ½ CUP PER SERVING

Note: To make 6 servings, this recipe may be halved. Bake the rice in a 1½-quart baking dish, checking after 45 minutes, for a total baking time of about 1 hour.

ROASTED WINTER VEGETABLES

This recipe is very similar to the Winter-Vegetable Stuffing that appears on page 164. Actually, the idea for the stuffing came from this recipe, and not the other way around. If you love winter vegetables, and particularly if rich, creamy vegetable mixtures leave you cold, this is a good, natural way to serve them. There are no exact measurements. You'll have to roast the vegetables by the seat of your pants, so to speak, but it's hard to go wrong, and you'll really feel that you've created something special when these aromatic vegetables come out of the oven.

Besides two ovens (if you plan to serve this for Thanksgiving dinner) you will need an assortment of winter root vegetables, such as potatoes, carrots, celery, fennel, onions, garlic, celeriac, winter squash, parsnips, turnips—whatever appeals to you or is available that has about the same density and character. Trim, scrape, or peel those vegetables that need it and cut them all into large bite-size pieces. Preheat the oven to 350°F. Melt a hunk of butter in a large roasting pan. Toss the vegetables around in the butter to coat them and then add a very little bit of chicken or beef broth and maybe some wine, just enough to moisten everything generously. You can add more later if you think the vegetables are drying out too much. If you like, you can stir a tablespoon or so of tomato paste into the broth, which will help the vegetables to brown later on. Add salt and pepper to taste and a generous sprinkling of crumbled thyme or oregano. Bake the vegetables for about an hour, stirring frequently, until they are tender and lightly browned. Stir in a handful of chopped fresh parsley just before serving. I also like to sprinkle a little balsamic vinegar over my own serving of the vegetables.

MARYLAND SCALLOPED OYSTERS

This is a dish that you may very well not want to consider for Thanksgiving dinner if you're not positive that there will be a fair number of oyster lovers with hearty appetites. However, it's about the nicest oyster recipe I know, and is a very American addition to the Thanksgiving dinner menu. The leftovers, gently reheated, are also wonderful the next day. Be ready to put this into the oven the moment the turkey comes out.

2 slices white bread, crusts removed and
whirled in a blender or food processor
to make soft bread crumbs (1 cup)
2 cups crumbled soda crackers
¼ pound (1 stick) butter, melted

2 pints stewing oysters with liquor,
reserving ½ cup of the liquor
Salt and freshly ground black pepper to
taste
½ cup heavy or whipping cream

Preheat the oven to 400°F. In a medium-size bowl, toss together the bread and cracker crumbs and butter. Pick over the oysters, removing any bits of shell. Sprinkle about 1 cup of the crumb mixture evenly over the bottom of a greased 1½-quart baking dish. Add a layer of half the oysters and a sprinkling of salt and pepper. Add another layer of about ½ cup of the crumb mixture and then a layer of the remaining oysters. Sprinkle with salt and pepper and finish with a layer of the remaining crumbs on top. Mix the reserved oyster liquor and cream together and gently pour over the whole thing. Bake for about 20 minutes, or until hot and bubbly.

YIELD: 6 SERVINGS

Note: This recipe may be doubled. In that case, use a 3- or 4-quart baking dish.

YORKSHIRE PUDDING

If you have opted to serve roast beef on Thanksgiving, this is the traditional English accompaniment. In the old days, the beef was cooked on a spit in the fireplace with a pan beneath it to catch the drippings. It was in this pan of hot drippings that the original Yorkshire pudding was cooked. When the batter was poured into the hot drippings, it puffed up gloriously as it baked. As you might suspect, Yorkshire pudding is a close relative of the popover, which is made essentially the same way, except that it's baked in muffin cups.

1½ cups all-purpose flour
¾ teaspoon salt
¾ cup milk

3 large eggs, beaten until frothy
¾ cup water
½ cup beef drippings

Mix the flour and salt together in a medium-size bowl until well blended. Make a well in the center of the flour mixture, pour in the milk, and stir together with a whisk until thoroughly combined. Beat the eggs into the batter. Add the water and beat again until frothy. Let the batter stand for at least 1 hour or, covered, overnight in the refrigerator. Beat again before using. When the roast beef has reached the desired degree of doneness, remove it from the oven and immediately increase the oven temperature to 400°F. Measure out ½ cup of the beef drippings from the roasting pan and pour into a 13- × 9-inch baking dish. Place the baking dish in the oven for about 10 minutes, or until the drippings are sizzling hot. Immediately pour the batter into the hot drippings and return the baking dish to the oven. Bake for 25 to 30 minutes, or until the sides of the pudding have risen and are crisp and golden brown. The beef should be carved and served when the pudding comes out of the oven. Serve immediately, straight from the baking dish, cut into squares.

YIELD: 8 SERVINGS

THE JEWELS OF THANKSGIVING: MOLDED SALADS

I work with some very talented food professionals with very sophisticated palates, and, of course, I queried each and every one of them about what they cooked for Thanksgiving dinner. Almost every one admitted to serving some sweet molded salad, a holdover in most cases from childhood, and an integral part of the menu that they would not dream of leaving out.

Here are several molded salads that I have enjoyed, in case you can't find the one you so fondly remember.

A small bowl of mayonnaise is the traditional accompaniment for most molded salads which were almost always served on or surrounded by iceberg lettuce.

LIB CURTIS'S GREEK SALAD

You tell me why this is called "Greek" salad, but that's what it says at the top of the loose-leaf page on which the recipe appears in Lib's handwriting. Stephanie, Lib's daughter, says her mother used to serve this every year when the whole family gathered for Thanksgiving, and she still does if there are enough people to eat it. Lib makes the salad in a 13- × 9-inch glass dish and cuts it into squares to serve, but we thought it looked prettier turned out of a decorative shallow mold.

One 3-ounce envelope cherry gelatin	*1 cup sour cream*
Two 3-ounce envelopes unflavored gelatin	*1 teaspoon vanilla extract*
¼ cup cold water	*One 3-ounce envelope lime gelatin*
2½ cups milk	*One 3-ounce envelope orange gelatin*
1¼ cups sugar	*One 3-ounce envelope lemon gelatin*

Make the cherry gelatin according to package directions, using all of the boiling water called for, *but only ½ cup of the cold water.* Pour into a shallow 10- or 12-cup mold that has been well oiled. Refrigerate until firm, about 1 hour. In a small bowl or cup, soften the unflavored gelatin in the cold water. In a medium-size saucepan, heat the milk and sugar over low heat just until the milk steams. Remove from the heat and add the softened gelatin, stirring for 3 or 4 minutes to completely dissolve the gelatin. Stir in the sour cream and vanilla until well blended and no lumps of sour cream remain. Set aside to cool to room temperature. Pour about 1¼ cups of the cooled milk mixture over the firm cherry gelatin and refrigerate until set. Continue layering the remaining gelatin flavors that have been made according to package directions, using all of the boiling water called for, *but only ½ cup of the cold water*, and ¼-cup portions of the milk mixture, refrigerating each time to firm, ending with a layer of gelatin. To unmold the gelatin, run a sharp knife around the edge, then dip the mold into warm water for a few seconds. Position a serving plate over the molded gelatin. Firmly grasp both the mold and the plate and invert the two. Remove the mold from the gelatin. Serve with dinner, cut into wedges.

YIELD: 12 TO 16 SERVINGS

Note: If the mold is shallow, each layer will set in about 30 minutes and the milk mixture can be left at room temperature until the layers are completed. However, if the mold is deep or if you have to stop for any length of time, the milk mixture should be refrigerated. Return it to its liquid state by rewarming it briefly in a microwave oven or over hot, not boiling, water. It will then need to cool to room temperature before continuing with making the salad.

CRANBERRY-WALNUT JEWEL

My friends Doug Flynn and Al Bolton, who have contributed a number of recipes in this book, served a salad similar to this one at a party they gave years ago while they were still our neighbors in New York. I still remember the salad, but when I asked Doug for the recipe he couldn't find it. Between the two of us, we came up with this one, which we both think is quite similar.

1½ cups fresh cranberries, rinsed and
    picked over
½ cup sugar
Two 3-ounce envelopes lemon gelatin
¼ teaspoon salt
2 cups boiling water
1½ cups cold water

1 tablespoon fresh lemon juice
¼ teaspoon ground cinnamon
⅛ teaspoon ground cloves
1 large navel orange, peeled, sectioned,
    and diced, or 1 cup diced apple
1 cup toasted (see pages 6–7) chopped
    walnuts

Place the cranberries in a food processor and chop into very fine pieces using a few on/off pulses, being careful not to puree the berries. Scrape into a small bowl. Stir in the sugar until well blended and set aside. Stir the gelatin and salt into the boiling water in a large bowl until the gelatin is dissolved. Stir in the cold water, lemon juice, cinnamon, and cloves. Chill until thickened to about the consistency of unbeaten egg white, about 30 minutes. Fold in the cranberry mixture, diced orange, and nuts. Spoon into a well-oiled 6-cup mold and chill until firm, about 8 hours or overnight. To unmold the gelatin, run a sharp knife around the edge, then dip the mold into warm water for a few seconds. Position a serving plate over the molded gelatin. Firmly grasp both the mold and the plate and invert the two. Remove the mold from the gelatin.

YIELD: 8 TO 12 SERVINGS

VIRGINIA CUCUMBER MOLD

This is a nice mold, not quite as sweet as some of them. I like it very much served with ham or other smoked meats.

One 3-ounce envelope lime gelatin
1 cup boiling water
2 teaspoons white vinegar
¼ teaspoon salt

2 large cucumbers, peeled if waxed,
    shredded, and drained in a colander for
    about 30 minutes
1 small onion, shredded (¼ cup)
1 cup sour cream
½ cup mayonnaise

Sprinkle the gelatin into a large bowl, add the boiling water, and stir until dissolved. Stir in the remaining ingredients, mixing until completely blended. Pour into a well-oiled 6-cup mold, then refrigerate until firm, about 8 hours or overnight. To unmold the gelatin, run a sharp knife around the edge, then dip the mold into warm water for a few seconds. Position a serving plate over the molded gelatin. Firmly grasp both the mold and the plate and invert the two. Remove the mold from the gelatin.

YIELD: 8 SERVINGS

PINEAPPLE CREAM

This is the molded salad that we serve every Christmas Eve to accompany a country ham and scalloped oysters, but it's also very good with turkey.

One 3-ounce envelope lemon gelatin
1 teaspoon salt
1 cup boiling water
1 tablespoon cider vinegar
1 tablespoon Worcestershire sauce

1 tablespoon grated onion
1 cup sour cream
¼ cup mayonnaise
Two 20-ounce cans crushed pineapple,
  very well drained

Sprinkle the gelatin and salt into a large bowl, add the boiling water, and stir until dissolved. Chill until the gelatin is the consistency of unbeaten egg white, about 1 hour. Beat the thickened gelatin with a rotary beater until smooth, about 1 minute. Add the vinegar, Worcestershire, onion, sour cream, and mayonnaise and beat until well blended. Fold in the drained pineapple, then pour into a well-oiled 4-cup mold and chill until set, about 8 hours or overnight. To unmold the gelatin, run a sharp knife around the edge, then dip the mold into warm water for a few seconds. Position a serving plate over the molded gelatin. Firmly grasp both the mold and the plate and invert the two. Remove the mold from the gelatin.

YIELD: 8 SERVINGS

WALDORF-SALAD MOLD

I can't help wondering what Oscar, the maître d'hôtel at the Waldorf-Astoria Hotel who invented the original Waldorf Salad, would have thought of this.

Two 3-ounce envelopes lemon gelatin
1 teaspoon salt
⅔ cup boiling water
3 tablespoons fresh lemon juice
2 small Red Delicious apples
1 cup heavy or whipping cream

½ cup mayonnaise
¾ cup seedless grapes, cut in half
3 or 4 celery ribs, finely chopped (1½ cups)
¾ cup toasted (see pages 6–7) chopped
  pecans

Sprinkle the gelatin and salt into a large bowl, add the boiling water, and stir until dissolved. Stir in 2 tablespoons of the lemon juice and chill until the gelatin is the consistency of unbeaten egg white, about 30 minutes. Core and dice the apples, then toss them with the remaining lemon juice to prevent darkening. Whip the cream in a cold medium-size bowl with cold beaters until stiff peaks form when the beaters are lifted. Stir the mayonnaise into the thickened gelatin, then add the grapes, celery, and nuts, stirring gently until well distributed. Fold in the whipped cream until no streaks remain. Spoon the gelatin mixture into a well-oiled 8-cup mold and chill until set, about 8 hours or overnight. To unmold the gelatin, run a sharp knife around the edge, then dip the mold into warm water for a few seconds. Position a serving plate over the molded gelatin. Firmly grasp both the mold and the plate and invert the two. Remove the mold from the gelatin.

YIELD: 8 TO 12 SERVINGS

EIGHT

Stuffings and Dressings

❦

THE SOUL OF THANKSGIVING DINNER

The most important thing to know about making poultry stuffing—or any stuffing, for that matter—is that it is not an exact science. Although volumes have undoubtedly been written about achieving the harmonious balance of flavors and textures that are necessary for the so-called perfect stuffing, my feeling is that these savory fillings are great places for novice cooks to play around and improvise without creating any serious culinary crises.

My own formal foray into the preparation of Thanksgiving dinner was making the stuffing. I was about fourteen, and I'd been watching my mother mix bread stuffing since I was first able to see over the kitchen counter. At the time I didn't understand why the bread had to be dry, or why my mother used her hands rather than a spoon for mixing. I just did what she did, confidently tasting as I went along. The stuffing turned out just fine—and I was hooked on cooking forever.

A stuffing can be as simple as sticking a few slices of apple or onion into the cavity of a chicken or some other bird for flavor. But more often, especially in connection with Thanksgiving, the word brings to mind moist, spoon-shaped dollops of a lovingly prepared mixture of bread, celery, onions, parsley, and butter, bursting with the pungent aroma of usually too much poultry seasoning. The ingredients will vary from family to family, and there may be the substitution of corn bread for white bread, or the addition of such traditional favorites as chestnuts or sausage or oysters, but then Americans aren't known for being particularly innovative when it comes to food on the Thanksgiving table.

For all the talk about it, the main functions of stuffing are to enhance flavor, prevent moisture from escaping, and help preserve the shape of the bird.

I filled a lot of turkeys before I finally realized that stuffings have four basic and interrelated components:

150

A base. Bread is the most common, especially for stuffings that are intended for the Thanksgiving turkey and other poultry. But cooked rice, pasta, grains, cooked and raw vegetables, as well as fruit and even meat, are other, less frequent choices, depending on what's to be stuffed.

Texture. Vegetables, fresh and dried fruits, nuts, meat, and other crunchy or chewy ingredients provide the critical contrast.

Flavorings. Herbs and spices, salt, pepper, and citrus fruit rinds are the most typical. Butter and other fats are also considered flavorings, and are excellent flavor carriers as well.

A binder. Water, milk or cream, broth, eggs, fruit juice, and wine, for example, pull the ingredients together, figuratively and literally, and can contribute more than a little flavor of their own.

Ingredients: Creating the Perfect Balance

When choosing the ingredients for stuffing, the idea is to achieve a pleasing balance of tastes and textures that will enhance the flavor of whatever is to be stuffed.

The first consideration is whether the stuffing should be *moist* or *dry*. Generally, but not always, a moist stuffing is used for those things that will not contribute much moisture of their own. The opposite is true for dry stuffings.

Turkey, especially the white meat, which tends to be on the dry side, no matter what the advertising people say, benefits enormously from an extremely moist, if not dripping stuffing. The juices from the turkey as it roasts will provide plenty of flavor, but not much in the way of moisture. (The fat that accumulates in the pan is mostly from the dark meat, which is *beneath* the stuffing.) Goose and duck, on the other hand, with their juicy dark meat and thick layer of self-basting fat just beneath the breast skin, will add lots of moisture and fat, so if the stuffing is too wet to begin with, it will simply turn into mush.

Flavor is another key factor. The subtle taste of turkey and chicken is easily over-powered by stuffings that are too intensely or dramatically seasoned, but because these birds add very little fat of their own to the filling, the stuffings for them usually benefit from some enrichment in the form of butter, sausage, or other high-fat ingredient.

The rich flavor of goose and duck stands up well to more assertive fillings. Tart ingredients and acidic binders tend to cut and complement the full, fatty flavor of these birds.

About the Ingredients

Bread or other base. When considering the amounts of ingredients for stuffing, figure on a ratio of roughly four parts base to one part texture and other ingredients.

Use good bread. Homemade and homemade-style breads have a firm texture that holds up well, but can sometimes be too sweet, so select these breads carefully. Breads, or bread cubes, that are packaged especially for stuffing seem, at least to me, to have no flavor at all. For my own bread stuffings, I usually use a high-quality sandwich bread, and I usually leave the crust on to give the stuffing a more interesting texture. During the weeks before Thanksgiving I hoard bread that has passed its prime, tightly wrapped, in the freezer.

If you're ambitious and want to experience the satisfaction of serving a real, from-scratch dinner, you might like to have a go at baking your own bread for the stuffing. The recipe on pages 156–57 makes two loaves of tasty white bread—one for the turkey and one for eating, preferably while it's still fresh from the oven.

Make sure that the bread is bone dry or close to it. The "day-old" bread that older recipes call for can't possibly be compared to today's bread, which stays "fresh" for days. If the bread is not dry, the liquid ingredients will not be absorbed properly, causing the bread to fall apart and the stuffing to be unappetizingly gummy.

The best way to dry bread is to spread it out on baking sheets or waxed paper, either in slices or cubes, and leave it uncovered for a day or two, turning every now and then. Or you can place the bread in the oven at a *very low* setting (you don't want toast), turning it frequently until it's dry.

Eggs. I used to taste my stuffing as I was making it, confident that my clean, uncracked raw eggs posed no health hazard. But because of the salmonella bacteria that is now inherently present in a relatively small number of eggs, I don't recommend doing that any more, although I expect that it's only a matter of time before the egg producers find an economical way to test the egg-laying flocks and are able to guarantee some, and eventually all, eggs to be salmonella-free. For now, the only way around the problem is to taste the stuffing before the eggs are added.

Fortunately, eggs aren't mandatory in stuffing, and as a matter of fact, some cooks believe that eggs make the stuffing pasty and prefer not to use them. In the recipes that follow, eggs are always optional, although if you choose not to include them you may want to increase the butter or other fat to make up for the fat provided by the egg yolk.

Onions, celery, and parsley. Unless the recipe calls for some other variety, ordinary yellow onions are the best choice. Select those that are very hard with dry, papery skin. One medium-size onion yields about ½ cup of chopped onion.

Choose heavy stalks of celery with good green color. The outer, more flavorful ribs are excellent for stuffing. Save the tender inside ribs and the hearts for the relish tray. Two to three celery ribs yield about 1 cup of chopped celery. Also, be sure to include some of the tasty celery leaves. (By the way, there's no need to scrape the celery if it's going to be chopped.)

Curly or flatleaf, it doesn't matter which parsley you choose as long as it's fresh (as compared to dried). The best way to store parsley is to rinse it, shake it dry, and stick it in a glass of water like a bouquet of flowers. Cover loosely with a plastic bag, and the parsley will stay fresh for days. Or you can rinse the parsley, shake it dry, wrap it in paper towels to absorb any excess moisture, and store it in the refrigerator crisper drawer.

I prefer to chop the vegetables for stuffing by hand with a chef's knife, but you can certainly use a food processor for the job as long as you're careful not to pulverize the vegetables.

Butter. For Thanksgiving stuffing, I never use anything but the real thing. Margarine can be substituted.

Poultry seasoning and herbs. Contrary to popular belief, dried herbs do not last forever, so replace them often, every year or so. This is particularly true of poultry seasoning, which is actually a blend of ground sage, rosemary, thyme, marjoram, savory, or other herbs, seeds, and salts, depending on who makes it. My personal preference is Bell's poultry seasoning, which is still packaged in the same friendly, little yellow cardboard box that I remember from my childhood. Poultry seasoning, in particular, loses its pungent flavor rapidly.

When using dried herb leaves, crumble them between your thumb and forefinger to bruise them and help release their flavorful oils.

And, by all means, if you can obtain fresh herbs when dried herbs are called for, use them. You will need three to four times as much of a fresh herb as dried.

I prefer to use freshly ground pepper, which has a coarser texture than prepared ground pepper, and certainly more flavor.

Nuts. Toasting brings out their best texture and flavor. There is simply no comparison between toasted and untoasted nuts, toasted nuts being much superior in every way. I almost never use nuts without toasting them first (see pages 6–7).

Too Much Stuffing, or Not Enough

Earlier on I wrote that stuffing making is not an exact science. This is never truer than when trying to decide how much is needed of what to have the final amount of prepared stuffing and the poultry cavity into which it goes come out even. It almost never will.

As a rule, you will need a generous ½ cup of prepared stuffing for each pound of poultry to be stuffed. Allowing this amount will give you little or no stuffing left over. One cup of prepared stuffing per pound of poultry weight will provide generous leftovers, which can be baked on the side in a greased pan, and which you may actually need if you're planning on getting the maximum number of servings from your turkey or other poultry at the Thanksgiving dinner.

Although it's not precise, this is my formula for getting things to come out right: One 1-ounce slice of bread per pound of poultry weight will yield about ½ cup of prepared stuffing and no leftovers; two 1-ounce slices of bread per pound of poultry weight will yield about a cup of prepared stuffing and fairly generous leftovers. This works beautifully with rather straightforward stuffing recipes, such as the Classic American Bread Stuffing on pages 158–59, but will have to be adjusted somewhat if there are other ingredients that will add much bulk, or if the bread weighs much more or much less than an ounce.

Mixing with a Light Touch

Making stuffing consists mainly of assembling the ingredients that go into it. Most often, the stuffing starts with the base ingredient, to which the other ingredients are added. The "moist" ingredients, such as chopped vegetables, cooked or uncooked, are added first, to moisten the base just enough to allow the seasonings to stick to it and the base ingredient and not fall into the bottom of the bowl. The liquid ingredients go in last. The amount of the final liquid ingredient is usually variable so that the finished stuffing is the right consistency.

Use a *big mixing* bowl that will give you lots of room to toss. If you don't have a big enough bowl, then use the roasting pan.

The best way to mix stuffing is with your hands, especially toward the end where the "feel" of it is so important. If you want to use a mixing utensil, a large wooden salad fork works well. While mixing, let the ingredients sort of fall between your fingers, and use a light touch. A lot of mixing and handling will cause the base, especially if it's a bread base, to break down, and the whole thing will become an amalgamated mess. The ingredients should remain more or less identifiable.

Matters of Safety

On pages 195–96 I have gone into matters of food safety in some depth as they relate to Thanksgiving dinner. But again, briefly, the cozy environment of a warm, moist, usually protein-rich stuffing is the ideal place for bacteria to multiply, so it's important not to mix the stuffing until just before it's put into the bird and then into the oven. To save time, all of the ingredients can be prepared ahead and held separately, but, please, mix, stuff, and roast at the very last minute.

Baking Leftover Stuffing

Stuffing baked outside the poultry cavity will never taste quite the same as that baked within, but there are a couple of tricks that will make it nearly as flavorful.

I don't recommend baking extra stuffing wrapped in aluminum foil unless it's just a handful or two. Instead, use a well-buttered casserole, into which the stuffing is spooned and not too tightly packed. You should also add a little more liquid to this portion of the stuffing since it will obviously not benefit from the juices the bird would provide. Cover the casserole tightly.

Because stuffing is essentially precooked, leftovers need only to be baked until heated through. At 325°F, 6 cups of stuffing will require about 1 hour of baking time; 3 cups will take about 45 minutes. I usually put the leftover stuffing in the oven along with the turkey during the last part of the roasting time, and after it has baked for a while I drizzle a spoonful or two of the juices and fat from the roasting pan over it for flavor. If the stuffing is not to be served with dinner, cool it down just a little, then refrigerate it promptly and use within a couple of days.

Leftover stuffing, or most leftover stuffing anyway, can be formed into balls and baked separately. They can be served as a side dish or even used to garnish the bird. Measure the stuffing by ¼ to ½ cupfuls and shape between your palms to make balls. Place in a greased baking pan and bake in a preheated 350°F oven for 20 to 30 minutes, or until heated through and lightly browned.

For quick reference

One 1-ounce slice bread — 1 cup cubed or broken bread
1 cup bread, plus other ingredients = ½ cup prepared stuffing
2 cups bread, plus other ingredients = 1 cup prepared stuffing
2 or 3 celery ribs = 1 cup chopped celery
1 medium-size yellow onion = ½ cup chopped onion
1 large yellow onion = 1 cup chopped onion
½ to ¾ cup prepared stuffing per pound of poultry weight = no leftovers
¾ to 1 cup prepared stuffing per pound of poultry weight = some stuffing left over to bake separately

Stuffing Mixes

I've used my share of stuffing mixes, and there's a lot to be said for them, especially if you're in a hurry and need only a small amount. However, since these are little more than seasoned dried bread cubes or crumbs, stuffing mixes are pretty ho-hum unless you take the time to add the optional ingredients that most of them call for on the package. In the end, all that's actually saved is the time it takes to dry the bread. Mixes can also be fairly pricey if you're stuffing a big bird.

I think most cooks resort to stuffing mixes, not so much to save time or labor, but simply because the thought of making stuffing from scratch the first time is scary. The recipes that follow should convince even the most timid cook that the mystique surrounding stuffing making is nonsense. However, if this is your first time out, you might like to do a dry run a week or two before Thanksgiving, using a whole broiler-fryer chicken as a stand-in for some of the stuffing and baking the rest on the side.

There is plenty of room in our workaday lives for convenience foods, and for many of us, who are already juggling too many balls, they are a godsend. But because the intent of this book is to present the familiar and traditional kinds of recipes that Mother or Grandma used to make for this one special day, I've decided not to include stuffing mixes. If you choose to use a mix, take the time to add some fresh ingredients, tasting discriminatingly, since most of the mixes with which I'm familiar are already somewhat overseasoned and oversalted.

Stuffing Versus Dressing

The difference between stuffing and dressing usually depends on who's being asked. To some, the terms are completely interchangeable, but if you ask me, stuffing goes into something and dressing, although usually of a similar nature, is served on the side.

Virtually all of the stuffings given here can be baked in a casserole and served as a dressing, if you like. A few stuffing-type dressings that are most often served on the side, such as the New Orleans Oyster Dressing (page 182) and Pennsylvania Dutch Mashed-Potato Dressing (page 181), follow the stuffings at the end of the chapter.

HOMEMADE WHITE BREAD FOR STUFFING

This recipe is the creation of my friend Carol Gelles, who used it in her book, *The Complete Whole Grain Cookbook* (New York: Donald I. Fine, Inc.), and who very kindly consented to allow me to use it here. Fortunately, the recipe makes two loaves, which you will probably need, since nothing draws people into the kitchen like the yeasty aroma of bread baking. Fresh from the oven and while it's still slightly warm, this bread is simply wonderful when it's spread with butter and honey.

½ cup very warm water (105° to 115°F)
1 teaspoon sugar
2 envelopes active dry yeast
5 to 5½ cups all-purpose flour

1 tablespoon salt
1 cup milk
¾ cup water

In a glass measuring cup, stir together the warm water and sugar. Stir in the yeast and set the cup aside until about ¼ inch of bubbly white foam forms on top. (This is called proofing, and if it doesn't happen it means the yeast has not been activated, usually because the water was too hot or too cold, or the yeast is out of date.) In a large bowl, mix together 3 cups of the flour and the salt. Stir in the yeast mixture, milk, and water. Stir in 1½ cups more of the flour to make a soft dough. Turn out onto a floured surface and knead in enough of the remaining flour to make a dough that is satiny and springy and no longer sticky. Place the dough in a large greased bowl, turning the dough once to grease the top. Cover and let rise in a warm, draft-free spot until doubled in bulk, about 1½ hours. Punch the dough down and cut it in half. Form the dough into two 8-inch loaves and place in two greased 8- × 4½- × 2¾-inch loaf pans. Cover and let rise again until doubled in bulk, about 50 minutes. Preheat the oven to 350°F. Bake for 50 minutes, or until the tops of the loaves are golden brown and sound hollow when tapped on the top. Remove the bread from the pans immediately and cool on wire racks. For a soft crust, brush the tops with melted butter as soon as the loaves have been removed from the oven. Slice when still slightly warm.

YIELD: 2 LOAVES, ABOUT 14 SLICES EACH

BASIC CORN BREAD FOR STUFFING

Don't try to save time by using ready-made corn bread or a corn bread mix. They're often too moist and too sweet. Make this corn bread ahead of time, if it's more convenient, and freeze it, tightly wrapped or in a plastic bag. Thaw the unwrapped corn bread in the refrigerator for several hours. Since this is a dry corn bread, intended to be used for stuffing, it's ready as soon as it comes from the oven and no further drying is necessary.

1 cup yellow cornmeal

1 cup all-purpose flour

4 teaspoons baking powder

1 teaspoon salt

¼ teaspoon freshly ground black pepper

1 cup buttermilk

1 large egg

⅓ cup vegetable oil

Preheat the oven to 425°F. Butter an 8- or 9-inch-square baking pan and set it aside. Combine the cornmeal, flour, baking powder, salt, and pepper in a large bowl with a wire whisk. Stir in the buttermilk, egg, and oil until the mixture is just combined. Do not overmix. Scrape the batter into the prepared pan. Bake for about 20 minutes, or until the top of the bread springs back when lightly touched. Remove from the oven and cool in the pan on a wire rack. If not using immediately, cover tightly and set aside until ready to proceed with the stuffing.

YIELD: 6 CUPS ½-INCH CUBED OR CRUMBLED CORN BREAD

CLASSIC AMERICAN BREAD STUFFING WITH VARIATIONS

FOR TURKEY OR CHICKEN

My grandmother was an excellent cook. This is her recipe, which I'm told she got from her mother, who was also a very good cook. It's the first stuffing I ever made and the one I use almost every year for Thanksgiving, at least in one turkey, since I often roast two smaller birds rather than one big one. We like it plain, with lots of butter and sage, and I always use the eggs. The recipe may be doubled, halved, or even quartered. If doubling the recipe, start with only one and a half times the amount of poultry seasoning; if quartering the recipe, use one egg.

Twenty-four 1-ounce slices white bread, dried and broken into postage stamp-size pieces

4 to 6 celery ribs, finely chopped (2 cups)

1 large onion, finely chopped (1 cup)

½ cup chopped fresh parsley

1 tablespoon poultry seasoning or to taste

1 teaspoon salt or to taste

½ teaspoon freshly ground black pepper or to taste

2 large eggs, beaten (optional)

¼ pound (1 stick) butter, melted (see note on page 159)

½ cup warm water

Mix the bread, celery, onion, parsley, poultry seasoning, salt, and pepper together in a large bowl, tossing with your hands until well mixed. Drizzle the eggs over the bread mixture and toss again. Mix the butter and warm water together and drizzle over the bread mixture. Toss again until well mixed. Continue to add more warm water, a little at a time, until the stuffing is moist and just holds together when lightly pressed between the palms of your hands.

YIELD: ABOUT 12 CUPS, OR ENOUGH TO fill a 14- TO 16-POUND TURKEY WITH 4 TO 5 CUPS LEFT OVER TO BAKE SEPARATELY

Note: If omitting the eggs, you may want to add another 3 to 4 tablespoons of butter to make up for the fat in the egg yolk.

Oyster Stuffing: Add 1½ pints oysters, drained and coarsely chopped, to the bread along with the celery and onions. Some of the oyster liquor can be substituted for the water.

Chestnut Stuffing: Add 1½ pounds (weight in shell) roasted chestnuts (see page 2) to the bread along with the celery and onions.

Sausage Stuffing: Cook 1 pound bulk pork sausage in a large skillet, breaking it up with the side of a spoon until no pink remains. Drain and add to the bread along with the celery and onions. Some of the sausage fat may be substituted for the butter.

Mushroom Stuffing: Finely chop ½ pound regular white mushrooms and ½ pound shiitake mushroom caps. Melt 4 tablespoons (½ stick) butter in a large skillet over medium-high heat. When hot, add the mushrooms and cook, stirring frequently, until most of the liquid has evaporated, about 15 minutes. Add the skillet mixture to the bread along with the celery and onions.

Corn Bread Stuffing: Substitute corn bread for all or half of the white bread.

BACON AND OYSTER STUFFING

FOR TURKEY

In the South, ham and oysters go together like Frick and Frack. If you happen to have some stray bits of ham in the refrigerator, especially a country-cured ham or, best of all, a Smithfield ham, by all means substitute it for the Canadian bacon.

½ pound (2 sticks) butter
½ pound Canadian bacon or slab
  bacon, diced
2 or 3 celery ribs, finely chopped (1 cup)
1 large onion, finely chopped (1 cup)
4 cloves garlic, minced
1 to 1½ pints oysters, drained, the liquor
  reserved, and coarsely chopped

Twenty-four 1-ounce slices firm white
  bread, dried, crusts removed, and
  broken into postage stamp-size pieces
3 tablespoons chopped fresh thyme or
  1 tablespoon dried leaves, crumbled
1 teaspoon salt
½ teaspoon freshly ground black pepper
½ cup warm water

Heat the butter in a large skillet until melted. Pour off and set aside ½ cup. Add the bacon, celery, and onion to the butter remaining in the skillet and cook over medium-high heat, stirring frequently, until the vegetables are tender-crisp. Stir in the garlic and cook, stirring, for 2 minutes more. Stir in the reserved oyster liquor and remove from the heat.

In a large bowl, combine the bread and the bacon mixture. Stir in the oysters and sprinkle with the thyme, salt, and pepper. Toss to thoroughly combine. Mix the remaining melted butter with the water and drizzle over the bread mixture. Toss again until well mixed. If necessary, add more warm water, a little at a time, until the stuffing is moist and holds together when lightly pressed between the palms of your hands.

YIELD: ABOUT 12 CUPS, OR ENOUGH TO FILL A 14- TO 16-POUND TURKEY WITH ABOUT 4 TO 5 CUPS LEFT OVER TO BAKE SEPARATELY

SAUSAGE, MINCEMEAT, AND CORN BREAD STUFFING

FOR TURKEY

Mincemeat gives this stuffing an interesting touch of sweetness and the sausage keeps it moist. The combination of sweet and salty is something I particularly like, a hangover from my years of living among the Pennsylvania Dutch, I suppose.

1 pound bulk pork sausage
3 or 4 celery ribs, finely chopped (1½ cups)
1 large onion, finely chopped (1 cup)
½ cup finely chopped green bell pepper
1 recipe Basic Corn Bread for Stuffing
  (pages 157–58), cut into ½-inch cubes
  (6 cups)

1⅓ cups mincemeat (half of a
  28-ounce jar)
1½ teaspoons poultry seasoning or to taste
¾ to 1 cup chicken broth (see pages 2–4)

In a large skillet, cook the sausage over medium-high heat, breaking it up with the side of a spoon until no pink remains. Remove with a slotted spoon to drain on paper towels. Drain off all but ¼ cup of the sausage drippings from the pan. Add the celery, onion, and green pepper and cook over medium-high heat, stirring frequently, until tender-crisp.

In a large bowl, combine the sausage, the skillet vegetables, corn bread, mincemeat, and poultry seasoning. Toss to mix thoroughly. Add about half of the chicken broth. Toss again until well mixed. Continue to add more chicken broth, a little at a time, until the stuffing is moist and just holds together when lightly pressed between the palms of your hands.

YIELD: ABOUT 8 CUPS, OR ENOUGH TO FILL A 14- TO 16-POUND TURKEY

CALVADOS RYE STUFFING

FOR TURKEY

A friend who spent some years living in the French province of Normandy, where apples, Calvados (apple brandy), and cream are daily staples, created this recipe. The Calvados provides an absolutely heady aroma when the stuffing is spooned from the cavity.

¼ pound (1 stick) butter
4 to 6 celery ribs, finely chopped (2 cups)
1 large onion, finely chopped (1 cup)
6 Golden Delicious apples, peeled, cored, and chopped (about 6 cups)
18 slices dark or light seedless rye bread, dried and broken into postage stamp size pieces (about 18 cups)

2 teaspoons dried sage leaves, crumbled
1 teaspoon salt
½ teaspoon freshly ground black pepper
⅔ cup light cream or half-and-half
⅓ to ½ cup Calvados or other apple brandy

Heat the butter in a large skillet until melted. Pour off ¼ cup and set aside. Add the celery, onion, and apples to the butter remaining in the skillet and cook over medium-high heat, stirring frequently, until tender-crisp. Combine the skillet mixture, bread, sage, salt, and pepper in a large bowl and toss gently until well mixed. Drizzle the cream over the ingredients and toss again. Add the reserved ¼ cup melted butter and ⅓ cup of the Calvados. Toss gently until well blended. If the mixture seems dry, add more Calvados or warm water, a little at a time, until the mixture is moist and holds together when lightly pressed between the palms of your hands.

YIELD: 12 CUPS, OR ENOUGH TO FILL A 14- TO 16-POUND TURKEY WITH 4 TO 5 CUPS
LEFT OVER TO BAKE SEPARATELY

FRESH SAGE, SAUSAGE, AND APPLE STUFFING

FOR TURKEY

A homey, hearty stuffing, full of old-fashioned flavors and ingredients that are so typical of autumn and Thanksgiving, and rich enough to stand on its own as a side dish.

1 pound bulk pork sausage

8 slices whole-wheat bread, dried and broken into postage stamp-size pieces

2 or 3 celery ribs, finely chopped (1 cup)

1 large onion, finely chopped (1 cup)

2 to 3 tablespoons minced fresh sage or 1 tablespoon dried leaves, crumbled

½ teaspoon caraway seeds (optional)

1 teaspoon salt

½ teaspoon freshly ground black pepper

2 Golden Delicious apples, peeled, cored, and cut into cubes (about 2 cups)

½ cup toasted (see pages 6–7) coarsely chopped walnuts

2 large eggs, beaten

¼ pound (1 stick) butter, melted

½ cup half-and-half or chicken broth (see pages 2–4)

In a large skillet, cook the sausage over medium-high heat, breaking it up with the side of a spoon until no pink remains. Remove the sausage with a slotted spoon and drain on paper towels.

In a large bowl, thoroughly mix together the sausage, bread, celery, onion, sage, caraway seeds, salt, pepper, apples, and walnuts. Drizzle the eggs and melted butter over the mixture and toss to combine. Slowly add the half-and-half, a little at a time, tossing until the mixture is very moist.

YIELD: ABOUT 10 CUPS, OR ENOUGH TO FILL A 12- TO 14-POUND TURKEY WITH 3 TO 4 CUPS LEFT OVER TO BAKE SEPARATELY

A RICH ITALIAN SAUSAGE STUFFING

FOR TURKEY

This is my Italian uncle Al Staiti's recipe. When his family came to the United States, like most newcomers they threw themselves wholeheartedly into all of our traditions and this is what his mother came up with when it was time to stuff the turkey. It is rich and delicious beyond indulgence, and because of its richness this stuffing is also wonderful baked in a casserole and served as a dressing.

1 cup heavy or whipping cream
3 cups crumbled, dry Italian bread
1 pound sweet Italian sausage (about 8
  links), removed from its casing
4 tablespoons (½ stick) butter
¾ pound baked or boiled ham, finely
  chopped
¼ pound prosciutto, finely chopped
¼ pound crimini mushrooms, finely
  chopped
¼ cup chopped fresh flatleaf parsley

¼ cup finely toasted (see pages 6–7)
  chopped pine nuts
¼ cup finely toasted (see pages 6–7)
  chopped walnuts
1½ teaspoons dried basil leaves, crumbled
½ teaspoon dried tarragon leaves,
  crumbled
⅛ teaspoon ground nutmeg
⅛ teaspoon ground ginger
1 cup grated Parmesan cheese

Drizzle the cream over the bread in a large bowl. Let stand while preparing the remaining ingredients.

Cook the sausage in a Dutch oven or other large heavy saucepan over medium-high heat, breaking it up with the side of a spoon until no pink remains. Add the butter and stir in the ham, mushrooms, parsley, pine nuts, walnuts, basil, tarragon, nutmeg, and ginger. Cook over medium heat for about 10 minutes, stirring frequently. Remove from the heat to cool. Mix the cooled sausage mixture and cheese together with the bread. Toss to thoroughly combine. If the mixture seems dry, add more cream or water, a little at a time, until the stuffing is moist and just holds together when lightly pressed between the palms of your hands.

YIELD: ABOUT 7 CUPS, OR ENOUGH TO FILL AN 8- TO 10-POUND TURKEY WITH 2 TO 3
CUPS LEFT OVER TO BAKE SEPARATELY

WILD RICE, PECAN, AND WHOLE-WHEAT BREAD STUFFING

FOR TURKEY, CHICKEN, OR CORNISH HENS

Using wild rice and pecans makes this a very patriotic stuffing since both are native American foods, pecans being our *only* native nut. The stuffing has a wholesome, natural flavor and crunchy texture that most people enjoy.

¾ cup uncooked wild rice

3¼ cups chicken broth (see pages 2–4)

6 tablespoons (¾ stick) butter

½ pound small regular white mushrooms,
   sliced (about 2 cups)

2 or 3 celery ribs, finely chopped (1 cup)

1 medium-size onion, finely chopped
   (½ cup)

½ cup toasted (see pages 6–7) chopped
   pecans

1 teaspoon poultry seasoning

8 slices whole-wheat bread, cut into
   1-inch cubes and dried

Rinse the wild rice in a sieve under cool running water and drain. In a small saucepan, bring 2¼ cups of the chicken broth to a boil. Stir in the wild rice and bring back to boiling. Reduce the heat to medium-low and simmer, covered, for 50 minutes to 1 hour, or until most of the liquid is absorbed. Remove from the heat and set aside, covered, for 10 minutes.

Heat the butter in a large skillet. Add the mushrooms, celery, onion, and pecans. Cook over medium-high heat, stirring frequently, until the vegetables are tender-crisp. Stir in the poultry seasoning and set aside.

Bring the remaining chicken broth to a boil in a small saucepan. Pour half the boiling broth into a large bowl. Add the wild rice, vegetable mixture, and bread cubes. Toss until well combined. Add the remaining chicken broth, a little at a time, until the stuffing is moist and just holds together when lightly pressed between the palms of your hands.

YIELD: ABOUT 7 CUPS, OR ENOUGH TO FILL A 12- TO 14-POUND TURKEY, A 6 TO 7-POUND CHICKEN WITH ABOUT 3 CUPS LEFT OVER TO BAKE SEPARATELY, OR 6 CORNISH HENS

WINTER-VEGETABLE STUFFING

FOR TURKEY, CHICKEN, OR CAPON

For vegetable lovers, here's a stuffing that's low in fat and high in flavor and texture. When I serve this, I usually carry out the low-fat theme with a light gravy made from the pan juices (see pages 216–17).

4 tablespoons (½ stick) butter

5 or 6 medium-size carrots, peeled and cut
into ½-inch pieces (2 cups)

1 pound small new potatoes, cut in half or
quarters if larger (2 cups)

8 to 10 shallots, cut in half (1 cup)

1 small fennel bulb, very coarsely chopped
(1 cup)

1 small knob celeriac, peeled and cut into
½-inch pieces (1 cup)

½ cup turkey or chicken broth (see
pages 2–4)

2 cups day-old French bread crumbs

½ cup chopped fresh parsley

2 tablespoons chopped fresh sage or
2 teaspoons dried leaves, crumbled

1 teaspoon dried thyme leaves, crumbled

1 teaspoon salt

¼ teaspoon freshly ground black pepper

Preheat the oven to 350°F. Melt the butter in a roasting pan in the oven. Remove the pan from the oven. Add the vegetables and broth, stirring to coat. Return the pan to the oven and cook, stirring occasionally, until the vegetables are tender and lightly browned, about 1 hour. Remove from the oven and toss in the remaining ingredients and mix until thoroughly coated.

YIELD: ABOUT 7 CUPS, OR ENOUGH TO FILL A 12- TO 14-POUND TURKEY, OR A 6-POUND CHICKEN OR CAPON WITH ABOUT 3 CUPS LEFT OVER TO BAKE SEPARATELY

DRIED TOMATO AND FRESH BASIL STUFFING

FOR TURKEY, CHICKEN, OR CAPON

It's fresh basil that gives this stuffing its special fragrance and flavor. Dried basil has a completely different taste and just doesn't do it in this case, at least not for me. As to whether this can be made at Thanksgiving, I'm banking on the fact that greenhouse basil, like parsley, is available most places year-round. The saltiness of the stuffing will depend on how salty the dried tomatoes are, and can be reduced a little by using sweet butter.

6 tablespoons (¾ stick) butter, melted

2 cups oil-packed dried tomatoes (see page
5), drained, 6 tablespoons of the oil
reserved, and chopped

8 cups ½-inch cubes Italian bread, dried
(the bread cubes should be really
hard-dry)

2 small fennel bulbs, finely chopped
(2 cups)

1 large onion, finely chopped (1 cup)

2 cloves garlic, minced

½ cup grated Parmesan cheese

1 cup chopped fresh basil leaves

½ teaspoon freshly ground black pepper

2 large eggs, beaten

¼ cup dry port wine

In a large skillet, combine 5 tablespoons of the butter and 5 tablespoons of the reserved oil over medium-high heat. When hot, add the bread cubes and cook, stirring and tossing, until they are lightly browned on all sides. Transfer the browned cubes to a large bowl. Heat the remaining butter and oil in the skillet over medium-high heat. Add the fennel and onion and cook, stirring frequently, until tender-crisp. Stir in the garlic and cook, stirring, for 2 minutes longer. Add the vegetables to the bread cubes. Stir the dried tomatoes into the mixture, along with the cheese, basil, and pepper. Drizzle the eggs and port over the mixture and toss to thoroughly combine. If necessary, add warm water, a little at a time, until the stuffing is moist and just holds together when lightly pressed between the palms of your hands.

YIELD: ABOUT 10 CUPS, OR ENOUGH TO FILL A 10- TO 12-POUND TURKEY WITH 4 TO 5 CUPS LEFT OVER TO BAKE SEPARATELY. IF STUFFING A 5- TO 7-POUND CHICKEN OR CAPON, CUT THE RECIPE INGREDIENTS IN HALF.

SPINACH AND PINE NUT STUFFING

FOR TURKEY, CHICKEN, OR CAPON

Also excellent as a side dish, but, in that case, make the final mixture a little wetter and reserve part of the Parmesan cheese to sprinkle over the top before baking.

2 tablespoons butter
4 to 6 celery ribs, finely chopped (2 cups)
2 large onions, finely chopped (2 cups)
3 or 4 cloves garlic, minced
12 slices whole-wheat bread, dried and
    broken into postage stamp-size pieces
    (6 cups)

Three 10-ounce packages frozen chopped
    spinach, thawed and squeezed dry
2 cups toasted (see pages 6–7) pine nuts
¾ cup grated Parmesan cheese
¼ teaspoon ground nutmeg
½ teaspoon salt
¼ teaspoon freshly ground black pepper
1 cup turkey or chicken broth (see
    pages 2–4)

Heat the butter in a large skillet over medium-high heat, then add the celery and onions and cook, stirring frequently, until tender-crisp. Stir in the garlic and cook, stirring, for 2 minutes more. Mix together the skillet vegetables and bread in a large bowl and toss to mix. Add the spinach, pine nuts, cheese, nutmeg, salt, and pepper and toss again. Drizzle about half of the turkey broth over the mixture and mix gently until thoroughly combined. If necessary, continue to add the remaining turkey broth, a little at a time, until the stuffing is moist and just holds together when lightly pressed between the palms of your hands.

YIELD: ABOUT 10 CUPS, OR ENOUGH TO FILL A 10- TO 12-POUND TURKEY WITH 4 TO 5 CUPS LEFT OVER TO BAKE SEPARATELY. IF STUFFING A 6-POUND CHICKEN OR CAPON, CUT THE RECIPE INGREDIENTS IN HALF, USING 1 PACKAGE OF SPINACH

HERBED CORN BREAD AND OYSTER STUFFING

FOR TURKEY, CHICKEN, CAPON, OR CORNISH HENS

The rich assortment of flavors in this stuffing doesn't overpower the delicacy of the oysters.

½ pound (2 sticks) butter

2 or 3 celery ribs, finely chopped (1 cup)

1 large onion, finely chopped (1 cup)

1 to 1½ pints oysters, drained, the liquor reserved, and coarsely chopped

¼ cup dry sherry

5 slices white bread, cut into ½-inch cubes and dried (2½ cups)

½ recipe Basic Corn Bread for Stuffing (see pages 157–58), cut into ½-inch cubes (3 cups)

1 cup chopped fresh parsley

1 tablespoon snipped fresh chives

½ teaspoon dried thyme leaves, crumbled

½ teaspoon dried rosemary leaves, crumbled

½ teaspoon dried chervil leaves, crumbled

½ teaspoon salt

½ teaspoon freshly ground black pepper

2 large eggs, beaten

Heat the butter over medium heat in a large skillet until melted. Pour off ½ cup and set aside. Add the celery and onion to the butter remaining in the skillet and cook, stirring frequently, over medium-high heat until tender-crisp. Stir in the reserved oyster liquor and the sherry and simmer over low heat for 5 minutes. Transfer the vegetable mixture to a large bowl and add the oysters, breads, parsley, and seasonings. Add the eggs and the reserved butter and toss to thoroughly combine.

YIELD: ABOUT 8 CUPS, OR ENOUGH TO FILL A 14- TO 16-POUND TURKEY, A 6- TO 7-POUND CHICKEN OR CAPON WITH ABOUT 4 CUPS LEFT OVER TO BAKE SEPARATELY, OR 6 TO 8 CORNISH HENS

CORN BREAD AND MUSHROOM STUFFING

FOR TURKEY, CHICKEN, CAPON, OR CORNISH HENS

The pleasantly bland and slightly mealy quality of corn bread is a good backdrop for mushrooms and currants. This stuffing should be very moist, especially if it is to be baked outside the poultry.

¼ pound (1 stick) butter, melted
2 or 3 celery ribs, finely chopped (1 cup)
1 large onion, finely chopped (1 cup)
½ pound small regular white mushrooms, sliced (about 2 cups)
1 recipe Basic Corn Bread for Stuffing (see pages 157–58), broken into small pieces (6 cups)
1 cup dried currants or golden raisins

2 teaspoons dried sage leaves, crumbled
2 teaspoons dried thyme leaves, crumbled
½ teaspoon salt
¼ teaspoon freshly ground black pepper
¼ cup dry port wine
1 large egg, beaten
¾ cup turkey or chicken broth (see pages 2–4)

Melt the butter in a large skillet over medium-high heat. When hot, add the celery, onion, and mushrooms and cook, stirring frequently, until the mushrooms are limp while some liquid remains.

Place the corn bread in a large mixing bowl. Stir in the skillet vegetables, currants, sage, thyme, salt, and pepper and toss to thoroughly combine. Drizzle the port, egg, and about half of the turkey broth over the mixture and toss again. If necessary, add more turkey broth, a little at a time, until the stuffing is moist and holds together when lightly pressed between the palms of your hands.

YIELD: ABOUT 7 CUPS, OR ENOUGH TO FILL A 12- TO 14-POUND TURKEY, A 6- TO 7-POUND CHICKEN OR CAPON WITH ABOUT 3 CUPS LEFT OVER TO BAKE SEPARATELY, OR 6 CORNISH HENS

BAKED POTATO AND BACON STUFFING

FOR TURKEY OR GOOSE

The roots of this stuffing are most assuredly planted in eastern Pennsylvania, where potato fillings and dressings find their way onto the table for Sunday dinner more often than not. After the potato pulp has been removed, wrap the skins and save them. Later they can be brushed with butter, baked in a 425°F oven for 10 minutes or until crisp, and served with sour cream and chives or caviar.

2½ pounds baking potatoes
½ pound bacon, cut into 1-inch pieces
3 medium-size onions, finely chopped
  (1½ cups)
2 or 3 celery ribs, sliced (1 cup)
¼ cup chopped fresh parsley
1 tablespoon dried sage leaves, crumbled

1½ teaspoons dried thyme leaves,
  crumbled
½ teaspoon salt
¼ teaspoon freshly ground black pepper
7 slices white bread, cut into ½-inch
  cubes and dried (3½ cups)
½ to ¾ cup warm water
4 tablespoons (½ stick) butter, melted

Preheat the oven to 425°F. Scrub the potatoes and pierce their skins in a couple of places with the tines of a fork (this is to prevent them from exploding in the oven). Bake for 35 to 40 minutes, or until the potatoes can be easily pierced with the tip of a knife. Remove from the oven and cool. Halve each potato and scoop out enough of the pulp to measure 4 cups.

In a large skillet, cook the bacon over medium-high heat until crisp. Add the onions and celery and cook, stirring frequently, for 2 minutes more. Break the potato pulp into small pieces and add to the skillet with the parsley, sage, thyme, salt, and pepper and toss to blend. Remove from the heat and set aside.

Place the bread in a large bowl. Combine the water and butter and drizzle over the bread, tossing to moisten evenly. Add the potato mixture and toss gently until combined.

YIELD: ABOUT 7 CUPS, OR ENOUGH TO FILL AN 8- TO 10-POUND TURKEY OR GOOSE
WITH 2 TO 3 CUPS LEFT OVER TO BAKE SEPARATELY

CRACKED WHEAT AND APRICOT STUFFING
FOR CHICKEN OR CAPON

For those Thanksgiving diners who are concerned about their diet (and even for those who are not), this is a *great* stuffing. It's moist, yet low in fat and high in fiber, with a satisfyingly rich flavor that's usually missing in stuffings with so little butter or other fat.

4 cups water
2 teaspoons salt
2 cups cracked wheat (available in Middle
    Eastern or health food stores)
2 tablespoons butter
1 or 2 celery ribs, finely chopped (½ cup)
1 medium-size onion, finely chopped
    (½ cup)

¾ cup dried apricots, quartered
¾ cup pitted prunes, quartered
2 teaspoons chopped fresh mint leaves
⅛ teaspoon freshly ground black pepper
4 cups chicken broth (see pages 2–4)
¾ cup dry port wine
¼ cup toasted (see pages 6–7) pine nuts

In a 4-quart Dutch oven or other large heavy saucepan, bring the water and 1½ teaspoons of the salt to a boil over high heat. Stir in the cracked wheat and boil for 2 minutes. Drain through a fine-mesh sieve and set aside.

Wipe the Dutch oven dry and melt the butter in it over medium-high heat. Add the celery and onion and cook, stirring frequently, until tender-crisp. Stir in the cracked wheat and continue to cook over medium heat, stirring, for 5 minutes. Stir in the apricots, prunes, mint, pepper, chicken broth, port, and the remaining salt. Cover and simmer over low heat, stirring occasionally, until the wheat is tender and most of the liquid has been absorbed, 20 to 30 minutes. Stir in the pine nuts.

YIELD: ABOUT 8 CUPS, OR ENOUGH TO FILL A 6- TO 7-POUND CHICKEN OR CAPON WITH ABOUT 4 CUPS LEFT OVER TO BAKE SEPARATELY

PEAR AND PINE NUT STUFFING

FOR CORNISH HENS

Pears and pine nuts are excellent stuffing companions, but fresh cilantro is the real flavor surprise here. This amount of stuffing is just right for an intimate Thanksgiving dinner—two Cornish hens—but the ingredients can be doubled, tripled, or even quadrupled. And since the stuffing is also quite healthy, a no-fat glaze, such as the Apricot-Orange-Brandy Sauce on page 226, would be a better choice than to serve gravy.

1 tablespoon butter
1 medium-size onion, chopped (½ cup)
1 Bartlett pear, peeled, cored, and chopped
    (1 cup)
⅓ cup dry bread crumbs

¾ cup toasted (see pages 6–7) pine nuts or
    walnut pieces
¾ cup minced fresh parsley
¼ cup minced cilantro
½ teaspoon salt
⅛ teaspoon freshly ground black pepper

Melt the butter in a medium-size skillet over medium-high heat. When hot, add the onion and cook, stirring frequently, until tender-crisp. Stir in the remaining ingredients. If the mixture seems dry, add a little warm water.

YIELD: ABOUT 2¼ CUPS, OR ENOUGH TO FILL 2 CORNISH HENS

MARYLAND PAN OYSTER STUFFING
❦
FOR CHICKEN, CAPON, OR CORNISH HENS

A stuffing from the Eastern Shore of Maryland, where succulent Chincoteague oysters manage to find their way into almost every winter meal. However, if you aren't lucky enough to live near the Chincoteague oyster beds, you can substitute almost any variety available to you locally.

¼ pound (1 stick) butter
2 or 3 celery ribs, finely chopped (1 cup)
1 medium-size onion, finely chopped (½ cup)
3 apples, peeled, cored, and chopped (3 cups)
1 to 1½ pints oysters, drained, the liquor reserved, and coarsely chopped
½ teaspoon grated lemon rind
½ teaspoon fresh lemon juice

⅛ teaspoon dried tarragon leaves, crumbled
⅛ teaspoon ground mace
⅛ teaspoon dried sage leaves, crumbled
½ teaspoon salt
¼ teaspoon freshly ground black pepper
8 slices white bread, cut into ½-inch cubes and dried (4 cups)
¼ cup chopped fresh parsley

Melt the butter in a large skillet over medium-high heat. When hot, add the celery, onion, and apples and cook, stirring frequently, until tender-crisp. Stir in the reserved oyster liquor, lemon rind, lemon juice, tarragon, mace, sage, salt, and pepper. Stir the oysters into the skillet, along with the bread cubes and parsley, and remove from the heat. If the mixture seems dry, add warm water, a little at a time, tossing until the stuffing is moist and just holds together when lightly pressed between the palms of your hands.

YIELD: ABOUT 6 CUPS, OR ENOUGH TO FILL A 6-POUND CHICKEN OR CAPON WITH ABOUT 3 CUPS LEFT OVER TO BAKE SEPARATELY, OR 6 CORNISH HENS

SHIITAKE MUSHROOM AND MATZOH CRACKER STUFFING

FOR CORNISH HENS

For centuries, Jewish cooks have been using matzoh for stuffing poultry at Passover. Whether it's for Passover or Thanksgiving, matzoh is an excellent and somewhat unusual base for stuffing. It has a nice mouth feel, keeps its own identity, and readily absorbs the flavor of other ingredients.

2 tablespoons butter
1 or 2 celery ribs, finely chopped (½ cup)
1 small onion, finely chopped (¼ cup)
1 cup sliced shiitake mushroom caps
   (about ¼ pound with stems)
½ cup chopped fresh parsley

½ cup toasted (see pages 6–7) chopped
   pecans
1 teaspoon salt
¼ cup chicken broth (see pages 2–4)
¾ cup crumbled matzoh crackers

Melt the butter in a large skillet over medium-high heat. When hot, add the celery and onion and cook, stirring frequently, until tender-crisp. Stir in the mushrooms and parsley and cook, stirring, just until the mushrooms are limp. Remove from the heat and let cool slightly. Add the remaining ingredients, stirring until well blended.

YIELD: ABOUT 2 CUPS, OR ENOUGH TO FILL 2 CORNISH HENS

APPLE, BACON, AND WALNUT STUFFING

FOR CORNISH HENS, CHICKEN, OR CAPON

Good and crunchy, with lots of companionable, homey flavors.

¼ pound sliced bacon
2 Granny Smith apples, peeled, cored, and
   coarsely chopped (2 cups)
1 large onion, coarsely chopped (1 cup)
1 cup toasted (see pages 6–7) chopped
   walnuts
2 tablespoons chopped fresh parsley
¼ cup dry sherry

1 teaspoon fresh lemon juice
½ teaspoon poultry seasoning
¼ teaspoon salt
¼ teaspoon freshly ground black pepper
4 slices light rye bread, crusts removed
   and whirled in a blender or food
   processor to make soft bread crumbs
   (3 cups)

In a large skillet, cook the bacon over medium-high heat until crisp. Remove from the skillet and drain on paper towels. Pour off all but 3 tablespoons of the bacon drippings. Add the apples and onion to the skillet and cook over medium-high heat, stirring frequently, until tender-crisp. Stir in the walnuts, parsley, sherry, lemon juice, poultry seasoning, salt, and pepper. Coarsely crumble the bacon, add it to the skillet mixture along with the bread crumbs, and stir until well blended.

YIELD: ABOUT 5 CUPS, OR ENOUGH TO FILL 4 CORNISH GAME HENS OR A 6- TO 7-POUND CHICKEN OR CAPON

GRAPE AND WILD RICE STUFFING

FOR CORNISH HENS, CHICKEN, OR CAPON

This is a low-fat stuffing with good flavor and texture that's also excellent as a side-dish dressing. The warm grapes add pleasurable little squirts of juice with every bite.

1 cup uncooked wild rice
3 cups chicken broth (see pages 2–4)
1⅓ cups water
⅔ cup uncooked long-grain white rice
2 tablespoons butter
1 or 2 celery ribs, finely chopped (½ cup)

1 medium-size onion, finely chopped (½ cup)
1 tablespoon finely chopped crystallized ginger (see note on page 174)
2 cups small seedless red or green grapes

In a sieve, rinse the wild rice under cool running water and drain. In a medium-size saucepan, bring the chicken broth to a boil over high heat. Stir in the wild rice and bring back to boiling. Reduce the heat to medium-low and simmer, covered, for 50 minutes to 1 hour, or until most of the liquid is absorbed. Remove from the heat and set aside, covered, for 10 minutes.

In a 2-quart saucepan, bring the water to a boil. Stir in the white rice, reduce the heat to medium-low, and simmer slowly, covered, for 15 to 20 minutes. Remove from the heat and set aside, covered, for 10 minutes.

Melt the butter in a medium-size skillet over medium-high heat. When hot, add the celery and onion and cook, stirring frequently, until tender-crisp. Stir in the ginger and set aside.

In a large bowl, combine the rices and grapes. Add the skillet vegetables and toss until thoroughly combined.

YIELD: ABOUT 7 CUPS, OR ENOUGH TO FILL 6 CORNISH HENS, OR A 6- TO 7-POUND CHICKEN OR CAPON, WITH ABOUT 3 CUPS LEFT OVER TO BAKE SEPARATELY

Note: One tablespoon chopped fresh ginger, or 1 teaspoon ground dried ginger and 2 teaspoons brown sugar, can be substituted for crystallized ginger. Crystallized ginger is found with the spices in most supermarkets.

GARLIC, LEEK, AND ONION STUFFING

FOR CORNISH HENS OR SQUAB

The sweet, bold flavor of three kinds of onions is just right as a stuffing for small birds, where more than a little might be too much.

1 cup pearl onions
24 small cloves garlic or 12 larger cloves
3 tablespoons butter
3 leeks (white part and 1 inch of the green part), thinly sliced (1½ cups)
2 tablespoons chopped fresh parsley

1 teaspoon dried thyme leaves, crumbled
½ teaspoon salt
½ teaspoon coarsely ground black pepper
2 slices white bread, crusts removed, and whirled in a blender or food processor to make soft bread crumbs (1 cup)

To loosen the skins from the onions and garlic, place them in a small bowl and cover with boiling water for about 1 minute. Drain and add cold water to the bowl. Slip off the skins and cut an X in the root ends of the onions. In a medium-size saucepan, cook the onions and garlic in lightly salted boiling water for about 20 minutes, or until barely tender. Drain into a colander. Melt the butter in a large skillet over medium-high heat. When hot, add the onions, garlic, and leeks and cook for 5 minutes, stirring occasionally. Stir in the remaining ingredients and toss until well blended.

YIELD: ABOUT 4 CUPS, OR ENOUGH TO FILL 4 CORNISH HENS OR 8 SQUABS

SWEETBREADS AND MUSHROOM STUFFING

FOR CORNISH HENS OR SQUAB

Sweetbreads are the thymus gland of a calf or other immature animal. They have a firm texture and an exquisite nutty flavor, but are moderately expensive, as are the shiitake mushrooms. These characteristics, coupled with the richness of the stuffing, make it ideal for smaller birds.

1 pound veal sweetbreads
2 tablespoons white vinegar
4 tablespoons (½ stick) butter

2 cups sliced shiitake mushroom caps
  (about ½ pound with stems)
¼ cup dry Marsala wine
2 tablespoons chopped fresh parsley

Soak the sweetbreads in cold water for about 1 hour, changing the water two or three times. Drain the sweetbreads and place them in a medium-size saucepan with the vinegar and enough cold water to cover by about an inch. Bring to a boil, then lower the heat to medium-low and simmer slowly, uncovered, for 2 to 5 minutes. Drain and immediately plunge the sweetbreads into ice-cold water. Allow to cool, then drain again. Carefully pull and cut away the fat, connective tissues, and any tough membranes. Break the sweetbreads into bite-size pieces.

Melt the butter in a large skillet over medium-high heat. When hot, add the sweetbreads and mushrooms and cook, stirring and tossing, until both are lightly browned. With a slotted spoon, remove the sweetbreads and mushrooms and set aside. Add the Marsala to the skillet, stirring and scraping with a spoon to loosen any brown bits that cling to the pan. Cook over high heat until the liquid is reduced by half. Return the sweetbreads and mushrooms to the skillet, stir in the parsley, and mix until well combined.

YIELD: ABOUT 3 CUPS, OR ENOUGH TO FILL 2 TO 4 CORNISH HENS or 6 SQUABS

PORCINI AND PÂTÉ STUFFING
FOR CORNISH HENS OR SQUAB

I get hungry just reading this recipe. It is intended to fill small birds, and I always regret that there is necessarily so little of it. Porcini mushrooms, a good pâté, and real Marsala wine are the secrets to the exquisite flavor of this stuffing. Don't substitute less expensive ingredients.

About ¾ ounce dried porcini mushrooms
  (available from specialty food stores)
1 tablespoon butter
¼ cup chopped shallots
Pinch of sugar
Few drops soy sauce
2 tablespoons chopped fresh parsley

3 slices white bread, crusts removed, and
  whirled in a blender or food processor
  to make soft bread crumbs (1½ cups)
1 to 2 tablespoons dry Marsala wine
6 ounces good-quality smooth liver pâté,
  cut into ¼-inch cubes

Brush away any bits of dirt from the dried porcini. Place them in a small bowl and add enough warm water to cover. Set aside for 30 minutes to rehydrate. Remove the porcini and pat dry with paper towels, straining through a fine-mesh sieve and reserving the water in which they soaked. Coarsely chop the porcini.

Melt the butter in a medium-size skillet over medium-high heat. When hot, add the shallots and cook, stirring frequently, until transparent. Stir in the porcini and cook until any liquid they give off has evaporated. Remove from the heat and stir in the sugar, soy sauce, parsley, and bread crumbs. Add the Marsala and just enough of the reserved mushroom liquid to moisten the mixture so that it barely holds together when lightly pressed between the palms of your hands. Gently fold in the pâté.

YIELD: ABOUT 2 CUPS, OR ENOUGH TO FILL 2 CORNISH HENS OR 4 SQUABS

BOCKWURST STUFFING

FOR GOOSE

Bockwurst is an almost-white veal sausage that is sold in links. The flavor can vary considerably, and it can also be quite spicy, depending on who makes it, so it pays to try the sausage from a few different places before settling on one you like. When I visit my daughter in Bel Air, Maryland, I buy my bockwurst from Peppi's, a small butcher shop where they make all their own sausage, and drag it back to New York in a cooler and then stash it in the freezer. Obviously, I have found more uses for bockwurst than stuffing a goose, and so will you.

¼ pound (1 stick) butter
1 large onion, finely chopped (1 cup)
1 clove garlic, minced
1 pound bockwurst sausage links, coarsely
  chopped
2 Golden Delicious apples, peeled, cored,
  and cut into cubes (2 cups)
¼ cup dry vermouth or white wine

8 or 9 slices light rye bread, dried and
  broken into postage stamp-size pieces
  (about 9 cups)
1 teaspoon chopped fresh rosemary
1 teaspoon dried sage leaves, crumbled
½ teaspoon salt
¼ teaspoon freshly ground pepper
Warm water

Heat the butter over medium heat in a large skillet until melted. Pour off ¼ cup and set aside. Add the onion and garlic to the skillet and cook over medium-high heat, stirring frequently, until softened. Add the bockwurst and apples and cook, stirring frequently, until the bockwurst is lightly browned. With a slotted spoon, transfer the mixture to a large bowl. Add the vermouth to the skillet, scraping with a wooden spoon to loosen any brown bits that stick to the pan. Add the pan liquid to the bockwurst mixture.

Add the bread, rosemary, sage, salt, and pepper to the mixture in the bowl. Toss gently until well combined. Drizzle the remaining ¼ cup melted butter over the bread mixture and toss again. Slowly add warm water, a little at a time, tossing until the mixture barely holds together when pressed between the palms of your hands.

YIELD: 8 CUPS, OR ENOUGH TO FILL A 10-POUND GOOSE WITH ABOUT 3 CUPS LEFT OVER TO BAKE SEPARATELY

PENNSYLVANIA DUTCH POTATO FILLING

FOR GOOSE OR TURKEY

Whether this stuffing will be used to fill a turkey or a goose depends upon the part of Pennsylvania in which you're dining.

2½ pounds all-purpose potatoes (about 5 medium-size potatoes), peeled and quartered	1 tablespoon poultry seasoning
	1 teaspoon salt
4 tablespoons (½ stick) butter	¼ teaspoon freshly ground black pepper
3 large onions, finely chopped (3 cups)	1 tablespoon cider vinegar
½ cup chopped fresh parsley	1 large egg, beaten
	16 slices white bread, dried

Boil the potatoes in lightly salted water to cover until they are just tender when pierced with a fork. They should *not* be on the verge of falling apart. While the potatoes are boiling, melt the butter in a large skillet over medium-high heat. When hot, add the onions and cook, stirring frequently for about 20 minutes, until the onion is soft and transparent. Remove from the heat and stir in the parsley.

Drain the potatoes and turn them into a large bowl. Immediately break them up into small pieces with a fork. Sprinkle with the poultry seasoning, salt, pepper, and vinegar and toss to blend well. Add the warm onion mixture and toss again. (The potatoes and onions should be mixed while they are both still fairly hot.) When the mixture has cooled slightly, drizzle the egg over it and toss again. (In the process of all this tossing, try not to mash the potatoes too much.) Dip each slice of dried bread into a bowl of water, squeeze most of the water from it, and then break it up into the potato mixture. When all the bread has been added, toss the mixture again to mix thoroughly. Since this stuffing expands more than the usual bread stuffing, be careful not to pack too much of it into the bird.

YIELD: 8 CUPS, OR ENOUGH TO FILL A 10-POUND GOOSE OR TURKEY WITH ABOUT 3 CUPS
LEFT OVER TO BAKE SEPARATELY

SAUERKRAUT AND APPLE STUFFING

FOR GOOSE OR DUCK

The sauerkraut base, mellowed by onions, apples, potatoes, and the incomparable flavor of rendered goose fat, is just tart enough to cut the richness of goose and duck. Also makes an excellent side dish.

¼ cup rendered goose fat or butter (see
    note below)
2 large onions, sliced (2 cups)
2 pounds fresh sauerkraut, rinsed and
    drained
2 Golden Delicious or Rome Beauty
    apples, peeled, cored, and shredded
    (2 cups)

2 medium-size (about ½ pound) potatoes,
    peeled and shredded (2 cups)
1 teaspoon caraway seeds
1 teaspoon salt
¼ teaspoon freshly ground black pepper
½ cup dry vermouth or white wine

Heat the goose fat in a medium-size skillet over medium-high heat. Add the onions and cook, stirring frequently, until tender-crisp. In a large bowl, combine the onions, with the remaining ingredients and toss to mix thoroughly.

YIELD: ABOUT 10 CUPS, OR ENOUGH TO FILL AN 8- TO 10-POUND GOOSE WITH 5 TO 6
CUPS LEFT OVER TO BAKE SEPARATELY, OR TWO 5- TO 6-POUND DUCKS

Note: To render goose fat, pull the solid fat from the goose cavities before roasting. Chop the fat coarsely and place it in a heavy pan over low heat until it is melted. Strain the fat into a bowl, where any solids will fall to the bottom. Use the clear fat on top for cooking. It will store in the refrigerator for several weeks and months in the freezer.

CHESTNUT AND DRIED-FRUIT STUFFING

FOR GOOSE OR DUCK

An upscale stuffing with lots of rich flavor, but maybe not for meals where young diners, or even old diners with underdeveloped taste buds, will be in attendance.

1 cup chopped pitted prunes
½ cup chopped dried pears
1 cup dry port wine
1 tablespoon butter
1 or 2 celery ribs, finely chopped (½ cup)
1 medium-size onion, finely chopped (½ cup)
1 apple, peeled, cored, and coarsely chopped (1 cup)

1 cup roasted (see pages 1–2) coarsely chopped chestnuts
2 tablespoons fresh lemon juice
1 tablespoon grated lemon rind
½ teaspoon ground mace
½ teaspoon salt
¼ teaspoon freshly ground black pepper
2 slices white bread, cut into ½-inch cubes and dried (2 cups)

Combine the prunes and pears in a small bowl, add the port wine, and let soak for at least 8 hours or overnight.

Melt the butter in a large skillet over medium-high heat. When hot, add the celery and onion and cook over medium-high heat, stirring frequently, until tender-crisp. Remove from the heat and turn into a large bowl. Stir in the apple, chestnuts, lemon juice, lemon rind, mace, salt, and pepper. Add the bread cubes and toss to combine. Drain the fruit (reserving the soaking liquid), add it to the mixture, and toss again. Gradually add the reserved liquid, tossing gently, until the stuffing is moist and just holds together when lightly pressed between the palms of your hands.

YIELD: ABOUT 6 CUPS, OR ENOUGH TO FILL AN 8- TO 10-POUND GOOSE WITH A CUP OR TWO LEFT OVER TO BAKE SEPARATELY, OR TWO 5- TO 6-POUND DUCKS

CORN BREAD AND KUMQUAT STUFFING

FOR GOOSE OR DUCK

You can't imagine how good this stuffing is with a spoonful or two of Traditional Orange Sauce or Cumberland Sauce (see pages 220 and 222–23, respectively).

1 recipe Basic Corn Bread for Stuffing (see
   pages 157–58), cut into ½-inch cubes
   (6 cups)
⅓ cup olive oil
4 to 6 celery ribs, finely chopped (2 cups)
1 large onion, finely chopped (1 cup)
1 cup sliced green onion (scallion) tops
1 clove garlic, minced
½ cup coarsely chopped kumquats
1 tablespoon grated lemon rind

1 tablespoon grated orange rind
¾ cup chopped fresh parsley
1 teaspoon salt
¼ teaspoon coarsely ground black pepper
¼ teaspoon dried tarragon leaves,
   crumbled
¼ cup fresh orange juice
2 tablespoons Grand Marnier or other
   orange-flavored liqueur
1 large egg, beaten

Preheat the oven to 350°F. Spread the corn bread cubes over two large baking sheets
and bake for 30 minutes, stirring a couple of times, until lightly browned. Heat the
olive oil in a large skillet over medium-high heat. Add the celery and onion and cook,
stirring frequently, until tender-crisp. Add the green onion tops and garlic and cook,
stirring, for 2 minutes more.

In a large bowl, combine the corn bread, skillet vegetables, kumquats, lemon and
orange rinds, parsley, salt, pepper, and tarragon and toss gently to blend. Mix the orange
juice and orange liqueur together and drizzle with the egg over the corn bread mixture.
Toss again to thoroughly combine.

YIELD: ABOUT 6½ CUPS, OR ENOUGH TO FILL ONE 10–12-POUND GOOSE OR TWO 5- TO
7-POUND DUCKS

RAISIN BREAD AND CRANBERRY STUFFING

FOR DUCK OR GOOSE

Sweet and fruity, just right for duck or goose. To stuff a goose, double the ingredients.

2 cups fresh cranberries, rinsed, picked
   over, and coarsely chopped
6 tablespoons sugar
8 slices raisin bread, cut into ½-inch
   cubes and dried (about 8 cups)

2 teaspoons grated orange rind
1 teaspoon salt
¼ teaspoon ground cinnamon
4 tablespoons (½ stick) butter, melted
½ cup fresh orange juice

Combine the cranberries and sugar in a large bowl. Add the bread cubes, orange rind, salt, cinnamon, and butter. Toss with enough orange juice so that the mixture is slightly moist and barely holds together when lightly pressed between the palms of your hands.

YIELD: ABOUT 4½ CUPS, OR ENOUGH TO FILL A 5- TO 7-POUND DUCK WITH A LITTLE LEFT OVER TO BAKE SEPARATELY

PENNSYLVANIA DUTCH MASHED-POTATO DRESSING

I could eat this dressing every day, and I have vivid memories of how impressed I was the first time I tasted it, even though I was just a kid. It was served at the home of the family who lived on and worked my parents' farm near Mohn's Hill, Pennsylvania. There was also a *very* freshly killed chicken to accompany the dressing, and a big bowl of mixed fresh corn and lima beans. The Dutch do love their starches! It also goes well with turkey, capon, or goose.

8 slices white bread, cut into ½-inch cubes and dried (about 8 cups)
2 pounds all-purpose potatoes, peeled and quartered
½ cup milk
3 large eggs, beaten

⅔ cup finely chopped fresh parsley
1 teaspoon salt
½ teaspoon freshly ground black pepper
12 tablespoons (1½ sticks) butter
3 large onions, finely chopped (3 cups)
4 to 6 celery ribs, thinly sliced (2 cups)

Preheat the oven to 300°F. Spread the bread cubes on one or two baking sheets and bake for 15 to 20 minutes, stirring once or twice, until lightly browned. Remove from the oven and set aside. Raise the oven heat to 350°F.

Place the potatoes in a large saucepan with enough salted water to cover them by about 1 inch. Bring to a boil and cook, covered, until tender, 20 to 25 minutes. Drain the potatoes and mash them coarsely. Add the milk, eggs, parsley, salt, and pepper and beat until smooth.

Melt 4 tablespoons (½ stick) of the butter in a large skillet over medium-high heat. When hot, add the onions and celery and cook, stirring frequently, until soft and lightly browned. Using a slotted spoon, remove the vegetables and add them to the mashed-potato mixture. Melt 6 tablespoons of the remaining butter in the skillet over medium heat. When hot, add the bread cubes and toss until well coated. Add the bread cubes to the mashed potatoes and stir gently until well mixed. Turn the mixture into a buttered 2½- or 3-quart casserole. Melt the remaining 2 tablespoons of butter and drizzle over the mashed-potato mixture. Bake for 25 to 30 minutes, or until the top is lightly browned and crusty.

YIELD: ABOUT 8 CUPS; ABOUT 12 SERVINGS

NEW ORLEANS OYSTER DRESSING

I cannot say enough good things about this recipe. If you like cooked oysters, this is your dressing. The consistency is wet, almost puddinglike, so, for the moment, forget all my cautioning about not adding too much liquid. This dressing is great with turkey and other poultry, but it's also good with beef or ham, or just by itself with a salad. I often make it especially to serve with turkey and other holiday leftovers.

¼ cup vegetable oil
2 large onions, finely chopped (2 cups)
4 or 5 celery ribs, finely chopped (1½ cups)
½ cup finely chopped green bell pepper
1 clove garlic, minced
1 pint oysters, drained, the liquid
    reserved, and coarsely chopped
One 4-ounce can mushroom stems and
    pieces, drained, the liquid reserved, and
    chopped

⅓ cup chopped fresh parsley
1 teaspoon salt
½ teaspoon freshly ground black pepper
⅛ teaspoon ground thyme
1 tablespoon butter
4 slices firm white bread, crusts removed,
    dried, and broken into postage stamp-
    size cubes

Preheat the oven to 325°F. Heat the oil in a large skillet over medium-high heat. Add the onions and cook, stirring frequently, until tender and lightly browned. Add the celery, green pepper, and garlic and cook, stirring frequently, until softened. Stir in the oysters, mushrooms, parsley, salt, pepper, thyme, and butter and remove from the heat. Drizzle the reserved oyster and mushroom liquids over the bread cubes in a large bowl and toss to moisten thoroughly. If necessary, add additional water. Add the skillet mixture to the bread cubes and toss gently to mix well. Turn into a buttered 2-quart baking dish, cover, and bake for about 45 minutes, or until hot through.

YIELD: ABOUT 5 CUPS; 6 SERVINGS

SAUSAGE, PECAN, AND WILD RICE DRESSING

It's okay to make this dressing ahead, if you want to, but be sure to warm it up slightly before serving, since cold isn't the best temperature for cooked sausage. It goes well with any kind of poultry.

1 cup uncooked wild rice
3 cups chicken broth (see pages 2–4)
2 tablespoons butter
1 large onion, finely chopped (1 cup)
1 or 2 celery ribs, sliced (about ½ cups)
1 pound bulk pork sausage

1 firm, tart apple, such as a Granny Smith
   or McIntosh, peeled, cored, and cut into
   ½-inch cubes
½ cup toasted (see pages 6–7) pecan
   halves

Preheat the oven to 350°F. In a sieve, rinse the wild rice under cool running water and drain. Combine the rice and chicken broth in a 3-quart casserole and cover tightly. Bake for 1½ hours, checking after 1 hour. If more liquid is needed, add a little water and fluff the mixture with a fork. Continue to bake for about 30 minutes. The rice should be moist, not dry. Remove from the oven and set aside, leaving the oven on.

Melt the butter in a large skillet over medium-high heat. When hot, add the onion and celery and cook, stirring frequently, for 1 minute. Add the sausage and cook, stirring and breaking it up with the side of a spoon until no pink remains. Add the sausage mixture, apple, and pecans to the rice, tossing to mix thoroughly. Turn into a buttered 2-quart baking dish, cover, and bake for about 45 minutes, or until hot through.

YIELD: 7 cups; 8 SERVINGS

ASIAN-STYLE DRESSING
❦

Fresh-flavored and healthy. A little sesame oil, if you like it, adds a slightly more dramatic taste. It goes well with any type of poultry, especially duck.

1 cup uncooked brown rice
2½ cups water
2 tablespoons butter
½ pound regular white mushrooms, sliced
   (about 2 cups)
2 or 3 celery ribs, diagonally sliced (1 cup)
About 4 green onions (scallions),
   diagonally sliced, including some
   of the green tops (about ½ cup)

⅔ cup toasted (see pages 6–7) walnut
   pieces
⅔ cup dried currants
½ cup chicken broth (see pages 2–4)
4½ teaspoons soy sauce
4½ teaspoons minced fresh ginger or
   1 teaspoon ground
2 tablespoons chopped cilantro or parsley

Combine the rice and water with a little salt in a medium-size saucepan. Bring to a boil, reduce the heat to very low, and cook, covered and undisturbed, for 45 minutes, or until the rice is tender and almost all of the water has been absorbed. Remove from the heat and set aside, covered, for 5 minutes.

Preheat the oven to 325°F. Melt the butter in a Dutch oven or other large heavy saucepan over medium-high heat. When hot, add the mushrooms, celery, and green onions and cook, stirring frequently, until the vegetables are tender-crisp. Add the walnuts and currants and continue to cook, stirring, for 3 minutes.

In a small bowl, combine the broth, soy sauce, and ginger. Stir into the vegetable mixture. Add the rice and cilantro and stir gently to blend. Turn into a buttered 2-quart baking dish, cover, and bake for about 45 minutes, or until hot through.

YIELD: ABOUT 6 CUPS; 6 TO 8 SERVINGS

RED CABBAGE AND CHESTNUT DRESSING

When all the ingredients for this dressing are finally mixed together, it will look like enough to feed a small army, but the cabbage will shrink down considerably as it bakes. Best served with duck or goose.

3 tablespoons butter
1 large onion, sliced (1 cup)
1 Golden Delicious apple, peeled, cored, and chopped (1 cup)
½ teaspoon salt
¼ teaspoon freshly ground black pepper
1 head red cabbage (1½ to 1¾ pounds), cored and shredded

One 16-ounce can whole chestnuts, drained and halved (see pages 1–2)
¼ cup red wine vinegar
6 tablespoons dry red wine
6 tablespoons orange juice
1 tablespoon sugar
½ tablespoon grated orange rind
¼ teaspoon freshly grated nutmeg
⅛ teaspoon ground cloves

Preheat the oven to 325°F. Melt the butter in a large nonreactive Dutch oven or other large heavy saucepan over medium heat. When hot, add the onion, apple, salt, and pepper and cook, stirring frequently, until tender-crisp. Add the cabbage and chestnuts and continue to cook, stirring, for about 5 minutes.

In a small nonreactive saucepan, combine the vinegar, wine, orange juice, and sugar. Bring to a simmer, stirring, over medium-low heat. Pour the hot mixture over the cabbage, then stir in the orange rind, nutmeg, and cloves. Taste and correct the seasoning, if necessary. Turn into a buttered 3-quart casserole, cover, and bake for 1 hour.

YIELD: ABOUT 7 CUPS; 8 SERVINGS

🍂

COUSCOUS AND PISTACHIO DRESSING

🍂

The Middle Eastern flavors in this pretty dressing complement dark-meat birds, such as squab and duck. For a spicier taste, substitute ½ to 1 teaspoon of crushed red pepper for the black pepper.

¼ cup olive oil
1 cup uncooked medium couscous
  (available in specialty food stores and
  many supermarkets)
2 cups water
1 cup coarsely chopped pistachio nuts
1 cup golden raisins

1 large red bell pepper, coarsely chopped
  (1 cup)
½ cup chopped fresh flat-leaf parsley
½ cup chopped fresh mint leaves
3 teaspoons ground cinnamon
3 teaspoons ground cumin
½ teaspoon salt
¼ teaspoon freshly ground black pepper

Preheat the oven to 325°F. Heat the oil in a large skillet over medium heat. Add the couscous and cook, stirring, until lightly browned. Stir in the water and cook over low heat, covered, for 5 to 10 minutes, lifting the cover and stirring occasionally, until the water is absorbed. Stir in the remaining ingredients. Turn into a buttered 2-quart baking dish. Bake, covered, for 45 minutes, or until heated through.

YIELD: ABOUT 6 CUPS; 6 TO 8 SERVINGS

CALIFORNIA PRUNE DRESSING

🍂

The first time I ate this it was served in a hollowed-out loaf of round Italian bread and it was quite a showstopper. The bread that had been pulled out of the loaf was used in the dressing. I still serve it this way now and then, but not for Thanksgiving. If you want to try it, you'll need a pound loaf of round Italian bread cut in half crosswise. Pull out the insides of the bread halves in large chunks, leaving bread shells about ½ inch thick. Break the bread taken from the inside into ½-inch pieces. Proceed as directed here to make the stuffing, then spoon it into one of the hollowed-out halves. Cover with the remaining bread half and brush all over with melted butter. Bake at 375°F for about 15 to 20 minutes, or until the stuffing is hot and the bread is crisp. After the stuffing is served, break up the crisp shell and serve it to eat along with the meal. It goes well with any type of poultry.

One 12-ounce box bite-size pitted prunes
(2 cups)
¾ cup hot chicken broth (see pages 2–4)
¼ pound (1 stick) butter
2 or 3 celery ribs, sliced (1 cup)
1 large onion, finely chopped (1 cup)

1 loaf (about 8 ounces) day-old Italian
bread, cut into ½-inch cubes (about
4 cups)
¼ cup chopped fresh parsley
1 teaspoon dried thyme leaves, crumbled
1 teaspoon salt
¼ teaspoon freshly ground black pepper
¼ teaspoon ground allspice

Preheat the oven to 325°F. Combine the prunes and broth in a small bowl and set aside. Melt the butter in a Dutch oven or other large heavy saucepan over medium-high heat. When hot, add the celery and onion and cook, stirring frequently, for about 5 minutes, or until tender-crisp. Stir in the bread, prunes and broth, parsley, thyme, salt, pepper, and allspice. Continue to cook, stirring gently, for about 2 minutes. Turn into a buttered 2-quart baking dish, cover, and bake for 45 minutes, or until heated through.

YIELD: ABOUT 6 CUPS; 8 SERVINGS

NINE

The Main Attraction

TURKEY AND OTHER ALTERNATIVES

Of course, it's usually turkey on the Thanksgiving table, but it can also be:

- *wild turkey*
- *chicken*
- *capon*
- *Cornish hens*
- *squab*
- *duckling*
- *goose*
- *or even beef rib roast and ham*

True or not, most of us learned at our mother's knee that the Pilgrims and their Indian friends feasted on wild turkey at that first Thanksgiving celebration. Consequently, turkey has always been the sentimental favorite for this strictly American holiday. Even those people who admit that turkey isn't one of their favorite foods end up serving or eating it anyway, simply because, for most of us, Thanksgiving wouldn't be Thanksgiving without it.

Nevertheless, there are often good, even compelling reasons for serving something other than The Big Bird on Thanksgiving, or maybe you're just ready for a change.

On the following pages we'll take a look at turkey, then some of the other poultry alternatives, and explain how to buy, prepare, and cook each of them.

TURKEY

Whether turkey was served at the first Thanksgiving is probably something we'll never know for sure. But a few lines in a letter from Edward Winslow, a founder of Plymouth

Colony, to a friend in England has inextricably and probably forever linked the bird with Thanksgiving: "Our harvest being gotten in, our governor sent four men on fowling so that we might after a special manner rejoice together." Since wild turkeys did inhabit the area, it was assumed early on that the fowl Winslow referred to was turkey, although it could just as easily have been ducks, geese, swans, or some other wild fowl.

In any event, there was certainly nothing "new" about turkey in 1621. The birds, which had roamed North and South America for aeons before the Pilgrims came to the New World, were commonplace in Europe. Along with gold and cocoa, Hernando Cortés took turkeys back to Spain from Mexico, where the Maya and Inca Indians had been raising them for nearly five hundred years. If there were any surprises at all connected with this showy bird when the Pilgrims landed, it was probably sheer joy in finding an unexpected but familiar source of food.

Until rather recently, turkey came only one way: big and rangy. After struggling home from the butcher under the tremendous weight of the bird (few turkeys ever weighed much less than 20 to 30 pounds in the good old days), the cook was faced with countless rinsings and more than a little pinfeather plucking and singeing. Then she was lucky if the bird would fit into the oven, and it was not unusual for the local baker to offer his services by roasting his customers' turkeys in the bakery ovens. After the turkey was finally cooked and served, the family faced endless days of eating the leftovers, for there were no home freezers in which to stash these remains for later meals.

For all of these privileges, your grandmother paid about the same price per pound for her turkey as you will for yours this year, and thanks to today's state-of-the-art turkey-raising and packing techniques, your turkey will be oven ready, considerably cleaner, more tender, and have a higher proportion of meat to bone. Turkey really is quite a bargain.

Buying a Whole Turkey

The only decision you'll have to make when selecting a commercially raised whole turkey is whether to buy it fresh or frozen. Either way you'll find ready-to-roast turkeys, ranging in size from a petite 4 pounds to an impressive 24, just for the picking at the supermarket, not only at Thanksgiving but any time of the year.

Fresh or frozen and the brand you eventually settle on are usually matters of habit or family custom, and sometimes price. The biggest advantage to buying a fresh turkey is that it won't take up valuable freezer space, or refrigerator space during the days it takes to defrost, but it will cost a little more than a frozen turkey. In either case, when you bring home a name-brand turkey, you'll always be assured of quality and wholesomeness, and since these birds have been raised in controlled environments to exacting standards, there aren't likely to be any roasting mishaps if you follow the packer's directions.

In addition to the well-known national and regional turkey brands, one option is to locate fresh-killed turkeys that have been hand-raised, so to speak, usually by a local turkey farmer. They may be marketed as "free-range" turkeys, or otherwise been fed some specially formulated diet that their producers believe will make them more tender and tasty. These pedigreed birds are usually sold fresh through specialty food stores and must often be ordered ahead of time. They are, understandably, more expensive than their mass-produced counterparts.

How Much Turkey Is Enough?

How large a turkey to buy usually presents a bigger dilemma for most cooks than which kind. For turkeys weighing 12 pounds or less, the rule of thumb is to allow ¾ to 1 pound of turkey per person for moderate leftovers, and 1¼ to 1½ pounds per person for generous leftovers. Turkeys weighing 12 pounds or more have more meat per pound, so these allowances can be reduced slightly.

Although setting a very large turkey on the table is certainly a spectacular sight, in reality a bird much over 18 to 20 pounds is hard to handle and may be difficult to fit into a roasting pan, to say nothing of the oven. If you're feeding a really big crowd, I think you'll find it more efficient to roast two smaller turkeys.

Turkey Parts and Products

In addition to whole turkeys, you'll find an ever-growing array of fresh and frozen turkey parts and products from which to choose:

Frozen stuffed turkey. If you have little time for preparation, consider a commercially stuffed and frozen turkey that goes straight from the freezer into the oven without thawing. Allow 1½ to 2 pounds per person when serving this turkey. (By the way, never attempt to stuff and freeze a turkey yourself. Home freezers are simply not sufficiently cold to freeze a stuffed bird quickly enough to avoid contamination.)

Boneless turkey. These are naturally proportioned with breast and thigh meat and are available fresh or frozen.

Turkey breast. For white-meat lovers, a bone-in breast, weighing between 3 and 9 pounds, is a good choice. The stuffing can be baked separately, or tucked under the breast as it roasts, and there will probably be enough drippings for gravy.

Boneless breast roast. Weighing from 1½ to 3 pounds, these small roasts are quick to cook and obviously easy to carve, and there are usually enough drippings so you can make your own gravy, but the stuffing will have to be baked on the side.

Turkey parts. These include breast halves, drumsticks, thighs, and wings. If your family is very partial to drumsticks, for instance, turkey parts might, in the end, be the smartest buy of all. On the other hand, if the idea of a pile of turkey parts just doesn't appeal to you for Thanksgiving, you can at least end family squabbles by adding a few favorite pieces to the whole-turkey roasting pan.

Turkey portions packed commercially will always include cooking directions, but occasionally you will find half and whole breasts, thighs, drumsticks, and wings packed loose with no other information other than the weight. For these, use the timetable that follows as a general guide.

Roasting Times for Turkey Parts

Whole breast	325°F	18 to 20 minutes per pound, or to an internal temperature of 170°F
Half breast	350°F	18 to 25 minutes per pound, or to an internal temperature of 170°F
Drumsticks	325°F	Loosely covered with aluminum foil for 1½ hours, then uncovered for 30 minutes to 1 hour
Thighs	325°F	Loosely covered with aluminum foil for 1¼ hours, then uncovered for 30 minutes to 1 hour
Wings	325°F	Loosely covered with aluminum foil for 1½ hours, then uncovered for 30 to 45 minutes

Thawing

If the turkey is frozen, place it on a tray (to catch any leaks) in its *unopened* wrapper in the refrigerator. Most cooks forget from year to year what a long time it takes to thaw a turkey and don't allow enough time.

Thawing Time in the Refrigerator

WHOLE TURKEY		TURKEY PARTS	
8 to 12 pounds	2 days	Half, quarter, half breast,	1 to 2 days
12 to 16 pounds	3 days	drumsticks, thighs	
16 to 20 pounds	4 days		
20 to 24 pounds	5 days		

If you're in a rush, or haven't allowed enough thawing time, you can hasten the process by placing a whole turkey, in its *unopened* wrapper, in a pan or bowl set in the sink and cover it with cold water. (If the wrapper is torn or has even the smallest hole in it, place the whole thing in another plastic bag and close the bag securely.) You will need to change the water frequently, about once every 30 minutes, until the meat feels soft but is still quite cool to the touch.

Thawing Time in Cold Water

8 to 12 pounds	4 to 6 hours	16 to 20 pounds	9 to 11 hours
12 to 16 pounds	6 to 9 hours	20 to 24 pounds	11 to 12 hours

You can also thaw a whole turkey (and turkey parts) in a microwave oven *if* the oven is large enough to accommodate it. Check the manufacturer's directions for times and power levels.

Once thawed, keep the turkey wrapped and chilled (but for not much longer than a day or two) until it's time to stuff and roast it.

Preparing the Bird for Roasting

Shortly before you plan to stuff and roast the turkey, unwrap it and remove the giblets and neck from the body and neck cavities (you'd probably be surprised—or maybe you wouldn't—to learn just how often these get roasted as is, especially the package of giblets, which is stuffed into the neck cavity and likely to be overlooked) and set these aside to use for making broth for basting and for gravy. Rinse the turkey inside and out with cold water and pat it dry with paper towels, inside and out. Lightly salt and pepper the neck and body cavities, if you like.

Stuff the turkey loosely, since stuffing expands some as it cooks. If you like, you can stuff the body cavity with one kind of stuffing and the neck cavity with another. (I hope by now that you know *never* to stuff the turkey, or anything else, until you're ready to roast it. Warm, moist stuffing, inside or outside of the turkey, is a much too friendly environment for bacteria. If you want to save time, mix the dry ingredients ahead of time, then add the liquid ingredients and mix just before stuffing.)

Draw the neck skin over the stuffing and skewer it to the back; fold the wing tips behind the shoulder joints. Now, depending on the way your turkey was dressed, push the drumsticks under the band of skin or metal clamp at the tail, or tie the drumsticks to the tail with string. If the opening to the body cavity is very large, you may want to run two or three small skewers across it and lace it closed with string, working from the top skewer down, catching the drumsticks with the ends of the string. If you don't bother to do all this, your turkey will emerge from the oven looking rather frightened, with wings and legs going every which way.

A Roasting Pan Is a Roasting Pan, or Is It?

One of the little surprises that often come with making one's first Thanksgiving dinner is the sudden realization that there is no roasting pan in the cupboard large enough to accommodate the turkey. The oven broiling pan, although expansive enough to hold most turkeys, is too shallow. If you use the broiling pan, or any other pan that is not at least a couple of inches deep, you'll have a mighty mess on your hands when the fat—and quite a lot of it—starts to drip from the turkey.

My advice to anyone who is equipping a kitchen is to buy high-quality cookware, and that includes a roasting pan. Look for a heavy pan with well-placed, well-designed handles. A pan measuring about 12 × 15 × 3 inches deep is large enough for most purposes, and will hold a 12- to 14-pound turkey comfortably. Although they're more expensive, roasting pans with a nonstick lining make cleanup a breeze.

You will also need a rack if the roasting pan is not equipped with one. It needn't be large, but it should be sturdy, and if it, too, has a nonstick coating, so much the better.

The disposable aluminum-foil pans that are sold at the supermarket are not a good investment. I've not found one that didn't buckle dangerously when the weight of the turkey (and the hot fat, I might add) was added to it. If you want to use one of these pans, buy two and use one inside the other for added strength.

Roasting the Turkey

Place the turkey, breast side up, on an oiled rack in the roasting pan. (Oiling the rack, if it doesn't have a nonstick coating, will hopefully prevent the back of the turkey from sticking to it after it's roasted.) Do not add water or cover the pan. (Actually, there is a covered-pan method for roasting turkey, but I find the finished bird, more steamed than roasted, so terrible that I refuse to discuss it.) Brush the turkey with softened or melted butter or margarine, or oil, or spritz it with vegetable cooking spray. Insert a meat thermometer into the center of the thigh next to the body, making sure that the bulb does not touch the bone. Some turkey brands have little pop-up thermometers inserted in the breast to indicate when the turkey is done. But in my experience the turkey is often too well done (for my taste, anyway) by the time it finally pops. Leave the pop-up thermometer in, if you want to, but rely on your own tests for doneness at the same time.

Roast the turkey at 325°F, following the packer's directions or the timetable that follows. (Don't be tempted to use some outdated roasting method, such as starting the turkey at a very low temperature and finishing it at a higher temperature some hours later, an extremely risky procedure if you value your health.) Remember that roasting timetables (like Amtrak's) are merely approximations, since such things as the temperature of the turkey when you put it in the oven, the accuracy of the oven, and other little variables will all affect roasting time.

This might also be a good time to mention that many home ovens, even very expensive ones, are not accurately calibrated, usually because of faulty thermostats, and can easily be off by as much as 50° either way. Obviously, the most careful timing is all for naught if the oven temperature is wrong. Invest in a glass mercury oven thermometer that registers from 100° to 650°F, and leave it on the oven shelf to double-check the temperature every time you roast or bake.

The times that follow are currently recommended by the United States Department of Agriculture. I'm certainly not an advocate of eating rare poultry, but frankly, I've found these times to be just a little too long, so I start testing 30 to 45 minutes before the lowest prescribed time has elapsed, and I would recommend you do the same. Remember, too, that the turkey will continue to cook some after it is removed from the oven.

Roasting Timetable for Stuffed Turkey at 325°F

READY-TO-COOK WEIGHT	APPROXIMATE TIME
6 to 8 pounds	*3 to 3½ hours*
8 to 12 pounds	*3½ to 4½ hours*
12 to 16 pounds	*4½ to 5½ hours*
16 to 20 pounds	*5½ to 6½ hours*
20 to 24 pounds	*6½ to 7 hours*

Roasting Timetable for Unstuffed Turkey at 325°F

READY-TO-COOK WEIGHT	APPROXIMATE TIME
6 to 8 pounds	2¼ to 3¼ hours
8 to 12 pounds	3 to 4 hours
12 to 16 pounds	3½ to 4½ hours
16 to 20 pounds	4 to 5 hours
20 to 24 pounds	4½ to 5½ hours

It's not really necessary to baste the turkey, except that it feels sort of good and Thanksgivingish to do it. (Remember that every time you open the oven door you allow heat to escape and increase the roasting time.) The skin is so tough that nothing can penetrate it. However, basting does help the bird to brown more evenly, so go ahead and spoon some of the drippings that accumulate in the roasting pan over the turkey a few times while it's roasting.

You can use melted butter or other fat, or some of the broth made from the giblets and neck that you will ultimately use to make the gravy, to baste the turkey while you're waiting for the pan drippings to accumulate. Some cooks like to cover the breast with oil- or butter-soaked cheesecloth and baste through that.

Once the breast has started to brown, make a little tent out of aluminum foil and set it lightly over the breast. Remove the foil during the last 30 to 40 minutes of roasting time to allow the breast to finish browning and to even out the coloring.

HOW TO TELL WHEN IT'S DONE

We all worry about undercooking turkey, but, in fact, most birds come to the table ready to collapse. There's almost nothing worse than an overcooked turkey, so it's important to watch the meat thermometer carefully and start testing during the last quarter of what you've judged the roasting time to be.

Admittedly, it's hard to know exactly when a turkey is roasted to perfection. The problem is that by the time the dark meat is cooked sufficiently, the white meat is often overcooked. Eventually, after you've roasted enough turkeys, you'll be able to trust your own instincts to be able to judge when it's done, but here are a few suggestions: The thermometer in the thigh should register about 180°F and the thickest part of the drumstick should feel soft when pressed with paper towel–protected fingers. You can also pierce the leg joint with a kitchen fork, and if the juices run clear, or even faintly pink, you'll know that the turkey is done. Still another way to check is to insert an instant-reading thermometer through the breast and into the center of the stuffing, where it should register 165°F.

Place the turkey on the serving platter to "rest" for 20 to 30 minutes while you make the gravy. This resting business gives the juices a chance to retreat into the meat and results in a more succulent turkey that is easier to carve. A hot turkey is almost impossible to carve.

HOT-LINE HELP

For years, the Butterball Turkey Talk-Line has been providing help for turkey consumers during the Thanksgiving and Christmas holidays. Every year specially trained, good-natured home economists take literally thousands of calls and answer thousands of questions about almost every aspect of turkey purchasing and preparation, from how to thaw the bird to what to do with the leftovers.

The toll-free line operates during business hours daily (central standard time) from the beginning of November right on through Christmas Eve, and also on the weekend prior to Thanksgiving.

The number has never changed, nor will it be, I am assured. Give these informed and helpful people a call if you have any questions: 1-800-323-4848.

A Few Last Words About Food Safety

Something that's been around for a long time, but didn't seem to get much press until relatively recently, is food poisoning. When we, or someone we know, gets food poisoning, we're inclined to blame everyone but ourselves. Since the improper handling and storage of poultry (and other raw foods of animal origin, by the way) are the leading causes of at least one form of food poisoning, salmonella, here are a few food-safety reminders to help you make sure your turkey and turkey leftovers are as safe to eat and flavorful as possible.

CLEANLINESS FIRST

You've probably heard or read by now that most of the bacteria deposited on food is put there by you or someone else working with less-than-immaculately clean hands, work surfaces, or utensils. So the first rule of food safety is clean, clean, clean for everything that comes in contact with your food.

Be aware of the dangers of cross-contamination. That means that any utensils or work surfaces (including the sink) that come in contact with uncooked poultry (or any other uncooked meat) should not come in contact with foods that will not be thoroughly cooked. These utensils should be washed—and not just rinsed—in hot sudsy water before they are used on foods that will not be cooked before serving.

STORING UNCOOKED TURKEY AND OTHER POULTRY

Store frozen turkey or other poultry in its unopened wrapper (or otherwise tightly wrapped) at 0°F, or lower, for no longer than six or seven months (much longer than this and flavor deterioration is rapid, although there's no actual danger in the eating).

Store fresh uncooked turkey in the coldest part of the refrigerator, usually the bottom, for no longer than four days, advises the United States Department of Agriculture.

Frozen turkey should always be thawed in its unopened wrapper in the refrigerator or in cold water. *Never* thaw turkey (or any other meat, for that matter) at room temperature.

Refreezing a turkey once it is thawed is not recommended, but if refreezing is absolutely necessary, safety will not be compromised if the turkey has been properly defrosted to begin with, and if it has not been held in the refrigerator for more than one or two days. Refreeze in the unopened wrapper (or rewrap tightly if the bag is torn or has been opened) in the coldest part of the freezer, usually the bottom.

SAFE HANDLING OF COOKED POULTRY AND STUFFING

Do not allow the turkey and the stuffing within to languish on the dining room table or on the kitchen counter, for even while you are debating about whether or not to have another piece of pie, the bacteria in your turkey are multiplying at a frightening rate. Let them multiply too much, and you and your dinner guests may soon be languishing in a sickbed.

Refrigerate or freeze turkey and stuffing, *separately*, within two hours after roasting.

Use refrigerated turkey and stuffing within three days. Use frozen stuffing within one month, and frozen turkey within two months, for maximum flavor and quality.

AND ONE MORE TIME

Never, for any reason, stuff a turkey, or any poultry or meat, until just before you're ready to roast it! And please remember that just because your mother or grandmother did things a certain way is not a good enough reason to compromise safety.

WILD TURKEY

If your aim is to serve something a little different for Thanksgiving, but not too different, consider wild turkey. Certainly nothing could be more traditional. These days wild turkeys are rarely found in their native habitats, and if they are, most are too wily to be hunted down successfully. Most, if not all, are raised on game farms and marketed primarily through specialty butchers and other purveyors of out-of-the-ordinary foods.

Wild turkey is smaller and shaped differently than domestic turkey, with a deep breast and longer legs, and weighs 7 to 10 pounds. It has only dark but extremely moist and succulent meat, not at all gamy tasting. As you might expect, wild turkey is expensive, as much as four to eight times what you'd pay for domestic turkey.

The preparation, stuffing, and roasting directions for a wild turkey are about the same as for a domestic bird. A plain turkey stuffing, made a little on the dry side, is the best choice, since it will pick up plenty of dark-meat moisture as it cooks inside the bird. Because wild turkey is leaner than domestic turkey—a big plus for the fat- and calorie-conscious—extra care should be taken not to overcook it.

CHICKEN

It's easy to understand why a roasting chicken, golden brown and crisp-skinned, is a popular choice for a celebratory feast. As good as turkey is, a plump chicken, perfectly roasted, may be one of the world's most perfect and satisfying foods.

Serving chicken for Thanksgiving has a lot going for it, especially when there are only a few sitting down to dinner. Although a big roasting chicken can be larger than a small turkey, the familiar chicken does not seem quite so intimidating, especially to the neophyte cook. Any stuffing that tastes good with turkey will probably taste just as good with chicken; chicken drippings make *great* gravy, and mashed potatoes and all the other traditional Thanksgiving trimmings, side dishes, and sauces are simply wonderful with chicken.

Buying a Roasting Chicken

Most chickens for sale these days are mass-produced, whether they are kosher, carry a premium brand name, or are purchased at a live-poultry market. What this means, of course, is that they are all pretty much alike, unless, of course, you have access to farm-raised, free-range chicken, and then you will probably discern some difference in texture and flavor. It may also be a bit tougher, since this bird has had to work harder for a living. However, you will, for sure, notice a difference in the price you pay for the home-raised bird, probably an additional dollar or more a pound.

Nowadays, roasting chickens can weigh as much as 7 pounds, but most are 5 or 6 pounds, which will provide six ample servings.

Freshness is the all-important factor when buying chicken. However, the vast majority of chickens sold nowadays are fresh and wholesome, having been packed under the watchful eye of U.S.D.A. inspectors, if the birds are intended for sale across state lines. If you have any doubts, look for the U.S.D.A. label. Virtually all chickens sold at retail are Grade A, which has more to do with appearance than anything else.

Aside from just *looking* fresh and clean, you'll want to make sure that the chicken you buy for this important meal has all its parts intact (no missing wing tips, etc.) and that the skin is free from tears and other blemishes. Chances are you won't be disappointed if you buy a brand that you like from a store that you trust.

Purchase a chicken as close to the time you plan to serve it as possible, preferably no more than a day or two in advance.

Preparation and Roasting

As soon as you arrive home from the market, remove the chicken from its wrappings. (There's no point in providing a cozy environment for the bacteria any longer than necessary.) Remove, too, the giblets and neck, which will be packed in the body cavity. Rinse the chicken in cold water and pat dry with paper towels. If you like, you can pull off the little wads of fat just inside the cavity opening. Wrap the chicken loosely in waxed paper and place it in the coldest part of the refrigerator, usually the bottom. Rinse the giblets, wrap them loosely, and store with the chicken.

Remove the chicken from the refrigerator just before you're ready to stuff and roast it. Prepare a broth for basting and gravy making with the giblets, following the directions on page 218. From this point on, the preparation and stuffing of a roasting chicken are exactly the same as for a turkey.

There is more than one school of thought about how to roast chicken. Most of these involve starting the chicken in a hot oven and finishing it off at a more moderate temperature, or roasting the bird at a relatively high temperature for a shorter time. These methods may work well for a whole broiler-fryer chicken, but for a large roaster, especially one that is stuffed, I prefer to stick with a constant temperature of 350°F.

Place the chicken on an oiled rack in a shallow roasting pan, breast side up. Roast a 5- to 7-pound stuffed chicken for 25 to 30 minutes per pound, or until the meat thermometer in the thigh registers about 175°F, or an instant-reading thermometer inserted through the breast and into the center of the stuffing registers about 165°F, or when the juices run clear, or even faintly pink, when the thigh is pierced. Baste the chicken frequently with the juices that accumulate in the pan, supplemented at first with melted butter or broth from the giblets. Place the chicken on a serving platter and allow it to rest for 15 to 20 minutes before carving.

CAPON

A capon is a neutered male chicken. This simple surgical technique (at least in everyone's opinion but the chicken's) originated in ancient Greece and was carried on by the Romans. The neutering process produces a large deep-breasted bird weighing up to 8 or 9 pounds, but more usually about 7 pounds, with all the tenderness of a very young chicken and all the flavor of a more mature bird. As well as lots of white meat, these birds have a thick layer of fat just beneath the skin, which melts during roasting and produces moist, tender meat. As you might expect, a capon costs more than a roasting chicken, an expenditure that the devotees of this delicate bird feel is more than justified.

Fresh capons are relatively easy to find, especially around holidays, and frozen capons are almost always available. Fresh capons should be purchased no more than a day or two before roasting.

Preparation and Roasting

Prepare capon for roasting following the instructions given for roasting chicken. If it is frozen, follow the instructions given for thawing turkey.

Roast a stuffed capon at 325°F for 25 to 30 minutes per pound. Subtract 30 minutes from the total roasting time for an unstuffed capon, regardless of the size. Other than the oven temperature and time, follow the same roasting procedure given for a roasting chicken.

CORNISH HENS

Sometimes called Rock Cornish hens or Rock Cornish game hens, these diminutive hybrids are an American innovation, the result of crossbreeding Cornish gamecocks and Plymouth Rock hens.

At one time Cornish hens came only one way: frozen. They were a handy size, barely over a pound, the perfect serving for one. Although these days fresh Cornish hens are almost always available at the supermarket, they seem to have gotten bigger and never weigh much less than 1½ pounds and usually closer to 2 pounds, a rather sumptuous single serving. However, for Thanksgiving, when we all eat too much anyway, go ahead and plan on one hen per person. Since Cornish hens are small, at least compared to turkeys, you can plan to fill them with an extravagant stuffing.

Buying, Preparation, and Roasting

Cornish hens are technically chickens, so all the same rules apply, and you can follow the guidelines given earlier for buying fresh chicken. Like chicken, Cornish hens should be purchased as close to serving time as possible, and they should receive the same meticulous home care.

Prepare each little hen for roasting just as you would a roasting chicken or turkey, bending the wing tips behind the backs, tying each pair of legs together, and buttering or otherwise oiling the skin. Place the hens together, breast side up, on an oiled rack in a shallow roasting pan in which they will fit comfortably.

Preheat the oven to 450°F. Place the hens in the oven and immediately reduce the heat to 350°F. Roast stuffed hens for 1 to 1¼ hours, and unstuffed hens for 45 minutes to 1 hour, or until tender and the juices run clear when a fork is inserted into the thigh. (Cornish hens are too small to use a meat thermometer.) Baste the birds often while they are roasting, first with butter and the broth made from the giblets (see page 418), and then with the accumulated pan juices. Allow the hens to rest on the serving platter for a few minutes before serving.

SQUAB

These tiny birds, rarely weighing much over ¾ pound, are immature domesticated pigeons. They are not to be confused with the wild variety, which has very dark meat and a decidedly gamy flavor. Although one squab hardly constitutes a hearty serving, if elegance is what is wanted, the tiny squab is worth considering.

Squab is not likely to be found at the supermarket, at least not in the supermarkets where I shop. But butchers who specialize in wild game and other exotic meats often have them on hand, fresh or frozen, or can order them for you.

One squab is usually considered a serving. Most of the richly flavored dark meat is on the breast. The meat on the legs is best described as skimpy, and it is almost nonexistent on the wings. Although you could certainly serve two squabs per person, I think you'll abandon the idea after you've priced them. Squab is expensive. What you might do is serve a small turkey or roasting chicken surrounded by squab. The squab could be eaten first, and the turkey or chicken would provide second helpings and leftovers.

Preparation and Roasting

Squab, whether it's fresh or frozen, usually comes in a little plastic bag. Thaw frozen squab, in its unopened bag, in the refrigerator for several hours. Rinse, dry with paper towels, and wrap loosely in waxed paper. Store in the refrigerator for no longer than a day before roasting.

Sprinkle the squab cavities lightly with salt and pepper. They may be stuffed or not. But since this is an elegant bird, and since the amount of stuffing needed to fill each one will be small (about ½ cup per bird), a rich mixture of luxurious ingredients is definitely in order. Tie the legs together and fold the wing tips behind the back.

If you want to, you can also give the bird a little help to keep it from drying out, either by inserting some softened butter between the breast skin and the flesh or by laying strips of bacon across the birds while they roast. If you use bacon, you must blanch it first in boiling water for a minute or two to eliminate its distinctive flavor, then drain and dry it on paper towels. For each squab, you will need one slice of bacon, cut in half and draped across the breast and thighs.

Place the squabs, breast side up, on an oiled rack in a shallow roasting pan. Roast at 400°F for about 40 to 45 minutes, or until the juices run clear when the thigh is pierced with a fork. Squab is one of the few birds where a little overdone is better.

Forget about serving gravy with squab. It's much too mundane. If you like, you can make a little deglazing sauce for four to six birds this way: Discard all but 2 tablespoons of the fat from the roasting pan and set the pan over medium-low heat. Add about a tablespoon of minced shallots and cook, stirring, until softened. Stir in 1 cup of chicken broth and ½ cup of Madeira or port. Raise the heat to medium-high and cook rapidly, stirring up the brown bits that cling to the pan, until the sauce is reduced to about ½ cup. Off the heat, swirl in a tablespoon of softened butter. Glaze each bird with the sauce before serving. A triangle of thin toast under each bird is a nice touch, too, and will serve to delicately mop up the sauce and the juices from the squab.

DUCKLING

I've always considered the word *duckling* to be too cute sounding to use in general conversation. Nevertheless, it is the proper name for a young duck, and a young duck is all you're ever going to find for sale in U.S. markets.

As well as being youthful, the duck (as it will henceforth be referred to here) you'll most likely purchase will be of the Long Island strain, which can trace its ancestral roots to nine White Pekin ducks that came to Long Island over a hundred years ago on a clipper ship from China—or so the story goes. Lately Muscovy ducks have become quite fashionable, but since these more closely resemble wild duck, leaner and less tender than their Long Island cousins, they're generally best when braised or otherwise cooked with moist heat.

Buying a Duck

Ducks have all dark meat and weigh between 3½ and 5½ pounds. Until recently, most of the U.S. population could live out their lives without encountering anything other than a frozen Long Island duck, tightly encased in a white plastic bag. Nowadays, fresh duck is more readily available, but, in most cases, the white plastic bag remains, so you can't see what you're buying. (The exception to this may be a specialty butcher shop that stocks fresh duck, but the chances are it will still be the same Long Island duck, only more expensive.) The good news is that through the years I've purchased dozens of frozen white-bagged ducks at the supermarket and haven't encountered a disreputable one in the bunch. However, because of its high fat content, duck takes well to being frozen, far better than other poultry, so don't worry inordinately about locating a fresh one.

Aside from its broad, flat breast, an almost tubular shape, and stumpy legs, ducks differ dramatically from most other poultry. Long Island ducks, which are raised in New York and several other states, have a large carcass for their body size and a thick layer of fat beneath the skin. The fat produces juicy, tender meat, but also a high ratio of fat and bone to meat. What starts out as a 5-pound duck ends up as a 3½-pound duck after the fat roasts out, so the number of servings per duck is not impressive. A small duck will serve two, but feeding four from a large duck is a stretch. I usually opt for a small duck and split it into two servings.

Duck skin should be off-white in color, smooth and almost silky looking. It is more elastic than chicken or turkey skin, and clings close to the body with no flabbiness. Like all other poultry, a duck should look clean and be odor free.

Preparation and Roasting

If the duck is frozen, thaw it in its unopened wrapper in the refrigerator for a couple of days, or by using the cold water method described for turkey on pages 190–91, which will take about three hours.

Rinse the duck inside and out and pat dry with paper towels. Wrap loosely in waxed paper and store in the refrigerator for no more than a day or two. Rinse the giblets and neck. Wrap and refrigerate these, too.

To prepare the duck for roasting, pull out the fat from just inside the body and neck cavities. If the neck is very long, chop it off close to the body and trim the neck skin. Chop off the wing tips at the second joint (they have virtually no meat on them) for a neater-looking presentation. You can discard the neck and wing tips, or save them for the stockpot, if you wish. Be sure to set the fat aside in the refrigerator or freezer, and consider using it just like goose fat, which is explained on pages 205–206.

Lightly salt and pepper the duck, inside and out, and loosely fill with stuffing. Since the vent opening in a duck is large, you will probably want to skewer and lace it shut, catching the legs and tying them together with the ends of the string, as described for turkey on pages 191–92.

Preheat the oven to 350°F. Place the duck, breast side up, on a rack in a roasting pan. Roast a stuffed 3½- to 4½-pound duck for 1½ to 1¾ hours; a 4½- to 5½-pound duck for 2 to 2¼ hours. After the duck has roasted for 30 minutes, prick the skin all over the top and sides (not too deeply) with a fork. This allows the fat to run off and makes the skin crisper. There is no need to baste a duck since the fat beneath the skin acts as a self-basting mechanism. The duck is well done when the juices run clear when the thigh is pierced with a fork, and the legs feel soft when pressed with paper towel–protected fingers. If you prefer your duck a little less well done (and many people do), lop off about 15 minutes from these cooking times and consider the duck done when the juices are still tinged with pink. Subtract 15 minutes from the total cooking time for unstuffed duck. Rest the duck for 10 minutes.

Saucing and Serving

You can make gravy for duck using broth made from the giblets (see page 218) the same way you would for any other poultry, but most connoisseurs feel that the flavor of a duck is better served with a tart sauce, usually flavored with wine or fruit. A number of sauces suitable for duck are given in chapter 10. In any event, don't discard the fat. Pour it off into a container with a tight-fitting lid and refrigerate it to use like goose fat.

Carving a duck is a devil of a job, although the French do it quite expertly and routinely, and even manage to eke out an extra serving or two by cutting the meat from the legs and breast into very thin slices. The most practical way to serve a duck is to cut it in half or quarters using a sturdy pair of poultry sheers. Since this is not a particularly pretty procedure, you might want to do it in the kitchen and arrange the halves or quarters on a serving platter with the stuffing, if any, tucked beneath them.

GOSE

If Thanksgiving were celebrated in Central Europe and Scandinavia, goose, not turkey, would undoubtedly be the bird of choice for dinner.

Just as turkey has never achieved booming popularity in Europe, goose has never found much favor here, despite the fact that the first geese may have landed in America with the Pilgrims, or certainly very shortly thereafter. A goose may even have been served at the first Thanksgiving dinner. Part of the reason may be that, until recently, a young, quality table goose was hard to find. Even now, it's not always easy to buy a goose, except around Thanksgiving and Christmas when they are in plentiful supply.

Buying a Goose

Much of what is said about duck can be said about goose. Most are sold frozen in the same sort of white plastic bag, although fresh ones are usually available from specialty butchers, especially around the holidays.

A goose can weigh as little as 6 pounds and as much as 14 pounds, but most are, in the range of 8 to 12 pounds, with most weighing about 10 pounds, large enough to serve eight reasonably generously. Like duck, the goose has a similarly large frame and a disproportionate amount of fat and bone to meat, which makes it not the most economical bird to serve. Count on at least 1 to 1¼ pounds of goose per serving and don't expect much in the way of leftovers. If there are many more than eight to serve, rather than roasting a very large goose, it would probably be easier to roast two 8-pound geese and serve them together.

Despite these small drawbacks, the dark meat is rich and moist, and almost nothing looks more beautiful and festive on the holiday table than a golden roasted goose.

Preparation and Roasting

If the goose is frozen, thaw it in its original, unopened wrapper, either in the refrigerator or by the cold water method given for turkey on pages 190–91. A 10- to 14-pound goose will take two or three days in the refrigerator or four to five hours in cold water to thaw.

Rinse the goose inside and out and pat it dry with paper towels. Wrap loosely in waxed paper and store in the refrigerator for no more than a day or two. Rinse the giblets and neck. Wrap and refrigerate these, too. Whether you decide to use the giblets or not, you will certainly want to save the goose liver. Although it can't compare to the foie gras (literally, "fat liver") of the geese raised in the Périgord region of France expressly for the purpose of producing huge livers, you can freeze the goose liver and add it to your next chicken-liver dish—maybe even make a pâté.

To prepare the goose for roasting, pull out the excess fat from the body and neck cavities and save it for rendering. Chop off the wings at the second joint to give the bird a better appearance, and save these for broth, if you like. Sprinkle the cavity with salt and pepper. Loosely fill the neck and body cavities with stuffing. Skewer and lace the vent opening closed, catching the legs with the ends of the lacing string, as described for turkey on pages 191–92 .

Preheat the oven to 400°F. Place the goose, breast side up, on a rack in a roasting pan. Insert a meat thermometer deep into the inside of the thigh muscle, being careful that it does not touch fat or bone.

Roast an 8- to 10-pound stuffed goose for 45 minutes at 400°F, then lower the heat to 325°F and continue roasting for 1½ to 2 hours. Roast a 10- to 12-pound goose for 1 hour at 400°F, then continue roasting for 2 to 2½ hours at 325°F. For an unstuffed goose, subtract about 30 minutes from the total cooking time. Because of its thick layer of fat, there is no need to baste the goose while it cooks. However, if you have plans to use the rendered goose fat, you may want to siphon it from the roasting pan every 30 minutes or so to keep it from browning too much. The goose is done when the thermometer registers 180°F and the thigh feels very soft when pressed with paper towel–protected fingers. The juices from the thigh, when pierced with a fork, should run clear. Rest the goose for about 20 minutes.

Carving and Serving

A roast goose is a glorious sight, so it would be a shame to carve it in the kitchen. Plan to bring it to the table. If you're serving two geese, a nice presentation is to serve a whole goose in the center of the platter and a carved goose around it.

Warn the carver that a goose is not constructed the same as a chicken or a turkey. The leg and wing joints are further under the body, so they should be removed before carving. You might also want to cut out the breast meat in one piece from each side and carve each of them into two to four equal serving pieces. The leg and thigh will make more servings, too, if the meat is carved from them. Crisp goose skin is a real delicacy, so be sure to include some of it with each portion.

Like duck, the flavor of goose meat responds well to a fruity sauce, although the drippings make good gravy. See chapter 10 for suitable accompaniments.

Goose Fat: A Golden Gift

In Europe, especially in certain parts of Germany and France, the most prized by-product of the goose is the pale gold fat siphoned from the pan while the goose is roasting. After it's chilled, the fat turns creamy white and has a texture that can only be described as silken. The solid fat pulled from the goose cavities before roasting can also be chopped and melted (rendered) in a heavy pan over low heat. Strain the fat through a cheesecloth or fine-mesh sieve into one or more storage containers where any remaining solids will fall to the bottom. The fat will keep for weeks in the refrigerator and for months in the freezer.

Spoon out the delicately flavored goose fat to use in nearly any suitable recipe calling for shortening or oil (breads and biscuits, for example), or to sauté almost anything, but especially potatoes. Admittedly, this is not something that you'll want to do very often, especially if you are concerned about saturated fat and cholesterol, but as an occasional treat, foods cooked with goose fat are indescribably delicious.

Duck fat, although not as fine as goose fat, can also be siphoned from the roasting pan, or rendered, and used the same way.

GOOSE LIVER PÂTÉ

If you like, the rendered goose fat and the goose liver can be used to make a tasty smidgeon of pâté.

2 tablespoons strained rendered goose fat
¼ cup chopped shallots or the white part
   of a green onion (scallion)
¼ teaspoon salt
⅛ teaspoon freshly ground black pepper
1 whole goose liver
1 tablespoon dry white wine or vermouth
2 tablespoons butter, softened

Heat the fat in a medium-size skillet over medium heat. Add the shallots, salt, and pepper and cook, stirring, until the shallots have softened. Remove the shallots with a slotted spoon and set aside. Place the whole liver in the hot fat remaining in the skillet and cook over medium heat, turning once or twice, until lightly browned but still pink and juicy inside. (Overcooking the liver will make the pâté grainy.) Spoon the liver and pan juice, along with the reserved shallots, the wine, and butter into a blender or processor and process for a minute or two, or until the mixture is smooth. Scrape into a small cup or ramekin. Chill until firm enough to spread, an hour or two. Serve with toast or crackers.

YIELD: ABOUT ½ CUP

GOOSE OR DUCK CONFIT

You can also make what the French call a *confit* with rendered goose or duck fat and the giblets. The French use *confit* as an ingredient in other dishes, mainly cassoulet, or sometimes they spread it on toasted French bread or crackers, which is what I suggest you do.

Rendered goose or duck fat

Goose or duck giblets (gizzard, heart, and neck, but not the liver)

2 teaspoons salt

1 teaspoon dried thyme leaves, crumbled

¼ teaspoon freshly ground black pepper

2 bay leaves

Combine the fat and the giblets in a large heavy saucepan or Dutch oven. The fat should just cover the giblets. Stir in the remaining ingredients. Cook over medium heat, stirring now and then, until the fat is just ready to come to a boil. Lower the heat so that the surface of the fat barely moves and a bubble breaks the surface now and then. (Cooking over too high heat will make the gizzards tough.) Cook for about 2 hours, uncovered, or until the gizzards are very tender. Remove the giblets from the fat with a slotted spoon. When cool enough to handle, pull the meat from the neck into small pieces. Cut the gizzard and heart into small pieces. Place the neck meat and giblets in a container with a tight-fitting lid that is just large enough to hold them without crowding. Strain the cooking fat through a fine sieve. Pour enough of the strained fat over the giblets just to cover them. Cover the container tightly and chill. *Confit* will keep for months.

YIELD: ABOUT 1 CUP

BEEF STANDING RIB ROAST

It is not an exaggeration to call this cut the king of roasts. From a prime or choice steer, well marbled and properly aged, many would agree that there is simply no better eating.

My mother either served turkey for Thanksgiving and roast beef for Christmas, or the other way around, but neither one was ever served on both occasions. Which one made it to the table on Thanksgiving usually depended on how many would be sitting down for dinner. Her reasoning for the times was sound: Turkey was more expensive than a rib roast—about the same price as it is today in 1930s and 1940s dollars (a rib roast, she recalls, cost about 29 cents a pound). Her second reason was even more compelling: No family should ever have to eat all those turkey leftovers for days on end *twice* in six weeks.

Preparation and Roasting

Should you decide to go with a standing rib roast this Thanksgiving, be prepared to pay dearly for it. So while you're at it, pay a little more and buy the roast from a butcher who is willing to trim and dress it properly. The instructions that follow are from my friend Merle Ellis, who is best known for his syndicated column and as "The Butcher" on television.

To serve eight, you will need a four-rib, first- or second-cut rib roast weighing about 9 pounds. When you order the roast, ask the butcher to loosen or completely remove the chine (back) bone by sawing across the ribs, and to tie it to the roast, if necessary. This one simple act makes carving the roast so simple that even the novice carver will look like an expert. Merle also suggests that you ask the butcher to remove the "lifter" meat, too. That's the thin layer of meat that's between the fat on the top of the roast and another layer of fat beneath it. (Merle says when you start talking "lifter meat" to a butcher you can expect to get his full attention, a fact that I can attest to.) Doing this eliminates most of the fat that will otherwise be trimmed away and left on everyone's dinner plate. The slice will look nicer, too. If you like, you can also request to have the short ribs removed, and save these to be braised or roasted for another meal. If you choose to leave the ribs on (they make *great* nibbling), the butcher can crack and fold them under the roast before he ties it to make it more compact.

Place the roast, straight from the refrigerator, in a shallow pan, fat side up. You will not need a rack since the rib bones form one naturally. Insert a meat thermometer into the meat so the bulb is centered in the thickest part of the meat, making sure that it does not rest on fat or bone. *Do not add water and do not cover the pan.*

Roast the beef to the desired degree of doneness at 325°F. The thermometer will register 130° to 140°F for rare; 150° to 160°F for medium, and 160° to 170°F for well done. Check the following chart for times.

Roasting Times for Standing Rib Roast per Pound

WEIGHT	RARE	MEDIUM	WELL
4 to 6 pounds	26 to 32 minutes	34 to 38 minutes	40 to 42 minutes
6 to 8 pounds	23 to 25 minutes	27 to 30 minutes	32 to 35 minutes
over 8 pounds	20 minutes	25 minutes	30 minutes

Although I have given the times for it, I simply cannot recommend a well-done rib roast for any reason.

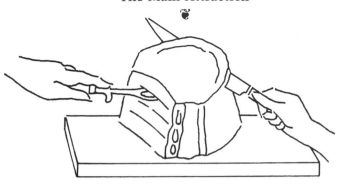

Serving and Carving

Place the roast on a platter to rest for 20 to 30 minutes before carving. This will give the juices an opportunity to retreat into the meat and makes the meat juicier.

To carve the roast, lay it on its side so that the ribs are to the left of a right-handed carver. Insert a carving fork between the ribs to hold the meat securely. Cut slices from the outer fatty edge in to the rib bones, making the slices no less than ¼ inch thick. Free each slice by running the point of the knife along the edge where it joins the rib bone and lifting it off before starting to carve the next slice.

A standing rib roast is traditionally accompanied by Yorkshire Pudding (see page 144) and often Horseradish Sauce (see page 227), with dark gravy (see page 219), made from the fat and drippings the same way as turkey or chicken gravy.

HAM

Ham is part of our national gastronomical heritage, even if it is not usually the first choice for Thanksgiving. However, many people, especially Southerners, feel that ham should be part of any feast, joining and complementing whatever else may be served in the starring role. Turkey and ham do have a special affinity for each other, and there's a lot to be said for having a ham on hand, especially if there are Thanksgiving-weekend guests to be fed.

Ham Products

There are a lot of smoked and cured meats on the market that are loosely referred to as *ham*. Nevertheless, only a smoked hind leg from a hog is actually entitled to use the name. Picnic hams, shoulder butts, and hocks aside, there is still a lot to know when it comes to buying a genuine ham.

Most hams today never see the inside of a smokehouse. All hams are cured, but few

210 THE THANKSGIVING COOKBOOK

are smoked. There are many kinds of cures for ham, but most fall roughly into two categories:

Dry cure. As the name implies, dry-cured hams are cured by a process that involves rubbing a seasoned-salt mixture into the fresh meat. After the curing mixture has permeated the meat, the ham is washed, dried, and aged. If they are smoked, this is done before aging. The dry-cure process is long and costly, and is used almost exclusively by the makers of specialty hams.

Wet cure. Hams cured this way have been immersed in a vat of seasoned brine. The ham can be eaten as soon as the cure is complete, or it, too, can be dried, aged, and sometimes smoked. Most commercial hams are cured using this technique.

COMMERCIAL HAMS

These are the hams you are most likely to find in the supermarket. The familiar cured flavor is imparted by pumping or injecting a curing solution into the fresh meat. After the cure these hams are either fully or partially cooked.

Commercial hams are sold whole or by the half. Sometimes the whole bone is left in, but more often, for ease in carving, the ham is semi-boneless, which means that only the round leg bone remains in the ham. In addition to these, you will find boneless, canned, and sectioned and formed hams, the last having been made from pieces of meat trimmed from the hind leg, which is then formed into a loaf or some other shape before curing.

SPECIALTY HAMS

The most famous of these is undoubtedly the Smithfield ham, which accounts for only a minuscule number of the specialty hams sold in this country. The name, designated by Virginia statute, is given to country hams, dry-cured, smoked, and aged by a special method by one of four companies in the town of Smithfield, Virginia. Not too long ago, all Smithfield hams had to be scrubbed, presoaked, and simmered for hours in barely moving water before they were skinned and baked. These old-fashioned hams are still available, but nowadays they are also sold in more "user-friendly" forms, fully or partially cooked, boned, etc. (By the way, the Queen of England serves Smithfield ham, a tradition handed down by her great-grandmother, Queen Victoria, who was said to have had a standing order of six per week.) Smithfield ham has a strong, distinctive flavor and a dry texture that makes true gourmets weak with joy, but that does, nevertheless, take some getting used to by the uninitiated. Smithfield hams are very often served with another, milder meat, frequently turkey, and *always* in small paper-thin slices.

Country hams, similar to Smithfield hams, that are also dry-cured, smoked, and aged, are sold throughout the South, usually under the name of the producer and the state from which they come. Each one of these has its own special cure, but they are not nearly as assertive or distinctive in flavor as a Smithfield ham.

There are also wet-cured specialty hams, very often from the North and often New England. Although these specialty-ham producers use essentially the same curing technique as the commercial packers, their hams are usually hand-selected, cured in a specially formulated brine for a particular flavor, then aged, and often smoked.

In addition to American hams, there are famous foreign hams, or foreign-style hams. These include prosciutto from Italy, Bayonne from France, Brandenham from the United Kingdom, and Westphalian Schinken from Germany.

Storing and Baking Ham

These days most hams are not cured in the sense that they can be kept without refrigeration, which used to be, of course, the whole point of salt curing. But they have been cured long enough to give them the familiar color and flavor of old-time ham. Some kinds of Smithfield and other dry-cured hams are the exception to this, but most hams, unless the packer advises otherwise, should be refrigerated until they are cooked.

Almost without exception, most hams you buy today, both specialty hams and those that are commercially packed, will come with the packer's recommended cooking or heating instructions.

Commercial hams are usually sold fully cooked. However, they will taste better if they are heated in a 325°F oven to an internal "eating temperature" of 130° to 140°F to further develop their flavor. Even cook-before-eating hams have been cooked to some degree and would be perfectly safe to eat. Cook these hams at 325°F to an internal temperature of 160°F to develop tenderness as well as flavor. Hams that are to be served chilled will also taste better if they are heated first.

GLAZING

These brief cooking or heating times will also give you an opportunity to glaze the ham, which should be done during the last 30 minutes of baking time so it doesn't burn. If the ham is covered or partially covered with a rind, about 30 to 45 minutes before the ham has finished baking (or when the thermometer registers 120°F), remove it from the oven and allow it to cool just enough to be able to handle it. Cut away the rind and the skin just beneath it to expose the layer of fat. Score the fat lightly in a diamond pattern, being careful not to cut into the meat. Stud the fat with cloves, if you like. Return the ham to the oven and start brushing it with a glaze.

A glaze can be as simple as a sprinkling of confectioners' sugar or a basting of Coca-Cola (very popular in the Southern states), or as elaborate as a mixture of jellies or jams, fruits, juices, and spices, all serving the same purpose of giving the baked ham an

appetizing, glistening appearance and adding a pleasant touch of sweetness to the saltiness of the ham. (See pages 230–31 for more glazing suggestions.)

A CARVING PRIMER

Whether you'll be using your grandmother's sterling silver carving set or a stainless
steel knife that's as sleek as tomorrow, *make sure it's sharp*. Use a knife-sharpening
gadget that you can buy in a housewares department or a sharpening steel, if you know
how to use one, to achieve a razorlike edge. If the knife is really dull, then have it honed
professionally. (Actually, home-sharpening devices can't actually sharpen knives. They
can only keep them sharp.)

Learning to carve at the table was a mandatory lesson for all young men a generation
ago. Nowadays, more often than not, the bird or roast is carved in the kitchen by whoever
has the most skill—or courage—and is brought forth in that rather unceremonious state
to the table.

Learning how to carve poultry and meat decently is not difficult. Follow the carving
steps as shown in the illustrations. For a little pre-Thanksgiving turkey-carving practice,
polish your skills on a couple of roasted broiling chickens in the weeks beforehand.

When the turkey or other roast will be carved at the table—and it really should be
on this special occasion—bring it to the table on a platter that is large enough to hold
it with a little room to spare. Platter garnishes should be kept to a minimum so that
they can be removed easily or pushed aside. In addition to the carving knife and fork,
a service plate and a long-handled spoon to remove stuffing should be provided.

How to Carve a Turkey, Chicken, or Capon

1. Remove the leg (thigh and drumstick) by holding the drumstick firmly with the
   fingers, gently pulling it away from the body. At the same time, cut through the
   skin between the leg and the body.

2. Press the leg away from the body with the flat side of the carving knife, then cut
   through the joint joining the leg to the backbone. Hold the leg on the service plate
   and separate the drumstick and thigh by cutting down through the joint.

3. If the drumstick is not to be served whole, stand it upright at a convenient angle to
   the plate and cut down, turning as you cut to get uniform slices.

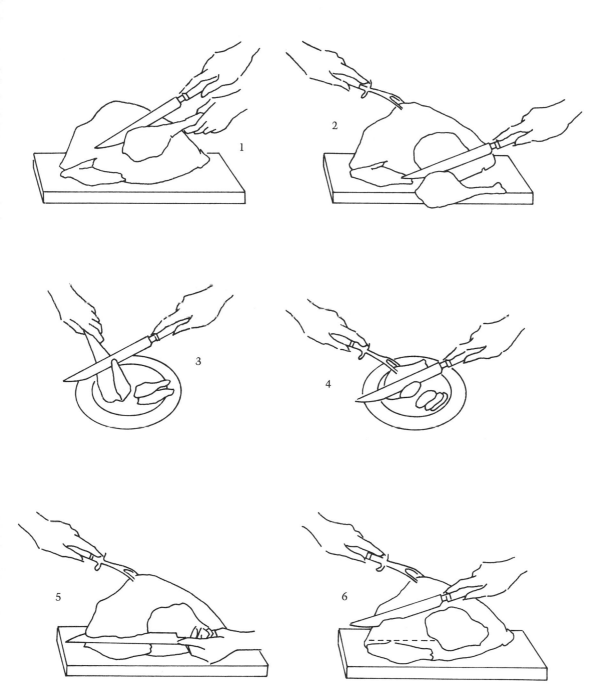

4. Hold the thigh firmly on the service plate and cut slices of meat parallel to the bone.

5. To slice the breast meat, make a deep cut into the breast, toward the body frame, parallel to and as close to the wing as possible. (Some carvers prefer to remove the wing before cutting into the breast.)

6. Starting halfway up the breast, cut thin slices of white meat down to the parallel cut. The slices will fall away from the turkey as they are cut. Continue until enough meat has been carved for first servings.

Note: Remove the stuffing from an opening cut into the side of the turkey where the leg has been removed.

How to Carve a Ham

1. Turn the ham, skin side up, with the bone facing the carver. Cut off a wedge from the right-hand side. This provides the ham with a firm base so that it does not slide around and should be done in the kitchen before placing the ham on the serving platter.

2. The ham should be set on the table with the bone to the right of the right-handed carver. Make one slanting cut down from the bone toward the left, and another perpendicular cut to make a wedge. Remove the wedge and set aside. Continue making perpendicular cuts down to the bone until you have as many slices as needed for first servings. Make one horizontal cut beneath the slices to free them.

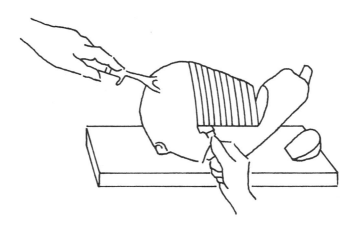

TEN

Gravy and Other Sauces
Savory and Sweet

If the recipes for all the sauces in the world were compiled in one book, I think a crane would be needed to lift it. There are literally thousands of recorded sauces in the world's cuisines, and probably thousands more that were made on the spur of the moment with drippings left in the skillet. It was the French, of course, who elevated the sauce to its noble standing.

The first sauce ever made undoubtedly enhanced and flattered whatever the food was for which it was created. As intrinsically important as they are, sauces have always played a secondary gastronomic role. But in the great restaurant kitchens, the saucier, the magician who whisks up the sauces, plays a secondary role to no one except the executive chef.

Lately, many of the great sauces have been relegated to the back burner, so to speak, victims of a weight-conscious and fat-conscious society that, more and more often, is opting to have its food served *au naturel*, or in sauces so light as to seem nonexistent.

Thanksgiving is the one day a year when gravy and other sauces shine again. After all, almost nothing is *so* good that a little sauce wouldn't make it better.

TURKEY AND CHICKEN GRAVY

The turkey is done to a turn, the stuffing is aromatic and moist, the mashed potatoes couldn't be fluffier, but if the gravy's not great, the dinner is less than perfect. Most of us would agree that much of the success of Thanksgiving dinner hinges on rich, brown, velvety gravy.

Although gravy making is based on the very simple principle of fat suspended in a thickener (usually all-purpose flour) that is thinned to a saucelike consistency with water or other liquid, most cooks—especially beginners—find that producing good gravy is more elusive than any other element in the meal.

Gravy tastes good because it contains fat and juices from the meat, the intense flavor of those little brown bits that cling to the roasting pan, and often a flavorful liquid that is used to thin the mixture.

Cornstarch as a Thickener

I prefer flour, but cornstarch can also be used to thicken gravy. It has *twice* the thickening power of flour and, hence, half the calories. But let me remind you that the preponderance of calories in gravy is not from the flour but from the fat. Cornstarch also makes a finer-textured gravy that is a little shinier and not quite so murky looking. However, cornstarch will not brown like flour, a big drawback, so if there are not enough brown solids in the pan drippings to color the gravy, you'll have to settle for a pale gravy or add a few drops of browning sauce, such as Kitchen Bouquet.

To substitute cornstarch for flour, use only half as much per cup of liquid. Otherwise, follow these instructions for flour-based gravy.

ROAST TURKEY OR ROAST CHICKEN PAN GRAVY LIKE GRANDMOTHER USED TO MAKE

The first rule for good gravy is to use the pan in which the turkey or chicken was roasted to make it. One of the biggest advantages to this technique may not be immediately apparent, but take my word that it will make the pan a whole lot easier to wash later on. The biggest culinary advantage is that the flavor of all those scrumptious-tasting little pieces of brown stuff that stick to the pan are sure to end up in the gravy and not down the sink.

The Rule. No matter how much gravy you're making, always use the same formula of 1 tablespoon of fat (from the drippings) and 1 tablespoon of all-purpose flour per cup of liquid. If you like a thicker gravy, use 2 tablespoons of flour per cup.

After the turkey has been taken from the oven and left to rest before it's carved, pour all of the fat and other liquid that's in the roasting pan into a large, heatproof measuring cup or bowl. Set aside until the fat floats to the top. The amount of liquid that's added to the fat-and-flour mixture determines the amount of gravy. Liquids that may be used include plain water, chicken broth, vegetable cooking water, or the broth in which the giblets and neck were simmered (see page 218). Some cooks also like to add a little dry white wine, vermouth, or dry sherry to flavor the turkey gravy.

Decide how much gravy you want to make. (Be sure to make plenty. You will be astonished at just how much gravy will be consumed at one sitting by otherwise health-conscious people, and you'll want some to serve with the leftovers.) For each cup of gravy, measure 1 tablespoon of fat from the measuring cup back into the roasting pan. Discard the remaining fat, but reserve the juices that have accumulated in the bottom of the cup.

Over medium heat, stir the flour into the fat in the roasting pan until it's smooth. (You may have to set a large roasting pan over both the front and back burners to obtain even heat.) Cook, stirring constantly, until the mixture bubbles. Remove the pan from the heat and steadily pour in the liquid (1 cup for each tablespoon of flour), stirring constantly. Also, stir in the reserved juices in the measuring cup. Return the pan to the heat and cook, stirring and adjusting the heat, if necessary, so that the mixture boils very slowly, until the gravy thickens and boils for 1 minute. Season to taste with salt and pepper. That's it. The gravy is ready to be poured into a gravy boat and served. However, if you're not ready for it, just let the gravy sit there in the pan until you are. The gravy can be reheated, but will thicken some as it cools, so a little more liquid may have to be added when it's reheated.

You can add things to the gravy after it's finished, if you like, most notably the chopped, cooked giblets (but not the liver since it often adds an unpleasant bitter taste, and many people don't like it) or browned, sliced mushrooms. A little chopped fresh parsley can be stirred in, too.

Note: Authorities on the matter advise that leftover gravy not be kept more than two or three days. It should also be brought to a full boil before serving.

LOW-FAT TURKEY GRAVY

Even without the fat, this gravy will still have a fairly rich taste from the flavor it picks up from the little brown particles that cling to the pan. Taking the time to brown the flour will also add character to this gravy, which can be used rather lavishly and guilt-lessly.

½ cup all-purpose flour
4 cups giblet broth (recipe follows) or
   chicken broth (see pages 2–4)

Dry sherry or white wine to taste
Salt and freshly ground black pepper to
   taste

After the turkey has been taken from the oven and left to rest before it's carved, pour off all of the fat and other liquid in the roasting pan into a large, heatproof measuring cup or bowl. Set aside until the fat floats to the top. Discard all of the fat, leaving only the meat juices in the bottom of the cup. Over medium heat, stir the flour into the roasting pan. Cook, stirring, until the flour turns golden brown. This may take a few minutes, so be patient. Remove the pan from the heat. Steadily add the broth and the sherry, stirring constantly. Return the pan to the heat and cook, stirring and adjusting the heat, if necessary, so that the mixture boils very slowly, until the gravy thickens. Season with the salt and pepper.

YIELD: ABOUT 4 CUPS

GIBLET BROTH

This is the broth that's used to make gravy and also to baste the turkey until enough drippings accumulate in the pan to use those. (If there's not enough broth to finish the gravy, use plain water. In fact, you can use plain water for the whole thing and it will still taste great.)

Place the giblets (except the liver) and neck in a medium-size saucepan and cover by a couple of inches with cold water. Season with a coarsely chopped small onion, a handful of chopped celery, including some leaves, and a few parsley sprigs. Bring to a boil over high heat, skimming the foam from the surface as it rises. Reduce the heat to medium-low, cover, and simmer slowly for 1½ to 2 hours, adding the liver, if using, for the last 20 minutes of cooking time. A little of the broth will boil away during cooking, but the amount of water you add in the beginning is roughly the amount of broth you'll have in the end. If the water seems to be boiling away too quickly, add a little boiling water. Strain the broth before adding it to the gravy.

The heart and gizzard can be very finely chopped and added to the gravy, but I don't recommend using the liver since it often gives the gravy a bitter taste.

GOOSE OR DUCK BROTH AND GRAVY

Giblet broth can be made from any poultry, and that includes goose and duck, although I never make either one since these birds don't require basting. Both birds are quite fatty, and consequently very moist, so to me pan gravy seems like fatty overkill. For my taste, goose and duck meat responds better to a lively, tart sauce.

ROAST BEEF PAN GRAVY

Roast beef gravy is made essentially the same way as roast turkey gravy, using water or beef broth (pages 2–4) as the liquid. The only problem you may encounter is that beef, especially if it is cooked to the rare or medium-rare stage, doesn't produce much in the way of brown drippings, so what you have in the roasting pan is mostly fat. However, as the roast rests before it's carved, quite a lot of meat juice will collect on the platter and this can be added to the finished gravy, which will give it some color as well as additional flavor. If the gravy is still not dark enough, a few drops of browning sauce will help and won't alter the flavor significantly.

MAKE-AHEAD BEEF GRAVY

Some years ago I started experimenting with a make-ahead gravy using canned beef broth. It evolved so well that now I serve it exclusively with standing rib roast. I especially like the convenience of being able to make it a day ahead.

6 tablespoons (¾ stick) butter
¼ pound small regular white mushrooms, trimmed and sliced (about 1 cup)
2 tablespoons minced onion
2 tablespoons minced fresh parsley
⅓ cup all-purpose flour

Two 13¾- or 14½-ounce cans ready-to-serve beef broth
¼ cup dry red wine (optional)
Beef juices
Browning sauce (optional)
Salt and freshly ground black pepper to taste

Melt 2 tablespoons of the butter in a large skillet over medium-high heat. Add the mushrooms and cook, stirring and tossing, until most of their liquid has evaporated and the slices are lightly browned. Remove from the heat and set aside. Melt the remaining butter in a heavy medium-size saucepan over medium-high heat. Add the onion and parsley and cook, stirring, until the onion has softened. Stir in the flour with a wire whisk and continue to cook, stirring constantly with the whisk, until the flour has turned a pale golden brown. Whisk in the beef broth all at once. Continue to cook, whisking constantly, until the mixture boils and is smooth and thick. Stir in the wine, then the mushrooms, along with any liquid that may have accumulated with them. Remove from the heat and set aside to cool slightly. Cover and refrigerate until the beef is removed from the oven. Reheat the gravy over low heat. As the beef rests, quite a lot of juice will accumulate on the platter. Add these juices to the gravy as it is being reheated. If the gravy is not dark enough, add a few drops of browning sauce. Season with the salt and pepper.

YIELD: ABOUT 4 CUPS

SAUCES FOR POULTRY, BEEF, AND HAM
TRADITIONAL ORANGE SAUCE
FOR DUCK OR GOOSE

The purist, of course, will eschew any sort of sweet sauce for the duck or the goose, but, frankly, I think just a little (don't overdo it; this is not gravy) does a lot for these birds. This sauce and the one that follows are easy. Make ahead, if you want to, and reheat gently over low heat before serving.

⅓ cup granulated sugar
⅓ cup firmly packed dark brown sugar
1 tablespoon cornstarch
¾ cup strained fresh orange juice
    (2 oranges)
1 tablespoon grated orange rind

¼ teaspoon salt
¼ cup orange liqueur
¼ cup very thin strips orange rind,
    dropped into boiling water for a minute
    or two and drained

   Mix both sugars and the cornstarch in a medium-size saucepan. Stir in the orange juice, grated rind, and salt and bring to a simmer over medium-high heat. Lower the heat to medium-low and simmer, stirring frequently, until the sugars have dissolved and the sauce is transparent, about 5 minutes. (May be made ahead up to this point and reheated.) Stir in the liqueur and orange strips.

YIELD: ABOUT 2¼ CUPS

QUICK ORANGE SAUCE

FOR DUCK OR GOOSE

*1½ cups strained fresh orange juice
  (4 oranges)*

*3 tablespoons honey
3 tablespoons orange liqueur*

Stir the orange juice and honey together in a small saucepan. Bring to a boil (be careful it doesn't boil over) and cook over medium-low heat, stirring frequently, until the mixture has reduced and thickened slightly, about 5 minutes. Stir in the liqueur. This sauce can be made ahead and reheated gently over low heat.

YIELD: ABOUT 1½ CUPS

MAHOGANY SAUCE

FOR DUCK OR GOOSE

I'm always a little suspicious of recipes that contain catsup, but trust me on this one. You'll find yourself making this sauce frequently because, as well as being good with duck and goose, it also goes well with game birds, chicken, roast pork, and even hot dogs.

*4 strips bacon, cut into ½-inch pieces
1 medium-size onion, finely chopped
  (½ cup)*

*2 tablespoons cider vinegar
1 cup grape jelly
1 cup catsup*

In a large skillet, cook the bacon over medium-high heat, stirring almost constantly, until it is just beginning to crisp. Add the onion and continue to cook, stirring, until the onion has browned. Stir in the vinegar, jelly, and catsup. Cook over low heat, stirring frequently, for about 5 minutes, or until the sauce thickens slightly. This sauce can be made ahead and reheated gently over low heat.

YIELD: ABOUT 1½ CUPS

BOURBON SAUCE

FOR DUCK OR GOOSE

This is a rather sophisticated sauce, certainly not suitable for children. I like the extra richness the liver provides, and that it has only a little sweetness. For some reason, duck and goose livers don't have the bitterness that turkey liver does.

1 juice orange	Three or four turns of a pepper mill
2 tablespoons butter	2 tablespoons orange marmalade
1 duck or goose liver	¼ cup bourbon whiskey
1 small clove garlic, minced	½ cup chicken broth (see pages 2–4)
3 tablespoons all-purpose flour	1 tablespoon grated orange rind

Squeeze the orange to make ½ cup of strained juice. Set aside. Melt the butter in a medium-size skillet over medium heat. Add the liver and cook, turning once or twice, until lightly browned but still pink and juicy inside. Remove the liver from the skillet and set aside. To the hot fat remaining in the skillet, add the garlic and cook briefly, stirring, until softened. Stir in the flour and pepper until well blended. Gradually stir in the orange juice, marmalade, bourbon, and chicken broth. Cook over medium-low heat, stirring, until the sauce has thickened and boiled for 1 minute. Remove from the heat. Finely chop the liver and stir it into the sauce along with the grated rind. (May be made ahead up to this point and reheated.) Return the pan to the heat, stirring until the liver is well mixed into the sauce.

YIELD: ABOUT 1½ CUPS

CUMBERLAND SAUCE

FOR GOOSE OR DUCK

This is the sauce that most often accompanies wild game, but it is also excellent served with goose or duck. It is my family's favorite sauce for roast goose.

3 large juice oranges	½ cup minced shallots or the white part
4 large lemons	of green onions (scallions)
1 tablespoon cornstarch	1 teaspoon dry mustard
½ cup ruby port	½ teaspoon ground ginger
One 10-ounce jar currant jelly	

Grate enough of the rind from one orange and one lemon to make 1 tablespoon of grated orange rind and 1 tablespoon of grated lemon rind. Squeeze the oranges and lemons to make 1 cup of strained orange juice and ½ cup of strained lemon juice. Before discarding the orange shells, cut a few thin slivers of the rind, making sure not to include the bitter white pith just beneath, and set aside. Stir 2 tablespoons of the orange juice together with the cornstarch in a small cup until smooth and set aside. Combine the remaining orange juice, the lemon juice, port, currant jelly, shallots, mustard, and ginger in a medium-size saucepan. Bring to a simmer over medium heat, stirring frequently and watching so that it doesn't boil over. Stir the cornstarch mixture into the sauce and cook, stirring constantly, until the sauce boils for 1 minute and thickens slightly. (May be made ahead up to this point and rewarmed.) Stir in the grated and slivered peels.

YIELD: ABOUT 3 CUPS

CURRANT SAUCE

FOR GOOSE OR DUCK

A rich, sweet sauce, but not quite so cloying as most of the orange sauces.

¼ cup dried currants
½ cup water
1 cup chicken broth (see pages 2–4)
1 tablespoon firmly packed light or dark brown sugar
1 small onion, peeled and left whole
1 small clove garlic, peeled and left whole
1 bay leaf
2 tablespoons red wine vinegar

⅓ cup currant jelly
2 tablespoons cornstarch
¼ teaspoon ground cloves
⅓ cup strained fresh orange juice (1 orange)
3 tablespoons black raspberry or black currant liqueur
Salt and freshly ground black pepper to taste

Combine the currants, water, broth, sugar, onion, garlic, and bay leaf in a small saucepan and bring to a boil over high heat. Reduce the heat to medium-low, cover, and simmer for 15 minutes. Strain the mixture through a fine-mesh sieve into a small bowl. Pour the strained liquid back into the saucepan and stir in the vinegar and currant jelly. Mix the cornstarch with the ground cloves and orange juice in a small bowl until smooth and stir into the currant mixture. Bring to a boil over high heat, stirring constantly. Reduce the heat to medium-low and simmer, uncovered, for 10 minutes. Remove from the heat and stir in the liqueur. Season with the salt and pepper. The sauce may be made ahead and reheated before serving.

YIELD: ABOUT 2¼ CUPS

CHERRY SAUCE

FOR GOOSE, DUCK, CHICKEN, OR CORNISH HENS

If serving this sauce with chicken or Cornish hens, you may wish to make it right in the roasting pan as you would gravy. In that case, pour off all of the fat from the roasting pan and set the pan over one or two stove-top burners. Reduce the amount of butter to 1 tablespoon and proceed as the recipe directs.

3 tablespoons butter
1 large onion, very finely chopped (1 cup)
One 10½-ounce can condensed consommé
3 tablespoons cornstarch

One 16-ounce can pitted tart red cherries, drained, reserving 2 tablespoons of the juice
¼ cup dry or sweet sherry
Salt and freshly ground black pepper to taste

Melt the butter in a large skillet over medium-high heat. When hot, add the onion and cook, stirring frequently, until softened. Stir in the consommé and simmer over low heat for 5 minutes. Stir the cornstarch into the reserved cherry juice to make a smooth paste and stir into the consommé mixture. Simmer for 5 minutes longer. Stir in the cherries and sherry. Season with the salt and pepper. This sauce can be made ahead and gently reheated.

YIELD: ABOUT 2½ CUPS

HOT CRANBERRY SAUCE

FOR TURKEY, CHICKEN, CAPON, OR CORNISH HENS

Use this sauce for a glaze, if you like, by brushing it on the turkey, chicken, capon, or Cornish hens during the last 20 to 30 minutes of roasting time. If you intend to make a pan gravy, don't use too much glaze or it will interfere with the flavor.

One 16-ounce can jellied cranberry sauce
One 6-ounce can frozen orange juice,
  thawed

¼ pound (1 stick) butter, cut into pieces

Mash the cranberry sauce in a medium-size saucepan over medium heat. Stir in the orange juice and the butter and cook, stirring, until the cranberry sauce and butter have melted and the mixture is smooth.

YIELD: ABOUT 2½ CUPS

A PAN SAUCE FOR SQUAB

This is the perfect sauce for squab stuffed with porcini mushrooms and pâté on pages 175–76, or other small birds.

2 tablespoons cognac or other good
  brandy
1 or 2 tablespoons butter

2 tablespoons minced shallots
2 tablespoons currant jelly
¼ cup port wine

After the squabs have finished roasting and the pan has been removed from the oven, barely warm the brandy in a small saucepan over very low heat. Touch a match to the brandy and pour, flaming, over the squabs. When the flames subside, remove the squabs from the pan and keep them warm. Set the roasting pan over one or two stove-top burners over medium heat and stir in the butter. When it is hot, add the shallots and stir until softened. Add the currant jelly and port and cook, stirring, until the mixture bubbles. Pour the sauce over the squabs and serve immediately.

YIELD: ENOUGH SAUCE FOR 6 TO 8 SQUABS

WILD MUSHROOM GRAVY

FOR CORNISH HENS OR CHICKEN

It's the wild mushrooms that give this gravy its rather exotic flavor. Regular white mushrooms won't do the job.

*1 ounce dried exotic mushrooms, such as
    morels or porcini*
1 cup boiling water
*¼ pound sliced bacon, cut into ½-inch
    pieces*
*Gizzards and hearts from the hens,
    chopped (see note below)*

1 small onion, finely chopped (¼ cup)
¼ cup all-purpose flour
¼ cup dry sherry
2½ cups chicken broth (see pages 2–4)
Freshly ground black pepper to taste

Brush away any bits of dirt from the dried mushrooms. Place them in a small bowl and add the boiling water. Set aside to rehydrate for about 30 minutes. Remove the mushrooms with a slotted spoon and pat dry on paper towels. Strain the liquid through a fine-mesh sieve and reserve it. Finely chop the mushrooms.

Remove the roasted hens from the roasting pan to a platter and keep them warm. Discard all but about 3 tablespoons of the drippings from the roasting pan and set the pan aside. In a large skillet, fry the bacon over medium-high heat until brown and crisp. Remove from the skillet with a slotted spoon and drain on paper towels. Discard all but about 2 tablespoons of the bacon fat in the skillet. Set the skillet over medium heat. When the fat is hot, add the mushrooms, giblets, and onion and cook, stirring frequently, for about 5 minutes, or until the onion is lightly browned. Set the roasting pan over one or two stove-top burners over medium heat. When the drippings are hot, add the mushroom mixture to the roasting pan. Stir in the flour. Cook, stirring almost constantly, until the flour has browned. Stir in the bacon, mushroom liquid, sherry, and broth. Bring to a boil over high heat, stirring frequently. Reduce the heat to medium and cook, stirring, until the sauce thickens and boils for 1 minute. Season with the pepper. The gravy can be made ahead and reheated.

YIELD: ABOUT 4 CUPS

Note: In most cases, I prefer not to use the liver in gravy, but it can be chopped and added to the giblet mixture, if you like.

APRICOT-ORANGE-BRANDY SAUCE

FOR CORNISH HENS, CHICKEN, OR CAPON

An excellent sauce that has no fat. Recommended for Cornish hens filled with Pear and Pine Nut Stuffing (pages 170–71).

⅔ cup apricot preserves
¼ cup frozen orange juice concentrate

¼ cup good brandy
2 fresh Bartlett pears, cored and quartered

In a medium-size bowl, combine the preserves, orange juice concentrate, and brandy. Add the pear quarters and refrigerate until ready to use. About 20 minutes before the hens are finished roasting, arrange the pears in the pan with the hens. Brush the pears and the hens with the glaze and return to the oven to finish roasting.

YIELD: ENOUGH GLAZE FOR 4 CORNISH HENS

HORSERADISH SAUCE

FOR BEEF

Whether to include the fresh bread crumbs in this sauce or not is a matter of personal preference. I happen to like the texture the crumbs provide. It's important to use a really pungent horseradish, the kind that burns your nose when you eat it. Plain prepared horseradish is also good with roast beef.

1 slice day-old white bread, crust removed and whirled in a blender or food processor to make bread crumbs (½ cup)
½ cup light cream or half-and-half

½ cup prepared white horseradish, drained and squeezed dry in a kitchen towel
¼ teaspoon salt
½ cup heavy or whipping cream
Paprika for garnish

Combine the crumbs, light cream, horseradish, and salt in a small bowl. Cover and refrigerate until shortly before serving time. Whip the heavy cream until stiff peaks form when the beaters are lifted. Fold into the horseradish mixture. If not serving immediately, chill until ready to serve. Turn into a serving bowl and sprinkle with paprika.

YIELD: ABOUT 2 CUPS

A QUICK HORSERADISH SAUCE

FOR BEEF

The old standby sauce that can be stirred together at the last minute.

½ cup sour cream

1 to 2 tablespoons prepared white horse-radish, drained and squeezed dry in a kitchen towel

Mix the sour cream with the horseradish in a small bowl. Turn into a serving bowl and chill until ready to serve.

YIELD: 1 cup

RAISIN SAUCE

FOR HAM

If you would prefer this rather sweet sauce a little less so, substitute lemon juice for some of the orange juice. This is also an excellent sauce for smoked tongue.

1 juice orange
2 teaspoons grated orange rind
1 cup golden or dark raisins
1 cup water
⅔ cup currant jelly

½ cup firmly packed light brown sugar
2 tablespoons cornstarch
¼ teaspoon salt
⅛ teaspoon ground allspice

Squeeze the orange to make ⅓ cup of strained juice. In a medium-size saucepan, combine the juice, rind, raisins, water, and jelly. Bring to a slow boil over medium-high heat. Blend the sugar, cornstarch, salt, and allspice in a small bowl and stir into the orange sauce. Reduce the heat to medium-low and cook, stirring, until the sauce thickens and clears. This sauce can be made ahead and reheated.

YIELD: ABOUT 2⅔ CUPS

CREAMY MUSTARD SAUCE

FOR HAM

1 cup sour cream
1 tablespoon Dijon mustard
1 tablespoon minced onion

⅛ teaspoon salt
One or two turns of a pepper mill

Combine all of the ingredients in a small saucepan. Heat gently (do not boil) just before serving.

YIELD: ABOUT 1 CUP

HOT AND SPICY MUSTARD SAUCE

FOR HAM

I always double this sauce since it keeps well for a couple of weeks in the refrigerator and we like it as an accompaniment to cold turkey as well as cold ham, and as a sandwich spread, too, in place of mayonnaise or mustard.

½ cup firmly packed light brown sugar
2 tablespoons dry mustard
1 chicken bouillon cube

¼ cup boiling water
¼ cup white vinegar
1 large egg, well beaten

Mix the brown sugar and mustard in the top of a double boiler. Dissolve the bouillon cube in the boiling water and stir in the vinegar. Stir into the sugar mixture, along with the egg. Set the double boiler over simmering water and cook, stirring constantly, until thick, about 5 minutes. Turn into a serving bowl. Cool, cover, and refrigerate until serving time. The sauce may be gently reheated or served chilled or at room temperature.

YIELD: 1 CUP

GLAZES FOR HAM

Many ham lovers enjoy the little bit of sweetness a glaze provides to offset the saltiness of the ham. At one time, especially for Easter dinner, it was not unusual to see a baked ham decorated as gaily as an Easter bonnet, with pineapple rings, cherries, and cloves covering every square inch of the diamond-patterned fat. Nowadays, with the de-emphasis of fussy food garnishes, hams are usually served in a more natural state, with only a glistening glaze, if that.

Since glazes are necessarily sugary, they should be lightly brushed onto the plain or diamond-scored fat on the top of the ham only during the last 20 to 30 minutes of baking time. Otherwise they tend to burn, both on the ham and in the roasting pan.

One-ingredient glazes for ham include Coca-Cola, maple syrup, light or dark corn syrup, honey, melted or softened canned cranberry sauce, orange marmalade (mixed with a little orange juice or orange liqueur to thin it slightly), cherry preserves (thinned with cherry liqueur), apple jelly, apple cider, orange juice or frozen orange juice concentrate, and other sweet fruit juices. My own favorite is just a light sprinkling of confectioners' sugar, which melts and forms its own glaze while the ham finishes baking.

There are also many simple glaze mixtures to enhance the flavor of ham. Here are a few that I've enjoyed on my hams over the years.

BOURBON GLAZE

½ cup bourbon whiskey
½ cup firmly packed light brown sugar

¼ teaspoon ground cloves
1 teaspoon grated orange rind

Combine all of the ingredients in a small bowl. Let stand, stirring occasionally, until the sugar is dissolved.

YIELD: 1 CUP

ORANGE GLAZE

¼ cup strained fresh orange juice
½ cup firmly packed light brown sugar

½ cup orange marmalade
¼ teaspoon ground mace

Combine the orange juice, sugar, and marmalade in a medium-size saucepan. Bring to a boil over high heat. Lower the heat to medium-low and simmer, uncovered, for 10 minutes. Remove from the heat and stir in the mace.

YIELD: ABOUT 1¼ CUPS

PORT-SYRUP GLAZE

½ cup light corn syrup   ½ cup port wine

Combine the syrup and port in a small saucepan and bring to a boil.

YIELD: 1 CUP

HONEY-MUSTARD GLAZE

½ cup honey   1 teaspoon dry mustard

Mix the honey and mustard in a small bowl.

YIELD: ½ CUP

SAUCES FOR VEGETABLES

A pat of fresh butter, a little salt, and a grinding of fresh pepper is probably the simplest sauce of all. A step beyond that is butter that has had some flavoring added to it.

MAÎTRE D'HÔTEL BUTTER

Also known as lemon sauce, maître d' hôtel butter can be flavored with any herb that goes well with the vegetable with which it is served, and it can be served hot or cold. Either way, it's good on just about any plain vegetable.

4 tablespoons (½ stick) butter
1 tablespoon fresh lemon juice
Pinch of cayenne (red) pepper

1 tablespoon minced fresh parsley, chives, or dill

To serve hot, melt the butter and stir in the remaining ingredients. To serve cold, work the butter in a small bowl with a wooden spoon until creamy. Gradually beat in the remaining ingredients.

YIELD: ¼ CUP

Herbed or Spiced Butter Sauce: Stir in about ⅛ teaspoon of the following dried herbs and other flavorings for a sauce perfect for these vegetables:

Asparagus: marjoram, savory, or tarragon
Beets: dill, ginger, savory, tarragon, or thyme
Broccoli: red (cayenne) pepper, rosemary, or tarragon
Brussels sprouts: caraway seed, dill, or sage
Carrots: ginger, dill, marjoram, mint, or nutmeg
Cauliflower: caraway seed, dill, mace, paprika, or rosemary
Green beans: dill, red (cayenne) pepper, sage, or tarragon
Mushrooms: oregano, rosemary, tarragon, or thyme
Onions: basil, oregano, sage, or thyme
Peas: basil, chervil, oregano, marjoram, mint, savory, or thyme
Spinach: allspice, marjoram, or rosemary

AMANDINE SAUCE

One of the most versatile and best-loved sauces of all. Other chopped nuts can be substituted for the almonds, but almonds are almost everyone's favorite.

4 tablespoons (½ stick) butter

½ cup toasted (see pages 6–7) slivered almonds

Heat the butter in a small skillet. When it is hot, add the almonds and cook over medium heat, stirring occasionally, for 3 or 4 minutes, or until the almonds are golden. Serve very warm.

YIELD: ABOUT ¾ CUP

SHARP SAUCE

Good over any vegetable that has enough flavor or texture to stand up to this assertive sauce—green beans and Brussels sprouts, for example.

½ cup mayonnaise
¼ cup cider vinegar
2 tablespoons sugar

2 tablespoons butter, melted
1 medium-size onion, minced (½ cup)

In a small saucepan, mix together the mayonnaise, vinegar, sugar, and melted butter until well blended. Stir in the onion. Set the pan over medium heat and stir until the mixture is hot. Serve the dressing very warm.

YIELD: ABOUT 1 CUP

SUPREME SAUCE

If this book had been written a mere year or two ago, undoubtedly I would have included a recipe for the greatest special-occasion sauce of them all: hollandaise. Unfortunately, because of the salmonella bacteria present in some eggs, I no longer consider it prudent to use undercooked eggs. So, for now, it must be the *late*, great hollandaise sauce. On the bright side, the egg industry has been down before, but never out, and, hopefully, safe hollandaise, eggnog, and three-minute eggs will be back soon. Until then, this mixture of butter and cream is a good substitute.

¼ pound (1 stick) butter
3 tablespoons fresh lemon juice
½ teaspoon salt

⅛ teaspoon ground white pepper
½ cup heavy or whipping cream

Melt the butter in a medium-size saucepan over medium heat. Stir in the lemon juice, salt, and pepper. Set aside to cool. Whip the cream until stiff peaks form when the beaters are lifted. Stir into the cooled butter mixture.

YIELD: ABOUT 1½ CUPS

CRÈME FRAÎCHE AND MUSTARD SAUCE

Good on beets and other root vegetables.

1½ cups crème fraîche (see page 4) or
   sour cream
¼ cup coarse-grain mustard

1½ teaspoons celery seed
1 teaspoon fresh lemon juice
Big pinch of ground white pepper

Combine all of the ingredients in a medium-size saucepan. Heat gently over low heat, stirring constantly, until warm.

YIELD: ABOUT 1¾ CUPS

WARM LEMON VINAIGRETTE SAUCE

Adds zesty flavor to almost any vegetable.

2 tablespoons fresh lemon juice
2 teaspoons Dijon mustard

2 teaspoons minced shallots or the white
   part of green onions (scallions)
¼ cup plus 2 tablespoons vegetable oil

Combine the lemon juice, mustard, and shallots in a small nonreactive saucepan. Stir in the oil. Just before serving, place over low heat and cook gently, stirring constantly, until warm.

YIELD: ABOUT ⅔ CUP

GOLDENROD SAUCE

On pages 116–17 I have given a recipe for Béchamel (white sauce) which lends itself nicely to just about anything you'd care to stir into it. This recipe and the one that follows are old favorites that can be spooned over or mixed with nearly any hot vegetable.

1 recipe Béchamel   *2 tablespoons chopped fresh parsley*
1 hard-cooked egg, finely chopped

    Make the béchamel according to the directions. Stir in the egg and parsley. Make ahead, if you like, but if you do, press a piece of plastic wrap directly on the surface to keep a skin from forming. Rewarm over low heat.

YIELD: 1¼ CUPS

ROQUEFORT SAUCE

1 recipe Béchamel (see pages 116–17)   *¼ cup crumbled Roquefort or other*
                                               crumbly blue-veined cheese

    Make the béchamel according to the directions. Stir in the Roquefort cheese. Make ahead, if you like, but if you do, press a piece of plastic wrap directly on the surface to keep a skin from forming. Rewarm over low heat. The cheese should not be dissolved completely.

YIELD: ABOUT 1¼ CUPS

Variation: 1 cup shredded cheddar, Swiss, or American cheese can be substituted for the Roquefort.

SAUCES FOR DESSERT

For those times when whipped cream is not enough!

EASY CHOCOLATE SAUCE

I'm sure you don't need me to tell you how to use chocolate sauce. This chocolate sauce and the two that follow can be made ahead and refrigerated after they are cool, but be very gentle when you rewarm them. To keep the sauce warm until you are ready for it, set the pan in another pan that is partly filled with warm water.

6 ounces semisweet chocolate, broken into pieces, or 1 cup semisweet chocolate morsels

½ cup heavy or whipping cream
½ teaspoon vanilla extract

Combine the chocolate, cream, and vanilla in a small heavy saucepan. Cook over low heat, stirring, until the chocolate is melted and the mixture is warm and well blended. This sauce may be made ahead and refrigerated. In that case, rewarm gently over low heat.

YIELD: ABOUT 1½ CUPS

GOOEY CHOCOLATE SAUCE

6 ounces semisweet chocolate, broken into pieces, or 1 cup semisweet chocolate morsels
½ cup light corn syrup

¼ cup light cream or half-and-half
1 tablespoon butter
¼ teaspoon vanilla extract

Combine the chocolate and corn syrup in a small heavy saucepan. Cook over very low heat, stirring constantly, until the chocolate is melted and the mixture is smooth. Stir in the cream, butter, and vanilla until well blended. This sauce can be served warm or cool. If made ahead, rewarm gently over low heat.

YIELD: 1¼ CUPS

A FANCY CHOCOLATE SAUCE

*6 ounces semisweet chocolate, broken
    into pieces, or 1 cup semisweet
    chocolate morsels*
2 tablespoons butter

1 cup water
1 cup sugar
2 tablespoons light corn syrup
¼ cup light cream or half-and-half

In a heavy medium-size saucepan, melt the chocolate and butter together over low heat, stirring constantly, and set aside. In a small heavy saucepan, combine the water, sugar, and corn syrup. Cook over medium heat, stirring until the sugar is dissolved. Raise the heat to medium and boil slowly until the mixture is thick enough to coat a spoon and a small amount dropped into a measuring cup of cold water forms a soft ball, about 8 minutes. Whisk the syrup into the chocolate mixture until well blended, then stir in the cream.

YIELD: ABOUT 2½ CUPS

Chocolate-Nut Sauce: Stir any variety of toasted (see pages 6–7) or untoasted chopped nuts that you like into the finished chocolate sauce, about ½ cup nuts for every cup of sauce.

VANILLA CUSTARD SAUCE

In cooking circles, this sauce is known as crème anglaise. It is the traditional sauce for most steamed and bread puddings, and I like it with many plain fruit pies, too.

4 large egg yolks
½ cup sugar

2 cups milk
1 tablespoon vanilla extract

Beat the egg yolks and sugar together in a large bowl until thick and creamy. In a heavy medium-size saucepan, warm the milk over low heat until it steams and small bubbles form around the edge. Gradually add the hot milk to the yolk mixture, beating constantly with a wire whisk. Pour the yolk mixture back into the saucepan. Set the pan over low heat and cook, stirring constantly with a wooden spoon, for about 8 minutes, or until the mixture coats the spoon. Stir in the vanilla. Set the pan in a large bowl that contains a tray of ice cubes and water. Beat the sauce until it cools down. This sauce may be made ahead and chilled. In that case, press a piece of plastic wrap directly onto the surface to keep a skin from forming. Reheat in a heavy saucepan over very low heat, stirring constantly to keep the sauce from curdling.

YIELD: ABOUT 1½ CUPS

HARD SAUCE

This is the classic accompaniment for plum pudding, but it is just as delicious with lighter puddings and pies, especially those that are served warm. To those who have never tasted it, the recipe for hard sauce may look obscenely sweet and rich, but to taste it is to love it, at least for most people.

½ pound (2 sticks) butter, softened
2 cups sifted confectioners' sugar

¼ cup good brandy or cognac
Ground nutmeg to taste

Beat the butter until creamy in a medium-size bowl with an electric mixer at medium speed. Gradually beat in the sugar until smooth. Stir in the brandy until well blended. Season with nutmeg. Turn into a serving bowl and chill until close to serving time, then set out for about 30 minutes to soften slightly.

YIELD: ABOUT 2½ cups

QUICK CARAMEL SAUCE

It's the heavy cream that makes this childishly simple sauce heavenly. Weight watchers can substitute milk.

½ pound packaged vanilla caramel
candies

1 cup heavy or whipping cream

Combine the caramels and cream in the top of a double boiler over boiling water. Cook, stirring constantly, until the caramels are melted and the sauce is smooth.

YIELD: ABOUT 1½ CUPS

CARAMEL CREAM

A rich topping for tarts and pies that goes one delicious step beyond whipped cream.

1 cup heavy or whipping cream   *2 tablespoons dark brown sugar*

Combine the cream and sugar together in a medium-size bowl. Let stand for 10 minutes, then beat with an electric mixer on high speed until stiff peaks form.

YIELD: ABOUT 1 CUP

RASPBERRY SAUCE

These days chocolate anything is the most frequent partner for this exquisitely fresh-tasting and delicate sauce. Raspberry sauce, for all its sweetness, can cut the richness of many creamy desserts.

One 12-ounce bag frozen raspberries,   *2 teaspoons fresh lemon juice*
  completely thawed   *1 cup fresh raspberries (optional)*
¾ cup sugar

Puree the raspberries in a blender or food processor. Push the mixture through a large strainer with the back of a spoon into a small saucepan, discarding the solids left in the strainer. Stir in the sugar and lemon juice. Cook over medium-low heat until the mixture comes to a slow boil. Boil slowly for 3 minutes, stirring constantly. Remove from the heat and cool. Serve at room temperature or chilled. Stir in the raspberries just before serving.

YIELD: ABOUT 1½ CUPS

A QUICKER RASPBERRY SAUCE

*One 10-ounce package frozen raspberries
in light syrup, thawed according to
package directions*

*⅓ cup light corn syrup
2 tablespoons black raspberry liqueur
(optional)*

Puree the thawed raspberries and their liquid in a blender or food processor. Push the mixture through a strainer with the back of a spoon into a small bowl, discarding the solids left in the strainer. Stir in the corn syrup and liqueur.

YIELD: ABOUT 1¼ CUPS

ELEVEN

The Bread Basket

❦

BISCUITS, MUFFINS, ROLLS, AND BUNS

The bread basket is probably the most reached-for serving bowl on the Thanksgiving table, so let's hope it's loaded with a selection of aromatic home-baked rolls, muffins, biscuits, and buns, some sweet, others savory.

What's hidden under the napkin can be a treat for the eye and the appetite, or it can be insufferably dull. A loaf of crusty bread may be just right for most meals, but Thanksgiving dinner demands that this part of the meal, like all the others, reflect a certain amount of bounty, as well as homemade goodness.

Filling the bread basket imaginatively can be fun, and all the oohs and aahs that it elicits make the extra effort worthwhile. The basket needn't contain an enormous selection, but if you can manage it, there should be some variety in flavor and texture, ranging from soft and sweet to crisp and savory.

If you're fortunate enough to have found a good bakery, one or two of these bread basket offerings can probably be purchased the day before, thus eliminating a little of the last-moment scurry that fresh-baked goodies require. In most cases, at least some preparation work can be done in advance, usually mixing the dry ingredients in the bowl and measuring out the others.

Whenever they are appropriate, I've included instructions for reheating. Unfortunately, most baked goods suffer at least a little when made ahead and rewarmed, especially biscuits, something to keep in mind when planning the final moments before dinner is served.

In addition to the recipes in this chapter, you will find an excellent white bread on pages 156–57, and Charlotte's Toasts on page 30, both good candidates for this once-a-year feast.

241

BISCUITS

It was my stepmother, Ellen Martin, who introduced me to the pleasures of homemade biscuits. As a Southerner she never felt that any dinner was quite complete without a few biscuits in the bread basket, and now I'm inclined to agree with her, especially for holiday meals. Ellen made wonderful biscuits, light and flaky, from a recipe that came from her family's cook in Birmingham, Alabama.

I have never had a problem making biscuits, nor should you, if you remember to restrain yourself and mix the batter only until it is moistened, no more than 30 seconds. Kneading the biscuit dough should also be a brief procedure, about ten times should do it, unless the recipe says otherwise. The dough can either be rolled out or pressed out with the palms of your hands, usually to a ½-inch thickness. Flour the biscuit cutter so it won't stick to the dough. Cut straight down and lift out. Twisting the biscuit cutter causes lopsided biscuits.

Ideally, biscuits should be served while they are still warm from the oven, but if you must, they can be made ahead and then tightly wrapped in aluminum foil and frozen or refrigerated. Reheat room temperature or chilled biscuits, loosely wrapped in aluminum foil, at 325°F for 10 to 15 minutes, about 5 minutes longer for frozen biscuits.

Serve the biscuits with softened butter, or they can be split and slathered with gravy. Plain honey, honey butter, or fruit butters are also good biscuit toppings.

HONEY BUTTER

Fruit preserves or jelly may be substituted for the honey.

¼ pound (1 stick) butter, softened   *¼ cup honey*

In a medium-size bowl, beat the butter and honey together with an electric mixer until light and fluffy. Spoon into a crock or small bowl. Soften slightly before serving.

YIELD: 1 CUP

Biscuit Variations

It's easy to vary the flavor of plain biscuits. A few minutes before removing them from the oven, sprinkle with grated Parmesan cheese or paprika. Or any one of the following may be stirred into the biscuit dough before the liquid ingredients are added:

- 2 to 3 tablespoons finely chopped fresh parsley or chives (other fresh herbs may be used, but the quantity will have to be adjusted depending on the pungency of the herbs)
- ½ cup shredded cheddar or other flavorful cheese
- ¼ cup chopped cooked ham or bacon
- ¼ cup chopped onion, lightly browned in a tablespoon of butter

Super Tip: If there's no time to roll and cut round biscuits, roll or press the dough into a ½-inch-thick square or rectangle and cut into squares or triangles with a long, sharp knife.

ELLEN MARTIN'S BAKING POWDER BISCUITS

These are the first biscuits I learned to make, and the ones I most often serve when I want a good, honest biscuit that can be made in a hurry.

2 cups all-purpose flour
1 tablespoon baking powder
½ teaspoon salt

¼ cup solid white vegetable shortening
About ¾ cup milk

Preheat the oven to 450°F. Combine the flour, baking powder, and salt in a large bowl with a wire whisk until completely blended. Cut in the shortening with a pastry blender or two knives until the mixture resembles coarse crumbs. Stir in enough of the milk to make a soft dough. Turn out onto a floured surface and knead briefly, about 30 seconds. Roll or pat the dough to a ½-inch thickness. Cut into rounds with a floured 2-inch biscuit cutter, placing the rounds on a baking sheet that has been lightly greased or coated with nonstick vegetable spray. Reroll the scraps and cut the remaining biscuits. Bake for 12 to 15 minutes, or until golden. Remove from the oven and serve immediately.

YIELD: ABOUT 16 BISCUITS

FLUFFY BUTTERMILK BISCUITS

A fluffier, lighter-textured biscuit than most, with just a hint of sweetness.

2 cups self-rising flour (not cake flour)
1 tablespoon baking powder
1 tablespoon sugar
⅛ teaspoon salt

⅓ cup solid white vegetable shortening
⅞ cup (1 cup less 2 tablespoons)
   buttermilk
Melted butter for brushing biscuits

Preheat the oven to 450°F. Mix the flour, baking powder, sugar, and salt with a wire whisk in a medium-size bowl. Cut in the shortening with a pastry cutter or two knives until the mixture resembles coarse crumbs. Add the buttermilk, all at once, and stir briefly with a fork just until the mixture comes together. Roll or pat the dough to a ½-inch thickness on a floured surface. Cut into rounds with a floured 2-inch biscuit cutter, placing the rounds on a baking sheet that has been lightly greased or coated with nonstick vegetable spray. Reroll the scraps and cut the remaining biscuits. Bake for 10 minutes. Brush the tops with the melted butter and continue to bake for 3 to 5 minutes longer, or until golden brown. Remove from the oven and serve immediately.

YIELD: ABOUT 20 BISCUITS

RAISIN BISCUITS WITH CHUTNEY BUTTER

These are my hands-down favorite biscuits. At one time I served them only with ham. Then I found that they were just as good with goose, so the next Thanksgiving I baked some to serve with turkey and they were practically inhaled. You don't have to bother with the Chutney Butter (recipe follows) if you're in a hurry, but without it the biscuits will be only half as good.

2 cups all-purpose flour
½ cup golden raisins
1 tablespoon baking powder

2 teaspoons sugar
1 teaspoon salt
1 cup whipping or heavy cream

Preheat the oven to 425°F. Combine the flour, raisins, baking powder, sugar, and salt in a large bowl until well blended. Make a well in the center of the flour mixture and add the cream. Stir with a fork, mixing just until moistened. Turn out onto a lightly floured surface and knead eight to ten times. Roll out or press to a ½-inch thickness. Cut into rounds with a floured 1½-inch biscuit cutter, placing the rounds on a baking sheet that has been lightly greased or coated with nonstick vegetable spray. Reroll the scraps and cut the remaining biscuits. Bake for about 10 minutes, or until golden. Remove from the oven and serve immediately.

YIELD: 18 TO 24 BISCUITS

CHUTNEY BUTTER

¼ cup golden raisins
¼ cup mango chutney, finely chopped
2 tablespoons Dijon mustard

2 teaspoons honey
½ pound (2 sticks) butter, softened

Combine the raisins, chutney, mustard, and honey in a small bowl. Let stand for 15 to 20 minutes to soften the raisins. Swirl the raisin mixture into the butter to create a marbled effect. Chill until about 1 hour before serving.

YIELD: ABOUT 1½ CUPS

SWEET POTATO BISCUITS

For me, these biscuits are something of a sentimental favorite. When my kids were little I sometimes cut out a few of these biscuits for them with a small turkey-shaped biscuit cutter. If there isn't time to bother with cooking and mashing a sweet potato, canned sweet potatoes or a cup of canned, solid-pack pumpkin can be substituted.

1 sweet potato (about 12 ounces), cut into
  large chunks
1 cup all-purpose flour
1 tablespoon baking powder
1 tablespoon sugar

½ teaspoon pumpkin pie spice
½ teaspoon salt
6 tablespoons (¾ stick) butter, at room
  temperature

Place the sweet potato in a small saucepan and cover with cold water by about 1½ inches. Bring to a boil, then cover and boil slowly over medium-high heat until tender, about 20 minutes. Drain the potato and mash until smooth. Measure out 1 cup and set aside. Preheat the oven to 425°F. Combine the flour, baking powder, sugar, pumpkin pie spice, and salt in a large bowl until well blended. Cut in the butter with a pastry blender or two knives until the mixture resembles coarse crumbs. Stir in the mashed sweet potato until well blended. The dough will be very soft. Turn out onto a floured surface and knead about ten times. Roll or press the dough to a ½-inch thickness. Cut into rounds with a floured 1½-inch biscuit cutter, placing the biscuits on a baking sheet that has been lightly greased or coated with nonstick vegetable spray. Reroll the scraps and cut the remaining biscuits. Bake for about 15 minutes, or until the biscuits are starting to color and are firm to the touch. Remove from the oven and serve immediately.

YIELD: ABOUT 28 BISCUITS

LITTLE DINNER SCONES

Scones are simply biscuits that have been enriched with egg and cream. These have been made smaller than regular scones, a better size to accompany dinner. This recipe was created by Anne Bailey, who developed and tested many of the recipes in this book. Her little daughter Megan pronounced the scones good, but thought they might be even better with mini chocolate chips instead of currants. So we tried it. And guess what? Megan was right.

1¾ cups all-purpose flour
2 tablespoons plus 2 teaspoons
    sugar
2¼ teaspoons baking powder
½ teaspoon salt

4 tablespoons (½ stick) cold butter
2 large eggs
⅓ cup heavy or whipping cream (see
    note below)
½ cup currants (optional)

Preheat the oven to 425°F. Combine the flour, 2 tablespoons of the sugar, the baking powder, and salt in a large bowl until well blended. Cut in the butter with a pastry blender or two knives until the mixture resembles small peas. In a small bowl, beat the eggs until well blended. Measure out 1 tablespoon of the beaten eggs and set aside in a cup or a small bowl. Stir the cream and currants into the eggs. Add the egg mixture to the flour mixture, stirring just until the dough comes together into a ball. Knead the dough in the bowl about four times. On a lightly floured surface, pat the dough into a 7-inch square. Brush with the remaining egg and sprinkle with the remaining sugar. With a long, sharp knife, cut the dough into 12 squares. Place the squares on an ungreased baking sheet and bake for about 10 minutes, or until pale golden. Remove from the baking sheet and cool on a wire rack.

YIELD: 12 SCONES

Note: For a lower-fat scone, buttermilk may be substituted for the cream.

SHORTNIN' BREAD
❦

The very same that Mammy's little baby loved so much, and so will you. These bite-size cookie-biscuits can be served in the dinner bread basket, but also as a light dessert, or an accompaniment to ice cream, fruit, or cheese.

¼ pound (1 stick) butter, softened
¼ cup firmly packed light brown sugar

1½ cups all-purpose flour
1 to 2 tablespoons milk

Preheat the oven to 350°F. Beat the butter and sugar in a medium-size bowl with an electric mixer until light and fluffy. Add the flour all at once and stir until the mixture just holds together. If the dough is too crumbly, gradually stir in the milk. Pat the dough out on a floured surface to a ½-inch thickness. Cut into rounds with a floured 1-inch biscuit cutter, placing the rounds on a baking sheet that has been lightly greased or coated with nonstick vegetable spray. Pat out the scraps and cut the remaining biscuits. Bake for 15 to 20 minutes, or until the biscuits are starting to color and are firm to the touch. Transfer to a wire rack to cool. Serve warm or cool

YIELD: ABOUT 32 BISCUITS

MUFFINS
❦

At one time it puzzled me that I could bake the same muffins at different times, using the same recipe, and one batch turned out perfectly while the other was lopsided or riddled with holes. Obviously I had not done my muffin-making homework or I would have known that I had either overworked the batter or baked the muffins at an oven temperature that was too high or too low. The perfect muffin rises out of the pan with straight sides and a rounded top. The texture, although not fine, should be even throughout with no holes or "tunnels," as they are called. When making muffins, remember these three rules:

1. Work the liquid ingredients into the dry ingredients with as few strokes as possible, no more than twenty to thirty. A few lumps in the batter don't matter. A correctly beaten muffin batter will not pour, but must be spooned into the cups.
2. Fill muffin cups only two-thirds. If empty cups remain in the pan, fill each of them with 2 to 3 tablespoons of water.
3. Unless the recipe says otherwise, bake at 400°F for about 20 minutes. Cool in the pans for about 5 minutes, then remove the muffins and cool on wire racks.

Muffins can be made ahead and frozen or refrigerated. Reheat frozen muffins, loosely wrapped in aluminum foil, for about 15 minutes at 350°F. To reheat refrigerated muffins, wrap loosely in aluminum foil and reheat for 5 to 10 minutes at 250°F. If the tops seem too moist, fold back the foil and bake a few minutes longer.

POPPY SEED–VANILLA MUFFINS

These are denser and richer than most muffins, almost like pound cake.

1¾ cups all-purpose flour
3 tablespoons poppy seeds
½ teaspoon salt
½ teaspoon baking soda
5 tablespoons butter, softened

½ cup sugar
2 large eggs
½ cup sour cream
2 tablespoons milk
1½ teaspoons vanilla extract

Preheat the oven to 400°F. Combine the flour, poppy seeds, salt, and baking soda in a large bowl. In a medium-size bowl, beat the butter and sugar with an electric mixer on medium speed until creamy. Beat in the eggs, sour cream, milk, and vanilla until well blended. Stir the egg mixture into the flour mixture just until combined. Spoon the batter into 12 muffin-pan cups that have been lightly greased or coated with nonstick vegetable spray, filling them two-thirds. Bake for 18 to 20 minutes, or until a wooden toothpick inserted in the center comes out clean. Cool the muffins in the pan for 5 minutes, then turn out onto a wire rack to cool completely, or eat while still warm.

YIELD: 12 MUFFINS

ORANGE-PECAN MUFFINS

A soft, cakelike muffin, and the recipe taste panel's favorite.

2 cups all-purpose flour
1 teaspoon baking soda
½ teaspoon salt
1 cup chopped pecans
¼ pound (1 stick) butter, at room
    temperature

¾ cup firmly packed light brown sugar
2 large eggs
1 tablespoon grated orange rind
1 cup buttermilk

❦

Preheat the oven to 375°F. Combine the flour, baking soda, salt, and ¾ cup of the pecans in a large bowl until well blended. In a medium-size bowl, beat the butter and sugar with an electric mixer on medium speed until light and fluffy. Beat in the eggs and orange rind until well blended. Stir the egg mixture and buttermilk into the flour mixture just until combined. Spoon the batter into 18 muffin-pan cups that have been lightly greased or coated with nonstick vegetable spray. Sprinkle the tops of the muffins with the remaining pecans, dividing evenly. Bake for 18 to 20 minutes, or until a wooden toothpick inserted in the center comes out clean. Cool the muffins in the pan for 5 minutes, then turn out onto a wire rack to cool completely, or eat while still warm.

YIELD: 18 MUFFINS

MAPLE-WALNUT MUFFINS

❦

For an intense maple flavor, you'll need to use the maple extract, but the more subtly flavored muffins are very good, too.

2 cups all-purpose flour
1 tablespoon sugar
1½ teaspoons baking powder
½ teaspoon baking soda
½ teaspoon salt
½ cup apple juice or cider

½ cup pure maple syrup
1 large egg
½ teaspoon maple extract (optional)
⅓ cup vegetable oil
1 cup chopped walnuts

Preheat the oven to 400°F. Combine the flour, sugar, baking powder, baking soda, and salt in a large bowl until well blended. In a small bowl, mix the apple juice, maple syrup, egg, and maple extract with a wire whisk until well blended. Whisk in the oil. Stir the egg mixture into the flour mixture, along with ¾ cup of the walnuts, just until blended. Spoon the batter into 12 muffin-pan cups that have been lightly greased or coated with nonstick vegetable spray. Sprinkle the tops of the muffins with the remaining walnuts, dividing evenly. Bake for 16 to 18 minutes, or until a wooden toothpick inserted in the center comes out clean. Cool the muffins in the pan for 5 minutes, then turn out onto a wire rack to cool completely, or eat while still warm.

YIELD: 12 MUFFINS

DOUBLE CORN MUFFINS

These not-so-sweet muffins are a far cry from the corn muffins most of us are used to for breakfast, but they're wonderful, and just right for dinner. If you have a few left over, serve them for breakfast with warm maple syrup.

1¼ cups all-purpose flour
½ cup yellow cornmeal
2 teaspoons baking powder
3 tablespoons sugar
½ teaspoon salt

1 large egg
⅔ cup milk
⅓ cup vegetable oil
One 8¾-ounce can whole-kernel corn, drained

Preheat the oven to 375°F. Combine the flour, cornmeal, baking powder, sugar, and salt in a large bowl until well blended. In a small bowl, combine the egg, milk, and oil with a fork or a wire whisk until well blended. Stir the egg mixture and the drained corn into the flour mixture just until combined. Spoon the batter into 12 muffin-pan cups that have been lightly greased or coated with nonstick vegetable spray. Bake for about 18 minutes, or until a wooden toothpick inserted in the center comes out clean. Cool the muffins in the pan for 5 minutes, then turn out onto a wire rack to cool completely, or eat while still warm.

YIELD: 12 MUFFINS

SOUR CREAM AND CHIVE MUFFINS

These muffins, which are very fluffy and more like biscuits, and the Seeded Buttermilk Muffins that follow are good bread basket companions.

2 cups all-purpose flour
2 teaspoons baking powder
½ teaspoon salt
½ cup sour cream, at room temperature
½ cup milk, at room temperature

4 tablespoons (½ stick) butter, melted and cooled to room temperature
1 large egg
2 tablespoons minced fresh chives

Preheat the oven to 400°F. Combine the flour, baking powder, and salt in a large bowl until well blended. In a small bowl, combine the sour cream, milk, butter, egg, and chives until well blended. Stir the egg mixture into the flour mixture just until combined. The batter will be very thick. Spoon the batter into 12 muffin-pan cups or 24 mini-muffin-pan cups that have been lightly greased or coated with nonstick vegetable spray. Bake the regular-size muffins for 18 to 20 minutes and the mini muffins for 15 minutes, or until a wooden toothpick inserted in the center comes out clean. Cool the muffins in the pan for 5 minutes, then turn out onto a wire rack to cool completely, or eat while still warm.

YIELD: 12 REGULAR OR 24 MINI MUFFINS

SEEDED BUTTERMILK MUFFINS

These muffins can only be described as elegant. Top them with different kinds of seeds so dinner guests can have a choice.

1¾ cups all-purpose flour
1 tablespoon sugar
1 teaspoon baking powder
½ teaspoon baking soda
½ teaspoon salt
1 cup buttermilk, at room temperature

1 large egg
2 tablespoons warm water
4 tablespoons (½ stick) butter, melted and cooled to room temperature
Poppy, caraway, or sesame seeds

Preheat the oven to 400°F. Combine the flour, sugar, baking powder, baking soda, and salt in a large bowl until well blended. In a small bowl, mix the buttermilk, egg, water, and butter with a wire whisk until well blended. Stir the egg mixture into the flour mixture just until combined. The batter will be very lumpy. Spoon the batter into 12 muffin-pan cups or 24 mini-muffin-pan cups that have been lightly greased or coated with nonstick vegetable spray. Sprinkle with the seeds. Bake the regular-size muffins for about 20 minutes and the mini muffins for 15 minutes, or until a wooden toothpick inserted in the center comes out clean. Cool the muffins in the pan for 5 minutes, then turn out onto a wire rack to cool completely, or eat while still warm.

YIELD: 12 REGULAR OR 24 MINI MUFFINS

CRANBERRIES-IN-THE-MIDDLE MUFFINS

The cranberry sauce in the middle of these muffins (which could just as easily be any firm fruit jelly or preserves) is a nice little surprise. This is the kind of recipe everybody wants to know how to make, so be prepared.

1½ cups all-purpose flour
½ cup whole-wheat flour
⅓ cup sugar
1 teaspoon baking powder
½ teaspoon baking soda
½ teaspoon salt

¼ pound (1 stick) butter, melted and
    cooled to room temperature
¾ cup orange juice, at room temperature
¼ cup unsulphured molasses
1 large egg
¼ cup whole-berry cranberry sauce

Preheat the oven to 400°F. Combine both flours, the sugar, baking powder, baking soda, and salt in a large bowl until well blended. In a medium-size bowl, mix the butter, orange juice, molasses, and egg with a wire whisk until well blended. Stir the egg mixture into the flour mixture just until combined. Spoon one heaping, measuring tablespoonful of batter into each of 12 muffin-pan cups that have been lightly greased or coated with nonstick vegetable spray. Make a small indentation in the batter with your finger or the handle of a wooden spoon. Carefully fill each indentation with about a measuring teaspoonful of cranberry sauce, making sure that the sauce is right in the center of the batter and not touching the sides of the cups. Gently spoon on the remaining batter, trying not to disturb the sauce. Bake for about 20 minutes, or until golden brown. Cool the muffins in the pan for 5 minutes, then turn out onto a wire rack to cool completely, or eat while still warm.

YIELD: 12 MUFFINS

DINNER ROLLS AND SWEET BUNS

I think those innocent-looking, little yeast packets sitting on the shelf in the supermarket would be greatly surprised to learn how many competent cooks are totally intimidated by the thought of using them. Time was when one day of the week was baking day, and even the youngest child was familiar with the magical action of yeast, swelling the bread dough to twice its size and filling the house with a wonderful aroma.

It's been a long time since most people have caught the smell of bread rising and baking on a regular basis, but experts that I've consulted on the matter agree that it's not necessary to know *everything* about baking with yeast in order to make good dinner rolls and buns.

Two things can happen that will ruin your efforts. Either the yeast doesn't activate or the dough is allowed to rise too much. Fortunately, both of these things can be avoided easily.

Remember that yeast is a living leavening agent (actually a very tiny plant in the fungus family) that requires air, warmth, moisture, and sugar or starch in order to grow.

Like every living thing, yeast gets old and dies. That's why there's a freshness date on the yeast envelope and it's very important to check that it's not expired.

The most common mistake beginning bread bakers make is to try to activate the yeast in water that is not warm enough. In order to start growing (activate), yeast needs very warm (105° to 115°F) liquid (usually water or milk). Most people equate warm with the temperature of a baby's bottle. Not so. *Very* warm water feels *hot* when you stick your finger into it, and remember that it will cool some when it is poured into the bowl. On the other hand, if the water is too hot, the yeast is killed.

If you don't have a kitchen thermometer, or are unsure about whether or not the yeast has been activated, it can be "proofed" this way. Sprinkle the yeast over the warm water as the recipe directs and then add a pinch of sugar. Stir until the yeast is dissolved and set the bowl aside. Within 5 to 10 minutes, the yeast mixture will start to foam or bubble, and you know the yeast is active. If this doesn't happen, throw it out and start over, checking the date on the yeast packet and the temperature of the water.

Once activated and mixed with the flour, the yeast begins to feed on the starch and to grow. The more sugar in the recipe and the warmer the environment in which the dough is left to rise, the more quickly the yeast grows and the dough rises. Growing yeast, or more correctly the gases that the yeast forms while it's growing, is what causes dough to rise. A warm spot is defined as between 75° and 85°F. If the room is cooler than 75°F, the dough will still rise, but it will take longer.

After the yeast has been rising for about 30 minutes, watch it carefully so that it does not rise too much. The test for dough that has doubled in bulk is to stick a couple of fingers straight down into the dough. If the indentation stays, the dough is risen.

All of the yeast recipes that follow call for active dry yeast, the kind that comes in a small packet. Compressed yeast cakes can be used interchangeably. There are also quick-rise yeasts on the market that you can use if you like. Follow the directions on the packets if you use these. Yeast can also be purchased in bulk in jars. In that case, use 2¾ teaspoons of yeast for each packet called for.

Hot-Roll and Other Mixes and Refrigerator Biscuits

There is at least one hot-roll mix on the market that, in my opinion, is a great product. Pillsbury makes it and the box includes a packet of yeast and a packet of flour mixture. You can do anything with this roll mix that you can with from-scratch dough. Follow the explicit directions on the box for exceptionally tasty dinner rolls. Frozen bread dough is another excellent product from which you can create all sorts of breads and rolls.

There are also shelves and shelves of muffin mixes, quick-bread mixes, and biscuits available that are worth a try. They're all easy to work with and provide the busy baker with the satisfaction of having mixed the dough or batter, if not from scratch, then pretty close to it, and they smell good when they bake, just like homemade.

Almost without exception, there are offers on these packages for booklets that will provide lots of information and recipes for using what's inside. If you like a particular product, these booklets are a small but good investment.

Glazing

Rolls and buns can be given different "finishes" by brushing them with one of the following just before they are put into the oven to bake:

- Melted butter helps brown the rolls and keeps them soft. For an even softer crust, brush again when the rolls are taken from the oven.
- Milk provides the most subtle shine.
- A whole egg, lightly beaten, with or without a tablespoon of water, gives a shiny, medium-brown color.
- An egg yolk lightly beaten with one tablespoon of water promotes a dark brown color with lots of gloss.

Shaping Rolls

Dinner rolls can be made in several shapes that add much to their eye appeal on the dinner table. Pan rolls are probably the most traditional shape, but there are others:

Pan rolls (figure 1). The dough is evenly divided and shaped into balls, which are placed in a square or round pan with the sides touching. Pull the rolls apart to serve.

Cloverleaf rolls (figure 2). The dough, after having been evenly divided, is formed into 1-inch balls. Three balls are placed in each muffin-pan cup, with each ball touching the bottom of the cup.

Crescents (figure 3). Roll the dough into a 9-inch circle using a pie pan as a guide. Cut the dough circle into twelve wedges. Brush the wedges with melted butter. Starting at the wide end, roll up each wedge, then place on a baking sheet, curving slightly to form crescents.

Fan-tans (figure 4). Roll the dough into a square about ⅛ inch thick and brush with melted butter. Cut into 1½-inch-wide strips. Stack six strips on top of one another,

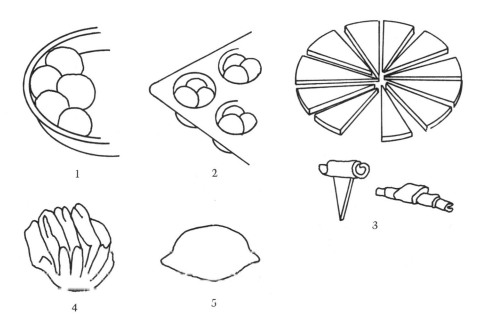

then cut the stacked strips into 1¼-inch pieces. Place the pieces, cut side up, in muffin-pan cups. They will fan out and brown beautifully as they bake.

Shaped dinner rolls (figure 5). Divide the dough evenly and roll each piece into a 2-inch ball. On a lightly floured surface, roll each ball until it is about 4 inches long with slightly tapering ends.

MICHELLE PAYNE'S WHOLE-WHEAT CLOVERLEAF ROLLS

Michelle is the sister of my good friend Stephanie Curtis, who worked so hard with me on this book. Good cooking, apparently, runs in the family. Michelle, who lives in Elkhart, Indiana, is a great baker, and these are the rolls she serves for Thanksgiving. They are very moist with lots of homemade flavor. For white dinner rolls, use 3½ cups all-purpose flour and omit the whole-wheat flour.

*1 all-purpose potato (about 6 ounces),
  peeled and cut into small pieces (about
  1 cup)*
1 envelope active dry yeast
6 tablespoons (¾ stick) butter, melted
¼ cup sugar
1 large egg, lightly beaten

1 teaspoon salt
½ cup milk
1 cup whole-wheat flour
2½ cups all-purpose flour
*1 large egg, beaten with 1 tablespoon
  water for glaze*

Cover the potato with water in a small saucepan. Bring to a boil, then lower the heat to medium and simmer until tender, about 7 minutes. Drain the potato, reserving ½ cup of the cooking water. Mash the potato in a small bowl and set aside. Cool the cooking water in a small bowl to a temperature of 105° to 115°F. Sprinkle the yeast over the cooking water and stir until it is completely dissolved. In a large bowl, stir the butter and sugar together until well blended. Add the mashed potato, the egg, and salt and beat until smooth. Place the milk in a small saucepan over low and heat just until small bubbles form around the edge. Add the milk and yeast water to the potato mixture, stirring until smooth. Add the whole-wheat flour and about two-thirds of the all-purpose flour to the potato mixture, stirring until well blended. The dough will be very moist. Turn out onto a floured surface and knead for 5 to 7 minutes, adding as much of the remaining flour as necessary to form a smooth, satiny dough. Form the dough into a ball. Place the dough in a greased bowl, turning to grease the top of the dough. Cover and let rise in a warm spot out of drafts for about 2 hours, or until doubled in bulk. Punch the dough down and cut it in half. Cut each half into twelve equal parts for a total of 24 pieces of dough. Cut each piece of dough into 3 pieces and roll the pieces into balls. Arrange 3 balls in each cup of two or three muffin pans that have been greased or coated with nonstick vegetable spray, making sure that each ball touches the bottom of the pan. Cover and let rise for 1 hour. Preheat the oven to 400°F. Brush the rolls with the egg glaze. Bake for 12 to 15 minutes, or until golden brown. Cool in the pans on a wire rack.

YIELD: 24 ROLLS

CRUSTY WATER ROLLS

These rolls are most like French bread, with a thin, crisp crust and soft, chewy insides. It's the steaming water in the oven that promotes this kind of crust, so don't eliminate it.

1 envelope active dry yeast
¼ cup very warm water (105° to 115°F)
¾ cup boiling water
2 tablespoons solid white vegetable
   shortening

1 tablespoon sugar
1½ teaspoons salt
2¾ to 3 cups all-purpose flour
2 large egg whites, lightly beaten

Sprinkle the yeast over the warm water in a small bowl. Stir until the yeast is completely dissolved. In a large bowl, combine the boiling water, shortening, sugar, and salt and stir until the shortening is melted. Set aside and cool until the mixture is lukewarm. Stir in 1 cup of the flour and beat until well blended. Stir in the egg whites, yeast water, and enough of the remaining flour to make a soft dough. Turn out onto a floured surface and knead the dough until it is smooth and satiny, about 5 minutes, adding as much of the remaining flour as necessary to keep the dough from sticking. Place the dough in a greased bowl, turning to grease the top of the dough. Cover and let rise in a warm spot out of drafts for about 1 hour, or until doubled in bulk. Punch the dough down and let it rest, covered, for 10 minutes. Cut the dough into 18 equal pieces and roll each piece into a ball. On a lightly floured surface, roll each ball until it is about 4 inches long, tapering the ends slightly. Place the rolls 2½ inches apart on a baking sheet that has been lightly greased or coated with nonstick vegetable spray. Cover and let rise for about 45 minutes, or until doubled in bulk. If you like, you can make a shallow slash on the top of each roll with a single-edge razor blade or a very sharp knife. Meanwhile, preheat the oven to 400°F and set a large shallow pan filled with boiling water on the bottom rack of the oven. Bake on the rack above the water for 10 to 12 minutes, or until the rolls are pale brown. Remove from the oven and cool on a wire rack.

YIELD: ABOUT 18 ROLLS

RICH PAN ROLLS

My favorite dinner roll, which may just as easily be shaped rather than baked in a pan. The dough is easy to work with, and the rolls it makes are soft and fragrant.

1 cup milk
¼ pound (1 stick) butter, softened
¼ cup sugar
1 teaspoon salt
2 envelopes active dry yeast

½ cup very warm water (105° to 115°F)
2 large eggs, lightly beaten
5½ cups all-purpose flour
Melted butter or 1 egg, lightly beaten,
   for glaze

Place the milk in a small saucepan over low and heat just until small bubbles form around the edge. In a large bowl, combine the hot milk, butter, sugar, and salt, stirring until the butter is melted. Set aside to cool to lukewarm. Sprinkle the yeast over the warm water in a large bowl, stirring until it is completely dissolved. Stir in the eggs, milk mixture, and about 4½ cups of the flour until a soft dough forms. Turn out onto a floured surface and knead the dough until it is smooth and satiny, 10 to 15 minutes, adding as much of the remaining flour as necessary to keep the dough from sticking. Place the dough in a greased bowl, turning to grease the top of the dough. Cover and let rise in a warm place out of drafts until doubled in bulk, about 45 minutes. Divide the dough into quarters, then cut each quarter into eight parts. Shape each piece of dough into a ball. Arrange the balls in two 8-inch square or round baking pans with the sides of the rolls just touching each other. Cover and let rise until doubled in bulk, about 40 minutes. Preheat the oven to 375°F. Brush the rolls with melted butter or beaten egg. Bake for about 20 minutes, or until golden brown. Cool in the pans on a wire rack. Pull the rolls apart to serve.

YIELD: 32 ROLLS

SMALL STICKY BUNS

If I could arrange it, my last meal on earth would include sticky buns. Although many people shrink from the idea of offering such an outrageously sweet roll on the dinner table, in many parts of the country it is quite expected. For a dinner accompaniment, I have reduced the size of the buns to about half of those I serve for breakfast or as a snack. By the way, this is the best sweet-roll dough you will ever eat.

DOUGH
¾ cup water
3 tablespoons sugar
3 tablespoons butter
2¼ cups all-purpose flour
1 envelope active dry yeast
½ teaspoon salt
1 large egg
1 tablespoon butter, melted

FILLING
½ cup firmly packed light brown sugar
½ teaspoon ground cinnamon
½ cup dark raising (optional)

TOPPING
½ cup firmly packed light brown sugar
2 tablespoons butter
1 tablespoon light corn syrup
1 tablespoon water
1 teaspoon white vinegar
1 cup chopped pecans

In a small saucepan over high heat, stir together the water and sugar. Bring to a boil and boil for 2 minutes. Remove from the heat, stir in the butter, and set aside for 20 minutes. In a large bowl, combine 1 cup of the flour, the yeast, and salt until well blended. Stir in the cooled sugar syrup and then the egg. Stir in 1 more cup of the flour. Turn out onto a floured surface and knead in as much of the remaining flour as necessary to make a dough that is just slightly sticky, about 7 minutes. (If you find that the dough is too sticky to knead and you've used all of the flour, dust your hands with flour, but don't add more to the dough; sticky dough is essential for a light and delicate bun.) Place the dough in a large greased bowl, turning to grease the top of the dough. Cover and let rise in a warm spot out of drafts until double in bulk, about 1 hour. Grease the bottom and sides of a 9- × 9-inch baking pan.

To make the topping, place the brown sugar, butter, syrup, water, and vinegar in a small saucepan. Bring to a boil over high heat, stirring until the butter is melted. Boil for 1 minute. Pour into the prepared pan. Sprinkle evenly with the pecans and set aside. Preheat the oven to 375°F. On a floured surface with a floured rolling pin, roll the dough into a 10- × 14-inch rectangle. Brush with the melted butter.

To make the filling, stir together the brown sugar and cinnamon in a small bowl until well mixed. Sprinkle this mixture evenly over the dough, then sprinkle with the raisins. Roll the dough up from a long side and seal by pinching the edge. With a sharp knife, cut the dough into 12 pieces. Arrange the pieces over the topping in the pan, cut side down. Cover the pan and let rise until doubled in bulk, about 40 minutes. Bake for about 25 minutes, or until nicely browned. Remove the pan from the oven and let stand for 5 minutes. Turn upside down onto a serving plate. Pull the buns apart to serve.

YIELD: 12 BUNS

SUGAR KNOTS

Sugar knots are something I learned to enjoy when I was a boarding student at Moravian Seminary for Girls (now Moravian Academy) in Bethlehem, Pennsylvania. The recipe that follows is more or less the way Maude, the school's cook, made the knots, but I think through the years I've improved upon Maude's recipe, probably because I don't have to worry about making a big enough batch to feed a hoard of hungry teenage girls.

2 envelopes active dry yeast

¾ cup very warm water (105° to 115°F)

½ cup warm milk

4½ cups all-purpose flour

¾ cup sugar

1 teaspoon salt

2 large eggs

2 tablespoons butter, melted

Melted butter for brushing rolls

Granulated sugar for sprinkling on rolls

In a small bowl, sprinkle the yeast over ¼ cup of the warm water, stirring until the yeast is completely dissolved. In a large bowl, add the yeast mixture to the warm milk and the remaining ½ cup warm water. Stir in 3 cups of the flour until well blended. Cover and let rise in a warm place out of drafts until doubled in bulk, about 40 minutes. Stir the sugar, salt, eggs, melted butter, and ¾ cup of the remaining flour into the dough. The dough will be quite sticky. Turn the dough out onto a floured surface. Knead gently, using a dough scraper to assist if necessary, adding only as much of the remaining flour as necessary until the dough can be handled easily but is still fairly sticky. Cut the dough into 18 equal pieces. With lightly floured hands, roll each piece into a rope about 9 inches long. Tie into a loose knot. As each knot is tied, place it on a baking sheet that has been lightly greased or coated with nonstick vegetable spray. Cover and let rise again until doubled, about 30 minutes. Preheat the oven to 375°F. Brush each roll with melted butter and sprinkle with sugar. Bake for about 15 minutes, or until pale gold. Immediately remove from the baking sheets and cool on wire racks.

YIELD: 18 ROLLS

QUICK CINNAMON TWISTS

Earlier in this chapter I discussed the merits of convenience products. The dough used in this and the following recipe is one of them. These twists have a good homemade flavor, not too sweet, of course, because bread dough isn't sweet. And they are quick. If you forget to thaw the dough overnight in the refrigerator, there are directions on the package for accomplishing the same thing in the microwave oven in just a few minutes.

¼ cup sugar

2 teaspoons ground cinnamon

One 16-ounce loaf frozen white or whole-

    wheat bread dough, thawed according

    to package directions until pliable

2 tablespoons butter, melted

Preheat the oven to 375°F. Mix the sugar with the cinnamon in a small bowl and set aside. On a lightly floured surface, roll the dough out to a 14- × 10-inch rectangle.

Brush with the melted butter and sprinkle with the cinnamon-and-sugar mixture. Cut the dough into 10-inch strips, each about ½ inch wide. Holding both ends of one strip, twist it. Bring the two ends together and twist again, placing the twist on a baking sheet that has been lightly greased or coated with nonstick vegetable spray. Repeat with the remaining strips, placing them 1 inch apart on the baking sheet. Do not let rise, but immediately bake for 10 to 12 minutes, or until lightly browned. Remove from the baking sheet and cool on a wire rack, or eat warm.

YIELD: ABOUT 28 TWISTS

SEEDED BREAD STICKS

A light coating of seeds and coarse salt gives these bread sticks lots of flavor. Frozen bread dough makes them quick and easy. Bake a day ahead of time and store tightly wrapped in aluminum foil until serving time.

One 16-ounce loaf frozen white or whole
wheat bread dough, thawed according
to package directions until pliable
Coarse (kosher) salt

Caraway seeds
Poppy seeds
1 large egg yolk, beaten with 1 tablespoon
water

Working on a *very lightly* floured surface, cut the dough into 12 equal pieces. Roll and stretch each piece, first rolling between the palms of your hands and then on the working surface to measure about 11 or 12 inches. (The sticks will probably be lumpy looking, and will undoubtedly stretch out into even longer lengths as you work with them, but that's okay.) Set aside on a lightly floured surface. Sprinkle a light coating of salt and caraway and poppy seeds on separate pieces of waxed paper. Brush the sticks on all sides with the egg mixture, then roll some of the sticks into each kind of coating. As they are coated, place the sticks about 1 inch apart on two baking sheets that have been lightly greased or coated with nonstick vegetable spray. (The waxed paper will have to be resalted and reseeded several times.) Cover the sticks with a towel and let rise in a warm place out of drafts until slightly puffy, about 15 minutes. Preheat the oven to 375°F. Bake the breads in the center of the oven for 15 to 20 minutes, or until lightly browned. Remove from the baking sheets and cool on wire racks. Store tightly wrapped. The sticks will keep well for a couple of days. Reheat at 350°F, loosely wrapped in aluminum foil, for about 10 minutes.

YIELD: 12 BREAD STICKS

❦

COLONIAL BROWN BREAD

❦

According to the late James Beard, brown bread is as old as our country, which makes it all the more appropriate for Thanksgiving dinner. Old-time recipes for brown bread always include some rye flour, and you can use it, if you like, but most people nowadays prefer milder-tasting whole-wheat flour. Brown bread can be sliced and served with dinner, or you may want to serve it for dessert. In that case, it can stand some sweet enrichment, such as Hard Sauce (see page 238) or sweetened whipped cream.

1 cup all-purpose flour
1 cup whole-wheat or rye flour
½ cup sugar
1 teaspoon baking soda
¼ teaspoon salt

1 large egg, lightly beaten
1 cup milk
½ cup unsulphured molasses
½ cup dark raisins (optional)

Mix both flours, the sugar, baking soda, and salt in a large bowl until well blended. Add the egg, milk, and molasses and stir until completely blended. Stir in the raisins. Pour the batter into a 2-quart soufflé dish or other deep casserole that has been lightly greased or coated with nonstick vegetable spray. (The dish will be only about three quarters full to allow for expansion as the bread bakes.) Cover very tightly with heavy-duty aluminum foil. Place the baking dish on a rack that has been set in the bottom of a Dutch oven or other large heavy saucepan. Add enough water to come a third to halfway up the side of the baking dish. Bring to a boil over medium-high heat, then reduce the heat to medium-low, or until the water barely moves. Cover the pan and steam for 1½ hours. Remove from the heat and set aside until cool enough to remove the baking dish from the Dutch oven. Run a sharp knife around the edge of the bread and unmold it onto a serving plate. Cut into wedges with a serrated knife and serve while still slightly warm. If the bread is not to be served immediately, while it is still warm, wrap it tightly in aluminum foil. Reheat, still tightly wrapped in the foil, in a 325°F oven for about 20 minutes.

YIELD: 8 TO 12 SERVINGS

CORN BREAD WITH CRACKLINGS

❦

This Southern-style corn bread may come as a bit of a surprise to Northern cousins, who generally expect a little sweetness in their corn bread. Nevertheless, this is great corn bread, even for those who are used to sweet breakfast corn breads. Serve it with plenty of softened butter.

6 *slices bacon, cut into ½-inch pieces*
1½ *cups yellow cornmeal*
½ *cup all-purpose flour*
2 *teaspoons baking powder*

½ *teaspoon salt*
2 *large eggs, well beaten*
2 *cups milk*

Preheat the oven to 400°F. Fry the bacon in a 10-inch (measured across the top) ovenproof skillet over medium-high heat, stirring frequently, until it is brown and crisp. (I use my grandmother's iron skillet.) Remove the bacon with a slotted spoon and set it aside in a small bowl. Measure out 3 tablespoons of the bacon fat from the skillet and add it to the bacon. Discard the drippings in the skillet, leaving a light film of bacon fat. In a large bowl, combine the cornmeal, flour, baking powder, and salt until well blended. Stir in the eggs and the milk and beat until smooth. Stir in the reserved bacon and bacon fat. Immediately pour the batter into the skillet. Bake for about 18 minutes, or until firm to the touch and just beginning to brown around the edge. Cool the skillet on a wire rack for 5 minutes, then cut the warm bread into wedges to serve. I don't recommend reheating corn bread.

YIELD: ABOUT 8 SERVINGS

IRISH SODA BREAD

This bread, in essence, is a big biscuit. Although it should be served very fresh, soda bread tastes good at room temperature, so there's no need for last-minute reheating.

2½ *cups all-purpose flour*
3 *tablespoons sugar*
2 *teaspoons baking powder*
½ *teaspoon salt*

¼ *teaspoon baking soda*
¾ *cup dark raisins*
2 *teaspoons caraway seeds*
1¼ *cups buttermilk*

Preheat the oven to 375°F. In a large bowl, combine the flour, sugar, baking powder, salt, and baking soda. Stir in the raisins and caraway seeds. Stir in the buttermilk to make a soft, sticky dough. Turn out onto a floured surface and knead three or four times. Shape the dough into a round loaf and place on a baking sheet that has been lightly greased or coated with nonstick vegetable spray. With a pair of scissors or a knife, cut an X ¼ inch deep in the top of the loaf. Bake for 35 to 40 minutes, or until golden. Remove from the oven and cool on a wire rack. Cut into wedges to serve.

YIELD: 1 LOAF; ABOUT 8 SERVINGS

QUICK ANADAMA BREAD

Like brown bread, this bread goes way back in American history. For all its simple ingredients, the bona fide recipe is a bit of a pain to make. This is Anne Bailey's quick and reliable version, with all of the flavors and a lot less of the work.

1¾ cups all-purpose flour
½ cup yellow cornmeal
1½ teaspoons baking powder
¼ teaspoon baking soda
½ teaspoon salt

6 tablespoons (¾ stick) butter, softened
½ cup firmly packed dark brown sugar
2 large eggs
1 cup milk

Preheat the oven to 350°F. Grease and flour an 8½- × 4½-inch loaf pan and set aside. Combine the flour, cornmeal, baking powder, baking soda, and salt in a medium-size bowl until well blended. In a large bowl, beat the butter and sugar together until creamy. Add the eggs and beat until the mixture is light and fluffy. Alternately beat the flour mixture and the milk into the butter-and-sugar mixture, beginning and ending with the dry ingredients, and beating only until well combined. Turn into the prepared loaf pan. Bake for 45 to 50 minutes, or until a wooden toothpick inserted in the center comes out clean. Cool the bread on a wire rack for 10 minutes. Remove from the loaf pan and cool completely on the rack. Wrap the bread tightly in aluminum foil or plastic wrap and refrigerate for one day. Bring to room temperature before unwrapping and slicing.

YIELD: 1 LOAF; 8 TO 12 SERVINGS

TWELVE

Desserts

❦

Dessert is the only food that is eaten solely for pleasure. It is the *pièce de résistance* at almost every meal, especially one that is in the least bit festive. Even those who generally decline to eat it on almost every other occasion will cave in on Thanksgiving. If the cook's reputation is not firmly established by the time this course is served, it should be afterward.

Like all the other parts of the Thanksgiving feast, tradition dictates and pumpkin pie, in one form or another, is always expected. The Pilgrims may, in fact, have served something vaguely similar, made from pumpkins, which they called *pompions*, that was sweetened with maple-tree sap. Then, besides any traditional family must-haves, almost anything goes. A fruit pie is always a good choice and, of course, anything made with the eternally popular chocolate is always enthusiastically received. Because Thanksgiving is the one meal of the year where no one feels naughty about overindulging, requests for small servings of everything that's offered can be expected. Undoubtedly there will be leftovers, so if you value your own waistline, be prepared to send home doggie bags with your guests.

In discussing other courses for the Thanksgiving dinner, I've stressed the importance of keeping a good balance, and this is especially so for desserts. Pumpkin pie is essentially bland and soft in taste and texture, as well as appearance, so go from there to colorful and contrasting, crunchy, tart and spicy, rich and light, and even warm and cold.

If you have the space in your dining area, you might even want to set the desserts out on display just before dinner.

How to Make a Pie Crust

"Easy as pie" is an expression that had real meaning about fifty years ago when house-wives turned out several pies a week almost as an afterthought. Nowadays, most cooks panic at the thought of producing a pie from scratch.

A good pie begins and ends with a good crust, and although producing a perfect pie crust is sometimes viewed as an art form, learning to make a tender, flaky crust from scratch is really rather simple. But perfect does entail practice, so I would not suggest trying your very first homemade pie the night you've got company coming.

I learned to make pie crust and pretty edgings by mixing up batches of pastry dough which I then rolled out and fitted into the pan several times, refrigerating the dough between each rolling and fitting. Of course, a pie dough that has been handled this much is not fit to eat, so dispose of it after the lesson is over.

Here is my recipe for a flaky pie crust. To make the crust even flakier, you can do as the old-time bakers did and substitute lard for some of the shortening. Please note that you will need slightly less lard than vegetable shortening, since lard has more shortening power.

Remember to keep the dough as cool as you can and handle it lightly. Handle the dough too much and it will toughen and certainly not be flaky after it's baked. The ingredient quantities are generous, so you won't have any problem getting the crusts to fit in the pan. In the beginning, your crusts may be a little thicker than the ideal ⅛ inch, but don't fret about it.

BASIC FLAKY PIE-CRUST PASTRY
❦
FOR A SINGLE-CRUST 8- OR 9-INCH PIE

1¼ cups all-purpose flour
¼ teaspoon salt

½ cup solid white vegetable shortening or
　¼ cup shortening plus 3 tablespoons
　lard, chilled
2 to 3 tablespoons ice water

FOR A DOUBLE-CRUST 8- OR 9-INCH PIE

2¼ cups all-purpose flour
¾ teaspoon salt

¾ cup solid white vegetable shortening or
½ cup shortening plus 2 tablespoons
lard, chilled
5 to 6 tablespoons ice water

Mix the flour and salt together in a medium-size bowl with a fork until blended. With a pastry blender or two knives, cut the cold shortening into the flour mixture until it resembles coarse crumbs. Drizzle 2 to 3 tablespoons of the ice water over the flour mixture. Toss with a fork to moisten evenly, adding more water, if necessary, a few drops at a time, just until the dough particles start to cling together and onto the tines of the fork. Gently gather the dough into one ball for a single-crust pie, or two balls, one just slightly larger than the other, for a double-crust pie (the larger of the two balls will be used for the bottom crust). Wrap in plastic wrap or waxed paper and chill for about 30 minutes before rolling (much longer than that and the dough will be too hard to roll). For longer storage, seal in a plastic bag. If you want to make the dough a day ahead, set it out at room temperature for about an hour before rolling.

FOOLPROOF PIE-CRUST PASTRY

This is a good pie-crust dough to have on hand when baking several pies for the holidays. It handles more easily than the Basic Flaky Pie-Crust Pastry, and can be tightly wrapped and refrigerated for several days, or frozen and thawed at room temperature for three or four hours. When refrigerated, the dough remains soft and can be rolled immediately.

4 cups all-purpose flour
1¾ cups solid white vegetable shortening
1 tablespoon sugar
2 teaspoons salt

1 large egg
½ cup cold water
1 tablespoon white vinegar

With a pastry blender or two knives, mix the flour, shortening, sugar, and salt in a large bowl until well blended and crumbly. In a small bowl, beat the egg with the water and vinegar. Stir into the flour mixture and mix with a fork until all of the ingredients are evenly moistened. Gather the dough into a ball, wrap it in plastic wrap or waxed paper, and chill for at least 30 minutes before rolling. For longer storage, seal in a plastic bag. If you want to make the dough a day ahead, set it out at room temperature for about an hour before rolling.

YIELD: MAKES TWO 9-INCH DOUBLE-CRUST PIES AND ONE 9-INCH SINGLE-CRUST PIE

Freezing. Pie-crust dough may be securely wrapped and frozen for up to two months. Thaw at room temperature for two to four hours before rolling. Or the pastry can be rolled to the desired size and then frozen. Place the dough circles on a sheet of heavy-duty aluminum foil with a piece of waxed paper between each circle. You can also sprinkle each circle with a light dusting of flour to make separation easier. Remove as many dough circles as needed and thaw for 10 to 15 minutes, right on the pie pan, easing the dough into the pan as soon as it is pliable. Single-crust pie shells can be frozen, too. In that case, it's probably a good idea to use disposable aluminum pie pans, stacking the shells on top of one another and separating them with sheets of waxed paper. It is not necessary to thaw frozen pie shells before filling.

ADDING FLAVOR TO A PIE CRUST

Depending on what the pie crust is to envelop, you may want to add a little flavoring to the dry ingredients before the shortening and water are added. Here are some suggestions:

- *½ cup grated cheddar cheese*
- *1 teaspoon ground cinnamon*
- *½ teaspoon ground nutmeg*
- *1½ teaspoons grated lemon or orange rind*
- *2 tablespoons minced nuts*

Rolling and Fitting a Single or Double Crust

To make a single-crust pie. Flatten the ball of chilled dough into a disk on a well-floured surface (see note on pages 269–70). With a floured rolling pin (or a floured, stockinette-covered rolling pin), roll the round of dough from the center to the outside in all directions to make a circle, keeping the pressure on the pin as even as possible and lifting the rolling pin just before you get to the edge of the dough so that the edge doesn't become too thin. If the edge cracks, immediately pinch it back together. Now and then, lift the dough with a pancake turner and peek under it to make sure it's not sticking. If it is, throw a little more flour under the crust onto the rolling surface. If the dough should stick and make a hole in the crust, cut a patch of dough from the edge. Moisten the edge of the area to be patched and press the patch into place.

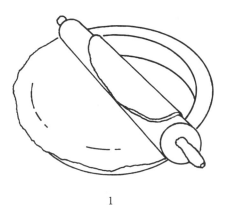

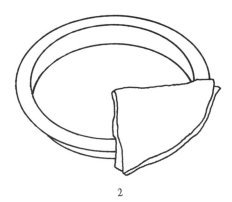

1

2

Roll the dough until it measures 2 inches larger all around than the size of the inverted pie pan in which it is to go, about 12 inches for a 9-inch pie. Loosely roll the pastry circle onto the rolling pin and unroll it into the pie pan—see figure 1. (Another way to do this is to carefully fold the pastry circle into quarters and place it in the pie pan with the point in the center—see figure 2—then unfold the pastry.) Ease the dough very gently into the pan, making sure that there is plenty of slack in the center. Holding up the edge of the dough with one hand, very gently ease and press the dough into the pan with the fingers of your other hand. (If your nails are long, you will have to use your knuckles. Or you can make a little ball of dough out of some scraps, flour it, and use that, a good idea no matter what the length of your nails.) The idea is to not stretch the dough, which will cause the crust to shrink. With scissors, evenly trim the over-hanging dough 1 inch from the edge of the pan. You're now ready to make the edging (see pages 270–71).

To make a double-crust pie. Roll out the slightly larger ball of dough and fit it into the pie pan as directed for a single-crust pie. Roll the second, smaller ball of dough the same way you rolled the bottom crust. (Since there is slightly less dough, the top crust will be a little thinner.) For a plain top crust, fold the dough into quarters. With a sharp knife, make three short cuts in the crust on either side of the point to allow the steam to escape. Place the folded crust over the filling with the point in the center. Carefully unfold over the filling. (Or you can use the rolling-pin method to place the top crust over the filling.) You're now ready to make the edging.

Note: Some bakers prefer to use the waxed-paper method for rolling out the crust. In that case, wipe the working surface with a damp cloth (to keep the waxed paper from sliding) and lay one 12-inch square of waxed paper on the dampened surface. Place the ball of chilled dough in the center of the waxed paper, pressing it to form a flat disk. Cover this with a second piece of 12-inch-square waxed paper. After the dough has been rolled to size, remove the top sheet of waxed paper. Pick up the bottom piece of waxed paper and the pastry (the pastry and waxed paper will stick together), and lay it over the pie pan, paper side up. Peel off the paper. Ease the crust into the pan.

Forming Elegant Edges

In the beginning, you'll probably be happy enough just to get an edible pie into and out of the oven and never mind how it looks. But as your pie crust–making skills improve (and they will, very soon) you'll start to be concerned with the appearance. That's when you'll want to experiment with fancy edges, sometimes called fluting or crimping, and pretty tops.

To prepare a single-crust pie for an edge, first fold the 1-inch overhang under the dough on the rim of the pie dish, making it flush with the edge of the pan.

To prepare a double-crust pie for an edge, fold the edge of the bottom crust under as directed above. Lay the top pastry over the filling and trim the overhang to 1 inch. Fold the edge of the top pastry under the edge of the bottom pastry, pressing the edges of the dough together with your fingers to seal it tightly.

When making a fancy edge, resist the temptation to keep going back over your work in order to make the edge picture-pretty. It may be pretty, all right, but it will also have all the flakiness and tenderness of cement. Practice doing edges on a pie crust that you will not be using.

Old-fashioned forked edge (for a single or double crust). This is the easiest edge of all, and a good choice for beginners, since it cannot be overworked. (This edge is not recommended for a very juicy pie that is likely to bubble over.) With the back of a floured four-tine fork, press the pastry onto the pie-pan rim around the edge. (Some bakers recommend first moistening the rim of the pie pan with water to help the crust adhere to it.)

Pinched or fluted edge (for a single or double crust). Turn up the pastry on the rim to make a stand-up edge. Place one index finger against the pastry on the inside of the pie pan. With the thumb and index finger of the other hand, pinch the pastry at that point. Repeat every ¼ inch. Leave the pinches rounded or pinch into points.

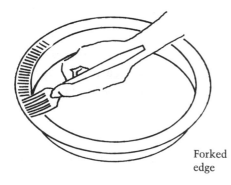

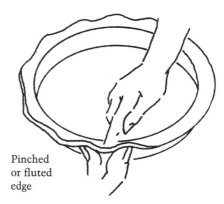

Forked
edge

Pinched
or fluted
edge

Scalloped edge (for a single or double crust). Make a rounded, pinched, or fluted edge, leaving ½ inch between each pinch. Flatten each pinch, or every other pinch, against the rim of the pan with a floured four-tine fork.

Roped edge (for a single or double crust). Turn up the pastry on the rim to make a stand-up edge. Press a thumb into the pastry edge at an angle, then pinch the pastry between the thumb and knuckle of the index finger, turning ever so slightly as you pinch. (Practice this edge by pinching your cheek. It works!)

Cutouts (for a single crust). With tiny cookie cutters (no more than ¾ inch wide), cut out circles, diamonds, hearts, leaves, stars, etc. from the pastry scraps. Moisten the pastry on the rim of the pie pan with water or milk and place the cutouts on the rim, overlapping slightly. Gently press into place.

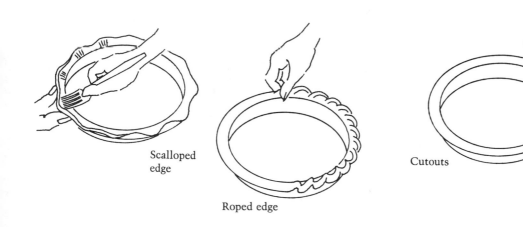

Scalloped
edge

Roped edge

Cutouts

Pretty Pie Tops

Silhouettes. There's nothing wrong with an ordinary top crust that simply has a few slits (straight or curved) cut into it to allow the steam to escape. But if you want to take the plain crust a little further, you can use a cookie cutter or a pattern to cut out designs from the top crust. For instance, an apple and a few apple leaves would be a nice cutout design to top an apple pie. You can also cut out letters and initials. Cut out the designs from the crust while it is still on the rolling surface.

Reverse silhouettes. Use the cutouts themselves to decorate the top of the pie, placing them on top of the filling. Or roll the top pastry crust into an 8-inch round, about ⅛ inch thick. Cut into six wedges and place the wedges on top of the pie.

Woven lattice top. Leave the 1-inch overhang on the bottom crust. Roll the top pastry dough into a 12-inch circle. Cut into ½-inch strips with a sharp knife, or a pizza cutter, and a ruler. Or use a zigzag pastry wheel to cut the strips for more decorative edges. Drape five to seven strips across the top of the filling. Weave one strip across the center by first folding back every other strip going in the opposite direction. Continue in this manner, folding back alternate strips each time a cross strip is added. Trim the strips to the same length as the overhanging bottom crust. Fold the bottom crust over the ends of the strips, building up a high edge. Seal by pressing the edges together, then make the edging.

Plain lattice. Lay the second half of the strips across the first layer without weaving them.

Woven or twisted lattice. Follow the instructions for making the woven or plain lattice, except twist the strips before they are placed on the filling.

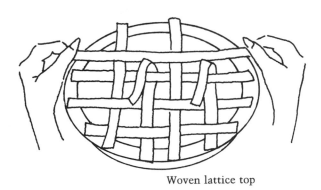

Woven lattice top

GLAZING

Before baking, brush the top crust and edge with a whole beaten egg or egg yolk, which will give the crust a dark, appetizing gloss. For more shine than color, brush with lightly beaten egg white, cream, or milk. For a sparkling effect, brush with any of these and then sprinkle with granulated sugar.

After baking, a warm crust may be spread or drizzled with a sugar glaze. To make a plain glaze, mix confectioners' sugar with enough milk or water to make a good spreading or drizzling consistency. A few drops of extract (rum, lemon, etc.) may be added to the glaze for flavor.

Baking Leftover Crust

It seems a pity to throw away perfectly good pie crust when it can easily be baked right along with the pie and eaten as a snack. (Or give it to the kids to use as play dough.) Cut the leftover crust into desired shapes and place on an ungreased baking sheet. Prick each piece several times with the tines of a fork and sprinkle with one of the following:

- *poppy or sesame seeds*
- *seasoned salts*
- *crumbled or ground dried herbs*
- *grated cheese*
- *cinnamon and sugar*

Bake along with the pie until lightly browned. Remove from the baking sheet and cool on a wire rack.

Storing Baked Pies

Most pies keep well at room temperature for a day, covered with aluminum foil or plastic wrap. (The notable exceptions are meringue pies or custard and cream pies.) Much longer than that and all pies should be covered and refrigerated. They can be refreshed by reheating at 325° to 350°F for 10 or 15 minutes. Meringue pies should be kept at room temperature, uncovered, and eaten on the day they are baked, and custard or cream pies should be refrigerated after they are baked and cooled.

Eliminating Soggy Crusts

For the crispiest crusts, use only glass or nonshiny, metal pie pans. Many experienced bakers also like to partially prebake the pie shell for an extra-crisp crust. To do this, lightly prick the bottom and side of the crust with the tines of a fork. Preheat the oven to 425°F and bake the unfilled crust for 6 to 8 minutes, or just until it is firm to the touch and has not yet started to brown. Take a peek after the first few minutes, and if there is any sign of puffing, prick these spots with the fork. Remove from the oven and fill. (Don't forget to reset the oven temperature, if necessary, before baking the pie.)

I have to tell you that prebaking a pie shell, even a little, is fraught with possible little problems that could ruin a busy day. The empty shell has a tendency to shrink and buckle and the side can slide down off the rim. A much simpler way to get nearly as good results (and the one I prefer) is to *lightly* brush the bottom of the crust with melted butter or lightly beaten egg white, or dust it with flour.

Baking the pie in the lower third of the oven helps, too. If the pie pan is metal, setting the pie shell on a baking sheet can also prevent the bottom from getting soggy. Place the unfilled shell on the baking sheet or slide the sheet under the pie after filling. A glass pie dish should be set directly on the oven rack. A piece of aluminum foil can be placed on the bottom of the oven to catch any drips.

Convenience Crusts

There are excellent convenience crusts on the market that can be a boon for the busy or less experienced baker. They are tasty, tender, flaky, and, quite honestly, about as good as most homemade pie crusts.

Frozen, ready-to-fill pie crusts in aluminum pans have to be the most convenient. They can go right from the freezer into the oven. The makers have even added extra dough on the rim that allows you to do your own stand-up edge after the crust has been thawed for a few minutes at room temperature. The brand I'm most familiar with (Oronoke) has an extra crust in the package to use when making a double-crust pie. *Warning:* Be sure to buy the "deep-dish" crust if you're making your own filling. The regular size is too shallow to hold most homemade fillings, and is intended for canned, ready-to-use pie fillings.

Refrigerated pie-crust rounds, ready for you to fit into the pan and make an edge, provide the extreme satisfaction of having done it yourself without actually making and rolling the dough from scratch.

The third option is pie-crust mix in a box. This stuff is great for the baker who wants to do it all, but doesn't have—or care to have—all the necessary ingredients on the shelf. All you add is water.

Tips for Perfect Pies

- Measure your ingredients carefully. That means use measuring spoons, glass measuring cups for liquids, and dry measuring cups for dry ingredients.
- Keep the dough as cool as you can and handle it as little and as lightly as possible.
- Use nonshiny metal pans or glass pie pans to help the bottom crust brown evenly. Bake a pie in a metal pie pan on a baking sheet, setting the pie shell on the sheet before it is filled or sliding it under the pie after filling. Glass pie dishes should be placed directly on the oven rack. Bake all pies in the lower third of the oven.
- Don't overfill the pie crust since most fillings expand some during baking. If there is too much filling for the shell, bake any extra in a custard cup along with the pie.
- Preheat the oven and make sure it's up to temperature before starting to bake. An oven thermometer is a mandatory kitchen accessory, not a gadget.
- If the top crust or the edge of the pie seems to be browning too quickly, lay a piece of aluminum foil over the whole pie, or cut a "wreath" from foil that just covers the edge.
- Cool the pie on a wire rack to help keep the bottom crust crisp.
- Serve the pie as soon as possible.

RITA MOLTER'S CRANBERRY AND MINCEMEAT PIE

Rita was my predecessor as the food editor at *Parents Magazine*, and she developed the recipe for this pie. Rita is a great baker and her creations are always as attractive as they are delicious.

2½ cups fresh cranberries, rinsed and
    picked over
1 cup sugar
¼ cup orange juice
One 28-ounce jar plain ready-to-use
    mincemeat
2 tablespoons all-purpose flour

Basic Flaky Pie-Crust Pastry for a 9-inch
    double-crust pie (see pages 266–67)
Milk and sugar for glaze
Hard Sauce (see page 238), Vanilla
    Custard Sauce (see pages 237–38), or
    vanilla ice cream

Combine the cranberries, sugar, and orange juice in a medium-size saucepan. Cook over medium-high heat, stirring frequently, until boiling. Reduce the heat to medium-low and simmer until the cranberries start to pop, about 5 minutes. Stir in the mincemeat and flour, then remove from the heat and set aside to cool.

Preheat the oven to 400°F. Prepare the bottom crust according to the directions on pages 269–70, trimming the dough but allowing it to hang over the edge of the pie pan. Spoon the cranberry mixture into the pie shell. Prepare a woven or plain lattice top according to the directions on page 272, making a high, stand-up edge. Brush the crust with milk and sprinkle with sugar. Bake for 40 minutes, or until the filling bubbles up between the spaces in the latticework. Cool on a wire rack. Serve warm or at room temperature with either of the suggested sauces or ice cream.

YIELD: ONE 9-INCH PIE; 6 TO 8 SERVINGS

WALNUT AND MOLASSES PIE

This is going to make you think of pecan pie, of course, but it's ever so much more interesting that I encourage you to try it. If you're really stuck on pecan pie, you can easily convert this into one by eliminating the molasses, increasing the corn syrup to 1½ cups, and substituting pecans for the walnuts.

3 large eggs
1 cup unsulphured molasses
½ cup dark corn syrup
½ teaspoon ground nutmeg
½ teaspoon ground cinnamon
¼ teaspoon salt
2 tablespoons butter, melted

2 tablespoons good brandy or cognac
  (optional)
2 cups coarsely chopped walnuts
Basic Flaky Pie-Crust Pastry for a 9-inch
  single-crust pie (see pages 266–67)
Lightly whipped cream for garnish

Preheat the oven to 350°F. Beat the eggs in a large bowl until frothy. Add the molasses, syrup, nutmeg, cinnamon, and salt and blend thoroughly. Beat in the melted butter and brandy, then stir in the nuts. Pour into the pie shell prepared as directed on pages 268–70 and finish with the desired edge. Bake for about 40 minutes, or until the center of the pie is firm to the touch. Remove from the oven and cool on a wire rack. Serve at room temperature or chilled, garnished with big dollops of whipped cream.

YIELD: ONE 9-INCH PIE; 6 TO 8 SERVINGS

CARAMEL AND PECAN APPLE PIE

Just reading over the ingredients should give you an inkling of the gooey delights in store if you should decide to bake this super-rich, crunchy apple pie.

Basic Flaky Pie-Crust Pastry for a 9-inch
double-crust pie (see pages 266–67)
¾ cup firmly packed light brown sugar
3 tablespoons all-purpose flour
¼ cup heavy or whipping cream
1 cup toasted (see pages 6–7) coarsely
chopped pecans

5 or 6 medium-size McIntosh apples,
peeled, cored, and sliced (about 6 cups)
3 tablespoons cold butter, cut into small
pieces
Milk and sugar for glaze
Lightly sweetened whipped cream or
vanilla ice cream

Preheat the oven to 400°F. Prepare the bottom pie crust according to the directions on pages 269–70. In a small bowl, mix together the brown sugar, flour, and cream. Stir in the pecans. Add to the apples in a large bowl, tossing lightly to mix. Spoon into the prepared pie crust and dot with the butter. Cover with the top crust according to the directions on page 269, finishing with the desired edge. Brush the crust with milk and sprinkle with sugar. Bake for 45 minutes, or until the filling bubbles up and the crust is golden. Remove from the oven and cool on a wire rack. Serve warm, at room temperature, or chilled with whipped cream or ice cream.

YIELD: ONE 9-INCH PIE; 6 TO 8 SERVINGS

DOUBLE-RICH PUMPKIN PIE

Crème fraîche is what gives this pumpkin pie its extraordinarily rich flavor and creamy texture, with an unusual consistency that is almost a cross between a pumpkin pie and a cheesecake. Crème fraîche is the thick, slightly sour cream that the French use about the same way we do sour cream or whipped cream, and it is now widely available in most specialty food stores, and even supermarkets. If you can't find it, see the instructions on page 4 for making your own.

Basic Flaky Pie-Crust Pastry for a 9-inch
  single-crust pie (see pages 266–67)
1 cup sugar
1 teaspoon ground cinnamon
½ teaspoon ground ginger
¼ teaspoon ground nutmeg
⅛ teaspoon ground cloves

One 16-ounce can solid-pack pumpkin
3 large eggs, separated
One 8-ounce container crème fraîche or
  1 cup homemade (see page 4)
Slightly sweetened whipped cream or
  crème fraîche for garnish

Prepare the pie shell as directed on pages 268–70, then partially prebake according to the instructions on page 274. Remove from the oven and set aside. Reduce the oven heat to 350°F. Combine ½ cup of the sugar with the cinnamon, ginger, nutmeg, and cloves in the top of a double boiler. Stir in the pumpkin, slightly beaten egg yolks, and crème fraîche. Set over hot but not boiling water and cook, stirring, until the mixture is hot and thick. Remove the top of the double boiler and set aside. In a medium-size bowl, beat the egg whites until they form soft peaks when the beaters are lifted. Gradually beat in the remaining sugar until thick and glossy. Fold the beaten whites into the pumpkin mixture until no streaks of white remain. Spoon the filling into the partially baked pie shell. Bake for about 45 minutes, or until the top is nicely browned. Remove from the oven and cool on a wire rack. Serve chilled with whipped cream or crème fraîche.

YIELD: ONE 9-INCH PIE; 6 TO 8 SERVINGS

LIBBY'S FAMOUS PUMPKIN PIE

The one and only. I've tried any number of plain pumpkin pies and this is the best.

PIE
2 large eggs, lightly beaten
One 16-ounce can solid-pack pumpkin
¾ cup sugar
½ teaspoon salt
1 teaspoon ground cinnamon
½ teaspoon ground ginger
¼ teaspoon ground cloves
One 12-ounce can undiluted evaporated
  milk (not condensed milk)

Basic Flaky Pie Crust Pastry for a 9-inch
  single-crust pie (see pages 266–67) with
  a fancy edge (see pages 270–71).

SPICED WHIPPED CREAM TOPPING
1 cup heavy or whipping cream
2 tablespoons confectioners' sugar
½ teaspoon pumpkin pie spice

Preheat the oven to 425°F. In a large bowl, combine the eggs, pumpkin, sugar, salt, spices, and evaporated milk with a wire whisk just until mixed. (Overmixing may cause unattractive bubbles on the surface of the pie.) Pour the pumpkin filling into the crust prepared as directed on pages 268–70. Bake in the lower third of the oven for 15 minutes, then lower the oven temperature to 350°F. Continue to bake for 40 to 50 minutes, or until a knife inserted between the center and the edge comes out clean. Remove from the oven and cool completely on a wire rack before cutting.

To make the topping, combine the cream, sugar, and spice in a small bowl. Beat until stiff peaks form when the beaters are lifted. Chill until serving time. Spoon over the cooled pumpkin pie before cutting, or serve the topping alongside the pie.

YIELD: ONE 9-INCH PIE; 6 TO 8 SERVINGS

ELIZABETH CROW'S PECAN TOPPING FOR PUMPKIN PIE

When I was the food editor at *Parents Magazine*, Elizabeth was the editor in chief and my boss. During one of our pre-Thanksgiving conversations Elizabeth told me that at one time she baked pumpkin pie from scratch, meaning she started with a big pumpkin. Later, as children were born and her career became more demanding, she started using canned pumpkin. That's when she hit on the idea for this topping. It was so popular with her family that it has gone on to become a Crow Thanksgiving tradition.

If time isn't on your side either, Elizabeth's sweet, crunchy topping can help even a store-bought pumpkin pie achieve homemade status.

1 cup pecan pieces
1 tablespoon minced crystallized ginger

¾ cup firmly packed dark brown sugar
4 tablespoons (½ stick) butter, melted

Preheat the oven broiler. Mix all of the ingredients in a small bowl. Spread evenly over the top of the pie and broil about 7 inches from the source of heat for about 2 minutes, watching carefully, until the topping is golden and the sugar is dissolved. Cool a little before serving.

YIELD: ENOUGH TO TOP ONE 8-, 9-, OR 10-INCH PUMPKIN PIE

AUTUMN CHERRY PIE

Everybody loves this pie, and they're also intrigued by the pleasantly sour flavor and slightly chewy texture of the dried cherries. Dark raisins could be substituted if dried cherries are not available, but it's the cherries that make this pie different and special.

2 cups dried cherries (see pages 4–5)
½ cup good brandy or cognac
1 cup heavy or whipping cream
½ cup sugar
3 tablespoons all-purpose flour
⅛ teaspoon salt

½ cup sugar
1 cup all-purpose flour
2 tablespoons butter
¼ teaspoon ground cinnamon
⅛ teaspoon ground nutmeg
Basic Flaky Pie-Crust Pastry for a 8- or 9-inch single-crust pie (see pages 266–67)
Whipped cream for garnish

CRUMB TOPPING
4 tablespoons (½ stick) butter, softened
½ cup firmly packed light brown sugar

Combine the cherries and brandy in a small bowl and set aside for 1 hour to soak. Preheat the oven to 450°F. Combine the cherries and brandy with the cream in a medium-size saucepan. Cook over medium heat until the mixture starts to boil, stirring almost constantly. Remove from the heat and set aside for 5 minutes. Strain the cherry mixture through a sieve into a small bowl. Set the cherries aside. Return the strained liquid to the saucepan. In a small bowl, combine the sugar, flour, and salt. Stir the sugar mixture into the cream mixture in the saucepan until blended. Return the cherries to the saucepan. Cook over medium heat, stirring almost constantly, until the mixture starts to boil. Remove from the heat and stir in the butter until melted. Let cool for 10 minutes then stir in the cinnamon and nutmeg. Pour into the pie shell prepared as directed on pages 268–70.

To make the topping, cream the butter and sugars in a medium-size bowl. Stir in the flour until the mixture is crumbly. Sprinkle evenly over the pie filling. Bake for 10 minutes, then reduce the oven heat to 350°F and continue to bake for another 15 to 20 minutes, or until the topping is flecked with brown and the edge of the crust is golden. Serve warm or at room temperature with a spoonful of whipped cream.

YIELD: ONE 9-INCH PIE; 6 TO 8 SERVINGS

"CHUST-RIGHT" SHOO-FLY PIE

My mother and I baked our first shoo-fly pie after I read an utterly charming book by Mildred Jordan, *The Shoo-Fly Pie*, published by Alfred A. Knopf in 1944. The story was about a little Pennsylvania Dutch girl named Debby Weissfinger, whose mother could never bake a shoo-fly pie to satisfy Debby's father. It was always too gummy or too dry, but never "chust right." In the end, of course, it's Debby who bakes the perfect shoo-fly pie. This is the shoo-fly pie I've been baking for years. For me, and for everyone else who's ever tasted it, it seems to be "chust right."

MOLASSES FILLING
1 cup unsulphured molasses
1 cup boiling water
1 teaspoon baking soda

CRUMB TOPPING
⅓ cup sugar
1 cup all-purpose flour

3 tablespoons solid white vegetable
  shortening
Pinch of salt

Basic Flaky Pie-Crust Pastry for a 9-inch single-crust pie (see pages 266–67)

Preheat the oven to 350°F. To make the filling, combine the molasses, water, and baking soda in a medium-size bowl and stir until well blended. To make the topping, combine the sugar, flour, shortening, and salt in another medium-size bowl and work together with a fork until crumbly. Pour the molasses filling into the pie shell prepared as directed on pages 268–70 and sprinkle evenly with the crumb topping. Bake for 25 to 30 minutes, or until the topping is lightly browned. Remove from the oven and cool completely on a wire rack before cutting. Since the Pennsylvania Dutch usually eat shoo-fly pie as an accompaniment to morning coffee, they serve the pie plain, but a little whipped cream or ice cream on the side couldn't hurt.

YIELD: ONE 9-INCH PIE; 6 TO 8 SERVINGS

GEORGE MINNEX'S BOURBON-PECAN PUMPKIN PIE

This old-fashioned Southern pie is the creation of the Reverend George Minnex, who, in addition to being a fine cook and host, is the curator of Ruthmere, an early twentieth-century house museum in Elkhart, Indiana, that was built by one of the founders of Miles Laboratories. The final step in the preparation of this pie is to pour burning brandy over the surface, which can be done at the table, if you like.

One 16-ounce can solid-pack pumpkin
3 large eggs, lightly beaten
1¼ cups firmly packed dark brown sugar
1½ cups half-and-half or light cream
¾ cup bourbon
1 teaspoon ground cinnamon
½ teaspoon ground ginger

¼ teaspoon salt
Basic Flaky Pie-Crust Pastry for two
    9-inch single-crust pies (see pages 266–
    67) with fancy edges (see pages 270–71)
4 tablespoons (½ stick) butter
2 cups pecan halves

Preheat the oven to 425°F. Combine the pumpkin, eggs, and ¾ cup of the brown sugar in a large bowl and stir until blended. Stir in the half-and-half, 3 tablespoons of the bourbon, the cinnamon, ginger, and salt until well combined. Divide the mixture evenly between the two pie shells prepared as directed on pages 268–70. Bake for 10 minutes. Reduce the oven temperature to 350°F and bake for an additional 30 minutes, or until the centers of the pies are set. Remove from the oven and set on wire racks to cool. Meanwhile, in a small saucepan, combine the butter and remaining brown sugar. Cook over medium heat, stirring, until the sugar dissolves. Stir in the pecans and ¼ cup of the remaining bourbon until well blended. Spoon the mixture evenly over the two baked pies. Just before serving, heat the remaining bourbon in a small saucepan just long enough to produce fumes, but do not allow the bourbon to boil. Remove from the heat and ignite the bourbon with a match. Carefully pour the flaming bourbon over the tops of the pies. Let the flames die down and serve immediately.

YIELD: TWO 9-INCH PIES; 6 TO 8 SERVINGS PER PIE

PLANTATION PEANUT PIE

Nut pies, not just pecan pies, have always been traditional Thanksgiving desserts, probably because in olden days nuts were cheap and plentiful, especially in the autumn when many other favorite pie-filling ingredients had gone out of season. Nut pies have remained popular through the years because, let's face it, nuts, sugar, butter, and other enrichments are an unbeatable combination.

1 cup chunk-style peanut butter
1 teaspoon vanilla extract
¼ teaspoon salt
2 tablespoons butter, melted
3 large eggs, lightly beaten

1 cup dark corn syrup
½ cup sugar
Basic Flaky Pie-Crust Pastry for a 9-inch
    single-crust pie (see pages 266–67)
Caramel Cream (see page 239)

Preheat the oven to 450°F. Combine the peanut butter, vanilla, salt, and melted butter in a medium-size bowl until well blended. In a large bowl, beat together the eggs, corn syrup, and sugar. Stir the peanut butter mixture into the egg mixture until thoroughly combined. Pour into the pie shell prepared as directed on pages 268–70. Bake for 10 minutes, then reduce the oven heat to 325°F and continue to bake for another 35 minutes, or until the filling is firm to the touch. Remove from the oven and cool on a wire rack. Serve warm or chilled with caramel cream.

YIELD: ONE 9-INCH PIE; 6 TO 8 SERVINGS

STEPHANIE CURTIS'S SWEET POTATO PIE

Stephanie is not a big fan of sweet potatoes, so all of us were pleasantly surprised when she produced this incredible pie. Like many good things, the pie has its little drawbacks, mainly that it must be made the same day it's to be served. However, it can be done early in the day and then set aside, uncovered, in a dry, cool place until serving time. Leftovers can be lightly covered and saved until the next day when it won't look like much, but it will still taste good. The other thing you should be alerted to is the matter of timing the making of the meringue so that it will not have to wait for the pie to come out of the oven. Better to have the pie wait a few minutes for the meringue. If the meringue is started about 20 minutes before the pie is ready it, things should work out fine.

1 orange
1 cup water
1 cup sugar
2 tablespoons finely chopped crystallized
 ginger
¾ pound sweet potatoes, cooked and
 mashed (2 cups)
¼ cup heavy or whipping cream

2 tablespoons butter, melted
1 teaspoon vanilla extract
6 large eggs, separated (read recipe
 through before separating)
Basic Flaky Pie-Crust Pastry for a 9-inch
 single-crust pie (see pages 266–67)
½ teaspoon cream of tartar

Cut off strips of the orange rind, being careful not to include any of the bitter white pith just beneath. Cut as much of the rind as needed into small slivers to make about 2 tablespoons and set aside. Squeeze the orange and strain the juice to make about ½ cup. Set the juice aside. In a small saucepan, combine the water and ½ cup of the sugar. Bring to a boil over high heat, then stir in the orange-rind slivers. Barely simmer over low heat, uncovered, until the mixture is syrupy, about 10 minutes. Stir in the ginger and set aside to cool to lukewarm.

Preheat the oven to 350°F. In a large bowl, beat the mashed sweet potatoes with the reserved orange juice, the cream, butter, vanilla, and 3 of the egg yolks until well blended. (The remaining 3 egg yolks will not be used and can be discarded or saved for another purpose.) Beat in the cooled syrup mixture. Place 2 of the egg whites in the large bowl of an electric mixer and beat just until soft peaks form. Stir (do not fold) the beaten whites into the sweet potato mixture. Turn the sweet potato filling into the pie shell, prepared as directed on pages 268–70, smoothing the top. Bake until the filling is set around the edge (a knife inserted comes out clean), but the middle is still slightly soft, 45 to 50 minutes. About 20 minutes before the pie is done, place the remaining egg whites and cream of tartar in the same mixer bowl. Beat at low speed until frothy. Increase the speed and very gradually add the remaining sugar, about a tablespoon at a time. Continue beating at high speed until the whites are very stiff and glossy. Don't rush this procedure. Done properly, it can easily take 15 minutes. When the pie is done, remove it from the oven and spoon the beaten egg whites over the filling in large cloudlike mounds. Return the pie to the oven and bake for an additional 10 to 15 minutes, or until the meringue is lightly tinged with color. Remove from the oven and cool on a wire rack. Because of the meringue topping, which does not keep well, this pie should be served the same day it's baked.

YIELD: ONE 9-INCH PIE; 6 TO 8 SERVINGS

LEMONY CRANBERRY-APPLE PIE

The cranberries add a pleasant tartness to this pie that's a good follow-up for a rich dinner.

Basic Flaky Pie-Crust Pastry for a 9-inch
  double-crust pie (see pages 266–67)
¾ cup firmly packed light or dark
  brown sugar
¼ cup granulated sugar
⅓ cup all-purpose flour
1 teaspoon ground cinnamon
4 or 5 McIntosh or Granny Smith apples,
  peeled, cored, and sliced (4 cups)

2 cups fresh cranberries, rinsed and
  picked over
2 tablespoons finely chopped lemon, both
  the rind and the pulp
2 tablespoons butter
Beaten whole egg or egg white and
  granulated sugar for glazing
  and sprinkling on pie crust
Vanilla ice cream

Roll and fit the bottom crust according to the instructions on pages 269–70. Preheat the oven to 425°F. Combine the sugars, flour, and cinnamon in a large bowl until well blended. Add the apple slices, cranberries, and lemon and mix well. Turn into the prepared pie shell and dot with the butter. Cover the filling with the remaining pie crust and make a pretty stand-up edge. Brush the top crust with beaten egg and sprinkle with sugar. Bake for about 40 minutes, or until golden. Remove from the oven and cool completely on a wire rack before cutting. Serve with a scoop of ice cream.

YIELD: ONE 9-INCH PIE; 6 TO 8 SERVINGS

DEEP-CHOCOLATE AND WALNUT PIE

A dessert that bridges the gap between elegant and traditional very nicely, so if your Thanksgiving dinner is an intimate one, this pie may satisfy all tastes.

3 large eggs
1 cup firmly packed light brown sugar
¼ cup light corn syrup
½ teaspoon baking soda
¼ cup good brandy or cognac
4 tablespoons (½ stick) butter, melted

5 ounces semisweet chocolate, coarsely
  chopped
1 cup coarsely chopped walnuts
Basic Flaky Pie-Crust Pastry for a 9-inch
  single-crust pie (see pages 266–67)
Plain or lightly sweetened whipped cream
Grated chocolate or chocolate curls (see
  pages 15–16)

Preheat the oven to 325°F. In a medium-size bowl, beat the eggs until pale and frothy. Add the sugar, corn syrup, baking soda, and brandy and stir until the sugar is dissolved. Stir in the butter, chocolate, and walnuts. Pour the filling into the pie shell which has been prepared as directed on pages 268–70. Bake for 40 to 45 minutes, or until the filling is firm to the touch and the edge is golden brown. Remove from the oven to a wire rack and cool completely before cutting. Serve with mounds of whipped cream sprinkled with grated chocolate or chocolate curls.

YIELD: ONE 9-INCH PIE; 6 TO 8 SERVINGS

MY FAMILY'S FAVORITE APPLE PIE

Years ago friends returning from their summer home on Long Island brought with them the most wonderful apple pie I ever tasted. I made many apple pies before I finally felt that I had reasonably duplicated this memorable pie. I must tell you that this is not a beautiful pie. The top crust rises and falls like the Rocky Mountains, but that's never seemed to matter to anyone who's ever eaten it.

CRUST
4 cups all-purpose flour
2 teaspoons salt
1⅓ cups lard or 1½ cups solid white vegetable shortening
½ cup plus 3 to 4 tablespoons ice water

FILLING
3 pounds McIntosh apples, peeled, cored, and sliced (about 8 cups)

1 tablespoon fresh lemon juice
1 teaspoon grated lemon rind
¾ cup sugar
⅓ cup all-purpose flour
1 teaspoon ground cinnamon
¼ teaspoon salt
3 tablespoons butter, cut into small pieces

Milk and sugar for glazing

Make a pie dough with the listed ingredients according to the instructions on page 267. After the pastry has chilled for about 1 hour, divide it into thirds. One third will be used to make the bottom crust and the remaining two thirds will be used for the top crust. Roll and fit the bottom crust according to the instructions given on pages 269–70. Do not trim the overhang just yet.

Preheat the oven to 425°F. In a very large bowl, toss the apples with the lemon juice and rind. In a medium-size bowl, combine the sugar, flour, cinnamon, and salt until well blended. Add the sugar mixture to the apple mixture and toss to coat the apples completely. Spoon the filling into the pie shell, mounding it high in the center. Pour over any juices that have accumulated in the bowl. Dot with the butter. Roll out the remaining dough, making the pastry circle at least 15 inches in diameter. Fold the circle in half and cut a few slits in it to allow the steam to escape. Place the folded pastry over one half of the filled pie shell. Unfold over the filling, pressing the top and bottom pastry together. Trim both overhanging edges with scissors, leaving a ½-inch overhang. Fold the overhang under on the rim of the pie pan, making it flush with the edge of the rim. Using a floured four-tine fork, firmly press the dough onto the rim of the pie pan. Brush the crust with milk and sprinkle with sugar. Bake for 40 to 50 minutes, or until the crust is appetizingly golden. Cool on a wire rack before cutting. Serve at room temperature or chilled with a scoop of vanilla ice cream.

YIELD: ONE VERY HIGH 9-INCH PIE; 8 TO 10 SERVINGS

TARTE TATIN WITH A CHEESE CRUST

This upside-down apple tart is a variation on the French classic. The secret to its richness is in cooking the apples very slowly on top of the stove in the caramel before baking them under a pie crust. The crust contains grated Emmenthal or other Swiss cheese, adding a cheesy chewiness that complements the caramelized apples, but a more conventional flaky crust could be substituted. Be sure to turn the tart out of the pan soon after it is baked or the caramelized apples will stick to the pan.

CRUST
1 cup all-purpose flour
¾ cup grated Emmenthal or other Swiss cheese
¼ teaspoon salt
2 tablespoons cold butter, cut into small pieces
1 large egg, beaten with 2 tablespoons cold water

FILLING
4 tablespoons (½ stick) butter
¾ cup plus 2 tablespoons sugar
3 tablespoons Armagnac or good brandy
4 or 5 Rome Beauty or Granny Smith apples, peeled, cored, and cut into 1-inch wedges (about 4 cups)

Crème fraîche (see page 4), whipped cream, or grated Emmenthal, Gruyère, or other Swiss cheese

To make the crust, combine the flour, cheese, and salt in a large bowl until well blended. Add the butter and blend with a fork until the mixture is crumbly. Add the egg and water and toss the mixture until it is well blended. Gather the dough into a ball. Wrap in waxed paper and refrigerate for 15 minutes.

To make the filling, melt the butter in a 9-inch round cake pan over medium heat. Stir in ¾ cup of the sugar and the Armagnac and cook over medium heat, stirring, until the mixture bubbles. Arrange the apple wedges in a spiral pattern over the bubbling mixture, packing them together as tightly as possible. (You should be able to fit all of the apple wedges into the pan if you stand the wedges up, core side down.) Cook over medium-low heat for 25 to 35 minutes without disturbing, watching carefully to make sure the sugar mixture does not start to burn, until the apple wedges have softened and cooked down and the sugar mixture has begun to caramelize. Don't rush this process. The apples should cook slowly in the bubbling sugar mixture, which may take up to 40 minutes. Sprinkle the remaining sugar evenly over the apples.

Preheat the oven to 350°F. Roll the pastry into a 9½-inch circle on a floured surface and place it over the apples, tucking the dough down between the apples and the side of the pan, and trimming away any excess dough. Bake in the center of the oven for 30 to 35 minutes, or until the crust is golden brown. Remove from the oven and let cool

☙

for 3 to 5 minutes before carefully inverting the pan onto a serving platter. Cut into wedges and serve warm or cool, topped with crème fraîche, whipped cream, or shredded cheese.

YIELD: ONE 9-INCH TART; 8 SERVINGS

DEEP-DISH APPLE PIE
☙

When there are a lot of people to feed and not much time for preparation, this is a good recipe to have on file, since it's nothing but a very good apple pie with no crust.

9 or 10 Golden Delicious or Rome Beauty
   apples, peeled, cored, and sliced
   (about 9 cups)
¼ cup Calvados, applejack, or apple cider
2 tablespoons fresh lemon juice
⅔ cup granulated sugar
½ cup firmly packed light brown sugar
3 tablespoons cornstarch
½ teaspoon ground cinnamon
¼ teaspoon salt

CRUMB TOPPING
1½ cups granulated sugar
¾ cup solid white vegetable shortening
4 cups all-purpose flour
½ pound (2 sticks) butter, melted

FLAVORED WHIPPED CREAM
1 cup heavy or whipping cream, whipped
   until stiff peaks form with 2 tablespoons confectioners' sugar and 1 tablespoon Calvados or apple brandy, if
   desired

Preheat the oven to 400°F. Place the apple slices in a large bowl, add the Calvados and lemon juice, and stir until the apple slices are well coated. In a medium-size bowl, mix both of the sugars, the cornstarch, cinnamon, and salt until well blended. Stir into the apple mixture until completely blended. Turn the apples into a 13- × 9-inch baking dish that has been buttered or coated with nonstick vegetable spray. Smooth the mixture with the back of a spoon to level the apples.

To make the topping, beat the sugar with the shortening in a medium-size bowl with an electric blender at medium speed until well blended. Gradually beat in the flour. Add the melted butter and beat again until well blended. The mixture will be more pasty than crumbly. Sprinkle evenly over the apple mixture. Bake for about 30 minutes, or until bubbling and the topping is browned. Serve warm or at room temperature with the flavored whipped cream. Rewarm, uncovered, at 325° to 350°F for about 15 minutes.

YIELD: ABOUT 12 SERVINGS

PEAR AND CRANBERRY CRISP

For those who are fond of homey, old-fashioned desserts, this one hits the spot. If you think it's not fancy enough for Thanksgiving dinner, serve the crisp with leftovers. It's easy and it's wonderful.

3 large pears, such as Anjou, Bosc, or Bartlett (about 1½ pounds), peeled, cored, and sliced
1 cup fresh cranberries, rinsed and picked over
¾ cup plus 2 to 4 tablespoons sugar
¾ cup all-purpose flour

½ teaspoon ground nutmeg
¼ teaspoon salt
¼ pound (1 stick) cold butter, cut into small pieces
1 cup coarsely chopped walnuts
½ cup uncooked regular or quick-cooking rolled oats (not instant)

Preheat the oven to 350°F. Arrange the pears and cranberries in the bottom of a shallow 1½-quart baking dish that has been greased or coated with nonstick vegetable spray. Sprinkle with 2 to 4 tablespoons of the sugar, depending on how sweet the pears are. In a large bowl, mix the remaining sugar with the flour, nutmeg, and salt. Add the butter and cut it in with a pastry blender or two knives until the mixture resembles coarse meal. Stir in the walnuts and oats until well blended. Sprinkle evenly over the fruit mixture. Bake for 35 to 40 minutes, or until bubbly and the top is lightly browned. This is best when served warm with a pitcher of cream or a scoop of ice cream.

YIELD: ABOUT 6 SERVINGS

BAKED CRANBERRY CUSTARD

Tart cranberries are ideal for this variation of the French dessert that is known as *clafoutis*. A *clafoutis* is traditionally made with sour cherries or other tart fruit, which provide a pleasant contrast to the sweet custard. The cranberries can be prepared ahead of time, but it must be mixed and baked just before serving.

2 cups fresh cranberries, rinsed and picked over
1¼ cups sugar
1 cup water
4 large eggs
¼ cup all-purpose flour

1 cup milk
¼ cup plus 2 tablespoons heavy or whipping cream
Confectioners' sugar, softly whipped cream, or crème fraîche (see page 4)

Preheat the oven to 400°F. Place the cranberries in a medium-size saucepan with ¼ cup of the sugar and the water. Bring to a slow boil over medium-high heat and cook for 5 minutes, stirring occasionally and reducing the heat if the mixture seems to be boiling too fast. Remove the cranberries with a slotted spoon and spread them evenly over the bottom of a shallow 2-quart baking or gratin dish that has been buttered or coated with nonstick vegetable spray. Boil the cranberry liquid over high heat until it is reduced to about ¼ cup. Combine the eggs and remaining sugar in a medium-size bowl until well blended. Gradually stir in the flour until smooth. Add the milk, cream, and reduced cranberry syrup and beat until well blended. Pour over the cranberries. Bake for 40 to 45 minutes, or until the top puffs and turns golden brown and the center is set. Remove from the oven and immediately spoon into individual bowls. Serve with a sprinkling of confectioners' sugar, whipped cream, or crème fraîche.

YIELD: 6 SERVINGS

PUMPKIN ICE CREAM

The goodness of this ice cream virtually depends on the quality of the vanilla ice cream you use, so choose carefully.

½ cup firmly packed dark brown sugar
½ teaspoon ground cinnamon
¼ teaspoon ground nutmeg

1 cup canned solid-pack pumpkin
1 quart vanilla ice cream, softened
    slightly in the refrigerator

Combine the sugar, cinnamon, and nutmeg in a large bowl, then stir in the pumpkin until well blended Add the ice cream in big spoonfuls, then beat with a big spoon until thoroughly combined. Turn into a 9-inch baking or pie pan. Cover tightly and freeze until ready to serve. Thaw slightly in the refrigerator before cutting into wedges to serve. Serve with Dainty Gingersnaps (see page 305).

YIELD: ABOUT 8 SERVINGS

MRS. HEFNER'S CHOCOLATE CAKE

The Hefners owned the redbrick-house-with-a-red-barn farm (I think the barn may have had hex signs painted on it) just down the road from us near Sinking Spring, Pennsylvania, when I was very young. There were a lot of kids in their family and all the action took place in a big square kitchen with a big square kitchen table and a black stove. I remember the day my mother wheedled this recipe out of Mrs. Hefner. It was a real cup-of-this-and-a-little-of-that recitation, but my mother got the recipe to work and the cake became a family favorite. I'd forgotten about Mrs. Hefner's cake until recently when my sister, Ruth Howard, mentioned that she'd found a copy of the recipe, baked the cake, and it was as good as she remembered. I must warn you that this cake is not of the high and handsome variety. In fact, it's quite flat and not very impressive looking, and is mixed together in a rather unorthodox manner. But as old-fashioned chocolate cakes go, there's none better.

1½ cups all-purpose flour
½ cup unsweetened cocoa powder
1 teaspoon baking powder
1 teaspoon baking soda
½ teaspoon salt
1¼ cups sugar
¾ cup solid white vegetable shortening
2 large eggs
1 cup hot tap water
2 teaspoons vanilla extract

WHITE BUTTERCREAM FROSTING
¼ pound (1 stick) butter, softened
One 16 ounce box confectioners' sugar, sifted
1 teaspoon vanilla extract
3 to 4 tablespoons milk

Preheat the oven to 325°F. Grease and flour two 9-inch round cake pans. In a medium-size bowl, mix the flour, cocoa, baking powder, baking soda, and salt and sift onto a sheet of waxed paper. In a medium-size bowl, beat the sugar and shortening until well blended. Beat in the eggs until the mixture is creamy. Gradually stir in the hot water. The mixture will look curdled. Gradually beat in the flour mixture and then the vanilla. Divide the batter between the prepared pans. Bake for 20 to 25 minutes, or until the layers are just beginning to pull away from the sides of the pans and a wooden toothpick inserted just off center comes out clean. Remove from the oven and cool on wire racks for 10 minutes. Remove the cakes from the pans and cool completely on the racks.

To make the frosting, beat the butter until creamy. Gradually beat in the confectioners' sugar. Beat in the vanilla and as much milk as needed to give the frosting a spreading consistency. Fill and frost the cake when the layers have cooled.

YIELD: ONE 9-INCH LAYER CAKE; 8 TO 12 SERVINGS

Variation: To make a chocolate buttercream frosting, beat in 2 tablespoons of un-sweetened cocoa powder before adding the vanilla and milk.

PUMPKIN SWIRL CHEESECAKE

For cheesecake lovers, this is the real thing, with no shortcuts or low-fat substitutes. Cheesecake is usually served ungarnished, in its pristine state. But, truthfully, a little chocolate sauce wouldn't hurt this cheesecake at all.

CRUST

¼ pound (1 stick) butter, softened
½ cup sugar
1 cup all-purpose flour
1 cup vanilla wafer crumbs (about
   23 vanilla wafers)
½ cup finely chopped walnuts or pecans

FILLING
Two 8-ounce packages cream cheese,
   at room temperature

1 cup sugar
¼ cup sour cream
2 large eggs
1 tablespoon all-purpose flour
¼ cup orange juice
1 teaspoon finely grated orange rind
1 cup canned solid-pack pumpkin
½ teaspoon pumpkin pie spice

Preheat the oven to 350°F. Lightly grease the bottom and sides of an 8½- or 9½-inch-diameter springform pan. To prepare the crust, beat the butter and sugar in a small bowl with an electric mixer on medium speed until creamy. With the mixer on low speed, beat in the flour, cookie crumbs, and walnuts. Spread evenly over the bottom of the prepared pan. Bake the crust for 15 minutes. Remove from the oven and set aside on a wire rack.

To prepare the filling, beat the cream cheese and sugar together in a medium-size bowl until creamy. Beat in the sour cream, eggs, flour, orange juice, and orange rind. Remove ½ cup of the filling and place in a small bowl. Spread the remaining filling evenly over the baked crust. Add the pumpkin and pumpkin pie spice to the reserved filling and stir to blend. Drop the pumpkin mixture by heaping measuring tablespoonfuls over the filling in the pan. With a rubber spatula, carefully swirl the mixtures together. Bake for 45 to 55 minutes, or until the edge is set and firm. The center may still appear to be a little soft. Turn off the oven and leave the cheesecake in the oven with the door ajar for 1 hour. Remove the cake to a wire rack and cool to room temperature. Cover and refrigerate overnight before removing the side of the pan and serving.

YIELD: ABOUT 16 SERVINGS

BREAD PUDDING WITH BOURBON SAUCE

This is not a dessert for children, or at least the sauce isn't. Sprinkle children's servings with confectioners' sugar or serve with ice cream.

One 8- to 10-ounce loaf day-old French
    bread, broken into small pieces
1 quart plus ½ cup milk
⅔ cup sugar
3 large eggs
2 tablespoons vanilla extract
½ cup dark or golden raisins
3 tablespoons butter, melted

BOURBON SAUCE
¼ pound (1 stick) butter
⅔ cup sugar
2 large eggs
⅔ cup bourbon or to taste

Preheat the oven to 350°F. Place the bread in a large bowl. Stir in the milk, then stir the mixture with a wooden spoon, or mix with your hands, until thoroughly blended. Add the sugar, eggs, vanilla, and raisins, stirring until well blended. Pour the melted butter in a 13- × 9-inch baking dish, tilting the dish to cover the bottom evenly. Pour the bread mixture into the baking dish. Bake for 50 minutes to 1 hour, or until very firm to the touch. Remove from the oven and cool completely on a wire rack before cutting.

To make the sauce, cream the butter and sugar until fluffy in a medium-size bowl. Beat in the eggs one at a time. Transfer the mixture to the top of a double boiler and set over simmering water. Add the bourbon and cook the mixture, stirring, until it is slightly thickened, about 5 minutes. The sauce should be served as warm as possible. If made ahead, press a piece of plastic wrap directly on the surface (this will prevent a skin from forming) and refrigerate. Reheat in a double boiler over hot water, stirring constantly, until very warm. Reheating much more than this may cause the sauce to curdle.

Cut the cooled pudding into 8 pieces. To serve, place the pieces of pudding in individual serving bowls and spoon the sauce over each serving, dividing equally.

YIELD: 8 SERVINGS; ABOUT 1¾ CUPS SAUCE

PLUM PUDDING TRIFLE

When Anne Bailey heard that I was not planning to include this trifle because I thought it was a little too "Christmasy," she changed my mind. Annie says she serves it for company frequently during the winter because it's fairly easy to make, most of it can be made ahead, and everybody agrees to seconds. "So, what could be better for Thanksgiving?" she asks.

1 cup sugar	2 tablespoons butter
3 tablespoons cornstarch	Two 15-ounce cans plum pudding
1¼ cups warm water	1 cup heavy or whipping cream
Grated rind of 1 lemon	2 tablespoons confectioners' sugar
¼ cup fresh lemon juice	½ teaspoon vanilla extract
3 egg yolks, lightly beaten	¼ cup seedless raspberry preserves

Combine the sugar and cornstarch in the top of a double boiler. Gradually stir in the water, then the lemon rind, lemon juice, egg yolks, and butter. Cook over simmering water, stirring constantly, until smooth and thick enough to mound when dropped from a spoon. Remove from the heat and set aside to cool. Crumble half of the plum pudding into the bottom of a large serving bowl. Top with the cooled lemon filling. Crumble the remaining half of the plum pudding over the lemon filling. Cover lightly and refrigerate until close to serving time. Two or three hours before serving, whip the cream with the confectioners' sugar and vanilla in a medium-size bowl until stiff peaks form. Cover and refrigerate until serving time. Just before serving, drop the whipped cream in mounds on top of the trifle, then drop a little of the preserves from the tip of the spoon here and there over the top of the whipped cream.

YIELD: 8 TO 12 SERVINGS

RUM-RAISIN CREPES

If you have a chafing dish in the back of the closet, it might be fun to assemble this at the table.

½ cup dark raisins
1 teaspoon ground cinnamon
¾ cup rum
1 cup all-purpose flour
1 cup sugar
2 tablespoons butter, melted

3 large eggs
½ cup milk
½ cup light cream or half-and-half
1 tablespoon vegetable oil
¼ pound (1 stick) butter

Combine the raisins, cinnamon, and rum in a small saucepan and set over low heat until the mixture simmers. Remove from the heat and set aside until ready to assemble the dessert. In a medium-size bowl, combine the flour and ¼ cup of the sugar. Combine the melted butter, eggs, milk, and cream in a small bowl. Beat with a wire whisk until well blended. Add the egg mixture to the flour mixture, beating until smooth. Chill the batter for at least 30 minutes, or cover tightly and refrigerate for up to two days. In that case, beat the batter to reblend it before using.

Set a 6-inch (measured across the bottom) nonstick skillet over medium heat. (The skillet is ready when a few drops of water bounce around when sprinkled in the bottom.) Brush the skillet lightly with oil. Measure about 2 tablespoons of the batter into the skillet. Immediately tilt the skillet until the batter covers the bottom. Cook for 30 to 40 seconds, or until the top looks nearly dry and the edge of the crepe is starting to brown. Turn the crepe (I use a long icing spatula) and cook on the other side for about 20 seconds, or until the underside is flecked with brown. Slide the crepe out of the pan and onto a plate. Repeat with the remaining batter, removing the skillet from the heat after making each crepe to keep it from overheating and lightly oiling the pan. Give the batter a stir from time to time to keep it well mixed. As the crepes are made, stack them on top of one another. You should have about 15 crepes. Cover the crepes with plastic wrap or aluminum foil and refrigerate. Bring to room temperature before assembling the dessert.

Just before serving, tear the crepes into 1½- to 2-inch pieces. Melt the butter in a large skillet or chafing dish over medium heat. Stir in the raisin-rum mixture. Add the crepe pieces. Sprinkle the remaining sugar evenly over the crepes and toss them over medium-low heat until the sugar and raisins are evenly distributed. Work quickly so that the sugar does not melt. It should retain a grainy texture. Spoon onto dessert plates and serve immediately.

YIELD: 8 SERVINGS

LIGHTER DESSERTS

As hard as it is for those of us with a sweet tooth to accept, there are some people who will decline even a small portion of rich desserts, and an accommodating host will want to have something more exciting on hand to offer them other than a two-week-old apple.

Most often, the people gathered around the Thanksgiving table are so well known to us that there's usually little doubt about what everyone will, or won't, eat. But if you have reason to feel that any of your guests might be more comfortable with a leaner dessert, the ones that follow are very light—some more than others—and very festive.

FRESH PEARS BURGUNDY

The intense flavor of these pears, accompanied by the reduction of their cooking liquid, can almost make a person forget that this dessert, except for a minuscule amount of oil from the almonds, is fat free. For a slightly richer version, add a small scoop of vanilla ice cream or serve in a pool of Vanilla Custard Sauce (see pages 237–38).

4 firm, ripe pears with stems
2 cups red burgundy wine
1 cup sugar
One 3-inch cinnamon stick

One 3-inch piece lemon rind
¼ cup toasted (see pages 6–7) slivered
*   almonds*

Peel the pears with a vegetable parer, leaving the stems on. Use an apple corer to remove the cores through the bottoms of the pears. Trim a thin slice from the bottom of each pear so it stands firm and straight. Combine the wine, sugar, cinnamon stick, and lemon rind in a Dutch oven or other large heavy saucepan. Bring to a boil over high heat. Reduce the heat to medium-low and simmer for 5 minutes. Add the pears and simmer over medium-low heat, basting and turning the pears often to color them evenly, until a wooden toothpick can be inserted easily into the bottom of each pear. This may take anywhere from 15 to 40 minutes, depending on the type and ripeness of the pears. Remove the pears as they are cooked and stand them in a shallow bowl. Cover and refrigerate until ready to serve. (If the pears are to be served within a few hours, there is no need to chill them.) Increase the heat under the syrup and boil until the mixture becomes syrupy and is reduced to about 1 cup. Serve the pears at room temperature or chilled with warm or chilled sauce, sprinkled with the almonds.

YIELD: 4 SERVINGS

❦

THANKSGIVING FRUIT BOWL

❦

When the fruits are served from a clear glass bowl, this is a very impressive-looking dessert, and those guests who are valiantly trying to reduce the sugar and fat in their diets will bless you for it.

5 large navel oranges
5 kiwi fruit

One 10-ounce jar lingonberries in syrup
(see note below)

With a vegetable parer, peel the oranges, making sure to cut away all of the bitter white pith just beneath the rind. Holding each orange over a medium-size bowl, cut between the segments, letting the segments and juice fall into the bowl. Peel the kiwi fruit and slice them into the bowl of segments. Drain the lingonberries in a sieve and rinse with cold water. Drain thoroughly. Arrange the orange segments and kiwi slices, and any juice that has accumulated with them, in a serving bowl, sprinkling in the lingonberries as you go so that they are evenly distributed throughout. Cover and chill until serving time.

YIELD: 6 TO 8 SERVINGS

Note: Lingonberries is available in specialty food stores. One cup fresh raspberries, the cleaned seeds from two pomegranates, or 1 cup Candied Cranberries (see page 19) may be substituted.

CARAMEL-APPLE SUNDAE

❦

If the caramel topping is kept to a minimum, this is a very conservative dessert.

For each serving you will need one soft eating apple. Cut the apple into six wedges using an apple coring and cutting gadget that does the job in one quick motion, or a sharp knife and a good eye. Brush the wedges with lemon juice to keep them from darkening. (Actually, the apples should be ready to go and sliced at the last minute.) Fan the apple slices on a dessert plate. Sprinkle with about 2 tablespoons of toasted (see pages 6–7) chopped walnuts. Drizzle a minimal amount of Quick Caramel Sauce (see page 238) over and around the apple and serve at once with a knife and fork.

YIELD: 1 SERVING

JOHNNIE'S JAM CAKE

This is an old recipe for a tender, moist, old-fashioned cake. Although I wouldn't exactly call this diet food, it is appealing to those who prefer their desserts less rich and gooey.

12 tablespoons (1½ sticks) butter, softened
¾ cup sugar
1 teaspoon vanilla extract
3 large eggs
1½ cups all-purpose flour
2 teaspoons baking powder
¾ teaspoon salt
½ teaspoon ground cinnamon
½ teaspoon ground cloves

½ teaspoon ground allspice
¼ teaspoon baking soda
¼ cup buttermilk
½ cup strawberry preserves
½ cup raspberry preserves
One 10- or 12-ounce jar plum jelly
Confectioners' sugar for dusting
1 cup coarsely chopped almonds or
    walnuts (optional)

Preheat the oven to 325°F. Grease two 9-inch round cake pans, line the bottoms with waxed paper, and set aside. In a large bowl, beat the butter and sugar until light and fluffy. Blend in the vanilla, then beat in the eggs, one at a time. In a medium-size bowl, stir together the flour, baking powder, salt, cinnamon, cloves, allspice, and baking soda until well mixed. Beat the flour mixture into the creamed mixture alternately with the buttermilk, beginning and ending with the dry ingredients. Stir in the strawberry and raspberry preserves until well blended. Divide the batter evenly between the prepared pans. Bake for 45 to 50 minutes, or until the cake layers start pulling away from the sides of the pans and the centers spring back when lightly touched. Remove from the oven to wire racks. Cool in the pans on the racks for 15 minutes, then turn out of the pans to cool completely on the racks.

When completely cooled, carefully peel off the waxed paper. Using a long, sharp knife, split each layer in half horizontally. (Because they are very moist, these cake layers are also extremely fragile. To handle them without breaking, slip a thin piece of cardboard between the halves after cutting in order to lift off the top. The cardboard is also helpful when stacking the jam-spread layers. The best way to do this is to lift each layer into position with the cardboard, and then carefully slide the cardboard out.) Spread about one third of the plum jelly over each of three cake layers. Stack the layers, ending with the plain layer, top side up. Generously dust the top with sifted confectioners' sugar. (For a very festive look, place a paper doily on top of the cake and dust through the doily. Lift off the doily, being careful not to disturb the design.) If you like, the side of the cake may be decorated with coarsely chopped nuts. In that case, spread a thin layer of jam around the side of the cake, then press the chopped nuts into the side of the cake with the palm of your hand.

YIELD: ONE 9-INCH LAYER CAKE; 10 TO 12 SERVINGS

EASY, ELEGANT APPLE TARTS
❦

These tarts are so *très chic* that you're likely to be accused of buying them. Even though these aren't exactly low-calorie, they are certainly not as indulgent as the usual Thanksgiving desserts, especially when a topping is declined.

1 sheet frozen puff pastry from a 17¼-ounce package, thawed according to package directions
6 medium-size Golden Delicious apples
¼ cup sugar

2 tablespoons cold butter, cut into small pieces
Coffee ice cream or Caramel Cream (see page 239)

Unfold the puff pastry and cut it into 6 equal parts. On a lightly floured surface, roll each piece so that it is large enough to make a 6-inch circle. Make a perfect circle by cutting around a 6-inch plate inverted on the pastry. As each circle is made, transfer it to an ungreased baking sheet with a pancake turner. Refrigerate the pastry while preparing the apples.

Preheat the oven to 450°F. Peel the apples, leaving them whole. Core each apple, then cut it in half through the stem. Lay each apple half flat on a cutting board and cut it crosswise into very thin slices. Lay the slices from each apple on one pastry circle, overlapping and fanning them out in a circular pattern. Sprinkle each apple-covered pastry with about ½ tablespoon of the sugar (using a total of 3 tablespoons of the sugar) and dot with the butter. Bake for about 10 minutes, or until the pastry is cooked through and the apple slices are tender. (The tarts may be prepared up to this point several hours ahead of serving.) Shortly before serving, preheat the oven broiler. Sprinkle the tarts with the remaining tablespoon of sugar, dividing evenly. Broil 4 inches from the source of heat to brown the tops, about 2 minutes, watching carefully so they don't burn. Serve with small scoops of ice cream or small dollops of caramel cream.

YIELD: 6 SERVINGS

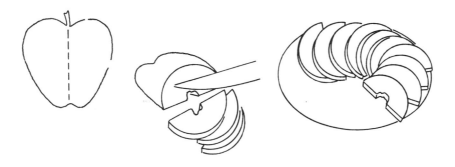

LINDA GREENHOUSE'S FRESH CRANBERRY SORBET

My friend and neighbor Linda makes the world's best sorbets and ice creams. In fact, at one time an impressive number of Upper East Side New York restaurants beat a path to her door after they tasted her wares. Whether you're dieting or not, the icy tartness of a sorbet is a pleasant counterpoint to a rich meal. Make the sorbet a couple of days before you plan to serve it to give it a chance to ripen in the freezer. Using an ice-cream maker, if you have one, will give the sorbet a finer texture.

1½ cups fresh cranberries, rinsed and
  picked over
¾ cup water
¾ cup sugar

¾ cup fresh orange juice
1 tablespoon orange liqueur (optional)
Mint leaves and Candied Cranberries
  (see page 19) for garnish

Place the cranberries and water in a heavy medium-size saucepan. Cook over low heat, stirring occasionally, until the berries are tender and starting to pop, about 5 minutes. Cool slightly, then puree the mixture in a food processor or blender. Press through a strainer, using the back of a spoon to extract as much of the liquid as possible. Discard the residue in the strainer and return the puree to the saucepan. Stir in the sugar and cook over low heat, stirring, until the sugar is dissolved. Remove from the heat and set aside to cool. Stir the orange juice and liqueur into the cooled mixture, then refrigerate until well chilled. Turn the cranberry mixture into an 8- or 9-inch square metal pan. Cover with aluminum foil and freeze until firm in the center, about 2 hours. Spoon into a chilled medium-size bowl and beat until fluffy with an electric mixer. Return to the pan, cover again, and freeze until nearly solid. Cover tightly and keep in the freezer until ready to serve. To serve, scrape across the mixture to create a sort of pebbly texture. Garnish with mint leaves and Candied Cranberries (see page 19).

YIELD: ABOUT 3 CUPS; 6 SERVINGS

GLAZED ORANGES

This is a dessert that you will find yourself serving again and again, sometimes in a pool of Easy Chocolate Sauce (see page 236), which makes it not quite so Spartan.

6 navel oranges	*2 to 4 tablespoons Grand Marnier or other*
2 cups sugar	*orange liqueur*
2 cups water	*Mint leaves and candied violets for*
Two 3-inch cinnamon sticks	*garnish (see note below)*

With a vegetable parer, peel the oranges, taking care to remove all of the bitter white pith just beneath the rind. Reserve a 3-inch strip of the rind, scraping away any pith on the underside. In a Dutch oven or other large heavy saucepan, combine the sugar, water, cinnamon sticks, and reserved orange rind. Bring to a boil over high heat. Lower the oranges into the boiling sugar mixture. Reduce the heat slightly and boil slowly for 5 minutes. Remove the pan from the heat and cool to room temperature. Place the oranges in a deep bowl and cover with the syrup. Cover and chill until ready to serve. To serve, place the oranges on individual dessert plates or shallow bowls. Stir the Grand Marnier into the syrup, then spoon some of the syrup over and around each orange. Cut the reserved orange rind into very thin slivers and use to garnish each serving. Decorate the top of each orange with a couple of mint leaves and a candied violet. Serve with a knife and fork, since the orange has been only partially cooked and needs to be cut to be eaten.

YIELD: 6 SERVINGS

Note: Candied violets can be purchased in food stores that specialize in confections.

SMALL INDULGENCES

Serving a small plate of sweet morsels after dinner is optional, and is certainly not necessary at all if the dessert course has been a lavish one. But if Thanksgiving dinner has been anything less than a banquet, such a small offering can be surprisingly welcome. The key word is small. I usually set out a cut-glass dish with just a few of my best truffles on a paper doily after nearly every company meal. Rarely do I have to return to the kitchen with them.

A little sweet is also nice to offer to those who have chosen a light dessert, such as sorbet or fruit, and it goes well with a tray of dessert cheeses.

SUGAR-SPICED PECANS

Just knowing that Thomas Jefferson planted the first pecan trees on the East Coast at Monticello, his home in Virginia, and that he gave a few pecan trees to George Washington, who planted them at Mount Vernon, makes these sweet nuts about as American as anything you could possibly serve.

¼ pound (1 stick) butter
2 cups pecan halves
1½ cups confectioners' sugar

1 tablespoon ground cloves
1 tablespoon ground cinnamon
1 tablespoon ground nutmeg

Melt the butter in a large skillet over medium-high heat. When hot, add the pecans and reduce the heat to low. Cook, stirring frequently, for 20 minutes. Remove the pecans with a slotted spoon and drain on paper towels. Meanwhile, mix the sugar, cloves, cinnamon, and nutmeg in a medium-size bowl. Add the warm pecans and toss until completely coated. When cool, store for up to a couple of weeks in a tightly covered container or plastic bag.

YIELD: 2 CUPS

SUGARED FIGS

Dried-fruit confections fell from favor for a long time, but now, with all the emphasis on healthy eating, they seem to be making a comeback. All you need to make sugared figs are an equal number of dried Calimyrna figs and pecan halves, honey, and confectioners' sugar. Trim the stems from the figs and cut a slit in the smooth side of each one, into which you stuff a pecan half that has been dipped in honey. Just before serving, sprinkle with a little confectioners' sugar.

OLD-FASHIONED SUGARPLUMS

Nearly everybody has read about "visions of sugarplums," but most people wouldn't recognize one if it hit them on the head. Sugarplums keep well for several weeks if they are stored properly and are nice to have around for both Thanksgiving and Christmas.

18 pitted dates (about 4 ounces), coarsely
  chopped
8 to 10 dried figs, stems removed (about
  4 ounces), coarsely chopped

½ cup toasted (see pages 6–7) chopped
  almonds
1 teaspoon fresh lemon juice
1 teaspoon mild honey
½ cup confectioners' sugar

Combine the dates, figs, almonds, lemon juice, and honey in a food processor. Process until very finely chopped and the mixture comes together. Roll into 1-inch balls. Sprinkle the confectioners' sugar on a piece of waxed paper. Roll the balls in the sugar. Wrap very tightly in colored plastic wrap or aluminum foil. Store in a cool, dry place, or refrigerate.

YIELD: ABOUT 2 DOZEN SUGARPLUMS

CHOCOLATE TRUFFLES

Ideally, chocolate truffles should be eaten soon after they're made and should not be refrigerated. But in this day of overheated houses, that's almost impossible, and who has time to worry about making truffles at the last moment?

⅓ cup heavy or whipping cream
6 ounces semisweet chocolate, chopped, or
  1 cup semisweet chocolate morsels

2 tablespoons unsalted butter, softened
⅓ cup unsweetened cocoa powder for
  dusting

In a small saucepan, warm the cream over low heat just until it begins to steam and small bubbles form around the edge. Remove from the heat. Add the chocolate and butter and stir until smooth. Pour the chocolate mixture into a shallow bowl. Cover and chill for several hours or overnight. Sprinkle the cocoa powder onto a piece of waxed paper. Spoon measuring teaspoonfuls of the chocolate mixture onto another piece of waxed paper. Quickly roll each truffle between the palms of your hands to form a ¾-inch ball, then roll each ball in the cocoa. Store in the refrigerator, tightly covered, for up to a week, or freeze for up to a month. If frozen, allow to thaw for 5 minutes before serving.

YIELD: ABOUT 2 DOZEN CHOCOLATE TRUFFLES

Raspberry Truffles: Stir 2 tablespoons seedless raspberry preserves into the cream with the butter and chocolate.

CAROL'S CRACKLING GOOD GRAPES

My friend, and extraordinary cook, Carol Gelles serves these candy-coated grapes as one of her dessert selections almost every time she entertains. Her guests (at least those who have eaten the grapes before) insist on it. But before you rush out to buy the grapes, you should know that, as good and essentially easy as they are, these grapes have one big drawback: They don't keep well at all. The thin, crisp, sugar-syrup coating that envelops each grape will not hold for more than a few hours at the most before it starts getting soft and sticky, so the dipping must be done within three or four hours before serving, not something too many cooks would want to fool with on Thanksgiving Day. But they are such a treat—especially when they are served with dessert cheeses—that I just had to go ahead and include them and leave the decision to make or not to make up to you. In any event, do at least one dry run before officially serving these grapes for the first time.

½ pound seedless grapes   ½ cup sugar
1 cup water

　　Rinse the grapes and drain them on a wire rack until *completely dry*. Cut the grapes into small clusters of two or three grapes each, leaving a stem that's long enough to hold onto while dipping. Combine the water and sugar in a heavy 1-quart saucepan. Bring to a boil, stirring constantly over medium-high heat. Stop stirring and boil undisturbed, watching carefully, until the syrup around the edge of the pan begins to acquire a pale yellow tinge, 10 to 15 minutes. Remove from the heat and set the pan in another pan that has been partially filled with warm water. Working quickly, dip each grape cluster into the syrup, holding it over the pan until the excess syrup has drained, then set aside on a piece of waxed paper, or a wire rack, to harden. Remove from the waxed paper just before serving.

YIELD: 12 TO 16 CLUSTERS

LITTLE ALMOND-BUTTER COOKIES

Because of all the butter in them, these cookies will keep for a long time, two or three weeks, in a covered container. They have a lovely delicate flavor, and are delicious with coffee or tea.

½ pound (2 sticks) unsalted butter,
  softened
½ cup sugar
¾ cup ground blanched (see pages 6–7)
  almonds (about ⅓ cup whole almonds)

2 cups all-purpose flour
½ cup seedless raspberry preserves
Confectioners' sugar for dusting

In a large bowl, combine the butter, sugar, ground almonds, and flour. Mix with your fingertips until the dough forms a solid ball. Cut the dough in half and shape each half into a cylinder measuring about 1¼ inches in diameter. Tightly wrap each cylinder in waxed paper or plastic wrap and refrigerate until firm, about 1 hour. Preheat the oven to 350°F. Cut the cylinders into very thin slices (about ⅛ inch) and place them on ungreased baking sheets. Bake for 10 to 12 minutes, or until the cookies are very lightly browned. Immediately remove from the baking sheets and cool on wire racks. After they are baked, the cookies must be handled very carefully. Gently spread the bottom side of one cookie with preserves and sandwich together with another cookie. You may lose a few during this process, but they taste just as good broken as they do whole. Sprinkle both sides of the filled cookies with confectioners' sugar. Store in a tightly covered container. A shallow tin is best so the bottom cookies don't have too much weight on them. Sprinkle with confectioners' sugar again before serving.

YIELD: 5 TO 6 DOZEN FILLED COOKIES

DAINTY GINGERSNAPS

I know two to three hundred cookies sounds like a lot, but they're very tiny cookies and very easy to make, so the whole project should take less than an hour, although the dough must be chilled overnight before baking. By the way, in case you've ever wondered, it's black pepper that gives gingerbread its characteristic bite.

2 cups all-purpose flour
2 teaspoons ground ginger
1 teaspoon baking soda
1 teaspoon salt
½ teaspoon ground allspice
¼ to ½ teaspoon freshly ground black
  pepper or to taste

¼ pound (1 stick) butter, softened
½ cup firmly packed light brown sugar
½ cup unsulphured molasses
¼ cup very finely chopped crystallized
  ginger

Combine the flour, ginger, baking soda, salt, allspice, and pepper in a small bowl and stir until well blended. In a large bowl, beat together the butter and sugar until blended. Beat in the molasses, then the flour mixture. Stir in the crystallized ginger. Divide the dough in half. Wrap the halves separately in plastic wrap or aluminum foil. Refrigerate overnight. Preheat the oven to 350°F. Lightly grease two large baking sheets, or coat them with nonstick vegetable spray. (Only one sheet of cookies can be baked at a time.) Roll half of the dough out directly onto one of the baking sheets until it is within an inch of the edges. Prick the dough all over with the tines of a fork; this allows the heat to penetrate the dough and makes the cookies crisp. Bake on the top oven rack for 10 to 12 minutes, or until firm. Remove from the oven and immediately cut the dough into small diamond shapes, using a pizza wheel or a small knife and working right on the baking sheet. The easiest way to do this is to cut the dough the long way into strips about 1 inch wide. Then, starting at one corner, cut into diagonal strips about 1 inch wide. Transfer the cookies to wire racks to cool completely. The cookies will become very crisp as they cool. Repeat with the remaining dough and the other baking sheet.

YIELD: MAKES 200 TO 300 TINY COOKIES

COFFEE: THE PERFECT ENDING

Coffee signals the end of the meal—it's usually the last thing served—and once it's on the table the cook has the chance to really relax, with no worry about what's coming next, except the dishes, maybe for the first time in one or two days. In the United States, coffee is generally served plain with cream or milk and sugar. I know that if you've cooked Thanksgiving dinner you've worked hard, no matter how simple you've tried to keep it. So make sure the coffee is as good as everything else.

Usually I serve a French-roasted coffee after dinner, which has a little more oomph than breakfast coffee. These days a vast array of coffees is available from every part of the world, flavored and unflavored, regular or decaffeinated. Whatever coffee you choose to drink, grind it, or have it ground for you, as close to brewing time as possible. It really does make a difference.

Aside from stirring brandy and cordials into the coffee to make it a little more exotic, spices and other flavorings that perk up a plain cup of coffee considerably can be added. For each cup of coffee being made, add one of the following to the coffeepot before brewing:

- *1 whole clove*
- *¼ teaspoon cardamom seed*

- *¼-inch cinnamon stick*
- *splash of white crème de menthe, orange liqueur, anisette, or kummel, for instance*

Or stir one of the following into each cup of coffee after brewing:

- *½ teaspoon semisweet grated chocolate*
- *⅛ teaspoon ground cinnamon*
- *twist of lemon or orange rind*

VIRGINIA PRESCOTT'S IRISH COFFEE

My mother always finds the easiest way to do everything without sacrificing too much of the integrity of whatever it is that she's shortcutting. This is her method for making and serving Irish coffee. The obvious advantage is that the coffee base can be made hours in advance, and the hot water and whipped cream added at the last minute, a real blessing on Thanksgiving. She always serves Irish coffee in heavy, pressed-glass goblets that have been in the family for generations (she always puts a silver spoon in the glass when she adds the hot water to absorb the heat so the glass won't break), but plain coffee cups will do fine.

1½ cups Irish whiskey
¼ cup sugar
¼ cup instant-coffee granules or powder

1 cup heavy or whipping cream
Boiling water

Into each of 8 coffee cups, place 3 tablespoons of Irish whiskey, 1½ teaspoons sugar, and 1½ teaspoons instant-coffee granules. You don't even have to bother to stir. Set aside until ready to serve. At some point not too long before the coffee is to be served, whip the cream just until it is very thick but not stiff. To serve, fill each cup with boiling water to within about ½ inch of the top, stirring until well blended. Float whipped cream on top of each coffee and serve immediately.

YIELD: 8 SERVINGS

THIRTEEN

The Leftovers

❦

My grandson Caleb reveals his true feelings about leftovers by referring to them as "remains." Unfortunately, he is not alone in his sentiment about this frequently necessary offshoot of eating well. After the first thrill of nibbling on cold turkey, the sight of the carcass perched on a refrigerator shelf is not a welcome sight to most cooks.

During the writing of this book a number of turkey and other poultry carcasses became leftovers in a relatively short time, not to mention dozens of thighs and more than a few breasts that were tested separately. The challenge of this chapter was to include recipes that would be good enough to stand on their own, and only half of those that were tried actually made it here.

The hope is that you will find the recipes that follow interesting and appetizing enough to tempt you to actually create a few leftovers of your own and serve at least some of these dishes at other times during the year. (If you do, directions for roasting turkey parts can be found on page 190.)

Good Recipes Start with Enthusiasm—and Good Ingredients

This is as true for leftover preparations as for any others. If they're thought of and handled as second-rate recipes, they're bound to look and taste that way, too.

Memorable leftover dishes start with the conscientious handling of the turkey (or other poultry) the moment Thanksgiving dinner is over. Remove the stuffing and refrigerate it separately to be eaten within a couple of days. Wrap the turkey as airtight as possible, whole or in parts, in heavy-duty foil and refrigerate promptly. (See page 196 for additional information on storing turkey safely.)

Turkey dries out fast, so plan to remove the meat from the carcass within a day or two and freeze it for later meals when it might be much more welcome. Turkey slices can be tightly wrapped and frozen, and the meat can also be cut into cubes and frozen in one- or two-cup portions, ready to be used. I used to use aluminum foil and plastic containers for turkey freezing, but now I freeze both slices and cubes in zipper-top plastic bags, making sure that all of the air is forced out of the bags before sealing. Also, be sure to date the bags—as if one is likely to forget! Thaw the bags or containers of frozen turkey in the refrigerator, or in a microwave oven if they are not packed in foil.

The secret to keeping leftover turkey meat as moist and tasty as possible is not to cook it further. It should only be heated. This is particularly true of the white meat, which is usually pretty dry to start with. Generally, I use dark meat, which holds up well in dishes that will be heated. The more delicate white meat is best for salads and other cold preparations, or where heating is minimal.

Since the quality of frozen cooked turkey meat deteriorates rather quickly, use it within a month or two for optimum flavor and texture. The bare-bones carcass, which is good for soup or broth, can be frozen, too, although you may prefer to make turkey soup (or broth) soon after Thanksgiving and then freeze it, ready to thaw and serve.

Although turkey meat is called for in these recipes, any leftover poultry meat can be used.

Super Tip: When cutting up cooked poultry, use scissors instead of a knife. Knives shred the meat; scissors (ordinary stationery-store scissors that you keep in the kitchen) cut neater, and much faster, too.

SECOND-DAY TURKEY DINNER

A good recipe to know about, especially if you went a little overboard on Thanksgiving and made too much of everything.

2 to 4 cups leftover stuffing
8 to 12 slices white and dark cooked
  turkey or chicken meat

2 to 3 cups turkey gravy
1 to 1½ cups whole-berry or jellied
  cranberry sauce

Preheat the oven to 350°F. Layer the stuffing, turkey slices, gravy, and cranberry sauce in a shallow, greased 1½- or 2-quart casserole. Cover and bake for 20 to 30 minutes, or until heated through.

YIELD: 4 TO 6 SERVINGS

TURKEY CURRY

If you have some cubed turkey meat stashed away in the freezer, this makes a good party main dish to serve during the Christmas holidays. Besides being delicious and easy, it is almost cost free. In addition to a fairly generous array of curry accompaniments (chopped green onion, radishes, peanuts, crystallized ginger, roasted red peppers, shredded coconut, and mandarin orange sections, for instance), I usually serve a chopped cucumber salad with yogurt dressing and lightly buttered pita or other flat bread. Other poultry meat can be used as well.

3 tablespoons butter
3 tablespoons vegetable oil
1 large onion, finely chopped (1 cup)
1 large tart apple, finely chopped
    (1¼ cups)
2 cloves garlic, put through a garlic press
2 tablespoons curry powder or to taste
½ cup heavy or whipping cream

¼ cup turkey or chicken broth (see
    pages 2–4)
¼ cup milk
¼ cup dry sherry
2 tablespoons finely chopped mango
    chutney
2 cups ½-inch cubes dark or white cooked
    turkey meat
Hot cooked rice

Heat the butter and oil in a 4-quart Dutch oven or other large heavy saucepan. Stir in the onion, apple, and garlic and cook over medium heat, stirring frequently, until the onion and apple are softened. Stir in the curry powder, reduce the heat to low, and continue to stir for 3 or 4 minutes. Add the cream, broth, milk, sherry, and chutney. Continue to cook, stirring, until the mixture simmers and thickens. (If the sauce seems too thick, stir in a little more broth or milk; if too thin, boil to reduce.) Stir in the turkey and cook until heated through. Serve over hot rice with additional chutney and other traditional curry accompaniments.

YIELD: 6 SERVINGS

TURKEY-MUSHROOM SAUTÉ

Quick sautés are among my very favorite supper dishes. They're easy to fix and are all more or less the same—two or three main ingredients tossed in butter and/or oil over fairly high heat. Serve the sauté with a green salad and crusty bread for soaking up the pan juices.

2 tablespoons butter
2 tablespoons olive oil
2 cups sliced shiitake mushroom caps
  (about ½ pound with stems)
2 or 3 large cloves garlic, minced
½ cup turkey or chicken broth (see
  pages 2–4)

2 cups ½-inch cubes dark cooked turkey
  meat
2 tablespoons balsamic vinegar
Salt and freshly ground black pepper to
  taste
¼ cup chopped fresh parsley

Combine the butter and oil in a large skillet over high heat. When hot, add the mushrooms and cook, stirring and tossing, until they are limp and have started to give up their liquid. Reduce the heat to medium, add the garlic, and continue to cook and stir for another 30 seconds to give the garlic a chance to soften. Stir in the broth and turkey and cook, stirring, until the turkey is hot. Add the vinegar and season with the salt and pepper. Stir in the parsley and serve.

YIELD: 4 SERVINGS

FUSILLI WITH TURKEY AND HAM
❦

Fusilli is the pasta that looks like spaghetti with a permanent wave, and it makes this dish look really special. If you can't find it, substitute fettucini or regular spaghetti.

2 tablespoons butter
1 medium-size onion, finely chopped
  (½ cup)
¼ teaspoon celery seeds
¼ teaspoon dried tarragon leaves,
  crumbled
¼ teaspoon ground white pepper

2 to 3 cups ½-inch cubes white cooked
  turkey or chicken meat
½ pound uncooked fusilli
½ cup sour cream
2 tablespoons all-purpose flour
1 cup turkey or chicken broth (see
  pages 2–4)
1 cup diced cooked ham

Melt the butter in a large skillet over medium-high heat. When hot, add the onion, celery seeds, tarragon, and pepper and cook, stirring frequently, until the onion is softened. Stir in the turkey and set aside.

Cook the fusilli in lightly salted boiling water according to the package directions. Drain well and transfer to a large serving bowl. Stir in the sour cream and set aside. With a slotted spoon, remove the onion mixture from the skillet to a small bowl. Over medium heat, stir the flour into the skillet. Gradually add the broth and bring to a boil over medium heat for 1 minute, stirring, until thick and smooth. Stir in the ham and reserved onion mixture and cook until heated through. Pour over the pasta and toss, mixing well. Serve immediately.

YIELD: 4 SERVINGS

TURKEY HASH

The secret to hash, all the old cookbooks say, is to dice everything the same size, so I did. The cilantro was an afterthought that I liked very much.

*4 to 6 unpeeled new potatoes, cut into
  ½-inch cubes (about 2 cups)*
3 tablespoons butter
*1 medium-size onion, coarsely chopped
  (½ cup)*
*1 small red bell pepper, cut into ½-inch
  pieces (about 1¼ cups)*

*2 cups ½-inch cubes dark cooked turkey
  or other poultry meat*
1 teaspoon salt
½ teaspoon dried thyme leaves, crumbled
¼ teaspoon ground white pepper
Pinch of freshly grated nutmeg
1 cup light cream or half-and-half
2 tablespoons chopped cilantro (optional)

Bring a medium-size saucepan of lightly salted water to a boil. Drop in the potatoes and cook just until fork-tender, about 10 minutes. Drain well and set aside. Heat the butter in a large skillet. Add the onion and red pepper and cook over medium-high heat, stirring frequently, until barely tender. Stir in the potatoes, turkey, salt, thyme, white pepper, and nutmeg, then add the cream and continue to cook, stirring, until most of the cream is absorbed. Stir in the cilantro and serve immediately.

YIELD: 4 SERVINGS

TURKEY PATTIES WITH TOMATO SAUCE

When I was growing up, these patties would have been smothered with hot, undiluted cream of mushroom, cream of chicken, or tomato soup. Need I say more?

3 slices firm white bread, crusts removed
¼ cup milk
3 cups dark or white pieces cooked turkey
    or chicken meat
1 tablespoon butter, melted
1 large egg

½ teaspoon salt
⅛ teaspoon freshly ground black pepper
⅓ cup light cream or half-and-half
⅓ cup dry bread crumbs
¼ cup vegetable oil
1 cup prepared marinara sauce, heated

Tear the bread into small pieces and place in a small bowl with the milk to soak. Place the turkey meat in a food processor or blender and process until finely chopped. Turn into a medium-size bowl. Add the soaked bread to the turkey along with the melted butter, egg, salt, pepper, and cream. Knead the mixture with your hands until completely blended. Place the turkey mixture in the freezer for 10 minutes to firm it up a bit. Spread the bread crumbs on a sheet of waxed paper. Shape the turkey mixture into four oval patties, each about ½ inch thick. If you like, taper the patties slightly at one end to resemble a chop. Dredge each patty in the bread crumbs, patting the crumbs gently so that they adhere to it. Place the oil in a large skillet over medium heat. When it is hot, add the patties and cook, turning once, until heated through and golden brown on both sides, 5 or 6 minutes total cooking time. To serve, spoon some of the hot marinara sauce over each patty.

YIELD: 4 SERVINGS

OLD-FASHIONED CREAMED TURKEY IN TOAST CUPS

My mother served lots of things in these toast cups, and whatever it was it seemed to taste better that way—at least to me.

12 slices very soft white bread, crusts
    removed
2 tablespoons butter, melted
1 tablespoon butter
1 small onion, minced (¼ cup)
¼ cup minced green or red bell pepper

One 10¾-ounce can condensed cream of
    mushroom soup
½ cup milk
2 cups ½-inch cubes dark or white cooked
    turkey or chicken meat
¼ cup diced pimiento
Chopped fresh parsley for garnish

Preheat the oven to 350°F. With a rolling pin, roll the slices of bread flat. Brush one side of each slice of bread lightly with the melted butter, then fit the slices into twelve 2½-inch muffin-pan cups, buttered side up. Bake for 12 to 15 minutes, or until the crusts are lightly browned. Cool before removing from the muffin pans.

Melt the butter in a large skillet over medium-high heat. When hot, add the onion and pepper and cook, stirring frequently, until softened. Reduce the heat to medium and gradually stir in the soup and milk until blended. Stir in the turkey and pimiento and continue to cook, stirring, until bubbly. Place two or three bread cups per serving on each plate. Spoon the creamed turkey into the cups and sprinkle with the parsley.

YIELD: 4 TO 6 SERVINGS

Variations: Instead of toast cups, the creamed turkey may be spooned over waffles, split biscuits, corn bread, rice, or mashed potatoes.

TURKEY STIR-FRY

Like me, you may actually find yourself roasting a couple of turkey thighs now and then just to be able to serve this stir-fry more often than right after Thanksgiving.

*⅓ cup plus ¼ cup sweet rice wine
  (available in Asian food stores)*

3 tablespoons light soy sauce

*2 teaspoons Oriental sesame oil (available
  in Asian food stores)*

*2 or 3 cloves garlic, put through a
  garlic press*

⅛ teaspoon freshly ground black pepper

*2 cups ½-inch cubes dark cooked turkey,
  chicken, duck, or goose meat*

2 teaspoons cornstarch

¼ cup water

2 tablespoons vegetable oil

*2 cups sliced shiitake mushroom caps
  (about ½ pound with stems)*

¼ pound snow peas, trimmed

*1 medium-size red bell pepper, cored,
  seeded, and cut into strips*

*1 bunch (about 6) green onions (scallions),
  cut on the diagonal into ¾- to 1-inch
  lengths, including some of the
  green tops*

Hot cooked rice

*2 tablespoons toasted (see note on page
  315) sesame seeds*

In a medium-size bowl, mix ⅓ cup of the rice wine, the soy sauce, sesame oil, garlic, and pepper. Add the turkey and stir until it is well coated. Set aside at room temperature for about 30 minutes, or up to 2 or 3 hours in the refrigerator, stirring occasionally. Mix together the cornstarch, water, and the remaining ¼ cup of rice wine in a cup and set aside. Place the vegetable oil in a wok or 12-inch skillet over high heat. When it is very hot, add the mushrooms and cook, stirring, until they are slightly limp, about 30 seconds. Add the snow peas, pepper strips, and green onions and stir-fry for about 3 minutes longer or until tender-crisp. Add the turkey mixture and continue to stir-fry until heated through. Stir in the cornstarch mixture and cook, stirring, until hot and bubbly. Serve the stir-fry over the hot rice, sprinkled with the toasted sesame seeds.

YIELD: 4 SERVINGS

Note: To toast sesame seeds, place them in a dry skillet and cook over medium heat, stirring, just until they begin to color and smell toasty, about 5 or 6 minutes.

BUFFALO TURKEY SALAD

❦

A salad by this name recently caught my eye on the menu of a very chic New York restaurant, a takeoff, undoubtedly, on the very popular Buffalo chicken wings. Although I didn't order the salad, the name did inspire this recipe that Roquefort cheese lovers will adore.

½ cup crumbled Roquefort cheese
½ cup light cream or half-and-half
½ cup mayonnaise
⅛ teaspoon liquid red pepper seasoning

2 cups ½-inch cubes white or dark cooked
  turkey or chicken meat
Lettuce leaves
Crumbled Roquefort cheese for garnish

In a medium-size bowl, combine the cheese with the cream until well blended. Stir in the mayonnaise and red pepper seasoning. Add the turkey and toss until well coated with the dressing. Serve the salad on lettuce leaves with a little more Roquefort cheese crumbled on top of each serving.

YIELD: 4 SERVINGS

CALIFORNIA TURKEY-AND-WALNUT SALAD

Joyce Goldstein, the chef of trendy Square One restaurant in San Francisco, created this recipe for the California Walnut Board.

¾ cup mayonnaise
2 teaspoons fresh lemon juice
2 teaspoons grated lemon rind
2 cups ½-inch cubes dark or white cooked
    turkey or chicken meat
1 large green apple, peeled, cored, and cut
    into ½-inch cubes (about 1 cup)

½ cup toasted (see pages 6–7) chopped
    walnuts
2 teaspoons chopped fresh chives or green
    onion (scallion) tops
¼ teaspoon salt
⅛ teaspoon freshly ground black pepper
Watercress sprigs

In a small bowl, mix the mayonnaise, lemon juice, and lemon rind. In a medium-size bowl, toss together the turkey, apple, walnuts, chives, salt, and pepper. Add the mayonnaise mixture and toss gently until well blended. Serve the salad on a bed of watercress sprigs.

YIELD: 4 SERVINGS

MEXICAN TURKEY SALAD

I love all the Mexican flavors, especially cilantro, which I know is not to everyone's taste. If that is the case, flatleaf parsley, which looks similar to cilantro, can be substituted. A little finely chopped fresh jalapeño pepper can also be added if you like fire in your Mexican food.

2 tablespoons fresh lime juice
2 teaspoons Dijon mustard
¼ teaspoon salt
⅛ to ¼ teaspoon chili powder
5 tablespoons vegetable oil
¼ cup coarsely chopped cilantro
2 cups ½-inch cubes white or dark cooked
    turkey or chicken meat
1 can (about 12 ounces) whole-kernel
    corn, well drained

6 green onions (scallions), sliced, includ-
    ing some of the green tops (about
    ½ cup)
1 small red bell pepper, finely chopped
    (about 1 cup)
1 small avocado, peeled, seeded, and
    diced (optional)
Lettuce leaves

Stir the lime juice, mustard, salt, and chili powder together in a small bowl. Add the oil in a thin stream, beating constantly until well blended and slightly thickened. Stir in the cilantro. In a large bowl, gently mix together the turkey, corn, green onions, pepper, and avocado. Add the salad dressing and toss gently until well mixed. To serve, spoon the salad onto lettuce leaves.

YIELD: 4 SERVINGS

TURKEY AND GRAPE SALAD

André Gilardin, a Belgian food photographer with whom I occasionally work, often serves this salad for lunch at the studio. His salad is made with white-meat chicken, but turkey works nicely, too. André also lays out plenty of good French bread, a soft cheese, bottles of mineral water, and he almost always serves moist, chewy brownies for dessert.

⅓ cup mayonnaise
⅓ cup sour cream
1 to 2 tablespoons snipped fresh dill (the amount depending on the pungency of the dill)
¼ teaspoon salt

2 cups ½-inch cubes white or dark cooked turkey or chicken meat
1 cup red seedless grapes, cut in half
Lettuce leaves
Toasted (see pages 6–7) almond slices for garnish

Combine the mayonnaise, sour cream, dill, and salt in a medium-size bowl. Add the turkey and grapes and toss gently until well blended. To serve, spoon the salad onto lettuce leaves and garnish with the almonds.

YIELD: 4 SERVINGS

FIVE-FLAVORS TURKEY SALAD

After all the rich, saucy food at Thanksgiving, this reasonably low-fat, high-flavor salad comes as a welcome change.

2 tablespoons soy sauce
2 tablespoons chopped green onion
  (scallion)
¼ cup red wine vinegar
½ cup peanut oil
1 teaspoon dry mustard
2 to 3 cups slivered dark cooked turkey,
  duck, or goose meat (see note below)

1 large cucumber
1 bunch watercress, tough stems removed,
  rinsed and drained
1 medium-size red bell pepper, cored,
  seeded, and cut into strips
¼ pound medium-size regular white
  mushrooms, trimmed and sliced
¼ cup chopped peanuts

In a small bowl, mix together the soy sauce, green onion, vinegar, oil, and mustard until well blended. In a medium-size bowl, mix half of the soy sauce dressing with the turkey and let stand at room temperature for 30 minutes, or in the refrigerator for 2 or 3 hours. Set the remaining dressing aside.

Peel the cucumber if it's waxed and cut it in half lengthwise. Scoop out the seeds with the tip of a spoon and cut the cucumber halves into ¼-inch slices. Place the turkey in a mound in the center of a serving platter and surround with the watercress. Arrange the cucumber, pepper, and mushrooms around the watercress. Sprinkle the peanuts on top of the turkey. Serve the salad with the remaining dressing.

YIELD: 4 SERVINGS

Note: To shred the turkey, pull off small sections going with the grain of the meat.

AL BOLTON'S WILD RICE AND TURKEY SALAD

Originally this was a wild rice and *shrimp* salad, but because Al usually accompanies the salad with cold sliced turkey breast, the switch seemed logical enough to me and it worked very well.

1 cup uncooked wild rice
2½ cups water
1 cup bottled chili sauce
2 to 3 tablespoons prepared horseradish
1 tablespoon fresh lemon juice

2 cups 1-inch cubes white cooked turkey
  or chicken meat
1 large avocado, peeled and cut into cubes
  (toss with 2 tablespoons fresh lemon
  juice if you like)
Spinach leaves

In a fine sieve, rinse the wild rice under cool running water. Bring the water with a little salt to a boil in a medium-size saucepan. Stir in the rice and return to boiling.

Reduce the heat to low, cover the pan, and barely simmer the rice for 55 minutes, or until most of the liquid has been absorbed. Remove from the heat and let stand, covered, for 10 minutes. Drain any excess liquid. Turn the rice into a large bowl.

Combine the chili sauce, horseradish, and lemon juice in a small bowl. Add the chili sauce mixture and the turkey to the warm rice and toss to mix well. Cover and chill until ready to serve. Just before serving, fold in the avocado. To serve, spoon the salad onto a bed of spinach leaves.

YIELD: 6 SERVINGS

SALMAGUNDI

Nowadays this is called Chef's Salad, but the basis for it has actually been around since Colonial times.

2 cups white or dark cooked turkey or chicken meat, cut into thin strips (½ pound)

2 cups cooked ham, cut into thin strips (½ pound)

½ pound sharp cheddar cheese, cut into thin strips

2 hard-cooked eggs, sliced or cut into wedges

4 small celery ribs with leaves

8 black olives

8 green olives

8 anchovy fillets (optional)

4 to 6 cups bite-size pieces mixed salad greens

Assortment of salad dressings

Artfully arrange the salad ingredients on top of the greens, on a serving platter or individual plates. Offer a selection of dressings, although good old Russian dressing is usually standard.

YIELD: 4 SERVINGS

TURKEY MUFFALETTO

An out-of-the-ordinary sandwich that feeds a crowd and simultaneously disposes of some of the little remainders on the relish tray. Serve with steaming mugs of soup.

½ cup pimiento-stuffed or pitted green
  olives, finely chopped
½ cup pitted black olives, finely chopped
2 or 3 celery ribs, finely chopped (1 cup)
3 or 4 green onions (scallions), thinly
  sliced
One 7-ounce jar roasted red peppers,
  drained and coarsely chopped
2 tablespoons drained capers
½ teaspoon dried oregano leaves,
  crumbled

⅛ teaspoon freshly ground black pepper
¼ cup olive oil
2 tablespoons red wine vinegar
1 round loaf Italian bread (about
  10 inches in diameter)
About 4 cups sliced dark or white cooked
  turkey or chicken meat (the pieces
  needn't be large)
¼ pound sliced provolone cheese

In a medium-size bowl, mix together both olives, the celery, onions, roasted peppers, capers, oregano, and pepper. Mix together the oil and vinegar in a cup. Set aside 2 tablespoons. Add the remaining oil and vinegar to the olive mixture and mix gently until well blended. Cut the bread in half horizontally and pull out some of the soft insides. Brush both cut sides of the bread with the reserved oil-and-vinegar mixture. Arrange the turkey slices on the bottom half of the bread. Spoon the olive mixture over the turkey. Arrange the cheese slices over the olive mixture and cover with the top half of the bread, gently pressing it down. Cut the sandwich into 8 wedges to serve.

YIELD: 8 SERVINGS

BARBECUED TURKEY ON HARD ROLLS

One of our tasters' favorite leftover recipes, and certainly one of the simplest to make.

1 tablespoon butter
1 large onion, chopped (1 cup)
2 cups shredded dark or white cooked
  turkey or chicken meat (see note below)

½ to ¾ cup prepared barbecue sauce
  (depending on how juicy you like your
  barbecue)
Freshly ground black pepper to taste
4 hard rolls, split
Dill pickle slices or spears for garnish

Melt the butter in a large skillet over medium-high heat. When hot, add the onion and cook, stirring frequently, until lightly browned. Reduce the heat to medium and stir in the turkey meat and barbecue sauce. Continue to cook, stirring, until heated through. Stir in the pepper. Divide the barbecue among the rolls and garnish with pickle slices.

YIELD: 4 SERVINGS

Note: To shred the meat, pull off small sections, going with the grain of the meat.

SPICY TURKEY IN PITA BREAD

Although the ingredients for this hot sandwich may sound a little strange, believe me, they taste good together.

2 tablespoons butter
1 medium-size onion, coarsely chopped (½ cup)
½ small red bell pepper, cored, seeded, and coarsely chopped (½ cup)
1 tablespoon tomato paste
¼ cup water
½ cup coarsely chopped stuffed green olives
½ cup golden or dark raisins

2 teaspoons Worcestershire sauce
¾ teaspoon chili powder
1 small clove garlic, put through a garlic press
½ teaspoon salt
¼ teaspoon freshly ground black pepper
2 cups ½-inch cubes dark cooked turkey, chicken, goose, or duck meat
4 pita breads, cut in half

Melt the butter in a large skillet over medium-high heat. When hot, add the onion and bell pepper and cook, stirring frequently, until softened. Stir in the tomato paste, water, olives, raisins, Worcestershire, chili powder, garlic, salt, and pepper. Cover and simmer over medium-low heat for 10 minutes. Add the turkey and continue to cook, stirring, until heated through. To serve, spoon the turkey mixture into the pita bread halves.

YIELD: 4 SERVINGS

HOT TURKEY–SOUFFLÉ SANDWICHES

Along with a cup of soup and a light dessert (sherbet or fruit salad and cookies, perhaps), this is an easy and impressive supper dish to serve over Thanksgiving weekend.

4 slices pumpernickel or rye bread, lightly
   toasted
¼ cup mayonnaise
4 or 8 slices white or dark cooked turkey
   or chicken meat
1 or 2 medium-size tomatoes, cut into
   8 thin slices

½ cup shredded Gruyère cheese
4 large egg whites, at room temperature
⅛ teaspoon cream of tartar
⅓ cup grated Parmesan cheese
⅛ teaspoon ground cayenne (red) pepper
Relish tray leftovers for garnish

Preheat the oven broiler. Spread each slice of toasted bread with 1 tablespoon of the mayonnaise. Divide the turkey slices evenly among the slices of toast, topping each with two slices of tomato. Sprinkle each sandwich with 2 tablespoons of the Gruyère cheese. In a large bowl, beat the egg whites and cream of tartar until stiff peaks form when the beaters are lifted. Gently fold in the Parmesan cheese and cayenne. Spoon the egg white mixture over the sandwiches, dividing evenly. Arrange the sandwiches on a baking sheet, then broil 6 inches from the source of heat until the topping is puffed and golden brown, about 1 minute. Serve immediately, garnished with celery ribs, carrot sticks, olives, and any other appealing leftovers from the Thanksgiving-dinner relish tray.

YIELD: 4 SANDWICHES

TURKEY CROQUE-MONSIEUR

Cole slaw, although not very French, does taste good with this.

8 slices firm white bread, crusts removed
8 thin slices Jarlsberg cheese
4 thin slices white cooked turkey or
   chicken meat

4 thin slices cooked ham
6 tablespoons (¾ stick) butter, melted

Preheat the oven to 400°F. Top four of the slices of bread with a slice of the cheese. Cover with a slice of the turkey and a slice of the ham and then a second slice of cheese. (The turkey, cheese, and ham should be trimmed to more or less fit the bread.) Top with the remaining slices of bread. Brush the top of each sandwich with melted butter. Generously brush the bottom of a large ovenproof skillet with melted butter. Set the skillet over medium heat. When the butter is hot, arrange the sandwiches in the skillet, buttered side down, and cook until lightly browned, about 20 to 30 seconds. While the sandwiches are browning, brush the unbuttered sides of the sandwiches with butter.

Turn the sandwiches with a wide spatula and brown the other side. Immediately place the skillet in the oven and bake until the cheese has melted. Cut the sandwiches in half and serve hot.

YIELD: 4 SANDWICHES

TURKEY AND WILD RICE CHOWDER

This chowder has always been one of my family's most requested leftover-turkey recipes. I usually make it on a cold night in January, finishing off the last bits of Thanksgiving turkey lingering in the freezer. This is a very rich soup. You won't need much to go with it except a loaf of good bread or some rolls.

1 cup uncooked wild rice (see page 9)
2½ cups water
2 tablespoons vegetable oil
½ pound medium-size regular white
  mushrooms, trimmed and sliced
1 medium-size onion, coarsely chopped
  (½ cup)
1 or 2 celery ribs, coarsely chopped
  (½ cup)
½ cup coarsely chopped red bell pepper
2 large cloves garlic, minced

4 cups turkey or chicken broth
  (see pages 6–7)
1 tablespoon chopped fresh basil or about
  1 teaspoon dried leaves, crumbled
½ teaspoon dried rosemary leaves,
  crumbled
½ teaspoon salt
¼ pound (1 stick) butter
½ cup all-purpose flour
2 cups milk
1 cup ½-inch cubes dark cooked turkey or
  chicken meat

In a fine sieve, rinse the wild rice under cool running water. Bring the water with a little salt to a boil in a medium-size saucepan. Stir in the rice and return to boiling. Reduce the heat to low, cover the pan, and barely simmer the rice for 55 minutes, or until most of the liquid has been absorbed. Remove from the heat and set aside.

Heat 1 tablespoon of the oil in a 4-quart Dutch oven or other large heavy saucepan. Add the mushrooms and cook over high heat, stirring and tossing, until they are lightly browned and all of their liquid has evaporated. Remove the mushrooms from the pan and set aside.

Heat the remaining tablespoon of oil in the same pan. Add the onion, celery, red pepper, and garlic and cook over medium-high heat, stirring, until tender. Return the mushrooms to the pan. Stir in the broth, basil, rosemary, and salt and bring to a boil. Reduce the heat to medium-low.

Melt the butter in a medium-size saucepan over medium heat. When hot, stir in the flour and cook, stirring constantly, until bubbly. Gradually stir in the milk. Add the flour mixture to the soup, whisking until blended and smooth. Stir in the rice and turkey meat and cook over low heat, stirring frequently, until the soup has thickened and is heated through.

YIELD: 8 SERVINGS

MY FATHER'S TURKEY SOUP (OR BROTH)

You have to remember that until relatively recently there were no large freezers in which to store Thanksgiving-turkey leftovers for a day when they might be more appealing. Those big turkeys (and they were all big in the good old days) had to be eaten day after day after day, until the mere mention of turkey set the family to groaning. So you can imagine how delighted we all were when the carcass was *finally* picked clean and then my father decided to make a big pot of turkey soup—his favorite part of the turkey—and we faced several more days of turkey soup. But it was good, and it's still good, especially now that I can freeze the soup in smallish containers and spread the soup meals over several weeks. Accompany this hearty soup with a good chewy bread. My own choice, although there's no particular reason for it, is pumpernickel-raisin bread with whipped butter or cream cheese.

Carcass from any size turkey
3 or 4 celery ribs and tops, coarsely
chopped (about 1½ cups)
1 large onion, coarsely chopped (1 cup)
½ cup chopped fresh parsley
1 teaspoon salt

½ teaspoon freshly ground black pepper
6 quarts water
½ to 1 cup uncooked medium pearl
barley, depending on how thick you like
your soup (see note on page 325)
Chopped fresh parsley for garnish

Break the turkey carcass in half through the backbone and place it in a large soup pot. Add the celery, onion, parsley, salt, pepper, and water and bring to a boil. (If you have a little gravy or stuffing in the freezer, add these, too.) Lower the heat to medium-low and simmer, covered, for 3 to 4 hours, stirring occasionally, until the carcass has almost completely fallen apart. Remove the pot from the heat and let cool to room temperature. Remove the bones, gristle, and anything else that looks unappetizing. This is easiest to do by simply going through the soup with your hands. Return the pot to the heat and bring the soup to a boil. Stir in the barley, lower the heat to medium-low, and simmer, uncovered, for about 30 minutes, stirring occasionally, until the barley is tender. Sprinkle the servings with parsley.

YIELD: ABOUT 4 QUARTS; 12 SERVINGS

Note: Noodles, rice, or other grains may be used instead of the barley.

LANCASTER COUNTY TURKEY POT PIE

A Pennsylvania Dutch pot pie is not a pot pie in the usual sense, since it does not have a crust over the top. Instead, thin, square egg noodles, called pot-pie noodles, are added to the broth. To save time, the noodles can be made ahead of time and refrigerated or frozen until you need them, or you can substitute packaged broad egg noodles, if you like. If you'd rather serve a more traditional pie, then spoon the filling into a deep baking dish and cover it with a pie crust, corn bread batter, or even puff pastry. Stretch the raw puff pastry tightly so it doesn't touch the filling; otherwise it won't rise properly.

NOODLES
1¼ cups all-purpose flour
¼ teaspoon salt
2 large eggs

FILLING
4 cups turkey or chicken broth (see pages 2–4)
4 tablespoons (½ stick) butter
¼ cup all-purpose flour

1 pound medium-size all-purpose potatoes, peeled and cut into 1-inch cubes
2 medium-size carrots, cut into ¼-inch slices
2 celery ribs, cut into ¼-inch slices
½ teaspoon ground sage
4 cups ½-inch cubes dark cooked turkey meat
Salt and freshly ground black pepper to taste
Chopped fresh parsley for garnish

To make the noodles, combine the flour and salt in a medium-size bowl. Make a well in the center of the flour and crack the eggs into the well. Using a fork, work the eggs into the flour mixture just until blended. Turn the dough out onto a floured surface and knead for about 10 minutes. Working with one half of the dough at a time, roll out on a generously floured surface with a floured rolling pin as thinly as possible (you should be able to see the shadow of your fingers through the dough), about ⅛ inch thick. Since this dough is particularly stiff, this may take a few minutes, and you may have to reflour the work surface and the rolling pin a couple of times. Trim the dough with the tip of a sharp knife or a pastry cutter into a rectangle or square, then cut into 2-

inch squares, placing the noodles in a single layer on a baking sheet as they are cut; set aside.

To make the filling, bring the broth to a boil over high heat in a 4-quart Dutch oven or other large heavy saucepan. Work the butter and flour together in a small bowl. When the broth comes to a boil, gradually stir in the butter mixture. Drop in the potatoes, carrots, celery, sage, and noodle squares. Lower the heat to medium-low to keep the broth at a slow boil. Boil gently, uncovered, for 10 to 15 minutes, stirring occasionally, until the vegetables and noodles are tender. Add the turkey and season with salt and pepper. Continue to cook just until the turkey is hot. Ladle into shallow bowls and sprinkle with the parsley.

YIELD: 4 TO 6 SERVINGS

GALE STEVES'S TURKEY FLORENTINE

Gale is one of the best cooks I know, so when she offered me a recipe for turkey leftovers I knew it would be good and I wasn't disappointed.

Two 10-ounce packages frozen chopped
  spinach
2 tablespoons dry sherry
¼ teaspoon ground nutmeg
5 tablespoons butter
2 cups sliced crimini or regular white
  mushrooms
3 tablespoons all-purpose flour
1 cup turkey or chicken broth
  (see pages 2–4)

1 cup light cream or half-and-half
½ cup shredded Gruyère cheese
½ teaspoon salt
⅛ teaspoon ground cayenne (red) pepper
2 cups ½-inch cubes dark or white cooked
  turkey or chicken meat
1 cup herb-flavored croutons
¼ cup grated Parmesan cheese (optional)

Preheat the oven to 350°F. Cook the spinach in lightly salted water as the package directs and drain thoroughly. Toss the spinach with the sherry and nutmeg in a large bowl and set aside. Melt 2 tablespoons of the butter in a large skillet over high heat. Add the mushrooms and cook, stirring and tossing, until their liquid has evaporated. Remove from the heat and set aside. Melt the remaining butter in a medium-size saucepan over medium heat. Stir in the flour and cook, stirring, until bubbly. Gradually add the broth and continue to cook and stir until the mixture boils and thickens. Stir in the cream, cheese, salt, and cayenne and cook, stirring, until the cheese melts. Mix ¼ cup of the cheese sauce with the drained spinach and spread the mixture in the bottom of a shallow, greased 2½- or 3-quart baking dish. Mix the turkey and the mushrooms with the remaining cream sauce and spoon over the spinach mixture in the baking dish. Scatter the croutons over the sauce. Sprinkle with Parmesan cheese and bake for 20 to 25 minutes, or until bubbly.

YIELD: 6 TO 8 SERVINGS

DEER VALLEY TURKEY CHILI

This is the chili they serve at Deer Valley Resort in Park City, Utah. No wonder the guests never want to leave. The night I served it, my guests didn't want to leave either, at least not until the chili pot was scraped clean.

1 pound dried black beans, picked over and rinsed
2 teaspoons salt
Two 10-ounce packages frozen cut corn, thawed
¼ pound (1 stick) butter
1 large red onion, chopped (1 cup)
2 or 3 celery ribs, chopped (1 cup)
1 medium-size red bell pepper, chopped (1 cup)
1 cup chopped mildly hot fresh chile pepper (see note below)
1 cup chopped leek (just the white part of 2 or 3 leeks)

2 cloves garlic, minced
2 tablespoons dried oregano leaves, crumbled
¼ cup all-purpose flour
4 cups turkey or chicken broth (see pages 2–4)
2 tablespoons ground coriander
2 to 3 tablespoons chili powder
½ teaspoon ground cumin
4 cups shredded dark or white cooked turkey meat (see note on page 328)
Salt and freshly ground black pepper to taste
Hot cooked rice

In a 6-quart Dutch oven or other large heavy saucepan, soak the beans overnight in enough water to cover them by about 3 inches. Skim off any beans that have floated to the surface. Drain the beans and sort out any debris, then add 10 cups of fresh water. Bring to a boil, then lower the heat to medium-low. Skim off any foam that rises to the surface with a large spoon. Simmer the beans, uncovered, for about 1½ hours, stirring occasionally, until the beans are tender but not too soft. During the last 30 minutes of cooking add the salt. Drain the beans, turn into a bowl, and set aside. Puree one package of the corn in a food processor or blender and set aside. In the same large saucepan in which the beans were cooked, melt the butter over medium heat. When hot, add the onion, celery, bell pepper, chile pepper, leek, garlic, and oregano, and cook, stirring frequently, until the vegetables are softened. Stir in the flour until well blended with the vegetables and cook over low heat, stirring constantly, for 5 minutes. Stir in the broth until well blended. Add the pureed corn, the remaining package of corn, the coriander, chili powder, cumin, and reserved beans. Simmer, stirring occasionally, for 10 minutes. Add the turkey and continue to cook for 5 minutes, or until heated through. Season with salt and pepper and serve over hot cooked rice.

YIELD: 8 TO 12 SERVINGS

Notes: In the West and Southwest, mildly hot chile pepper varieties, such as California, Anaheim, or Poblano peppers, are readily available. However, in other parts of the country finding a decent selection of chile peppers is more difficult. If all else fails, substitute one 4-ounce can of chopped green chiles, drained, and add them along with the final ingredients at the end of the cooking time.

To shred the turkey meat, pull off small sections, going with the grain of the meat.

A SORT-OF TURKEY CASSOULET
❧

We didn't want to call this dish a cassoulet since the French are very sticky about having their classic recipes Americanized, so to speak, and I don't blame them. But after Stephanie Curtis, an American food writer who lives in Paris, finished developing and cooking this recipe, we thought it was worthy of the name. Leftover duck or goose meat would be particularly good in this recipe.

1 pound dried Great Northern beans
½ pound bacon slices, cut into 1-inch pieces
1 large onion, chopped (1 cup)
1 or 2 celery ribs, chopped (½ cup)
1 small carrot, scraped and chopped (½ cup)
8 cloves garlic, minced (about 3 tablespoons)
½ teaspoon dried thyme leaves, crumbled
¼ teaspoon salt
¼ teaspoon freshly ground black pepper

1 bay leaf
4 cups chicken broth (see pages 2–4)
1 can (about 15 ounces) whole peeled tomatoes, drained
1 pound garlic sausage or kielbasa, cut into ½-inch cubes
⅓ cup dry vermouth or white wine
2 to 3 cups bite-size pieces dark cooked turkey, duck, or goose meat
½ cup dried French-bread crumbs
1 tablespoon butter, cut into small pieces

In a large bowl, soak the beans overnight in enough water to cover them by about 3 inches. Discard any beans that have floated to the surface. Drain and sort out any debris.

Preheat the oven to 375°F. In a 4-quart Dutch oven or other large heavy ovenproof saucepan with a tight-fitting lid, cook the bacon over medium-high heat until almost crisp. Remove the bacon with a slotted spoon to drain on paper towels and set aside. Pour off all but about 3 tablespoons of the bacon drippings from the pan. Heat the remaining drippings over medium-high heat. Add the onion, celery, and carrot and cook, stirring frequently, until softened. Stir in the garlic and cook, stirring, for about 2 minutes longer. Add the thyme, salt, pepper, bay leaf, and the drained beans. Cook, stirring, for about 4 minutes longer. Stir in the chicken broth and cover the pan tightly. Place the pan in the oven and bake for 1 hour and 20 minutes, or until the beans are tender. Stir in the tomatoes, garlic sausage, and vermouth and continue to bake, uncovered, for 30 minutes. Stir in the bacon and turkey, sprinkle the bread crumbs evenly over the top of the casserole, and dot with the butter. Return to the oven and continue to bake, uncovered, for 30 to 45 minutes, or until the crumbs are lightly browned and the mixture is bubbly.

YIELD: 8 TO 12 SERVINGS

Index

ɸ